TAL-Y-LLYN
RAILWAY.

The timeless Talyllyn train, little changed for eighty years, leaves Rhydyronen, some passengers clearly preferring the open wagons at the back to the almost-empty carriages.

L. T. CATCHPOLE

THE TAL-Y-LLYN RAILWAY.

J. I. C. BOYD

Ein Gwlad
Ein Hiaith
Ein Cenedl

(One Land, One Language, One Nation)

[From a graffito incised on coping stones of Hendy Bridge]

WILD SWAN PUBLICATIONS LTD.

ISBN 0 906867 46 0

To the memory of our daughters,
ELIZABETH and DIANA
who shared our experiences
of The Talyllyn Railway

Waiting for the train — the Boyd family epitomise the informality and tranquillity of the Haydn Jones regime. 1949. AUTHOR

Designed by Paul Karau
Printed by Amadeus Press, Huddersfield

Published by
WILD SWAN PUBLICATIONS LTD.
1—3 Hagbourne Road, Didcot, Oxon OX11 8DP

CONTENTS

TALYLLYN RAILWAY COMPANY

Registered Offices include: 30 Pall Mall, Manchester
King's Station, Towyn
22 High Street, Towyn
Arthur & Co., Solicitors, Machynlleth

London Gazette (notice re Bill for Talyllyn Railway Company)	25 Nov. 1864
Act: 28 & 29 Vic. Cap. CCCXV	5 July 1865
Authorised Capital: £15,000 in 750 shares of £20 each	(all issued)
Authorised Loans or Debentures: £5,000	(not raised)
Dividends: none paid	
Ownership: Up to 1911, the Company exclusively the property of the Directors	
Commencement of construction of railway:	app. Apr. 1864
Opened as Mineral Line (no Act yet obtained):	by mid-May 1865
Board of Trade Reports following inspection:	25 Sep. 1866
	8 Nov. 1866
Opened as passenger line under Act:	(unofficial) 1 Oct. 1866
	by Dec. 1866
Length of line authorised under Act: Towyn King's to Abergynolwyn:	6 m 50¾ chains
Official total mileage returned in 1922:	10 m. 27 chains
Maximum gradients officially returned:	1 in 60 (1866)
	1 in 77 (1891)
['One sixth of the length is at 1 in 77–100' – Board of Trade 1891]	
Minimum curve:	6 chains (1866)
Speed Limit under Act:	15 m.p.h.
Speed Limit under Board of Trade ruling in lieu of fitting continuous brakes, 1891:	12 m.p.h.
Last use of Village Incline:	Winter 1946*
Last Down slate loadings:	1948
Last train under Henry Haydn Jones' regime:	6 Oct. 1950

* Last of series of regular 'runs' carrying four barrels of beer, which had obtained for some years.

AUTHOR'S NOTE

In 1946 I set myself the task of writing about certain narrow gauge railway systems in a form which I have followed since that time, and which has been imitated by many in the interim. With experience I have moved further from the railway itself to the more fascinating study of personalities which lay behind the promotion of railways. For me, railways have become people. The Talyllyn Railway had no competitor where people are concerned. Promoters, directors, management, employees – they were A Race Apart. In consequence the format of my story herein is quite different: not only this, but the personalities caught up in the saga have equally made it more difficult, and yet more enjoyable to relate. Who could resist the 'owner' who kept no records, called no meetings of shareholders, destroyed documents to ensure their disappearance ... or employees who, out on the line, were grandees in their own departments ...?

Underlying it all are the unsolved mysteries, some basic questions as to why, how and when which remain unanswered; those same fundamental facts about origin which the appropriate page in *Bradshaw's Railway Manual* would usually recall, fail to inform in this instance. How much is fable, how much is what in Ireland would be called 'Blarney', how reliable are the sometimes conflicting memories of those involved? Mistrusting anything which cannot be supported by documentary evidence leads nowhere. My doubting approach to the folklore, mythology, and traditional tale has changed from mistrust to one of mature acceptance. 'There is no smoke without fire', and following up some of the more unlikely fables has shown their fundamental rightness. No less the people of this Railway have proved difficult to probe too; even the complex character of Haydn Jones is remembered, sadly, almost without warmth in view of all he felt he was doing for the neighbourhood and its people. Over the years, despite its public status, 'his' Railway was a most private affair; throughout, owners kept their cards pressed closely to their chests and died in the same position. It is probably fitting that I have been unable to tear those cards from their grasp, and so some secrets remain.

PREFACE

There is nothing unique in the general background to this narrative: to walk the hills of Wales is to find the ground littered with past exploits of Victorian times where demand for minerals, which lay beneath the surface, was created by the Industrial Revolution. These riches were not only bound for England, for beneath the hatches of sailing ships outward bound across the Irish Sea might be found coal for Kinsale or Ballycastle, roofing slates for Dublin, bricks and tiles for Waterford: inward-bound ships would be making for Aberdovey from Arklow with limestone, pit props and copper ore for Swansea from Cappoquin. Paving setts, ornamental slabs, rails, foundry products in general – the list is endless – owed their origins to the Welsh landscape. Markets were found far beyond the British Isles and Welsh-built ships traded the world over.

Our concern here is with a Manchester cotton-spinning business, wooed from its concern with yarns, and tempted to try its hand in the slate industry and – like many another speculator – having had its fingers burned, withdrawing after bitter disappointment. Not ending there, the tale is taken up with the purchase of the business by a local landowner who, with local issues and personal esteem to bolster him, and a seat in the Commons, kept something of that slate business in being for another forty years or thereabouts. By then, the business and its owner were mutually exhausted.

From its hiding place lurking among the Merioneth hills, the Quarry business provided egress by a railway to link it with the Irish Sea at Aberdovey, and so enable its products to reach the markets of the world. That railway still survived to become the subject of the first railway preservation movement; it is in this particular that the story moves from the conventional to become an epic.

I became familiar with this last decade of that Old Order of Things until one day, while visiting the railway, I learned that Sir Henry Haydn Jones had died; it was inevitable that it – for the Quarry had already closed – would cease to operate and its title would be added to the lengthy list of highly individual systems which, though surviving through the Second World War, were succumbing monthly. For someone with little opportunity, limited funds and no influence whatever, the knowledge that so many such features of our national life were now unable to continue, was a most depressing one and left me with the camera, the interview and long hours of research to compensate for their loss ... and it must be acknowledged, that whilst the Talyllyn Railway still operated, it was far from being in the forefront of my attentions!

Almost forty years after the period of this book terminated, The Talyllyn Railway Preservation Society still succeeds in encapsulating something of the past and continuing a trend which many others have followed (not always successfully). Difficulties have been overcome and much of the character of the Old Order – so difficult to retain whilst operating a railway business – has been secured: the saga of these last forty years is yet to be written.

More urgently, it is for those of us who recall the Railway as it was between 1865 and 1950 – remarkably little altered over that long time – to set down what is known about that singular institution. The manuscript for this book has been in preparation for many years and the problem of where to end the narrative was long discussed; but the attractions of continuing it into the first years of the Preservation Society (and so recording the link between the Old and the New), were resisted. The death of Haydn Jones on 2nd July 1950 was the signal of the end of an era, and an appropriate issue to determine this memorial.

**Winding eastwards but hidden from view, the Talyllyn Railway makes its way towards the Quarry;
Rhydyronen station nestles among the trees to the left.**   W. H. DAVIES

INTRODUCTION

There is a fold in the bare hills where two streams converge; hard by a considerable disturbance of those windswept, treeless slopes reveals where Man has burrowed beneath in a search for slate. Like an iceberg, what is evident above ground is as nothing when compared with that below. Some long gone, the tumble of rubbish tips, the empty shells of ruinous buildings, the drunken slab pillars which, once vertical, carried water in wooden troughs to the water wheels, the mawkish underground passages with their drowned tramways leading to the working chambers . . . all these and more besides – are fast disappearing under an umbrella of afforestation as effectively as the waters of a new reservoir drown a whole valley. The rumble of shafting and machinery, the whine of cutting machines opening up the rock, the slap, slap, slap of the drooping leather driving-belts, the hum of water turbines and the constant roar of water as it falls from the paddles of water wheels – all the noises brought by Man to this remote place have been silenced and the sounds of nature are reinstated once more. Today, only the crescendo and diminuendo of the wind as it moans through the awesome piles of slate rubbish, and which lately whistled through glassless window frames and around decaying roof timbers (the object of their support long collapsed), is heard among the bleating of the mountain sheep. Occasionally the cry of the solitary curlew or mew of seagulls coming in off the sea will disturb a silence which can almost be touched. The days when the sound of cannonades of subterranean explosions rumbled upward, and the atmosphere was acrid with gunpowder smoke which rose up the airshafts to hang about the workings on a still day, are recalled by few. The damp air is clean again and the burial place of the defunct slate mine is already carpeted by the incoming forester; soon there will be little to reveal this small encapsulation of the Industrial Revolution.

So lies another example of English penetration into Wales, of the ambitious Victorian period when capital was available for speculation and speculators knew little or nothing about the destination of their savings. The passing of the Bryneglwys Quarry has left many mysteries unsolved; even the Umbilical Cord of the Quarry, the Talyllyn Railway, which linked it to the outside world (and which survives), also enjoys its share of unravelled lore. If a neatly simple and easily-explained story is the one preferred by readers, then this tale is not for them!

Just at the start of World War II I came to know the Talyllyn Railway, and the three men who were then the embodiment of it. Seen against the background of those times it appeared to be hardly a contender for my interest as were other systems – and there were many of them at that time – which were shortly to be dubbed 'Lines of Character'.* A decade later, with the death of Sir Haydn Jones, the position was very different, for the end of the war had brought *finis* to so many which we thought to be inviolate in 1940. So in consequence, when services had finished on the Festiniog, the Vale of Rheidol had only just re-opened after the Emergency, and the remainder of the Welsh Highland was being dismantled (one might go on!), I turned to an equal love, the railways of Ireland. Throughout that pleasant distraction, the old Talyllyn carried on as it had always done, and ever with more difficulty as we shall read. Now and again Towyn would be revisited, a tedious task with meagre main line train services during coal shortages and all private motoring forbidden; under such restrictions and discouragements did the seeds of interest swell.

Perhaps a personal reminiscence of these times is opportune. Information about the Talyllyn Railway in particular and Welsh narrow gauge railways in general in those times was very meagre: the only periodical of value was *The Railway Magazine,* at that time under the editorship of that charming personality whom I had had the pleasure of meeting, W. A. Willox. Under him the *Magazine* was a blend of the historic, technical, travel-bound and topical and perhaps these were then its consummate years. However, its current news relied heavily on correspondents, and the Talyllyn saw few of these, so reports were sparse. There was always the unreliable guidance of gossip at one of the three railway societies then active in our part of the North-West, but one was considered very odd therein if the offerings of the main line – almost anywhere – did not command one's first attention, and questions were asked about unpronounceable places. Fortunately, one could always fall back on one of those pocket bibles, published (however primitively by modern standards) by The Oakwood Press, and they were invaluable. It would be hard not to admit that the core of the few then investigating what the majority considered a trifle of little remark, was centred on any other source of information. From our part of the country, the Talyllyn was probably the most difficult to reach but having heard rumour that things were not too healthy and the future might beckon the wartime scrap merchant's torch (then enjoying a field-day), I

---

* *Lines of character* by L. T. C. Rolt and P. B. Whitehouse (1952) [Constable & Co. Ltd. London]

felt it would be worth what might prove to be something of an endurance test to reach, and might in the event prove a wise way of spending a precious day of army leave.

Though I had seen the Railway albeit sketchily on previous outings, the postcard from Mr. Edward Thomas had made up my mind, 'We will hold the train for you'. Obviously the reliability of the morning train which met the overnight Aberystwyth Mail from Whitchurch at Machynlleth, was not to be trusted. Drowsily I walked from the mainline station to the Wharf; either Mr. Thomas had forgotten I was coming or the Talyllyn train had not yet arrived. The latter proved to be the case. I was greeted warmly in the office, as a doctor might converse with a new patient in his surgery. Yes, there had been one other enthusiast this year (it was now March): yes, there were many doubts about the future of the line though Sir Haydn kept up the reassurance that he would see things through in his lifetime. Yes, there was a slight delay this morning, some trouble with the engine. Did I know anything about engines, and would I like to walk up the track and talk to the driver who would be working on the engine at the next station? I did just that, and was in time to see Hugh emerging from the pit with a broad grin and the assurance that we should at least be able to get down to Wharf and then see how things looked at that stage. The yard contained one coach, already standing and blocking the running line. The engine backed down onto it and coupled up. I was shown the First Class compartment, and, having gently buffed my vehicle, we simpered down the length of the cutting and hooked up onto one or two empty slate wagons. The driver went into the office, as I did and was given a ticket; I don't think it ever left my pocket again that day. The scudding clouds gave brief glimpses of sunshine but it would clearly not be a day for photographs (not that I could take many for film was expensive and in very short supply – I was already trying to cut sheet RAF film into strips in the darkness of the wardrobe to fill the gap in normal supplies; my efforts were unrewarding).

I stood in the office doorway for a moment; *Talyllyn* was shrouded in a cloud of wet steam blowing in all directions from the safety valves. The engine was an island in the middle of the most colossal puddle, partly from the injector but mainly from overnight rain. I tiptoed through the water to reach the carriage. With the driver was a man in an old raincoat. Three aboard;

we were off, only an hour late. I glimpsed Mr. Thomas check our departure through the office window, and I think I read his thoughts.

We pulled up at Pendre; I was so astonished to find the doors of the carriage only opened on the one side, and that the platform was so short and on that same side as the opening doors, that I never fully-noticed the shed and Works on the other side of the train. I had forgotten that the Railway boasted two stations in Towyn, so utterly unalike. Why? Beyond Pendre, (which seemed to be on the edge of nothingness with mist-covered mountains – so I judged – way, way ahead) the route stretched into a countryside which had little to commend it. For a moment I asked myself if it wasn't all a mistake to come here after all . . . that was, until the train started again. With gentle rise and fall, the carriage rolled its way as if a boat meeting the swell bow-on. Sitting in the corner seat, I caught sight of the cab of the engine leaning outwards as the engine too, was uplifted by another oncoming wave; the cab then rolled back and out of sight, 'now you see me, now you don't'. I could not sit through this! Jumping up, I went to the northside window and looked out – the other being inconveniently barred. The driver shouted encouragingly at me but I could not understand him – obviously he meant to emphasise that his engine was responding to his treatment. The slate wagons bobbing about at the back were like a string of lighters behind a tug on the choppy waters of the Mersey alongside the floating landing stage at Liverpool – a familiar sight for me. Doubts were gone, of the narrow gauge railways then experienced, this was going to be the most exceptional. . . .

About 1950, L. T. C. Rolt and his associates became aware of the Railway; by then I was well-acquainted! Today, almost four decades since then, it is difficult to reconcile what a 'Preservation Society' has actually preserved, with what I knew before Sir Haydn's death. However, one must accept that if 'perpetuation' be substituted for 'preservation', then those who have nurtured the opportunity to experience the Talyllyn Railway right up to the present have done so with more success than any other similar concern in the Principality. The craft of marrying the old with the new without insensitive destruction of the historic past is not lightly learned.

Colwall, Herefordshire   J. I. C. Boyd
1988

TALYLLYN RAILWAY
ANNUAL STATISTICS EXTRACTED FROM THE ANNUAL RETURNS OF THE BOARD OF TRADE AND MINISTRY OF TRANSPORT

Year Ending	GROSS RECEIPTS Passenger train traffic £	Goods traffic £	Total Receipts (e) £	EXPEN-DITURE £	SURPLUS £	DEFICIT £	Operating Ratio (k)	PASSENGERS CARRIED 1st class	2nd class	3rd class (b)	Total	GOODS CARRIED Coal (c) tons	Other mineral traffic tons	General merchan-dise tons	TRAIN MILES OPER-ATED
30 Sep 1867	328	1,133	1,461	1,740	–	279	119	74	–	11,490	11,564	510	4,284	153	7,950
31 Mar 1869	351	1,422	1,773	1,639	134	–	92	183	–	15,129	15,312	6,199		120	10,620
31 Mar 1870	404	X	1,738	1,820	–	82	104	X	–	X	X	X		X	10,724
31 Mar 1871	434	1,317	1,768	1,697	71	–	96	271	–	16,333	16,604	X		X	11,270
30 Sep 1871	443	1,202	1,645	1,810	–	165	110	275	–	16,118	16,793	6,863		(d)	10,789
30 Sep 1872	457	1,232	1,845	1,961	–	116	106	107	–	17,680	17,787	7,170		X	10,688
30 Sep 1873	491	1,070	1,679	2,047	–	368	122	86	284	17,470	17,840	6,622		X	10,619
30 Sep 1874	535	1,007	1,675	2,034	–	359	121	–	232	19,838	20,070	6,301		X	10,262
30 Sep 1875	524	1,236	1,903	1,411	492	–	74	–	312	19,073	19,385	7,463		X	9,990
30 Sep 1876	600	1,074	1,838	1,631	207	–	89	–	324	21,940	22,264	6,541		X	10,480
30 Sep 1877	646	1,465	2,337	1,836	501	–	79	–	324	22,945	23,269	8,444		X	11,341
30 Sep 1878	669	1,283	2,181	1,767	414	–	81	–	406	23,096	23,502	7,633		X	10,308
30 Sep 1879	557	889	1,646	1,523	123	–	92	–	220	20,699	20,919	5,815		X	10,023
30 Sep 1880	568	1,214	1,963	1,418	545	–	72	–	253	20,561	20,814	7,088		X	9,592
30 Sep 1881	589	1,017	1,671	1,608	63	–	96	–	369	19,742	20,111	6,756		X	9,870
30 Sep 1882	521	1,267	1,799	1,785	14	–	99	–	206	19,863	20,069	7,248		405	10,116
30 Sep 1883	430	1,501	1,959	1,543	416	–	79	–	202	20.747	20,949	7,641		1,052	9,844
30 Sep 1884	453	1,276	1,755	1,507	248	–	86	–	134	21,220	21,354	9,044		816	10,047
30 Sep 1885	461	770	1,252	1,423	–	171	106	–	199	21,514	22,713	6,825		454	10,054
30 Sep 1886	492	885	1,397	1,746	–	349	125	–	176	25,091	25,267	8,197		344	9,945
30 Sep 1887	476	758	1,263	1,364	–	101	108	–	236	24,132	24,368	6,605		380	10,655
30 Sep 1888	457	726	1,203	1,421	–	218	118	–	184	22,754	22,938	6,458		370	10,733
30 Sep 1889	497	642	1,159	1,421	–	262	123	–	337	24,254	24,591	5,433		396	11,354
30 Sep 1890	499	638	1,160	1,381	–	221	119	–	257	25,333	25,590	6,442		284	11,434
30 Sep 1891	453	584	1,055	1,580	–	525	150	–	182	21,741	21,923	4,866		390	11,103
30 Sep 1892	473	651	1,137	1,357	–	220	119	–	208	23,933	24,141	6,191		373	12,040
30 Sep 1893	519	892	1,428	1,607	–	179	113	–	212	25,849	26,061	7,678		390	11,851
30 Sep 1894	566	856	1,436	1,349	87	–	94	–	163	28,338	28,501	7,455		561	10,878
30 Sep 1895	582	805	1,408	1,448	–	40	103	–	260	28,263	28,523	7,491		589	10,732
30 Sep 1896	607	745	1,368	1,528	–	160	112	–	267	30,244	30,511	6,970		616	11,168
30 Sep 1897	620	782	1,418	1,527	–	109	108	–	283	30,354	30,637	6,892		745	12,080
30 Sep 1898	640	837	1,490	1,560	–	70	105	–	322	30,596	30,918	7,221		417	10,972
30 Sep 1899	639	801	1,453	1,679	–	226	116	–	308	30,345	30,743	6,853		432	11,036
30 Sep 1900	579	949	1,539	1,754	–	215	114	–	349	28,309	28,658	5,920		546	11,275
30 Sep 1901	560	1,101	1,676	1,681	–	5	100	–	600	27,811	28,411	6,880		668	11,368
30 Sep 1902	532	1,239	1,656	1,782	–	126	108	–	474	26,259	26,733	8,310		453	11,110
30 Sep 1903	521	918	1,451	1,444	7	–	99	–	686	24,171	24,857	4,953		576	11,156
30 Sep 1904	507	951	1,470	1,556	–	86	94	–	486	24,137	24,623	5,135		827	11,156
30 Sep 1905	450	1,111	1,573	1,574	–	1	100	–	464	21,384	21,848	6,666		483	10,983
30 Sep 1906	452	827	1,291	1,242	49	–	96	–	534	21,525	22.059	4,560		588	10,865
30 Sep 1907	454	798	1,264	1,500	–	236	119	–	436	21,797	22,233	4,547		465	11,209
30 Sep 1908	453	678	1,143	1,447	–	304	127	–	429	22,163	22,592	3,719		525	11,130
30 Sep 1909	420	659	1,091	1,190	–	99	101	–	469	21,226	21,695	3,972		311	10,958
30 Sep 1910	413	452	877	1,208	–	331	138	–	438	20,281	20.719	2,221		376	10,004
30 Sep 1911	412	176	602	790	–	188	131	–	433	21,740	22,173	332		410	9,765
30 Sep 1912	465	177	661	998	–	337	151	–	440	27,726	28,166	353		417	9,898
30 Sep 1913	No Return submitted														
(h)												General merchan-dise	(f)	Total	
31 Dec 1921	∅	∅	∅	∅	–	176	–	193	–	28,566	28,759	2,206	435	2,641	10,494
31 Dec 1922	1,050	471	1,595	1,720	–	125	108	125	–	25,716	25,841	2,103	368	2,471	10,242
31 Dec 1923	1,008	651	1,701	1,883	–	182	111	148	–	24,456	24,604	2,169	252	2,421	10,480
31 Dec 1924	837	869	1,706	1,901	–	195	111	78	–	21,157	21,235	2,685	319	2,904	10,282
31 Dec 1925	832	713	1,589	1,685	–	96	106	66	–	21,155	21,221	2,956	211	3,167	10,560
31 Dec 1926	728	735	1,501	1,905	–	404	127	63	–	19,065	19,128	3,087	106	3,193	10,666
31 Dec 1927	679	736	1,478	1,796	–	318	122	51	–	17,585	17,636	2,975	283	3,258	10,931
31 Dec 1928	571	552	1,181	1,493	–	312	126	52	–	13,909	13,961	2,229	196	2,425	10,904
31 Dec 1929	450	415	947	1,315	–	368	139	16	–	10,286	10,302	1,619	240	1,859	10,030
31 Dec 1930	372	320	836	1,108	–	272	133	26	–	8,781	8,807	1,249	224	1,473	10,083
31 Dec 1931	367	472	971	1,064	–	93	110	26	–	8,659	8,685	1,853	208	2,061	10,100
31 Dec 1932	356	308	791	1,167	–	376	148	–	–	8,034	8,034	1,178	216	1,394	9,421
31 Dec 1933	322	330	780	1,012	–	232	130	–	–	6,746	6,746	1,278	200	1,478	8,891
31 Dec 1934	278	312	715	974	–	259	136	–	–	6,110	6,110	1,244	150	1,394	7,963
31 Dec 1935	238	409	787	917	–	130	117	–	–	4,615	4,615	1,639	140	1,779	5,684
31 Dec 1936	226	411	786	954	–	168	121	–	–	4,341	4,341	1,643	145	1,788	5,618
31 Dec 1937	223	452	827	952	–	125	115	–	–	4,054	4,054	1,803	147	1,950	5,538
31 Dec 1938	223	455	832	1,141	–	309	137	–	–	3,904	3,904	1,822	148	1,970	5,565

NOTES

(a) The Returns are for the year ending 31st December, but in each year's Returns up to 1912 a note indicates that the T.R. figures are for a different year-end, as shown here. There seems to be a gap between the figures appearing in the 1867 and 1868 Returns (the first two lines in this table) and an overlap between the figures in the 1870 and 1871 Returns (lines 4 and 5).

(b) Including Parliamentary.

(c) Coal is not shown as a separate heading in the Returns from 1868 to 1913 inclusive.

(d) From 1872 to 1881 no figures are shown for General Merchandise traffic on the T.R. This has presumably been included with Mineral Traffic.

(e) The 'Total Receipts' figures include certain miscellaneous receipts besides passenger and goods traffic (e.g. rent). From 1921 there are slight differences in some of the items included under these headings.

(f) From 1921, slate does not seem to be regarded as mineral traffic. The 'other' goods traffic is mostly coal (there are several additional sub-divisions in the actual Returns).

(h) The Returns were not published between 1913 and 1921.

(k) Expenditure divided by Receipts, and expressed as a percentage. Not always shown in the Returns, but the missing figures have been calculated for this table.

X No figures are shown for the T.R. under these headings in these years.

∅ The layout of the 1921 Returns differs considerably from the others. Comparable figures for these headings cannot be extracted.

ROLLING STOCK FIGURES

The following are shown throughout in every year from 1867 to 1938:
2 locomotives, 4 coaches, 1 other passenger train vehicle.

WAGONS The figures for wagons are as follows:

1870: 109	1924: 93	1935: 98
1871-1914: 114	1925-1926: 99	1936: 92
1910-1912: 100	1927: 95	1937: 86
1921: 86	1928-1931: 99	1938: 80
1922: 88	1932: 98	
1923: 95	1933-1934: 96	

These figures include 'service vehicles' which total 2 from 1922 onwards. A detailed analysis of wagon stock is given in the Returns from 1921 onwards: for instance in 1921 the figures are:

10 open goods   70 mineral
3 covered goods   3 service

30227. F.F.& Cᵒ.

Towyn before the turn of the century, with its ring of surrounding hills for a backdrop, is here but hardly touched by the arrival of the Railway Age.

F. FRITH & CO.

CHAPTER ONE

THE RAILWAY COMES TO TOWYN

EARLY visitors to Towyn were at least agreed on one issue – it was a dirty little place. As long ago as 1789 Pennant wrote:

'... scarcely so worthy of an appellation so lofty as 'town'. As to streets it has none and what the inhabitants would willingly term as such are merely lanes bordered by wide and dirty ditches. It has a few good houses and a church with no pretensions to elegance ...'

All seaside places have two things in common – the sea on one side and the land on the other. Towyn is the creation of these two environments and over the years it has demonstrated which of the two is the dominant one. The town stands on an historic site for the place has an ancient background – quite unlike neighbouring Aberdovey, for instance, which was virtually non-existent before 1810 and had no church. Towyn stands on a part of the coast where a number of river estuaries flow into Cardigan Bay and make land travel along that coast impossible without long detours inland to cross such rivers. These rivers divide the coast into separate economic units, each with its own centre, of which Towyn is one. North of Towyn the Dysynni river forms a barrier to the north and the road has to make inland to Bryncrug in order to cross it. Such obstacles and the poor state of the roads made the small boat the ideal way in which to pass along the coast. In more general terms the local farming community seldom needed to move far from its birthplace and might never know the countryside which lay more than ten miles beyond its own doorstep. At the mouths of the local estuaries some ship-building took place; Towyn was always a market town and never a port but had a small boatyard. In those times there was a channel to the open sea via the Dysynni which was closed off when the land to the north of the town was reclaimed by the Corbets in the late eighteenth century.

Towyn was in fact the first place hereabouts to lose its shipyard which lay at the end of Gwalia Road where a dyke now leads out towards the Dysynni; building was mainly of brigs and ceased about 1820. There were sixteen shipwrights and carpenters at work in the district in the period 1744–87; this figure includes yards around the coast nearby and does not refer exclusively to Towyn.

Former shore lines have undergone immense changes through the ages, and the sea, though presently receding, will advance from time to time to damage promenade and foreshore. Occasionally it retreats to display traces of the old 'shore route'* and trunks of trees from an ancient submerged forest.

Traces of this old shore road, by the glimpse of an occasional milepost, can be seen whenever abnormal tides clear away the sand. The sea level along here is calculated to have fallen 30–60 feet over the years.

The coming of the railway changed the way of life for few in the district but everyone was affected by the improved links with the hinterland and the benefits this brought about – it was the first shock-wave of an industrial revolution which had long changed some other parts of Wales but had left the Towyn district untouched up to then. Links with the sea, however, had been lost long before the railway came.

There were three ancient arteries overland hereabouts. The northerly one made its way from what must have been an historic haven known as the Broad Water on the Dysynni and then up onto the shoulder of the hills to make its way above the shoreline, working north and east to reach Dolgelley, another bridge town. This natural line of communication is at least 3,000 years old and known here as Y Ffordd Ddu – related pre-historic cairns mark its course. To the east of Towyn another route led towards central England by climbing over the Bwlch Llyn Bach Pass and dropping to Cross Foxes. The new railway invasion was to come from the south along the coast and from this direction there was no land route until what had been a rough track was turned into a turnpike road up the 'Happy Valley' towards Machynlleth in 1775. Later this was replaced by a coastal road through Aberdovey by one Corbet, commenced in 1805, (resited in 1827) and a mail coach set upon it.

In the early part of the last century there was a marshy tract to north and south of the town. Ships of up to 15 tons burthen could reach the weir on the Dysynni near the ancient mansion of Peniarth, on the Spring Tides. Even in 1850 this area was mostly uncultivated and had not been affected by the Enclosure Acts – it was used mainly as a source of peat for fuel. Most of the local woodlands had disappeared long ago as fuel. Corbet, the landowner of nearby Ynysymaengwyn Estate, had carried out improvements such as drainage and cultivation, and attempted to find coal among the peat beds. Out at Aberdovey, also on his lands, he was working copper and lead.

---

*Not a road proper but a well-used route when circumstances allowed.

Turning now to people who were beginning to discover Towyn as a resort (the modern interpretation to that word should not be applied in this instance!), we read that it attracted 'moderately prosperous and leisured people ... many respectable families frequent this place in preference to Aberystwyth because of its cheap and excellent provisions'. Was this 1910? No, it was, preposterously, in the decade 1810–20, and ten years later it was suggested that such families came not from the west midlands of England, but rather, mainly from Llanidloes, Newtown and Montgomery. Were these engaged in the busy wool and allied industries of those parts? Certainly Aberdovey was eschewed by some as being too commercial – boat building activities on the shore were not attractive whilst that which was carried on in the Gwalia creek at Towyn was on such a small scale as to be passed unnoticed.

The little town was so much a part of the Ynysymaengwyn Estate as to hardly enjoy a separate existence, and the drainage improvements, which Edward Corbet created from 1788 by the building of embankments, was largely for his own benefit: though he allowed the local peasants to cut turf on his marshland, this was done in such a way as to clear drainage channels to allow boats to work along them in the form of narrow canals and so assist in clearance.

However, agriculture was predominant. The procuring of peat gave employment to a large number of persons. Though families were large, each farm had a considerable number of hired servants: on 12th May each year there was a Hiring Day for such, the hire having to be renewed annually.

The beginnings of modern Towyn may have been the work of one man, Edward Corbet (1743–1820), but the greatest effect (and none has subsequently exceeded it) was due to the building of the Aberystwyth & Welsh Coast Railway linking Aberdovey and Llwyngwril between April 1862 and October 1863. To achieve this an embankment was thrown across the mouth of the Dysynni and adjoining marshland and over the years this work has been protected by an enormous bastion of boulders brought by train and craned off onto the seaward side. At the north end a bridge crosses the tidal Dysynni below the Broad Water.* An effect of this was to create an attractive area of water behind the embankment which the later tourist trade developed with a small steamboat service during summer months. So whilst the sea once lapped on a shore just behind the cottages to the side of St. Cadfan's Church, (an important centre of the Celtic Church since the fifth century and suggestive of Royal Bounty in its features) these buildings are now almost a mile east of the shore. Construction of the main line embankment was hampered by a strong

---

* Rebuilt in its present form in 1910 at a cost of £4,500.

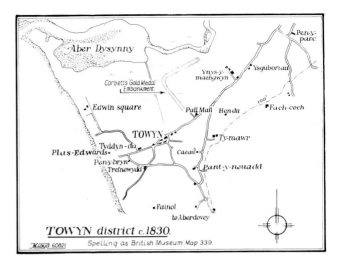

TOWYN district c.1830.

Spelling as British Museum Map 339.

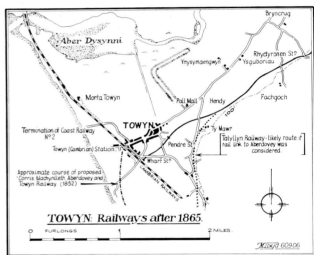

TOWYN: Railways after 1865.

tidal race as the arms of the new work extended towards each other and narrowed the gap between them. In winter storms of 1865/6 a 'pile engine' and other materials were carried out to sea, and though passenger trains were already running along this length, the work was clearly incomplete. Trains could only run to either side of a breach in the embankment 'and passengers had to walk' (though perhaps this meant 'swim'!) Note that the Talyllyn Railway was also in building at this time.

Public concern for the state of the town was stirred up by the coming of the railway. New Year 1866 was marked by the start of street gas lighting though it was remarked 'that the lights were not very brilliant as the pipes are still full of air'. Later that year the gas was taken into shops and hotels. At this time, too, the health-giving properties of the town were being extolled – a popular form of 'Come hither' advertising used until recent times. At the same time, the popu-

Aberdovey Ferry awaits its passengers; the men hold the vessel off the low-tide rocks along the south shore of the Dovey.

Hardy late-Victorian holiday-makers sample the delights of the Broad Water near the Rhydygarnedd Ferry.

F. FRITH & CO.

As yet undeveloped, Warwick Place and the new Promenade are a foretaste of a forthcoming evolution.

The evolution takes place; quiet pastures become Promenade Shelters and Boarding Houses in the late Victorian era.
F. FRITH & CO.

lation was bracing itself against a plague called Rinderpest, which affected cattle, with Wynne of Peniarth (the local MP) taking a fine stand to counteract it.

We read, 'The great salubrity of the climate', and 'hundreds resort to Towyn where evidently is found that which catered for the restoration of the patient'. Fears were expressed that accommodation fell short of the desirable.

So Towyn found itself, with its new railway connection, at the threshold of the new holiday boom. The nearby development of the Bryneglwys Quarry and its connecting Talyllyn Railway which was also coming into the town to make junction with the Coast Line was hardly to be noticed.

Perhaps fortunately, though Wales was much sought after by the diarists of those times, Towyn was largely missed on their excursions. Those who did find it were not impressed. Open drains, poor lodgings and that same wretched state which showed itelf in Irish towns after the great famine of the late 1840s, seemed to have invaded Towyn also. In 1819 it was written 'that dirty ditches meandered along the centres of lanes which the locals called streets – a dull and secluded place as to be very rarely honoured by foreign visitors'. The courses of the open drains which served the town until the 1860s may still be followed, though now long superseded!* *The Cambrian Quarterly* in 1829 thought it a 'poor and secluded place . . . situated at one end of

the extreme points of the county possessing in itself but few resources of wealth, it serves no other purpose than that of a mart to which a portion only of the produce of neighbouring lands is brought for sale.'

There was already the beginnings of a summer visitor business before the railway came. Families from the Midlands would spend a number of weeks there in the better months; at first they took lodgings but later many actually built their own residences. What had once been a weary trek by private carriage from England became a trouble-free journey for their transmutation, by the new Cambrian Railways system. So the basic pattern of business on which the town was to depend for its future, began its life. Agriculture, slate quarrying and landowners might go their own way, but the prosperity of the district now depended on the ability of the town to sell itself to the English visitors. Even the now-complete new Talyllyn Railway could never have foreseen that a century hence, it would be this business which ensured its survival, for its builders were only concerned, at this juncture, with transport for their quarry enterprise. Accepting this, we may consider how this change in priorities came about.

The form of this summer influx had important effect on the way in which the town and subsequent Talyllyn Railway passenger business developed. Whilst coastal resorts such as Blackpool, Barry Island, Rhyl, or Whitley Bay, were near the great manufacturing areas, there was another type of resort such as Southport, Scarborough or Llandudno which catered for the 'polite society'. To the surprise of the local residents, such visitors were even interested in making the adventurous ride by train and walking up to the Bryneglwys Quarry '. . . these were English people and never

---

* In the manner of most towns of the period, it was the local brook which became an insanitary ditch. Brook Street, a post-1865 diversion route, forms part of its course and beyond the boundary of the town it still runs in the open though not in an unsavoury state. (The Brook Street section was built in a slabbed wall on either side of the stream where it passed along the street, and then slabbed over the top. The road surface was then made up to the level of the covering slabs. More recently, it has been piped.)

Welsh'. And they were always curious. The local Guide Books extolled the pier (which was never finished), the racecourse which had such a short life (meetings were held in early September), the 18-hole golf course which could not compete (in the opinion of a regular influx from the Midlands) with that at Aberdovey ... 'and there is boating, close to the new parade, about a mile from the town'. Other accounts more truthfully warned that Towyn was not an ideal place for boats and that two persons in a rowing boat had gone out and were found – fortunately alive – three days later, on Bardsey Island. There were also boats on the Dysynni but they 'have to be hailed by much shouting as they lie on the opposite side of the stream; it is not well to choose very windy weather for this expedition.' But it was the promise of health which was the over-riding issue in the advertising of those times, recommending people with delicate chests to take up winter residence in the place, 'for the weather is so mild that myrtles will grow out of doors all year round.' Such claims were always backed by statements from medical men who were probably well rewarded. The state of the excellent drinking water, the sewage system, the beneficial effect on wheezy chests and the opportunities for convalescence, were trumpeted *ad nauseam*.

Have these things changed? Not a bit! Ask today what Towyn people do in the wintertime, and the answer will be. 'Look forward to the spring and the coming of the visitors'.

Where did Towyn come in the league of resorts along this coast? Certainly not at the top, for it was too far away for the day excursionist and only attracted the middle stream of society. These people were informed and wooed by a pullulation of pocket guide books in which the delights of what would then be considered to be a rare opportunity to ride on a small railway were colourfully set out. The Talyllyn Railway quickly adapted itself to this new development, and encouraged travellers to continue their journey beyond Abergynolwyn by foot or road vehicle to sample the delights of Talyllyn Lake, Bird Rock, Castellybere and even the summit of Cader Idris! To consider the latter might be achieved within a day's outing by train is mental extravagance indeed.

The basis of Talyllyn Railway holiday traffic, which soon outgrew the limited number of passenger vehicles that it owned (to the effect that empty slate wagons were pressed into service in the high season), was founded on the pattern of visitor who returned year after year, mainly in families. It was their habit to meet other families at the same period each summer, and enjoy the same pursuits together, annually. Thus the outing on the Talyllyn Railway became part of a social practice rather than the spontaneous decision of a day

tripper looking for unusual excitement ... the customary desiderata of most seaside resorts were hardly to be found at Towyn – Talyllyn Railway platforms were not cluttered with coin-operated machines to check one's weight, inspect what was seen by the butler, or purchase a bar of chocolate. In this it differed from other local railways such as the Festiniog or Vale of Rheidol where such machines were hired and formed part of the furniture to allure the tripper. But then the Festiniog was drawing its business from *hoi polloi* on the North Wales coast, and Aberystwyth catered for some types of ragbag visitor which Towyn did not encourage!

The foregoing has been considered at some length, for the Talyllyn Railway came to be more dependent on passenger numbers as tonnages of slate fell away. To understand the nature of this seasonal business is to appreciate why the Railway stood in a class by itself in this as in many other ways.

Let us now consider the actual arrival of the railway into the district. The Railway Age was approaching from the east; the line had opened between Newtown and Machynlleth in January 1863 and this was extended to Borth – *en route* for Aberystwyth – on 1st July 1863. Thus by the summer of 1863 the tracks were ready on the south shore of the Dovey opposite to Aberdovey, so near yet so cut off from the coast to the north of that small town. The Aberystwyth & Welsh Coast Railway planned to build an embankment on a grade of 1 in 100 from the south shore, culminating in a 280-yard viaduct, off the north end of which the line would curve westwards through Aberdovey – there would be an opening span. It would then only be 2 miles from the start at Caepenmochno and so across to Aberdovey. For years, a ferry (the property of the Corbets) had plied across this estuary and this work would replace it; thence the new railway would continue northwards up the coast via Towyn and make for Dolgelley. (The line did in fact reach Pwllheli in 1867 via Barmouth and Portmadoc.)

Accordingly, a pier was built at Aberdovey and materials ferried across; it would become a bridgehead from which the new line to the north would strike out. The first sod had been cut at Towyn on The Green near the 'Corbet Arms' (later the 'Corbett & Raven' for a time) Hotel by Mrs. Ffoulkes of Aberdovey in April 1863, which seems a curious place for the ceremony as the railway was to run nowhere near the spot. Towyn's original station opened in November 1863, but services between Aberdovey Pier and Towyn had begun on 24th October and were extended to Llwyngwril in November. Meanwhile there was trouble with the building of the Dovey embankment and bridge so the ferry continued to enjoy an unexpected extension of life. In the end, ideas for crossing the Dovey were given up altogether and powers obtained for a railway alternative along the coast from Glandovey to Aberdovey to link with the existing railway where it came up from the pier. This line was opened on 14th August 1867 and dubbed The Deviation. From that time Towyn was really in physical rail contact with the rest of the country, and the uncertainties of a sea crossing at the mouth of the Dovey became but a memory. Passenger trains ceased to use the pier line from 14th August 1867, and goods trains from 4th May 1964. In the interim the pier and its rail link was the intended goal for slate wagons loaded with Bryneglwys Quarry products and consigned to ship there, so saving the transfer of contents of Talyllyn wagons onto the standard gauge, but rather conveying wagons bodily on the standard gauge to the ship's side at Aberdovey. Of this, more anon.

Lest it should be wrongly construed that the A & WCR was the first scheme to bring the railway to Towyn, it should be pointed out that a Corris, Machynlleth, Aberdovey and Towyn Railway was projected in 1852 which would have come down the Dovey valley as far as the north bank of the river close to Machynlleth and then worked westwards along the river to Aberdovey, thence north to Towyn. The purpose of this railway could have been no other than to tap those districts with isolated slate quarries. There was also to be a line down to a pier at Aberdovey. Arthur Causton of Gloucester was the Engineer, he who had had close links with waterway schemes near that city, e.g. a survey for the Ledbury–Hereford section of canal in 1838 and for Gloucester Docks in the 1840s.

This dream of a railway to Towyn did not materialise but Causton had been involved with a Corris, Machynlleth & River Dovey Tramroad scheme of October 1850 which would replace cart transport from the Corris quarries to the banks of the Dovey at Derwenlas, and for which there was much local support. Causton's plan supplanted another by Thomas Nicholls for a tramroad – based on his visit to the Festiniog Railway – from the Corris district and down the Dulas valley to Pant Eidal where a quay would be built on the north shore of the river. Backing for this survey was a Montgomeryshire Railway, details of which would only serve to confuse! The Nicholls plan was discarded in 1852, leaving the way for Causton's CM & RDT scheme which, backed by an Act of 12th July 1858, would in due course take substance and leave the Bryneglwys Quarry at the mercy of Corris competition when the Corris Tramroad opened in April 1859. This line ran down to Quay Ward west of Derwenlas and even then plans were afoot to extend further westward towards the open sea and better trans-shipment facilities. Nor were these

all its territorial ambitions, but they have no place here! By its Act the minimum gauge was fixed at 2 ft. 3 ins., perhaps a significant figure for the later Talyllyn Railway? Traffic began to reach Quay Ward from 30th April 1859.

Under the A & WCR Act of 1865 that company was empowered to amalgamate with the Corris Railway. This did not take place, however. (From 1864, the CM & RDT had become The Corris Railway with permission to use steam power.) Due to developments up on the Festiniog Railway, it is significant that this Bill also appealed successfully against the 10 mph restriction on the Corris line and unsuccessfully against the prohibition of passenger trains. On 28th October 1865 the *Aberystwyth Observer* stated that goods and passenger services had begun to run between Machynlleth and Corris (but not beyond Machynlleth towards Derwenlas?) on 21st October, an announcement which has so far escaped notice. The rail-isolated Bryneglwys slate quarry which is at the centre of this account, would clearly have been at a disadvantage had not its own railway been almost ready. (Into this same atmosphere the quarries around Mawddwy were also involved, and they too would be developed around the purchase of the Plas Dinas Estate by Manchester entrepreneur, Edmund Buckley who would, contemporarily with the projection of a Talyllyn Railway, promote his own Mawddwy Railway – to standard gauge.)

It is helpful to add a little flesh onto the bones of the outline to the coming of the Coast Railway just described. Whilst the interim period was running its course, and The Deviation was not yet ready, the Cambrian Railways was having special difficulty with the southern end of the rail access to the intended Dovey viaduct. On the south side of the river there was the 'Penrhyn branch' (Report of 1st August 1868) 1 m. 56 ch. long. On the north was the Aberdovey landing stage branch 35 ch. long. The Cambrian engineer pointed out that the course of the Lerry river on the south shore was constantly changing and they might anticipate having to carry out some expensive work there in due course (this was in fact necessary in later years when the mouth of the river was channelled into its present position, entirely obliterating the evidence of the Penrhyn branch). In 1869 it was reported that the branch near Ynyslas, not used for some time, had been built by Savin the contractor and might be rented by Jones & Griffiths, timber merchants, for their private use. It was recommended that the old landing stage be offered for sale 'as the planking is being rapidly carried away'. So came about the railway map as we know it at the present time.

An almost forgotten aspect of the coming of the railways was that many places adopted 'London

The grimmer face of the expanding town could be seen from the Cambrian station overbridge, looking inland along the main street; as yet pavements and a macadamised road surface are in the future.   F. FRITH & CO.

Railway Time'; for instance the Great Western Railway put a clock on every station for the benefit (first of all) of its employees. At this time it did not give pocket watches to its drivers. Its timetables stated that 'London time kept at all stations' (June 1841). Certain companies eschewed London time: such was the Taff Vale which, being standard gauge, was unconnected with the other railways initially, and kept its own time. With the arrival of the Coast Railway, Towyn adopted London time too. Another effect was to cause the district to become bi-lingual and Anglicize the narrow coastal strip.

As to the ferry, *Bradshaw's Timetable* shows 'Ynyslas Ferry for Aberdovey' with three crossings a day in June 1864; beyond this the table continues as a railway timetable for Towyn and Llwyngwril only. Stations beyond Llwyngwril appear first in August 1865, and August 1867 shows ferry times for the last occasion, viz:

Aberdovey	dep.	8 a.m.	12.04 p.m.	5.15 p.m.
Ynyslas	dep.	8.40 a.m.	2.10 p.m.	6.10 p.m.

In the early 1860s there had been changes to the ferry which the timetables do not reveal, for, in connection with the building of the Coast Line, a small paddle steamer had been chartered by the railway to ferry materials across the estuary to Aberdovey. The *Elizabeth* was little more than a steam smack with clipper bow and was registered at 86 tons with a 30 ton burthen: she was 121 ft. long, breadth 20 ft. with a depth of 6 ft.; and there were two oscillating steam engines giving a nominal 30 horsepower. She had been built by Lewis & Stockwell of London, with engines and boiler by James Watt & Co., Soho Foundry, Birmingham. From November 1863 she took over the passenger ferry duties as well, and sailing times were linked to train connections. This continued until August 1867 when The Deviation (often called facetiously The Doveyation) was opened. She was disposed of in December 1869.

(A ship of 6 ft. draught could not use the estuary today: has the river silted further, or was *Elizabeth* subject to tide times?)

With the establishment of rail services, by which Towyn became part of the great railway map which was to join almost everywhere of importance together, the townspeople were not slow to add the attractions of the Talyllyn Railway to the potential of a holiday in the vicinity, and this aspect is covered when considering the Guide Books' coverage.*

---

* Wrexham Weekly Advertiser advertises seaside excursions to Towyn (etc) every Saturday and Monday, 28th April 1866.

CHAPTER TWO

THE SAGA OF BRYNEGLWYS

PUBLISHED in Dolgelley in 1890, *Cantref Meirionedd* by Robert Prys Morris includes an account – in Welsh – of Bryneglwys:

'The name Bryn-yr-Eglwys i.e. Church Hill, is borne by a dwelling which was once a farmhouse and is situated a mile and a half from Abergynolwyn. Close to it is another house which was erected for the manager of the slate mine or mines which lie around about this spot. This latter house also bears the name Bryn-yr-Eglwys but with the addition of The English word 'Hall'. There is no doubt that the old farmhouse mentioned above got its name from the hill on the side of which it stands, and the hill itself is so-called because the church formerly stood in the neighbourhood. According to tradition the church site was on the Cantrybedd side of the stream which flows past the foot of the hill, and a short distance from the stream ... place is supposed (now) covered with rubbish from the mine, but a lot of crumbling stones have been moved away from a nearby spot which was called 'The Old Graveyard' (Yr Hen Fynwent) ... to a place out of reach of the rubbish, by forming a sort of enclosure and planting trees around it like a churchyard ...*

'... the first lease ... was obtained thirty one years back from 12 May 1874† ... mining began in that same year ... the lease was held by three men but some years before that the land was owned by ... Robert Roberts. It was sold for £120 by the three men to the late Mr. John Pugh, Craig-y-Don, Aberdovey who worked it on a small scale for some years; after his death his widow carried it on for a while. After that the mine was closed down for some time; then in or about ... 1857 it was sublet to five Welshmen, and they worked it for three years. It was closed a second time until it came into the possession of Mr. John Lloyd Jones, Nantlle, Llanllyfni who began to work it in November 1862 and carried on for some time. Later he sold his rights to the late Mr. T. H. Maconal (sic) who formed a company to open the mine on an immense scale. By the terms of the sale he came into possession on January 1st 1864. In May of the same year work was started on the railway along which run the trains carrying the stone down to Towyn station, and the line was completed in 1865 ...'

Perhaps it is unwise to begin this narrative with an account which is untrustworthy in several respects, but is typical of the contemporary 'histories' of Welsh quarrying, in the native language, and is similar to other local 'hanes' where an author has perhaps been moved to set down the legends of his native district, on the realisation that up until that time there was no written record of the recent past.

This tale also perpetuates the story of St Cadvan (St Cadfan) who is said to have passed by Bryneglwys on his journeys to Cwm Cadian, and the averment that the said enclosure is 'reported to be an ancient burial ground and rightly or wrongly connected with St Cadfan'. The Parish Church in Towyn bears the name of this saint and the surviving Scots Pine and Monkey Puzzle Tree at Bryneglwys are said to mark the site of a small and ancient stone circle there. The old house,

Bryneglwys Hall, is said to have been roofed by 'slate from the Pont-y-Garth Mine ... and an old lady to be resident until the First War'.

Allowing for lapses which may occur in the foregoing tale, it typifies the speculative years in Welsh mining, and the fervour of those, misled by thinking fortunes might be made, and putting their capital into crankish enterprises which started off with such elan, supported by prospectuses which were seldom based on more than flimsy anticipation of what might be expected but, in fact, never turned out to exist. Bryneglwys Quarry was quite typical of that situation. Reports supplied by surveyors to accompany the prospectus of companies often formed to take over the sites of those who had failed there previously, were closely followed by speculators who were quite ready to hand over their money on a 'Jam Tomorrow' venture.† 'Venture Capital' spelled the enlargement of Bryneglwys, the formation of what became the Talyllyn Railway, and, after a brief flirtation with slate quarrying lasting only from 1864 to 1881, those 1860s venturers retired with their fingers badly burnt. From 1881 to 1946 and under fresh ownerships, the Quarry continued to operate – in part by members of the 1864 outburst – but the 'once bitten, twice shy' atmosphere was ever-present in its doings, and both Quarry and Railway showed, more and more as years went by, the signs of parsimonious ownership.

Another form of the same background to the Quarry is summarised by Llewellyn Davies in 1927 in an equally doubtful account of beginnings, Davies maintaining the site was discovered by a man named Smith from Corris who took a lease about 1843, sold it to John Pughe in the same year, whilst Pughe's widow Jane worked it only to sell to John Lloyd Lewis in about 1862. Another local source records that a John Williams worked the upper part (only) of Cantrybedd from 1834. In short, there is clearly an element of truth in these traditions but it would be a brave writer who today could set down the precise order of events!

Like so many of his contemporaries, Pughe was full of enterprise, but so too was the Bryneglwys Estate landowner, Lewis Morris of Machynlleth, who was prepared, somewhat surprisingly, not to saddle Pughe's endeavours to his (Morris) financial advantage by drawing up a lease which left the entrepreneur but scant room for manoeuvre. In this instance, John Pughe, a native of Carmarthen but of Bronhaulwen, Penegoes, Aberdovey, was treated reasonably well, being given a 50 year lease on 12th November 1844 to work the site exclusively for an annual rental of £40. Clearly there were a number of men already on the

---

* Said to be done in order to sink a shaft on that spot (Royal Commission of Ancient Monuments). An old tradition says this enclosure was formed when St Cadfan's Chapel was moved from Cantrybedd in ruined state, by T. H. McConnel on the instructions of Rev. G. R. G. Pugh.

† The dates in this account should be compared with those that are given later.

site (perhaps the three men led by Smith from Corris?) for Pughe is said to have had to buy them out from their pioneer excavation for £120, their authority possibly being a Take-Note from Morris which gave them the right to prospect for a limited period. Pughe's ambition lay beyond the site then working; the watercourses hereabouts marked the boundaries of estates, three in all and under each of which Pughe intended to mine for slate. To complicate matters further, the geological strata of the slate below ground was formed in three distinct bands – not conforming in the least, of course, to the boundaries of the three landowners! Pughe's lease with Morris only gave him the right to quarry without paying royalty on slate extracted on Bryneglwys land (the name Bryneglwys being later given as a collective title to the whole Quarry but strictly applying but to a part of the area of the estate of that name). The second adjacent estate where good slate might be mined was Cantrybedd, then owned by Rev. Richard Pugh, and, after negotiation, John Pughe was given a 60 year lease from 31st December 1846 to work slate there. Unlike Lewis Morris, Rev. Pugh was not a local man but incumbent of Llanfihangel-y-Gwynt in Montgomeryshire.

John Pughe would be aware of the potential of Cantrybedd slate as his fellow-townsman John Williams had worked there previously and is reputed to have owned the land, too, from 1834. After Williams died, his widow sold it to Rev. Pugh in 1843. (Traditionally this area formed the oldest part of the Quarry and comprised the levels at the south-west corner of the site on the slopes of Taren-Hendre.)

Complexities in local lore now set in (!) for Mrs. Williams is also said not to have sold *all* her interest to Rev. Pugh but that some went to John Lloyd Jones of Nantlle for £3,000* (some accounts give £5,000) who continued trial excavations on that estate without increasing output. If true, this would explain Lloyd Jones' interest when John Pughe's widow advertised the adjacent Bryneglwys workings. More probably, however, John Pughe's widow had lease of the *whole* Quarry and sub-let to John Ll. Jones!

The watercourse separating Bryneglwys and Cantrybedd became known as the Boundary Stream, but locally is Cwm Cwm. So John Pughe obtained the right to quarry in two estates and like the ant, to work underground with little evidence on the surface of his activities, to the consternation of respective landowners who could not tell if they were being cheated of their royalties! With some sense of posterity, he had a slab set into the wall of the mill, reading:

These premises were erected
by JOHN PUGHE and
the Machinery fixed up
therein in the Year 1847
much to the credit of
Person who bore
he expence

(the bottom left hand corner of the slab has broken off.†)

Pughe placed two advertisements in *The Mining Journal* during 1847 at six and a half month intervals; on 10th April 'the proprietor (lessee) Mr. John Pughe of Brynawel, Aberdovey states that in six months time he will offer to the public 2,400 of the 5,000 shares into which the concern is divided, he retaining 2,600, he having a 50 year lease . . . since commencement . . . has been removing covering of peat and earth, driving levels, making roads, bridges etc. as well as digging for and obtaining great quantities of slates and slabs of first rate qualities . . . colour is a beautiful light blue . . . they rise in rocks generally from 2 to 8 ft. in length and $1\frac{1}{2}$ to 4 ft. in breadth . . . now preparing a large building to contain machines etc. Two powerful streams run through the works . . . never failing supply . . . Road soon to be commenced from quarries to edge of River Dovey, 4 miles, from that spot slates will be taken on boats to the port of Aberdovey at an expense of 18 pence per ton . . . Only reason for parting with shares is infirmity of body and increase of age . . . very deep level could be driven . . .' The second advertisement appeared on 26th September.

At a later date the machinery was expected to be ready in three months and 'shares would only be sold to respectable applicants, in lots of not less than twenty'.

If such information as can be gained is collated, it may be inferred that Pughe was already elderly in 1847, and after his death and a period when his widow ran the business, it was ultimately sold in 1862 to John Lloyd Jones of Nantlle, Caernarvonshire who brought his Manager/Agent Robert Williams to develop the site.‡

The Machynlleth Deeds (National Library of Wales) suggest that one Edward Davies of Dolcaradog, Machynlleth ('a cunning operator' according to one opinion) engaged in metal-mining, began to seek sale of the Quarry from 1859 on behalf of Mrs. Pughe. In early 1863 a group of Manchester industrialists and businessmen, under the leadership of Thomas Houldsworth McConnel,§ had their interest focused on the site.¶ This link is also shrouded in mystery for though his brother, William McConnel was the undoubted ringleader, the means whereby he was introduced to the site, his objective in forming a company at such a distance from his usual business in those times (a railway did not reach Dolgelley until

---

* Recorded on tablet in Quarry, so it is said.

† The tablet was found by L. T. C. Rolt and J. B. Snell in the Quarry Office in 1951.

‡ See 'Quarryman's Autobiography' (Robert Williams).

§ Until about 1840 invariably spelt M'Connel.

¶ Text of correspondence William Lloyd (on behalf Mrs Pughe) and Edward Davies.

The seeds of the Bryneglwys Quarry venture's development, and the building of the Talyllyn Railway, were sown in the cotton mills of north Manchester during the 1860s. This was the seat of the McConnels' industrial empire. FINE COTTON SPINNERS

the summer of 1868) is not known for certainty. William was a partner in the cotton spinning business of McConnel & Co.

So, in short, he may have simply wished to be involved with a venture outside the cotton trade with its traditional 'one good year and two bad' syndrome, and interest himself in speculation further afield. Had he known, slate quarrying (with its beckoning gamble that gold might be found in these Merioneth workings!) was even less reliable than the cotton trade. There is no doubt that with his resources, he could well afford to put his capital at the disposal of the new development, but the air of a confidence trick remains concerning the deal.

He may have come to know of the site through meeting such men as Edmund Buckley or others like him who would be personal friends at John Shaw's Club in Manchester, and fellow-members of the Royal Exchange, the market place there of the cotton industry.

At this time the Quarry output was low but development costs were high; in the outside world there was plenty of money looking for quick profits and some outrageous plans were spread before an uninformed public; they had an adventurous ring about them. With purchase agreed and T. H. McConnel at the helm, the new Bryneglwys scheme announced it intended to produce £5,000 worth of slate per annum for the next

15 years . . . and perhaps in this respect only it did not disappoint its owners.*

In Ancoats, north Manchester, a large cotton spinning mill, known as Sedgwick Mill, had been built in 1818–20 by Messrs. McConnel & Kennedy. By 1833, this company had become the largest cotton spinners in the country and the biggest importers of American cotton. James McConnel was the Chairman. Three of his sons, Henry, James, and William, became partners in the business when their father died in 1831. Henry and James retired in 1860 and 1861 respectively, leaving William the sole proprietor. Whilst this might have been advantageous to William in normal circumstances, it occurred during a very bad period for the Lancashire cotton industry. The American Civil War, beginning in 1861, cut off all supplies of raw cotton for spinning, and without their basic commodity, the Lancashire mills starved for supplies. McConnel's mill held vast stocks and managed to carry on by restricting usage, whilst half the mills of the county closed down completely. The years 1863 and 1864 gave no better promise and it seems at this time William McConnel felt compelled to widen his interests and make a move so familiar in industry today where a wide spread of diversified subsidiaries make for less vulnerability.

---

* In 1861 Bryneglwys Farm was still unconnected with the quarry business and occupied by Samuel Williams who farmed 40 acres.

It is unfortunate that the circumstances which gave the McConnels the introduction to Bryneglwys are not known. The years of the Civil War had given William second thoughts and learning that Pughe and his successors in title were not only extracting slate successfully but might have hopes of finding gold (first discovered in the Dolgelley area in 1844 and reaching a climax in 1860–61), he and others formed the Aberdovey Slate Co. Ltd. on 23rd January 1864, which included a lease of land containing the Bryneglwys Quarry. The capital was £75,000, increased in 1865 to £112,500, of which £15,000 was earmarked for the construction of a railway to connect the Quarry with the outside world. McConnel's relatives and friends in Manchester formed the first Board of Directors.

In 1865, McConnel & Co., (as it now was) became a Limited Liability Company. The War ended and cotton imports were resumed. William McConnel continued to control McConnel & Co. Ltd. until 1878 when he retired; he died, aged 93, in 1902. His son, John William, became Managing Director in 1880 but was not associated with the Talyllyn Railway at any time; it was his brother, William H., who was to be connected with the Railway and Quarry, and have no association with the mill. Thus the two lines of business went their separate ways. To complete the cotton mill story, in 1898 the company became the first associated business of Fine Cotton Spinners & Doublers Association Ltd.

What of T. H. McConnel's fellow promoters and the first six directors of the Aberdovey Slate Co. Ltd. (registered 23rd January 1864)? They included his brothers William (then sole proprietor of McConnel & Co.) and James (the younger) who had retired from the mill in 1861. When T. H. McConnel was to die of consumption in 1873, William would become Chairman of the follow-up company. At the start, the McConnels owned almost one third of the equity.

They began by retaining Robert Williams as their Manager/Agent;* they paid an enormous sum for their speculation as Jane Pughe received £11,850 for her share and John Lloyd Jones netted £27,000 for his part. A sum of almost £40,000 underlines the optimism of the incomers for Robert Williams maintained that his employer had spent less than £1,000 on the site. The new owners were never to be rewarded and the quarry undertaking never paid a dividend. The Talyllyn Railway Company, an essential by-product of the scheme, was to be a separate undertaking, separately financed and only profitable from time to time!

Incorrectly, Charles Barker & Sons Joint Stock Companies Directory of 1867 records the Aberdovey Slate Co. Ltd. as established 1863. Other particulars are accurate:

Capital	£112,500
Paid up capital	99,000
Shares	750 of £100 each 750 of £50 each
Directors:	James Murray*, Murray Gladstone*, James McConnel*, Edward Hardcastle, John Lawson Kennedy, Samuel Holker Norris*, Thomas Houldsworth McConnel*, Thomas Swanwick*, James Worthington, Thomas Dudley Ryder, William McConnel.
Bankers:	Manchester & Liverpool District Bank.
Secretary:	T. R. P. Cannan.
Registered Offices:	30 Pall Mall, Manchester: Towyn, Machynlleth.

*Those so marked were also directors of the Talyllyn Railway Co. in 1867.

The new Coast Railway was to prove to be the objective of the Bryneglwys Quarry rail link to the outside world. In this wise McConnel would score heavily over his nearest competitors who only 'owned'* a horse tramway down the Dovey valley to the main line at Machynlleth, whereas McConnel planned a steam-operated railway for his purposes, the first Welsh narrow gauge railway to be planned and built as a locomotive-worked line from the start. Surviving evidence points to the fact that a railway had been begun about April 1864 (within weeks of the Slate Company being formed in the previous January) and that by September it was passing Fachgoch, references suggesting this main line was in building from the Towyn end. It is possible that a tramway may have already existed from the foot of an incline called Alltwyllt in the Nant Gwernol gorge to carry away slate products and replace sledge haulage on the narrow roadway up from Abergynolwyn to the workings. An extension of this suggestion would be that in order to bring Quarry output down to road level in that village, a further incline (The Village Incline) had been built. In the village the slate could be transported by carts, along the Parish Road between Rhydyronen and Ty Mawr (where horses were exchanged) thence along the road to Aberdovey, the traditional place of shipment.†

The Village Incline may pre-date the building of the main line, but there are reasons for believing it was an afterthought.

Continuing this hypothesis to a logical conclusion, as the new railway made its way up the valley from Towyn, (perhaps faltered by delays in completing the viaduct at Dolgoch) the tramway would be continued westwards to meet the new construction which would benefit from having an access point near the Abergynolwyn – Towyn present road at a point now

---

* There is a press reference to Richard Lewis 'for the brief period in which he held the superintendence & management of the works' being given a testimonial at the new Market Hall on 3rd July 1866 . . . nothing else is known.

* Correctly, the line up to Corris was not actually owned by the quarry operators.
† This method replaced the earliest route from the Quarry, which was to take products on horseback out over the mountain ridge, down to Pennal and thus along the coast road to Aberdovey.

occupied by Abergynolwyn station. Somewhere along this route the Quarry tramway would meet the line coming up from Towyn.

Before leaving this suggestion, it may be asked why the Village Incline (of whatever date of build) was necessary if road interchange with convenient nearness to the village was available at the site of Abergynolwyn station? It could be explained by the provision of the tramway system within the village, extending from the foot of its incline. An early incline link, i.e. before the building of the main line from Towyn, would enable the development of the village in pace with the enormous growth it sustained as families moved in from elsewhere and their menfolk took up employment at the Quarry. The requirement to send building materials from Quarry into village would certainly justify the building of an incline down into the community.

Be all this as it may, the building of these rail links was achieved by agreement with the relevant landowners, thus avoiding the necessity, the consumption of time and the expense of going to Parliament for statutory authority to build. In this regard, had the contemporary Festiniog & Blaenau Railway Co. Ltd., registered under the Limited Liability Act of 1862 of 7th August that year, influenced those at Bryneglwys? Its prospectus read '. . . the Promoters of the Company are land-owners, quarry proprietors and other persons interested in the prosperity of the neighbourhood . . .' and in this wise the McConnel faction may have seen a reflection of their own role and intended to do the same.

On 1st August 1865 the Quarry Company increased its working capital by £37,500 in 750 shares of £50 each as a Rights Issue (1 share for every £100 held) and there was a further change on 24th August 1867 when the title was altered to The Abergynolwyn Slate Co. Ltd. with further financial changes.* The Quarry was getting off to a promising start and developing its production quickly; by the early 1870s output was 8,000 tons a year, requiring the Talyllyn Railway (as the rail link had formally become) to carry an average of 500 tons of stone per month, mostly in the form of roofing slates, but even this tonnage was insufficient to secure an adequate financial return on the heavy capital expenditure involved in developing the Quarry. One in three wagons of slate was often required to pay the landowner's royalty.

On the Cantrybedd Estate, the Rev. Richard Pugh's interest had passed to his seven children following his death in 1858; the new Company considered the

existing lease with Cantrybedd to be penal and negotiated a new one for six of the children, and a separate one for Charlotte, whose share had been incorporated in her marriage settlement.

The Company also intended to work the Broad Vein and part of Hendrewallog was leased for 45 years from 1st May 1866. It was also necessary to make a lease with the third estate involved, that of the Ruck family who owned part of the Narrow Vein – this was for 29 years from 12th November 1865.

Nor was this all! They also leased Bryneglwys Farm in 1866 ('a convenience for having produce for their horses'), an important advantage as it enabled the Bryneglwys community to enjoy the benefits of a nearby farm, not overlooking the facilities for stabling Quarry horses. Furthermore, from 25th March 1864 they leased land to enable them to tip rubbish outside the entrance to The Long Tunnel, and also to build a tramway from the foot of an incline to be built at Cantrybedd to the head of another incline to be built at Alltwyllt, and then extend to a point where the passing loop at the east end of the track arrangements at the Village Incline winding drum began. They went on to make a freehold purchase of land from Rev. G. R. G. Pugh (Richard's son), to give the Company freedom to provide houses for their workers, whilst at the same time the Pughs had the right to use the tramway at minimal cost – this further tramway was, in fact, the essential length of track to link up the end of the already-authorised tramway east of the Village Incline drum, and the termination of the statutory Talyllyn Railway Company a few yards east of Abergynolwyn station. The same purchase of land also included the Village Incline and land in the village. (A suggestion that all the foregoing tramways were already in existence before these formalities took place has already been discussed.)

There was no end to the greed of the Quarry for more development cash. As the underground trial bores crept forward, the original optimism faltered and then waned. The quality of material was becoming worse and it was inescapable that the enterprise had over-reached itself. Facing up to an impossible situation, and with the death of two McConnels (one having no links with the Quarry), and having its funds exhausted, the proprietors decided to pull out and sell the undertaking for the best price. W. Dew & Son auctioned Estate, Quarry and Railway at the Queen's Hotel, Chester on 9th October 1879. The sale catalogue mentions '. . . the RAILWAY INN, WRITING SLATE MANUFACTORY and EIGHTY EIGHT COTTAGES in the Village of Abergynolwyn, and the FARMS known as PANDY and NANT-LLWYN-Y-GWEDD containing altogether about 240 acres . . . also the FARM and MINERAL LEASES held by the Company, and 750 fully paid up SHARES of £20 each in the TAL-Y-LLYN RAILWAY COMPANY'.

---

* There was a Rights Issue of £50,000 in 7½% Preference Shares to existing members (or power to borrow £50,000 at interest not exceeding 7½%). On 6th October 1869 there was a further increase in capital by £16,500 in 350 shares of £50 each which took the total beyond its registered amount of £112,000 – a timely warning!

The Quarries 'might be viewed on application to Mr. Evan Evans ... and Mr. John Roberts at The Slate Wharf, Towyn, will answer any queries as to the Railway and other properties involved in the Sale'. Messrs. Orford & Milne, solicitors to the Company were acting, as was James Stevens, architect and surveyor who supplied a somewhat inaccurate map of the Quarry premises to accompany the catalogue.

Despite this evidence that the proprietors wished to sell, due to slackness of trade the Chester auction did not produce a buyer (a repeat auction on 16th March 1881 at The Mitre Hotel, Manchester, achieved the same non-result). Earlier some outward pretence of assurance was maintained: in an exchange of letters between Charles Holland and his nephew, Charles Menzies Holland, the former wrote (23rd November 1871) on Girvan & Portpatrick Railway notepaper (!):

> 'McConnel, writing to me the other day said his Abergynolwyn Quarry is doing very well on the make of slates 'which however is only about 500 tons per month – but that he has any demand for slates and thinks the prices should be raised. I do not generally notice any remarks of this sort beyond very generally ... he wrote on some engineering matter and is at Ben-Rhydding now ...'

(Holland continues with the contention that a man who was 'never doing better' is probably ready to sell! But then Holland was ever a cynic.)

On the subject of tonnages, at this time Bryneglwys had 30% of all local quarries' output and by 1883 its highest annual tonnage of 7,996 tons was reached. The following year the Talyllyn Railway would carry its highest-ever tonnage of minerals, 9,044 tons. This figure might have been better had not, in August 1880, some of the best workings been flooded when part of the large Llaeron Reservoir embankment collapsed in a storm. The exploit of an elderly quarryman named Watkins who ran from the foot of Cantrybedd Incline to the top of the Village Incline and shouted to warn inhabitants of impending disaster is still a strong local recollection. Concerning the mishap, the Abergynolwyn Police Constable's Journal reads:

> '7 August 1880 Saturday: about 3.30 p.m. the lake at Bryneglwys Quarry broke down its embankments and rushed in force sweeping down everything before it all the bridges between here and the quarry except the County bridge in the village were washed away. Robert Price, the butcher, warehouse and contents, knocked down the new wall at the new Police Station house to the foundation and carried away a large quantity of timber belonging to the contractor.'

After the failure of the auction, 'the highest bid being £10,000 though the property cost £200,000', William McConnel bought the set-up personally for £18,000. On 14th March 1882 the ASCL was wound up and in due course Thomas Aldred was appointed as liquidator. McConnel now set to work with a certain vigour by building the Cantrybedd Mill and expanding the latent Broad Vein workings. The high tonnage of the early 1880s did not last and by 1905 had declined to about 5,500 tons.

When William McConnel died in 1902 W. H. McConnel, his son, continued as sole owner, the while looking over his shoulder at the approaching date of 31st March 1910 when his three quarry leases were due to expire; these were in fact extended by twelve months. He allowed the business to run down and introduced no new capital – worse, he began to work slate in the cheapest way he could by paring down the supporting pillars which divided the working chambers underground to the point where their safety was greatly reduced. In 1909 he approached his sons about the business but none of them showed any interest and so he gave his Manager Agent, Meyrick Roberts, instructions to tell the men on 17th December 1909 the place would close from the following day. The gloom which spread throughout the village from this news, coming just before Christmas, may be imagined. In the weeks that followed, stocks were cleared from the yards and carried by Talyllyn Railway, the storage space at the Towyn Wharf being inundated with materials. Then came the dismantling of machinery and quarrymen began to move away from Abergynolwyn. Amidst a most depressing atmosphere throughout the district, the works were silent for almost twelve months but at least dismantling ceased for the moment as there was rumour that a certain party was interested in purchase.

Relief did come in due course from a purchase by Mr. Henry Haydn Jones, a businessman of Towyn who, in the General Election of January 1910, had defeated his Conservative opponent and become Liberal MP for Merionethshire. In a second election during December the same year, he was returned unopposed, and continued to hold the seat until his retirement in 1945, being knighted for his services in 1937. Of his background, lifestyle, family and links with the Quarry etc., detail is given elsewhere. He had spent some months attempting to find a purchaser for the undertaking without success. He was aware that stocks in the Quarry had been high and that demand was low; the building trade was in a deep recession due to effects of the 1910 Finance Act and slate was not a popular roofing medium, the setback being due to imports of cheap foreign slates of wretched quality rather than faults in the Welsh, which suffered with the majority. In considering the purchase, Haydn Jones knew he could not employ more than 150 men and that he was bound to be criticised – should he purchase – for taking it on as a bolster to his political aims. In the event, he borrowed £5,250 and in January 1911, bought Railway, Quarry and Village for what even then was a pathetic sum; his apparently impetuous gesture was accelerated by McConnel's removal of machinery. The property was conveyed to him on 25th March 1911.

The Abergynolwyn Slate & Slab Co. Ltd. was formed on 2nd November 1911 with a capital of £5,000 in £1 shares: Haydn Jones was its Life Director. Taking the three lapsed leases in hand he was able to obtain fresh ones on competitive rates after protracted negotiations with the successors of landowners who, when located, were faced with virtually no option but to re-let on terms which were clearly of a 'take it or leave it' basis. These leases gave Haydn Jones access until 29th September 1941.

Haydn Jones' path to obtaining these new leases had been 'oiled' by a Report on the workings from Tapp Jones & Son of Westminster (10th May 1910) which was made for Rev. Pugh's son. This Report was not of course made available to Haydn Jones, but it maintained that the only practicable future for the Quarry was to extend the workings westward on the workable floors 'as there is practically no profitable slate rock available in the existing workings ... the condition in which the Quarry has been left will undoubtedly materially injure the prospect of again leasing it as a slate quarry, and the condition of the Cantrybedd portion applies equally (if not more so) to ... the Bryn Eglwys ...'.

The sale was arranged, but complicated by a desire to sue McConnel for compensation to the landowners relative to the damage he had wreaked and not rectified under the terms of Pugh's lease at expiry. This injury was met by his having to leave machinery, tramway, drums etc. on site without compensating payment to the incoming tenant.

As for feelings in Abergynolwyn, the relief at the news that the Quarry had been sold to Haydn Jones, was immediate, for here was an owner in the person of a local man whom many knew. Appreciation came instantly in the words of a song which the villagers used for a number of years afterwards:

> Wel, hen dren bach yr Aber
> Chwibiana heddiw'n dwt
> Daw eto fwg i'r awyr
> O ben dy getyn pwt
> Bydd Tywyn, Rhydyronen,
> Dolgoch a'n H'Aber ni
> Yn rhedeg i'th gyfarfod
> I roi lwc dda i ti.
> Cytgan:
> Byw byth fo Haydn Jones
> Wel ia'n ddigon siwr
> Bydd trichant o ebillion
> Yn canu clod y gwr.

The subscribers to the new Company were Haydn Jones (1,000 shares) and Ellis William Davies (MP for Caernarvon and Haydn Jones' solicitor) (one share). The Registered Office was at 'The Wharf, Towyn'. On 25th November 1911 a new Agreement between the Company and Haydn Jones(!) was made to the effect that he personally owned the machinery etc. on the premises leased to the Company 'in consideration of the Sale to the Company of these items'. In view of this, the Company was prepared to allow him £1,500 in shares, credited as fully paid. So was marked the

first of many 'deals' between the man, the Quarry Company, the Estate, and the Railway which would need so much unravelling almost half a century later. David Jones was made local Manager.

Immediately before the First War there were about 130 men and boys at work; the war reduced the workforce to one of elderly men and boys only; the numbers fell to about 40. Unfortunately for Haydn Jones, the upsurge of Trade Union interest among slate quarrymen which had been fuelled by the long Penrhyn Slate Quarry dispute (1900–1903) grew strongly to the point where in 1911 the North Wales Quarrymen's Union (formed in 1874) adopted a charter setting out minimum conditions of employment and basic wages for their members. Quarry operatives had themselves formed a countering body, The N. Wales Slate Quarry Proprietors Association. By 1918 well over half Bryneglwys employees were in the Union and they approached Haydn Jones as the Association had previously agreed with the Union; on one point there was an unusual facet in that Bryneglwys had worked a five-day week since 1889 – possibly the only site in the industry – and the men were now asking for a five and a half day week! Haydn Jones was not a member of the Association and he explained to his employees that he considered arrangements between them were a private matter and in any case his outgoings in keeping the business at work and his willingness to carry losses in the hope of an improvement in trade, made it impossible for him to meet their wishes. Bitterness followed and Haydn Jones being a man of principle, was ready to close the Quarry; though he was paying lower rates than customary they must continue on his terms. Younger men, reacting to the vision of the brave new world fit for heroes which the ending of war had created were bitter at this disappointment. The men would not give him the undertaking of support for which he called and the Quarry was closed on 31st January 1920. Matters cooled for a time whilst men and management reflected on the situation; Haydn Jones held the trump cards and after maintaining that 'he who paid the piper called the tune', the men went back to work on the original terms one month later.

There was to be another closure the following year over membership of the Union. There was a meeting but Haydn Jones was adamant; if those who wished decided to join the Union, he would close the Quarry. He would accept no comment and the men, defying his intentions, joined the Union. Haydn kept his word and one Friday he closed the Quarry. For three or four weeks nothing transpired then a few of the older men came back and asked to work. They were allowed to begin. A number had gone over to Braichgoch and started work there and others started a small quarry at Dolgoch but were soon disillusioned and asked Haydn if they could return. In due course they all came back, but those who had joined the Union were taken on the

To mark Queen Victoria's Diamond Jubilee in 1897, the Bryneglwys quarry-men were assembled on the rubbish tips at Beudybach and photographed for the occasion. TALYLLYN RAILWAY CO.

last – the stoppage lasted almost four months overall. Working hours at this time were 7 a.m. to 12 noon, and 12.30 p.m. to 5.30 p.m. with no Saturday work. R. O. Williams now became Manager.

In 1931 Haydn Jones appointed Daniel Evans of Penygroes, Caernarvonshire, a quarry-owning man and slate agent in Caernarvon, to be Quarry Manager 'in absento'. Evans might bring Robert Jones with him to work at Pendre. Evans would go up in the train and so into the Quarry accompanied by Haydn Jones: a housekeeper resided there to give them lunch. 'He was a gentleman' recalls Mrs. Mathias. The train would convey them to the foot of Alltwyllt Incline and there they would be hauled up in a wagon, thence horsed along the level and so up Cantrybedd to the Bottom Level.

Haydn had a good business sense; all tools used in the workings came through Messrs. D. & J. Daniel, his own ironmonger's business in the Towyn High Street. Candles were supplied in 2 dozen bundles and hung from roofs of buildings or underground workings to stop the rats from reaching them. The men had to buy their own tools; but by and large, Haydn enjoyed good relations with them. However between the men themselves was much bad feeling, particularly between the Rockmen, who made the 'bargains' monthly with the management (and were remunerated accordingly), and the lowly labourers, who only had a fixed basic rate.

The summer of 1932 was notable for the lack of rain, and dependent as it was upon water for power, the Quarry looked anxiously towards the level in the reservoir. In October, the one hundred employees were laid off to await rain! At an earlier time, McConnel had brought portable steam engines to the Quarry to

overcome a drought – they were said to have been sold by Haydn during World War I.

Now and again good orders appeared but the district was rife with rumour that Haydn Jones turned them away because he was unwilling to develop the Quarry to the scale where such increased business might be accepted. He was certainly aware of the limited potential for developments but, nonetheless, his slates shared part of the new roof of a section of Westminster Hall, went to some new works in the Manchester area, and a new High School in Sheffield was roofed throughout despite the preference of architects to use other materials.*

After a short-lived resurgence after the First War, orders fell short again and the hand of death began to pinch the life from the place; Haydn continued the easy way of reducing still further the widths of the 'pillaring' as McConnel had done and collapses began. The annual visit from the Mine Inspectorate was accompanied by the fear that he would close down the whole Quarry to the loss of all the locality. The Inspector was faced with the continuing enigma of following what he felt was his duty and the problems of the consequence of exercising it.† Stocks down at

---

* Trading under the name VAENGALED ('Welsh Grey Slates') the Quarry had many buildings roofed with its slates (in some instances the order was shared between several quarries). Up to 1925 these included:– Westminster Hall; Goldsborough Hall; National Library of Wales; Kirk Braddan, Isle of Man; St. David's Hotel, Harlech; Sherborne Hospital, Durham; Star Chamber (Court side); Princess Mary's residence. At this period the Sale Office & Registered Office was divided; the former was c/o Daniel Evans, Grove Chambers, Caernarvon, the latter at Slate Wharf, Towyn. The shipping port is given as ABERDOVEY and rail loading charges were 3/2d per ton.

† Slate Mines had been placed under the jurisdiction of the Inspector of Mines by the Metalliferous Mines Act of 1872.

the Railway wharf grew as sizes, unattractive to the building industry, accumulated there, but these were happily and unexpectedly cleared when the effects of German bombing on English cities during World War II created a demand for slates of any size to make good the damage, and the stock yard was completely cleared. There was then enough work for about a dozen to continue in the Quarry for, in 1942, Haydn Jones had been able to obtain an annual tenancy following the expiry of his three leases.

On Boxing Day 1946 the prediction of the Mines' Inspector came true when the men were approaching the Quarry for the day's work. There was a loud rumble like thunder as the roof of the underground chamber, where the men were currently working, collapsed; the Inspector was called and he instructed that the roofs of all other unreliable chambers be dynamited. This resulted in the wholesale fall of that part of the Narrow Vein where the best slate occurred. Up until and after then the local quarrymen maintained there were still many good, workable faces (probably on the pillars!). Between then and September 1948 the last of the stocks held in the Quarry were loaded into the train and stacked at the Wharf station. Haydn Jones gave notice to his solicitor H. M. Arthur of Machynlleth of formal intention to quit the Quarry on 1st December 1948; this was served on W. A. Pugh whose death followed a little while afterwards and whose brother Rev. Richard D. A. Pugh succeeded to the estate. A curious example of renewed interest was to come through Mr. Arthur in 1952 on behalf of a client who wished to explore the possibilities of the site; was the Rector prepared to sell at a reasonable price? Nothing further was heard, and the Rev. Richard Pugh died on 10th May 1955.

Sir Haydn wrote a form of epitaph to the owner of the freehold (Pugh) in 1948 ... 'In my opinion the Quarry can never be made to pay ... my predecessors spent much money in testing the vein and so did I. The vein contains useless rock and rubbish and the cleavage is so difficult that it can never be made a financial success'. He added that his loss the previous year 'due to unreasonably high wages' had involved him in a sum of £1,600.

With stocks of slates now gone, the Quarry hibernated until W. O. Williams of Harlech moved in during 1952 and removed, to sell as scrap metal, all available items such as machinery, rails, wagons, ropes, shafting; it was the *coup de grâce*. The access tramway from Alltwyllt Incline top into the Quarry was also taken up.

It has been written of the Quarry that its survival after 1910 'in the face of increasing competition from manufactured roofing tiles and in spite of the best rock being already worked out, was remarkable. It was essentially a job-creation exercise and depended on the willingness of the men to accept low wages and working conditions which were primitive even by the standards of the slate industry. . . .'* and it would be difficult to improve on that succinct statement.

The Abergynolwyn Slate & Slab Co. Ltd. remained in business at least on paper: the Registered Office was removed from the Wharf to 11 Penrallt Street, Machynlleth in 1954 and Lady Haydn received her husband's shares and became a director at his death on 2nd July 1950. Edward Thomas was Secretary. On 23rd March 1956 Lady Barbara and Edward Thomas resigned; on 5th May the Registered Office moved to Moorgate, London and on the 28th following the name was changed to the Aberllefenni Slate Quarries Ltd. Since 1st December 1972 its Holding Company has been The Bow Slate & Enamel Co. Ltd.

Throughout the saga the complexities of land ownership have not received mention as they are tedious to most and are only partially relevant to the story. Undoubtedly they influenced the Quarry owners, put up costs and deterred investment for the future; some of the reasons why the Talyllyn Railway remained for all this period in a virtually unchanged condition from the day it opened can be laid at the door of this consequence, in that firstly the Quarry, not developing as it was hoped, never offered more traffic than the Railway could carry so that railway facilities were always adequate, and secondly, when additional capital was required, it was always directed to the Quarry's demands rather than the Railway. It should be remembered that for the Quarry to show a profit to its operators it did not necessarily have to be sending down large tonnages of slate – in fact there is ample evidence that in the days of the largest tonnages, profit margins did not rise in line with them. As to the state of play on the ground – so to speak – the Quarry's physical and landownership problems were set out succinctly in 1910 ...

'... the Quarry is situated upon three different properties ... the produce of Cantrybedd (property) has to be brought from the Upper to the Lower Mills by means of an incline over the Bryn Eglwys and Ruck Estates ... the entrance to the Quarry on Floor 20 is entirely on Bryn Eglwys property ... that on Floor 50 is partly on Bryn Eglwys and partly on Cantrybedd ... a large expense [would be] incurred to bring out the Cantrybedd produce within its own boundaries ... the Mills are all on Cantrybedd property and the Tramroad and Inclines to connect with the Talyllyn Railway are principally on the Pugh Estate [i.e. Cantrybedd]'.

The freehold property involving a railway commenced at the summit of the Alltwyllt Incline on the Quarry Tramway and led down The Mineral Line to Abergynolwyn station, which was also laid out upon the same freehold. But more of this elsewhere!

---

* *Slates From Abergynolwyn* (Alan Holmes) Gwynedd Archives Service.

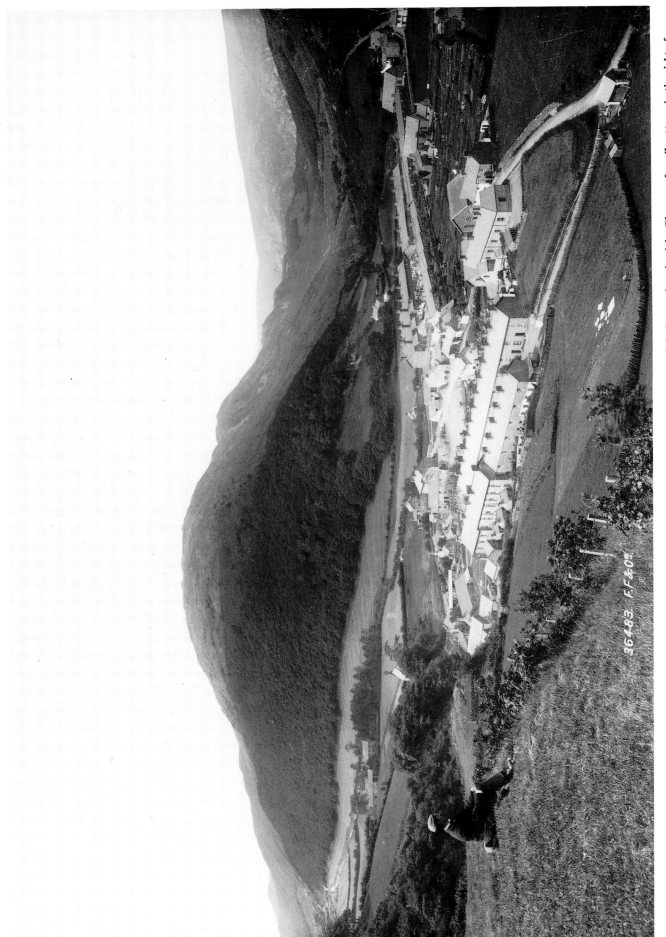

James Stevens' Abergynolwyn lies below to the north-west. The valley of the Afon Fathew runs to the left, that of the Dysynni to the right. The row of small cottages in the right of the picture mark the initial beginnings of the village.

F. FRITH & CO.

CHAPTER THREE

WORKING THE BRYNEGLWYS QUARRY

THE JOHN PUGHE PERIOD (1844– c. 1857)

To comprehend how the rock was extracted, something of the nature of the ground where slate occurs, must be understood. There are three veins of slate which traverse this southern part of the former county of Merioneth; they appear on the coast just below the promenade at Towyn and stretch eastwards for almost twenty miles as far as Dinas Mawddwy, taking in workings at Dolgoch, Bryneglwys, Glyniago, the Corris district, and so on, *en route*. At Bryneglwys we may imagine the surface of the ground as being the top layer of a three-decker cake which has tilted sideways so that if a section was cut away across the ground worked by the Quarry, the three layers would rise up to ground level at an angle and, at ground level, would expose the three layers of the 'cake' as they come to the surface. If we consider the layers to be veins of slate rock, then three veins come to the surface being named The Broad (or Hard), The Middle (or Red) and The Narrow. These veins are inclined somewhat south-east, being 50–60 degrees angle to the horizontal. They are parallel to each other throughout. This 'tilting' of the veins presented one of the first problems Pughe had to face, but he was on equal terms with any other quarry working the same veins elsewhere.

Pughe got off to a promising start though by evidence of the Census Returns for Abergynolwyn (then but a hamlet) in 1851, only two slate quarrymen were then resident, most of his labour coming from elsewhere and even one of the two had but recently come from Llanbedr, Caerns. Population figures for the whole parish of Llanfihangel-y-Pennant (which includes Abergynolwyn) show the effect of slate quarrying in the district:

1841 (375)   1851 (376)   1861 (368)
1871 (731)   1881 (784)   1891 (648)

The population almost doubled in the sixties. This increase for the same reason affected the nearby parishes of Talyllyn, Llanegryn and Llangelynin.

However, there were clearly other quarrymen living in the parish and one combined his work as a dressmaker, and another as a shoemaker; even then (1851) the preponderance of men was living up at Bryneglwys itself where we find four men lodging with the shepherd at Beudynewydd, three with the farmer at Hendrewallog, all of these but one being Caer-narvonshire men. At Bryneglwys itself lived George Smith aged 61 (Pughe's Agent) from Amport (*sic*), Hants., and he had a slatemaker lodging there, also from Caernarvonshire. Smith's son, William aged 23 and born in Chelsea, lived with him; he was the 'slate packer'. There were no more than three other men living locally who described themselves as quarrymen, and it is not known if they worked at Bryneglwys. So the picture is that the scale of Pughe's work was a modest one, though he had 24 men working under him – a considerable force for these parts but insignificant compared with quarries in Caernarvonshire. It will be seen that as was customary, Pughe employed an English Manager or Agent which in this instance, seems a little strange for an undertaking worked by a Welshman.

Pughe began work in The Narrow Vein (approx 55 ft. thick) which was then most suited to the end products for which there was a market: it was the most southerly of the three. The Broad Vein was approx 1,500 ft. thick and The Middle approx 1,350 ft. thick, but the latter was never worked at Bryneglwys. He probably followed earlier trial workings and went downwards from ground level until he had created a substantial pit; as he went down, then so did the overhang, caused by the tilting of the slate bed, become more menacing on the one side, and one day, shorn of support, it fell into the pit. Allowing that this had been anticipated, it did oblige Pughe to work 'sideways' so as not to increase an overhang, and to work on the other side where there was no such danger. This sideways working was enhanced when Pughe dropped a shaft into the Vein, from inside of which he could work both across the width and along the length of the vein. These shafts (of which more followed) spread out to the surface as pits. By 1857 there were three such pits, all connected to the original shaft by a horizontal tunnel. These shafts had an added duty in that they provided essential ventilation to clear the underground workings of the smoke created by the powder used to dislodge the rock. In fact, overground of these shafts, on a windless day, the land was clothed in a low-hanging smoke.

As to the original shaft, Pughe cut a tunnel, drift or adit from alongside his small mill on the Bryneglwys Level so as to meet the shaft almost 70 ft. below ground. In due course, the shaft was enlarged and became itself a pit, open to the sky; the tunnel was thus given daylight at both ends, and took the name The Daylight Adit. In course of time it grew to become a large bore carrying a double line of tramway in Talyllyn Railway track materials but without chairs; its floor was so sloped as to carry away any penetrating water. At least until 1857 this tunnel tramway must have been the principal means of removing rock, as Smith's report of that year says there was no lifting haulage in the original shaft.

The men's equipment would be basic and the pay was 8/6d. a week. The end product was the time-honoured Blue Vein slate most suited to roofing purposes. At first, Pughe's only machinery was one dressing table and slate saw. The finished slates were packed into panniers which were slung, one each side of a mountain pony and then carried over the Tarren-y-Gesail backbone approximately to the south, and so down into Pennal for shipment at the small river quay there. There was once a tavern between Abergynolwyn and Pennal.

Things were on a small scale. With 25 men, only a few hundred tons would be produced annually; the carriage of slates to the waterside would be hampered by bad weather and as transport costs caused quarries to close down (for almost any quarry produced slate at approximately the same cost) it was the cost on board ship which determined the survival of the site. Pughe's Mill was also small, but 48 ft. × 47 ft., a simple span-roofed structure which would later form part of the larger Old Mill. It stood just inside the boundary of the Cantrybedd Estate and on the west bank of the Boundary Stream; on the other bank of that stream was the Bryneglwys Estate. The buildings had two openings each side and by dint of them tramways passed through the building; along their tracks passed the flat frame trolleys which brought the large undressed slabs from underground for processing in the mill, to be finished perhaps as roofing slates, mantel-pieces, windowsills and so on. The mill was some 200 yards downhill from The Narrow Vein.

The foregoing comprised the extent of the enterprise of John Pughe. Further afield, the quarries over the ridge at Corris were now enjoying the benefits of rail haulage down to the Dovey-side at Derwenlas – an important competitive factor – and launched in 1853 at that same Derwenlas, was the sailing ship *Seven Brothers* which was destined to carry much Bryneglwys slate. Of this more anon.

Were it possible to go back in time and see the Quarry at the period Pughe was at work, the site would be something of an anticlimax. The only access was along the rough road, up the Nant Gwernol gorge from near Abergynolwyn (then not much more than a farmstead) to the quarrying site some 750 ft. above sea-level. Above ground, apart from the newly-created rubbish tips which now appeared on the flanks of the hill, and the small mill building, there would be little evidence of what was taking place below. There was a small yard beside the mill where finished materials were stacked by size, awaiting transport over the mountain. From time to time a wagon, pushed by three or four men, would leave or enter the mouth of The Daylight Adit with its entrance cutting – so much like the small entrance to a wasps' nest. Or occasionally a train of ponies would leave the premises and set off up the mountain path with its ship-bound load (or a caravan would return single file down the narrow path). On the ridge those bound for Pennal and beyond would obtain a wonderful southward vista of sea and mountain – when the weather allowed! This is an age-old primitive route* which climbs for $\frac{3}{4}$ mile south-east from Bryneglwys at 775 ft., to the ridge of Moel-y-Geifr at 1,393 ft.; here, having climbed very steeply from Pont Llaeron south-eastwards to that ridge, it re-doubles westward along the contour, and re-doubles again, falling from the col (703046) just to the west of the dome of Mynydd Cefncaer (701033) and so down to Esgairisaf (702019), thence to Pennal, the historic crossing of the Dovey almost three miles south-west of Machynlleth. Thus was Pughe using an existing and well-known artery. The tale of a family moving from Bryneglwys to Pennal within the last century or so emphasises the traditional use in these parts of sledges; all the family belongings (furniture etc.) were piled up onto one of these and hauled by two horses. At Pont Llaeron the sledge overturned ... Pennal was, of course, a Roman crossing of the Dovey and they had a nearby fort to safeguard it. Vessels that loaded at Pennal were mainly small craft, and Pughe's slate would be again transferred into sea-going vessels at Aberdovey, thus adding to the cost of the product.

Oddly, when Mrs. Pughe advertised the Quarry for sale in 1859, Derwenlas ($4\frac{1}{2}$ m. away) is specially mentioned as having shipping facilities. It was the highest point on the river to which ordinary tides reached. Does this infer the Quarry had used either or both for shipment?

Here, presumably, 'Mrs. Pughe's ship' the *Seven Brothers* (it was not her property but built in her time of ownership of the Quarry lease) would begin to ply the seas from Aberdovey, and it may well be that the introduction of this vessel in 1853 marked the end of the use of the packhorse route in favour of sledging or cartage down to Abergynolwyn, and thence by carts to Aberdovey wharf, changing horses at Ty Mawr – an event recalled in Towyn fifty years ago. There are

---

* A traditional land-link used by pack animals, but often impassable in winter when, for instance, Pennal men would remain in Bryneglwys barracks.

cuts in the Quarry road down to the village which are said to have been caused by spragging the wheels of carts.

The motive behind the building of the *Seven Brothers* is not clear. It may have been confidence in the future of the Quarry, and accelerated by a plan of November 1850 to build a railway to link the quarries up the valley in the Corris district, with Machynlleth, Pennal, Aberdovey and Towyn, with a wharf branch at Aberdovey. Following on the heels of this dream, came the Shrewsbury & Aberystwyth scheme which would also have had a feeder branch up to Corris. Such competition would have eclipsed Bryneglwys transport, and another tradition that the *Seven Brothers* was part of a 'package deal', which would have included a direct rail link from Bryneglwys to Aberdovey, could be the basis of the oft-told tale that the Talyllyn Railway would not have entered Towyn at all! But all these plans failed to fructify.

Cartage to Aberdovey was done along the 'improved road' (turnpike) which could be followed down to Croes-Faen, thence past Ty Mawr (the section known as Lovers' Lane) and out onto the main coast road of today, bypassing Towyn altogether.

[On the subject of roads, *The Merionethshire Herald* writes (14th November 1863):

'Towyn – our roads again. Our roads are in a horrible state, partly owing to the state of the weather; partly owing to the increased heavy traffic by the cartage of slates from Bryneglwys Quarry, and the railway contractors heavy wagons; but especially owing to the road surveyors' great neglect of repairs ...'

Unfortunately we cannot deduce if it was the Coast Railway or the Talyllyn Railway contractor who was guilty, but by date it is likely to be the former. The matter appears again in the same paper (23rd April 1864):

'Tallyllyn and Towyn turnpike road ... part of the road between Penyparc (near Towyn) and Minffordd was not put and kept in proper repair ... The traffic along the road consists of slates from near Abergynolwyn and materials carried to and from farms ... Mr. Jones (solicitor) received a message from Mr. McConnel of the slate quarry ... stating that he would give £10 to assist the funds of the trustees for every £50 they spent on the road.'

So at least we know that McConnel had begun his links with Bryneglwys by carting slate – whether to Aberdovey or Towyn or both, is not known. Robert Williams (Quarry Manager who continued under McConnel) in his diary writes of sledges bringing down slate from the Quarry; it is suggested this was only so far as the village.]

Jane Pughe, who took over the business, had been born a Williams and a sister of Hugh Williams who was concerned with lead mining at the well-known site of Dylife in Montgomeryshire. This undertaking brought its products to Derwenlas for shipment, so Pughe would probably know the port well and through his wife's connections he became a partner in the Dylife venture. So connected through marriage, they were connected in commerce also. Dylife was never to have rail links, but in steam days transport was done by steam traction engines and trailers.

By the late 1850s Bryneglwys was said to be idle. It may be that business was hit by the opening of the Corris Machynlleth & River Dovey Tramroad in 1859, which gave Corris area quarries a rail link with Derwenlas and cut their transport costs considerably. If Robert Prys Morris' account is valid 'in or about 1857 it was sublet to three Welshmen who worked it for three years ... and closed a second time'.

THE JOHN LLOYD JONES PERIOD (1862–63)

In 1862 the opportunity of acquiring Pughe's business came to the notice of John Lloyd Jones (1826–1893) of Baladaulyn near Llanlyfni. Jones was the son of the noted Nantlle Methodist preacher and quarryman, Rev. John Jones of Talysarn, who had been involved in setting up a workers' co-operative at the Dorothea Quarry nearby. His mother, Fanny, had for her father Thomas Edwards who had worked both for Garnons and Turner as a quarry manager.* Though John Lloyd began his career in quarrying as deputy for his father (who was Manager of the Dorothea Quarry) in 1851–57 whilst his senior was away on preaching engagements, his real capacity was as salesman and haulage contractor for Dorothea. With good business sense he became Chairman of Dorothea, but sold out to his brother-in-law in 1861. In the early 1860s he was then involved with the Pantdreiniog and Fron

Quarries; he was owner of the lease of Penyrorsedd Quarry and sold it to W.A. Darbishire in 1863 (staying on as his Manager for a time); he was also involved in Ty Mawr East and Tynyweirglodd Quarries – all the foregoing were in the Nantlle region and even then the list is incomplete! His forte seems to have been timely purchase and opportune selling! With such a background one might have expected him to develop Bryneglwys with cunning experience but it seems to have been cut short, for about eighteen months after acquisition he sold it to the McConnel interest, reputedly for a considerable profit.

Before he came to Bryneglwys these 'butterfly tactics' were well known. He would purchase a quarry, make a few improvements and re-sell shortly afterwards; it would seem he had, until then, insufficient capital (and perhaps desire also) to develop fully a site, that is until Bryneglwys came into his hands. Here, he set to work with a will and may have intended to

* See *Narrow Gauge Railways in North Caernarvonshire* Vol. 1 p.7 etc. (J. I. C. Boyd)

continue had not a spider-and-fly situation appeared, and probably Jones considered that the McConnels, with cash ready to speculate, were too good a prey to let pass!

His first visit to Bryneglwys, in company with Robert Williams, his Manager and also from Llanlyfni, was under the aegis of The Britannia Slate & Slab Co., the operating name of the Dorothea Quarry, and in due course the site on the Cantrybedd Estate was worked by him. Williams was installed as Agent or Manager and the undertaking was styled 'Britannia Slate & Slab Co., Bryneglwys and Cantrybedd Quarries'. Pughe's workforce of over twenty had been reduced to about six when Jones began work in October 1862, and such was the rapid development that by December twenty-three were engaged. Williams encouraged any Caernarvonshire quarryman to come to Bryneglwys but the slate cutters soon found they were not as efficient with the local rock as they had been back at home, and that the local men could do the work better!

Exploitation now took on a quite different form under Williams, who not only extended the workings along The Narrow Vein but began to work downwards below the level of Pughe's Mill and, by doing so, opened up two new working faces, one on the Cantrybedd Estate and the other on the boundary between it and Bryneglwys. Soon The Daylight Adit was too high above the working area to be an effective exit from the workings, so Williams, using the same techniques so effective at Nantlle, placed a 30 ft. diameter water wheel between Pughe's original pit and his mill; between 1864–67 a second similar wheel was erected alongside. On the nearby edge of the pit he built a massive headframe which enabled large pulley wheels at its top to be suspended over the edge of the pit. A haulage chain, driven by the water wheels was then taken from a winding drum over pulleys and down into the pit. Empty wagons were lowered, and full ones raised by an appliance similar to a pulley block and having 'spreaders'. In the case of wagons, four short spreaders, each with a hook at its end, were passed through the eyes in each upper corner of the wagon body. Bearing in mind the pit was not vertical, it was essential to take heavy, inclined fixed chains from the surface (at the headgear landing-platform) down to a low point in the pit on the opposite side, where they were securely anchored. These chains were used solely as a guide.

Of this development, a nice account appeared in *Y Cymro* during 1900, when Williams' diaries were published.

'Nothing much happened whilst the quarry was being worked by John Ll. Jones save that I opened two new faces, one at the end between Bryneglwys and Cantrybedd, and one in Cantrybedd. Also a water wheel was erected, thirty feet in diameter and three feet wide, and it was connected to the machines which were necessary to raise the stone and rubble and pump water. It was also necessary for me to effect substantial repairs to the road from the quarry down to Abergynolwyn in order to make it suitable for those who wished to carry slates down to Aberdyfi in their sledges (pedrolfenni) from which Port were transported hundreds of tons, some to Germany and some to London and various other places. It was a very expensive exercise to move the slates by means of these contraptions, but as Mr. Jones had been so fortunate in selling the quarry and having such a good price for it, the country was as fortunate as he was, as he had organised gentlemen of sufficient means to enable the quarry to be opened on a grand and effective scale in order to produce hundreds of tons a month, when it became necessary to have a better method of transporting the slates to the harbour and so it was determined to have an iron way (ffordd haiarn) from the quarry down to Towyn, and this decision was carried out effectively. A railway was made the full way from the quarry down to Towyn in a very short time, the whole being completed in a little over one year.

'I should explain that the Company had recently asked me if I would stay to serve them at the quarry as their Agent. I said I would provided that the terms and payment reflected the responsibility being placed upon me. Successful terms were agreed between us and I worked for them for several months working according to the plan given to me by Mr. Wyatt, Lord Penrhyn's old Agent, for it was he who had been chosen by the Company to do so. Whilst carrying on with Mr. Wyatt's plan, I saw that it was completely opposed to the best way of opening the quarry in my opinion. My new master's name was Thomas H. McConnell. In considering the responsibility which could have descended upon me in proceeding in that way I decided it would be better for me to outline my plan to Mr. McConnell before things went too far to be improved. Accordingly I wrote to him explaining that I thought I could produce a better plan than Mr. Wyatt's, and saying that if I had to proceed with Mr. Wyatt's plan I would not hold myself responsible for the consequences. I had made up my mind that it would have been better for me to have left if I couldn't open the quarry in the best way according to my own plan and in truth I had a place to go to at that time ... He wrote to Mr. Wyatt warning him that I had condemned the whole of his plans. Mr. Wyatt came to Bryn Eglwys to meet him and I was obliged to stand face to face with the old gentleman in connection with his plans, but as Mr. Wyatt was a wily old bird he gave no sign of offence because he knew that I would have known more than he about the best and cheapest way to exploit the quarry, and indeed he was so generous as to confess that to my master in recommending my plans and saying that I was paying proper regard to my duties and that it would be better for me to carry out my own plans (praise which I may or may not have deserved). Therefore I was allowed to open the quarry entirely according to my own plan and many have judged my work from that time until now, and I know of no one who has condemned my work.

'I opened twenty chambers in less than thirteen and a half years, and many improvements were made. Many houses were built by the Quarry Company, and as the Company had bought the lands around Abergynolwyn they were able to lease land for other people to build houses which has improved things immensely for the inhabitants compared with things as they were when I came to this neighbourhood. Also a railway was built from the quarry to Towyn to carry the slates and goods which has given facilities to residents nearby which they had never had before.

'Also in the quarry everything has been done in the best possible way as far as the workplaces of the quarrymen are concerned, and in order to carry out from the chambers the huge blocks of three or four tons each, some more and some less. All these are worked in warm buildings which have been built in the best possible manner, with plenty of light coming into them, such as quarrymen had not previously encountered, and indeed which quarrymen in past ages would not have dreamed about, and yet it is not in all quarries that such advantages are to be had ...

'The person who had acted as master to me had died, and this was a great loss to me as the Company sent an Englishman by the name of James Stevens* to be its representative with me in

---

* Surveyor to the McConnels' scheme, from Manchester.

the quarry, and as every quarryman in every quarry in Wales knows, when an Englishman comes in as an official in a Welsh quarry he generally feels obliged to show himself to be superior at all times, and as I was of the opinion that I was the chief official at the Bryn Eglwys Quarry, I did not submit to the Englishman. It was rather an effort, but it was the Englishman who lost the day. But immediately after the effort, I gave up my post as I had indeed intended to do before the dispute. But I was determined to leave as the victor with the crown on my head, having served the McConnells and the Company for fully twelve years and before then in the same quarry under John Ll. Jones for a year and a half.'

Supporting the headframe and working platform, Williams built a massive slab footwall on the north side of the pit. The landing platform was fitted with an ingenious trap in the floor; this was hinged up to clear a wagon rising from below so that when it reached ground level the trap could be dropped, and the wagon, now hanging above it, could be lowered down onto a steel sheet. It was then run off along an overground tramway. To supply the large overshot water wheels with water, the Llaeron and Boundary streams were diverted into a wooden trough or lander carried on slab piers to the tops of the wheels. The use of sledges drawn by men is recalled, the driver (with helper?) having to drag the sledge uphill again.

Methods of working are only known in the most general of terms; later developments have destroyed earlier workings save for Pughe's Mill which had an additional 88 feet put on it, having three tramway openings on each side. It was readily identifiable, as the roof had a lower pitch than the other buildings.

THE ABERDOVEY SLATE CO. LTD. PERIOD (1864–67)

The above Company was formed in 1863 but did not acquire the property until 1st January 1864, and they set about the works in a most energetic way. The open pit method was abandoned completely (with its dangerous overhangs) and the system of working in underground chambers, as at Blaenau Ffestiniog, was adopted. These chambers were cut on floors at 25-yard vertical intervals and at each floor a 'working tunnel' parallel to, but about 18 ft outside of the vein, was dug; at regular intervals along one side of each tunnel an opening was made into The Narrow Vein. In the area concerned at this time, three such tunnels would be made: at such openings the first job was to cut a 'roofing shaft' upwards along the edge of the vein, to reach either the floor above or the surface of the ground. This was essentially a ventilating exercise, but in time blocks of rock might be hauled up the slope of the shafts. As the off-tunnel openings were enlarged beneath and beyond these shafts, a chamber was formed by the Miners, whose job it was to open up the vein rapidly before handing over to the Rockmen. Explosives were used to urge on the work so that the roofing shafts poured out smoke continuously above ground. Whilst the Miners' task was to prepare the chambers for the Rockmen, the latter worked differently, using intuition and skill to bring out large slabs rather than to blow them to smithereens; they used the 'grain' of the rock to split it away from the working face, using large chisels and bars and only a minimal amount of explosive where essential, poured into carefully positioned holes made by a 'jumper' (a long steel rod carefully sharpened at one end and driven in by hammer blows). In this way the fragmentation of the rock was minimal. Further splitting might be necessary, using wedges and hammer, to bring the rock slabs down to a size where they could be lifted by tripod derrick and loaded onto a flat wagon and so by rail to the mill. The main tramways were laid in c.40 lb.* flat-bottomed rails (identical in section to those on the Talyllyn Railway) and lesser tramways in 27 lb. (or less) bridge rails, all supported on 'sleepers of the best construction' (i.e. wooden).

The foundation of this system lay in the provision of two principal features; firstly a long adit ('Long or Main Tunnel'),† level with the 50 yards-depth 'working tunnel' (684 yds. long) ‡ which ran along the side of and about 18 ft. outside the vein: secondly, a deep or Main Shaft§ which fell beside the ground-level opening of Pughe's original pit, to reach this Long Tunnel. This tunnel or adit, known as 'The Long Tunnel' (Lefel Fawr) to distinguish it from the working tunnel beforementioned, is quite straight from its entrance beside the Lower Mill on the Cantrybedd Level, to the foot of the second feature, the deep shaft; it is 615 yards‡ long, i.e. approaching one third of a mile. At the shaft foot it turns left to meet The Narrow Vein at right angles – the tunnel at the 50-yard depth cutting through it. It ends on the working floor of the 50 yard-depth tunnel. The yardage depth in these instances was not measured from ground level but from John Pughe's Daylight Adit, which hereafter became the 'Adit Level' or Base Level from which all later vertical distances were taken. Floors were subsequently begun at 25 yard-depth intervals above and below Adit Level and each given a short tunnel to connect it to the deep shaft, the purpose being to allow each floor to drain into the deep shaft, the water then falling down to the bottom of that shaft where it met The Long Tunnel. The latter, being constructed with a slight slope to its floor, thus drained the whole of the workings and by turbines

---

* Sale Catalogue quotes 45 lbs.
† Nominally 6 ft. wide × 6 ft. high.
‡ These figures are distance reached by 1879 – not at period above.
§ Varying 6–8 ft. square.

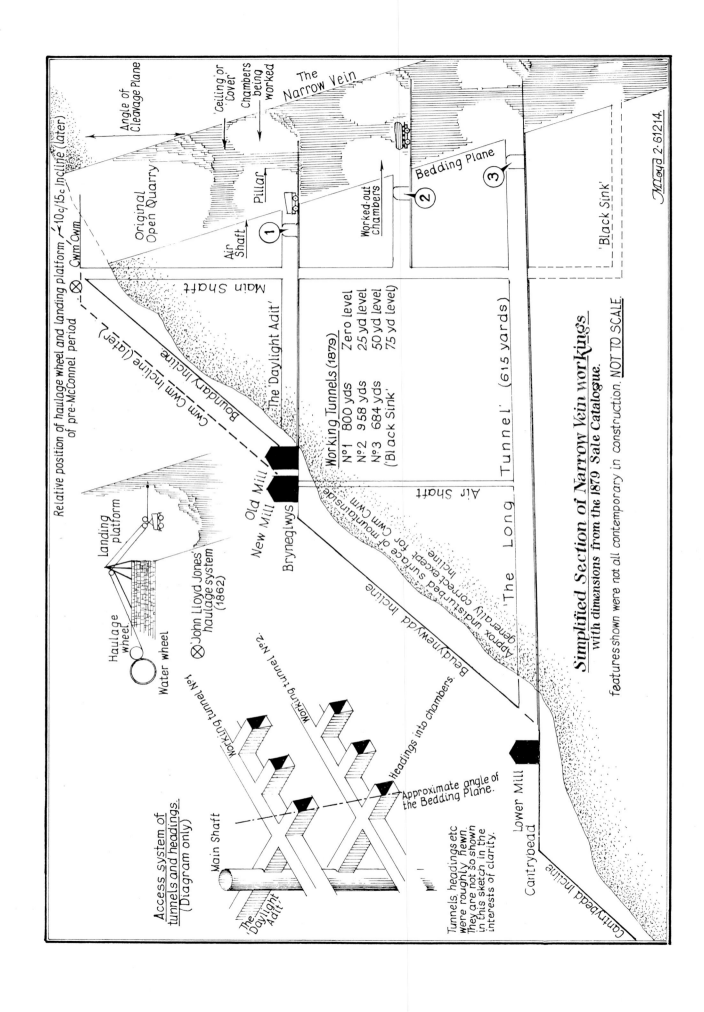

Simplified Section of Narrow Vein workings
with dimensions from the 1879 Sale Catalogue.

features shown were not all contemporary in construction. NOT TO SCALE.

M.Lloyd 2·61214.

discharging water out onto the Cantrybedd Level and so into the river. (In later times, The Long Tunnel was unable to drain the workings which were opening out *below* it and this would cause problems.)

Referring momentarily to the three 'working tunnels' parallel to the vein: the lowest (50 yard-depth to which The Long Tunnel was connected) was 684 yards * long; 25 yard-depth above this the tunnel was 958 yards * long; the third and highest – connecting and level with The Daylight Adit – 800 yards * long. (There were also c. 242 yards * on Cantrybedd and c. 275 yards on Bryneglwys plus c. 684 yards of additional tunnelling off The Long Tunnel.)

These lengths were not reached until 1879, some sixteen years after the period under review, but they are pertinent at this stage as they demonstrate the scale of underground work almost $1\frac{1}{2}$ miles of essential underground tunnelling besides the actual excavations made in extracting the slate rock! The Daylight Adit carried a double track tramway, and all others a single line of rails.

A numbering system was evolved in due course; the Adit Level became 20 and the levels below 25 and 50 had the suffix B or C added to denote which estate they were on (Bryneglwys or Cantrybedd).†

A chamber might become 30–40 yards long, extend across the full width of the vein and reach up to 20 yards in height. Each was therefore a gigantic underground cave, separated from adjoining chambers by intervening rock, known as a pillar. The pillars were about 10 yards wide and were left intact (or should have been . . . !) and in the honeycomb of underground cavities thus formed, it was the pillars which supported the whole. All chambers/pillars followed exactly the slope of the vein around.

It has already been appreciated that The Aberdovey Slate Co. Ltd. was not only concerned with these great works, but was also building a linking railway, and developing a village. Also on the surface of the Quarry. additional mills and other working features appeared. It was a decade or so of remarkable expansion, the like of which would never be seen again.

---

* These figures are distance reached by 1879 – not at period above.

† In practice, Floor 20 did not extend north-eastwards beyond The Daylight Adit as, the ground being sloped, there was insufficient depth below ground. In consequence, Floor 15 was next above Floor 25 on that side of the workings; on the Cantrybedd side, Floor 15 succeeded 20. Two further floors, 10 and 5, were driven both sides of the valley and retained the 25 yard vertical interval.

THE ABERGYNOLWYN SLATE CO. LTD. PERIOD (1867–81)

The change of title did not bring about any great changes – not unexpectedly. As work in developing The Narrow Vein progressed, it became increasingly evident, as working tunnels became longer and further trial bores were made, that the early expectations for the Quarry would never be fulfilled. But at first, development was still the keynote. The second 30 ft. water wheel was erected beside the first, and now, instead of drawing wagons destined for the mill by headframe up to the surface, a new double-tracked incline was made within the vein itself, and the water wheels coupled to it by an ingenious system of chains running just below ground level, though the original Nantlle-pattern headframe with its guiding chains was retained for bringing to the surface wagons of rubbish which were then pushed to a tipping area. It was whilst handling such wagons on the landing of the headframe that an accident occurred: a man engaged in this work lost his footing and fell into the workings below, being injured fatally and confirming the method was still in use at that time. The new incline did not reach the surface but only to the double line of tramway in The Daylight Adit, and blocks *en route* for the mill travelled this way. It served the workings on the north-east side of the Quarry.

The momentous year of 1879 when the undertaking was put up for auction has already received mention. Fortunately the sale catalogue still exists and provides the first full-scale account of the Quarry, above and below ground. Much of its contents have already been described as they were all developed in the 1864–79 period. By this latter date one open pit and sixteen chambers on Bryneglwys and eight chambers on Cantrybedd, all on The Narrow Vein, had been created. Rubbish was cleared, as just described, on the chain hoist and tipped out around the area where the two water wheels stood. When they were in danger of becoming engulfed it became necessary to build a 30 ft. high slab protecting wall around them to prevent such a calamity! Whilst it was not so convenient to have slab blocks *en route* for the mills by this method (The Daylight Adit was much more convenient and saved handling), such flat wagons as came up the chain hoist loaded had to be put onto a tramway leading down the Boundary Incline to Bryneglwys Mill at its foot (the incline so-named as it stood on the boundary of Bryneglwys and Cantrybedd Estates).

There was, in fact, a further short incline above the Boundary Incline, in order to reach Floor 15 and, beyond this again, a longer incline climbed to give access to Floor 10. Both 10 and 15 had adits opening out on the hillside above and to the south-west of Bryneglwys Mill, and were served by tramways; these two inclines were abandoned many years ago in favour of taking material out through lower level tunnels. Fieldwork at the head of the last-mentioned incline will produce evidence of still higher grass-covered tips and trial workings, Floor 5. These were never developed but tradition has it that this area was that in which John Williams did his earliest work in the 1830s.

To cater for this substantial increase in through-put, Bryneglwys Mill was enlarged in the 1860s to a total area of 17,500 sq. ft., though this includes a room used as a repair shop. When a later building nearby was put up opposite and became the New Mill, this edifice became the Old Mill; in due course a lean-to was built against the east end of the Old for a Blacksmith's Shop and Machine Shop.

More may be said about the above-ground scene at the Quarry, largely accomplished between 1864 and 1867. In the Old Mill the hand-operated machinery had given way to water-powered drive by turbine; the roof trusses were a convenient way to carry a long line of shafting which was revolved by a belt off the turbine, and belts in turn were brought down from the shafting to the various machines. In those days of almost 'care less' conditions, accidents caused by unprotected belting were frequent and often fatal. In this mill a wall-pit was built against the wall of the central room and in it there was a vertical-axis turbine; this was supplied with water most economically from the tail-races of the two water wheels, where, having done its work there, it was carried on a wooden troughing to enter the mill at roof ridge height. To conserve water for this extended use, a storage system of two reservoirs was commenced in 1865–66. The larger one held 15 million gallons and involved the building of a sub-stantial earthen dam with stone pitching on the inner face. There was a prominent central tower resembling a small stone lighthouse standing in the water not far from this earthwork; it was reached by a catwalk from *terra firma* and contained the water outlet valves which could be worked by two handwheels at its top. This was the Llaeron Reservoir. When water was released from here it flowed along a surface channel into a small holding reservoir created by damming up the Boundary Stream just above The Narrow Vein and from here it could be led directly to the Old Mill turbine. This small reservoir also acted as a 'buffer zone' as the design of the water supply (not relevant in detail here) meant there was always a flow down into it even when the Llaeron valves were closed. Two other water wheels, one of 16 ft., the other 10 ft.

diameter, were used to drive pumps to aid the clearing of water.

Soon the Old Mill no longer stood in isolation: behind and around it a considerable 'delta' of rubbish continued to grow, covering the bed of the Boundary Stream as well. Thirty yards away the New Mill was built, a simple span-roofed slab-walled building with, in its south-west corner, the top of a shaft leading straight down to The Long Tunnel. This shaft is likely to date from the building of the tunnel and would expedite its construction, for having been sunk to the level of that tunnel, it would be possible to work out in each direction from there and so double the number of working faces and prosecute the work. Actually the first 20 ft. of that shaft is above natural ground level, so had had to be slab-walled – the ground around became part of the rubbish tip so this fact is not readily apparent. Part way down was a platform on which another turbine was carried for driving the New Mill; its waste water dropped down the shaft and escaped via The Long Tunnel below. As the turbine was fed from the tail-race of the turbine in the Old Mill, this might have been a third opportunity to drive from it, a particular advantage in time of drought. There was insufficient work for the New Mill even before the First War, and it was out of regular use from that time.

Where The Daylight Adit emerged beside the Old Mill, the flat trolleys were weighed; the blocks on the trolleys would be marked according to the Rockmen underground who had supplied it. (These two would be teamed up with two slatemakers in the mill, the team striking a 'bargain' every month with the Manager – this was based on the number of slates it might be expected they would produce in the next month and a price was then agreed upon between Manager and team. Each block so weighed would be identified by mark by the two men of the team employed in the mill as produced by their partners. Other men in the organisation like labourers and jour-neymen were paid on a daily basis.) Wherever such wagons appeared from below there was, as here, a small building with weighing table and accompanying office where records were kept. The delicate part of the weighing mechanism was therefore under cover; there would also be a fireplace in the corner and one of the loads of incoming wagons to the Quarry would be to carry coal for distribution to numerous weighing offices on various levels/floors.

Additionally hereabouts was a larger office building where wages were calculated and time books kept. There was a bell hung from the gable end outside; when rung it marked the start of each shift and to qualify a man had to be inside the boundary wall when the bell ceased to be sounded; otherwise he was

Looking almost due east in the Quarry, with the Old Mill and its storage yard in the foreground; the Gunpowder Magazine is the small building in the centre. The Manager's House is on the extreme left.   BURRELL'S SERIES

'carpeted' in front of the Manager. Some men who were close friends of the bell-ringer would have the bell rung long enough for them to reach the boundary!

The Quarry used a considerable quantity of explosives and near here was an unremarkable building with two unequal rooms inside used as a magazine; the larger was for kegs of powder and the other for dynamite or nitroglycerine used by the Miners. The building was lined inside with softwood to eliminate the risk of sparks. Some explosives were also stored in a small building at the Railway's Wharf station and into each building a tramway was led, conveyance by special vans belonging to the Quarry being part of the railway traffic. From time to time the Police Sergeant at Abergynolwyn would make routine inspections of magazines in the adjacent quarries.

Accommodation was provided in Welsh slate quarries for both men only or whole families who might either reside permanently in the quarry precincts or simply be lodged by the week; at Bryneglwys the five day week (the earliest example) began in 1889 and so employees enjoyed two days at home each weekend. There was a barrack for the men; some three or four families lived in two houses beside the drum house at the head of Cantrybedd Incline, a none-too-large building; rent was 1/- a month in the 1890s. Some men lodged in nearby farmsteads or in Abergynolwyn

village. By the late 1870s the original Caernarvonshire labour force had been mixed by the addition of others from the Dysynni and Dovey valleys (the latter mainly from Upper and Lower Corris) who lodged by the week, together with Cornish tin miners whose own native occupation was uncertain. Numbers employed reached the 350 mark and in the mills slate dressers made up to 1,000 roofing slates in one day, mainly in the large 'Countess' size, 20 ins. × 10 ins. – the largest slates commanded the higher prices.

Near The Daylight Adit weigh house stood the carpenter's shop to which an upper floor had been added to make a barrack for 24 beds (the Big Barrack); access was by external stairway. There was another barrack having 18 beds (the Water Barrack) with a dining room, all on the first floor and divided into three by partitions. A family lived downstairs where there was also a large mess room with a big brick fireplace which held a communal soup tureen, kettle etc., and also doubled up as a school, Sunday School and meeting place. Here such men as ate there might be addressed by the 'Chairman' of the barracks at mealtimes but there were other eating places (each was called a 'caban') and the 'Savoy Cafe' at the Abergynolwyn end of the Cantrybedd Mill. Lighting was wholly by candle or oil lamps and though surrounded by water – which was used as a source of power – there was no domestic electrical supply. There were also gardens, a bakery etc., in fact the whole community was self-supporting.

The Manager was accommodated in a house ('Bryneglwys Hall') with a smack of Victorian suburbia about it; it was of slab but faced with hung slates at the front; it included the usual offices of those times – laundry, bakery, walled yard, and a separate farm adjacent. There were sufficient rooms to accommodate ten lodgers, even though the Meyrick Roberts family had ten children of its own! Behind the house was the Quarry Office, arranged so as to give views of the workings on three aspects. The house, built in the 1860s, became vacant in the late 1930s.

The nearby farmhouse of ancient origin, a string of cottages (to which an upper floor had been added in the 1860s) which included a small shop, all pre-dated the Quarry.

THE WILLIAM AND W.H. McCONNEL PERIOD (1881–1902)

Some of the events mentioned in the foregoing have taken the saga well beyond the period in question, and the years must now be rolled back.

The Quarry was now equipped with a considerable length of tramway, permanent tracks of about 2 miles and approximately 4 miles in total assessed at 188 tons of rail. At the entrance to the main exits, weigh houses (supplied with weighing tables by Pooley & Sons) were traversed by the loaded wagons leaving the chambers *en route* for the mills; from these figures actual production (against rubbish) could be calculated. Mostly in the area of the mills, there were about twenty wagon turn-tables.

Money had been poured into the undertaking and it was all to no avail. William McConnel bought the concern from the liquidator for a mere £18,000 and made further trial workings on The Broad Vein whilst directing most of his attention to The Narrow Vein on the Bryneglwys side; he was now financed in such a way that so long as business held up, there was sufficient profit to keep 'in the black'. The stumbling block lay in the date on which leases would terminate, but after a number of hiccoughs and much parry and thrust between the legal representatives of all parties, leases were so arranged as to all terminate in 1909. Details of these events make tedious reading, but on Bryneglwys the young Lewis Morris was as equally stubborn as had been his father. Some of the early leases had been drawn up in such a way they were a hindrance even to the landowners who wished to be moderately helpful!

So it was mid-1881 when William and his son, William Houldsworth, could operate the reformed undertaking; as mentioned, they began in a small way to develop The Broad Vein near the head of the Beudynewydd Incline, and a larger mill on the Cantrybedd Level to serve it. A tablet dated 1881 on the adjacent stable building may confirm work had begun before the change in company ownership. This memorial had been removed at the time the workings were dismantled after the death of Sir Haydn, but it was typical of other nice touches, professionally done or simply 'doodled' in slate, which could be found not only in the Quarry, but for the sharp-eyed, along the Railway too. The tablet in question read:

> W. H. McConnel, Esqr
> 1881
> M. R. Manager

and 1881 is flanked by a hammer on the left and a trowel on the right both impressions being initialled 'J. W.' Is this that same 'John Whiting 1866' cut into the stonework so neatly elsewhere? The previous decade had seen some development on The Broad Vein and there were several galleries above ground to show for it: in due course five levels in the vein were established, two below the level of the main tramway on Beudynewydd Incline, the lowest being connected to the main tramway by a junction halfway down that incline. (There had been other small workings on this vein but these have not been fully traceable as they are mostly buried by rubbish from above.)

The new Cantrybedd Mill was to become one of the largest in the industry, being at first 155 ft. long by 40 ft. wide with a smithy and stable at the upper east end (a 'landslide' in about 1930 carried part of the west end away due to the collapse of a spoil tip washed down by a release of trapped water from a trial adit above) whilst at the other end a turbine was installed to drive the shafting, supplied by water coming from a small reservoir fed by a channel taken off the Boundary Reservoir; it drained through a culvert into the river. Later the Mill was again extended to 452 feet.

Clearly the spirit of the age had penetrated into the Welsh valleys with an enthusiasm which has seldom been felt in this country since the ending of the last World War for there was general pleasure over the coming Diamond Jubilee of Queen Victoria. Many business proprietors were anxious to display their love of Queen and Country in a manner which would echo in their neighbourhoods. Hence the announcement in

With the Barracks (left) and Smithy (right) as background, employers and employees pose for a group photograph. McConnels, father and son, are be-hatted and seated to the right of the front row. The occasion is said to be one marking the purchase of the Quarry by William McConnel.

TALYLLYN RAILWAY CO.

the *Towyn on Sea and Merioneth County Times* for 3rd June 1897:

'The owners of the Bryneglwys Quarry, Abergynolwyn have decided to celebrate the Diamond Jubilee of Her Majesty by giving a trip to London to the whole of their employees who with much pleasure have accepted the offer. To quarrymen and others of the Abergynolwyn district this will be a great treat to be enjoyed once in a lifetime as a great many of them have never been outside the boundary of Wales. This action on the part of the managers is sure to increase the good feeling that exists between masters and workmen.'

However, it is still recalled that McConnel's good-will gesture was not unanimously acceptable, for in the same newspaper of 12th August following there appears:

'Jubilee – On Thursday 5th inst. the employees of the Abergynolwyn Slate Company were presented with their Jubilee gift. Owing to the men failing to show unanimity on any place for a trip Mr. Meyrick Roberts, the manager, with the sanction of Mr. McConnel decided to give two days pay to all the men and boys employed on the railway, wharf and quarry. The quarrymen being desirous of showing their appreciation of such liberality have decided to present Messrs. McConnel and Mr. Roberts with an address which will take the form of a photograph of the men and a lithographed address together with photographs of Mr. McConnel, Mr W.H. McConnel and Mr. Roberts which is being prepared by Mr. Young, Towyn.'

The *actual payment*, well-remembered, was two gold sovereigns to each adult employee – wages had always been paid in gold coin.

Back underground, The Narrow Vein was driven deeper to create a floor at the 75 yard-depth, in two disconnected sections. Unhappily it lay, of course, below the level of The Long Tunnel so extra pumps had to be installed to drain it, together with a special haulage system worked by water wheel to bring wagons up to the Tunnel level. As the quality of slate was good here, work was carried out in damp, dark and dangerous conditions, well named as 'The Black Sink' and giving the Quarry a bad name throughout the industry (Sinc Dial – 'Devil's Sink' was another title!). Ultimately Cantrybedd would contain a further 12 new chambers, making 28 in all. To avoid tramming rubbish out into the open, old chambers were filled with rubbish, a policy disliked by the Mines' Inspectors as they could not ascertain the condition of the pillaring if buried. At the Merionethshire Slate Mines Enquiry (April 1894) it was said there were 15 and 11 chambers in Bryneglwys and Cantrybedd respectively, and that of these 9 and 8 respectively, were working.

An account of an underground visit in the 1950s said:

'On my last visit I was fool enough to go underground at Bryneglwys, led by an ardent potholer; we went in at the western arm of the top level access tunnel (the eastern having been destroyed in the collapse) and passed seventeen walled-off chamber entrances before finally reaching one intact chamber at the very end of this tunnel which had been used for dumping rubbish and was half-filled. The intact and abandoned chamber lies one beyond this, one Level down . . . so I am told!'

THE W.H. McCONNEL PERIOD (1902–1909)

When his father died aged 93 in 1902, William Houldsworth continued to operate the business as Managing Owner. As the time for expiry of the leases drew near, no new developments were taking place – in fact, McConnel was fast developing interests elsewhere and the amount of time he spent on Quarry business was small, leaving matters overall largely in the hands of R.B. Yates (Meyrick Roberts was the Resident Quarry Manager). The risky habit of continuing to pare down the pillars between the chambers as an inexpensive way of winning good slate from old chambers, threatened still further the safety of the mine; this was said to have saved £600–800, being the cost of opening up a new chamber. This policy by McConnel was encouraged not only by the lease position, but also by the fact that his son, invited to take over the business, had shown no interest. There was no point in throwing good money after bad, and, with only thought for the day, the work of winning slate in the cheapest manner possible, no matter the ultimate risk was pursued.

In December 1909 he stopped work completely and shortly began to remove machinery with a view to putting up the business for sale. The saga of the next twelve months has already been described and there was to be a nail-biting twelve months for the 71 employed in 1909 (compared with 114 the previous year), for there was little other work in the immediate district. Luckily, fortune smiled, and once more, without any external changes in the Quarry itself, the men were able to return thankfully to work, with Henry Haydn Jones, their new Member of Parliament for Merionethsire, now the sole owner of Quarry, Talyllyn Railway and the village estate. Instead of an absentee owner, however paternalistic for those times he might have been, the men saw in their new employer not only the promise of continuing paternalism, but a man of themselves, a native of Wales, a successful businessman, a Liberal and non-conformist. The auguries were good – but the new owner was to see his purchase in quite a different light.

THE HENRY HAYDN JONES PERIOD (1911–1948)

The doubts expressed by Haydn Jones as to the possible profitability of the Quarry in the future have previously been ventilated; but nothing has yet been said of the condition of the workings, a report on which had been prepared for the enlightenment of Rev. G.R.G. Pugh who was being exhorted by his lawyer to allow Haydn Jones to enjoy a new lease on the easiest of terms, his Reverence having had the social problems explained to him in great detail. The report includes:

' . . . we are informed that nearly all the chambers have been worked out and there is practically little or no rock available in the developed part of the property and that no further developments have taken place by the extension of channels or the opening out of new chambers for a very long time . . . some of the chambers have been choked up with rubbish and the supporting pillars removed.'

An instance of the dangers of working the pillars at this mine was the collapse of a chamber – luckily on a Sunday – which buried everything. It was one of the most profitable sites and for a time it stopped work there as the men had to be sent home by the Manager.

Another issue concerned an interesting feature of the lease between Rev. Pugh and McConnel on 20th February 1866. This gave Pugh the right to use any tramways built by McConnel on Pugh's land (or 'running powers reserved by Rev. G. R. G. Pugh') in this particular instance included the tramway from the Quarry down Nant Gwernol on Pugh's land: ' . . . it forms the link in the chain whereby slates and other minerals may be conveyed from the quarry to the Talyllyn Railway and along that railway to Towyn . . .' and at the same time could be made valueless if the railway owner ceased to operate a train service!

At this stage our story has only covered events so far as they concern the Quarry and not the Railway, though out of context it should be added that McConnel not only intended to give up the Quarry

The yard in front of the Lower Mill with shunting horse. The Beudynewydd Incline rises behind the farmhouse of that name in the extreme left of the picture. TALYLLYN RAILWAY CO.

In the Lower Mill the two men on the left are making slates by splitting the slab with hammer and chisel; the man on the right trims them to size on the guillotine. TALYLLYN RAILWAY CO.

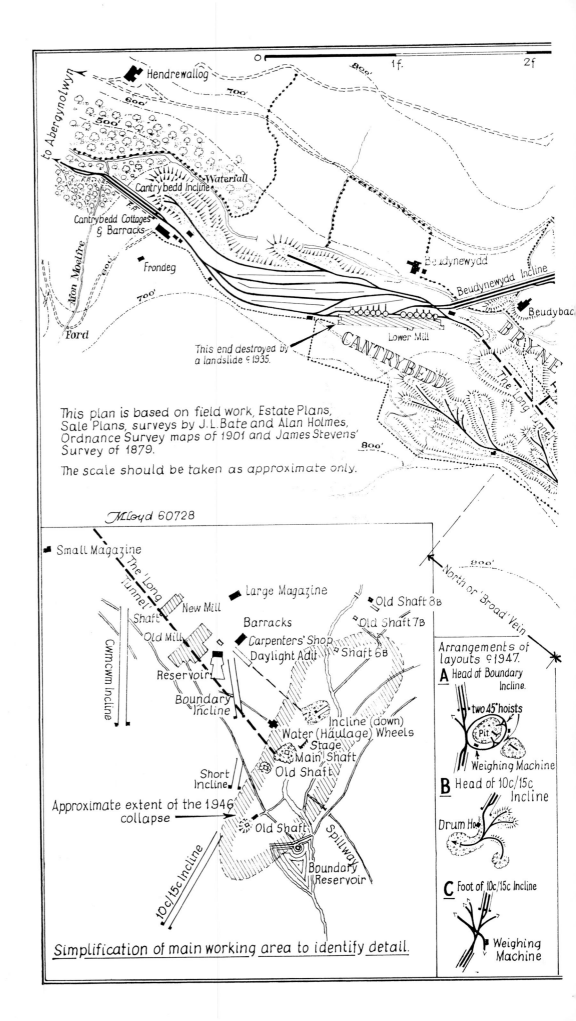

Hendrewallog

to Abergynolwyn

Afon Moelre

Waterfall

Cantrybedd Incline

Cantrybedd Cottages
& Barracks

Frondeg

Ford

Beudynewydd

Beudynewydd Incline

Beudybac

Lower Mill

CANTRYBEDD

BRYNE

The Long Tunnel

This end destroyed by
a landslide c 1935.

This plan is based on field work, Estate Plans,
Sale Plans, surveys by J.L.Bate and Alan Holmes,
Ordnance Survey maps of 1901 and James Stevens'
Survey of 1879.

The scale should be taken as approximate only.

J.Lloyd 60728

Small Magazine

The 'Long Tunnel'

Shaft

New Mill

Large Magazine

Old Shaft 8B

Old Shaft 7B

North or 'Broad' Vein

Cwmcwm Incline

Old Mill

Reservoir

Boundary
Incline

Barracks

Carpenters' Shop

Daylight Adit

Shaft 6B

Incline (down)

Water (Haulage) Wheels

Stage

Main Shaft

Old Shaft

Short
Incline

Approximate extent of the 1946
collapse

10c/15c Incline

Old Shaft

Spillway

Boundary
Reservoir

Arrangements of
layouts c 1947.

A Head of Boundary
Incline.

two 45" hoists

Pit

Weighing Machine

B Head of 10c/15c
Incline

Drum Hoist

C Foot of 10c/15c Incline

Weighing
Machine

Simplification of main working area to identify detail.

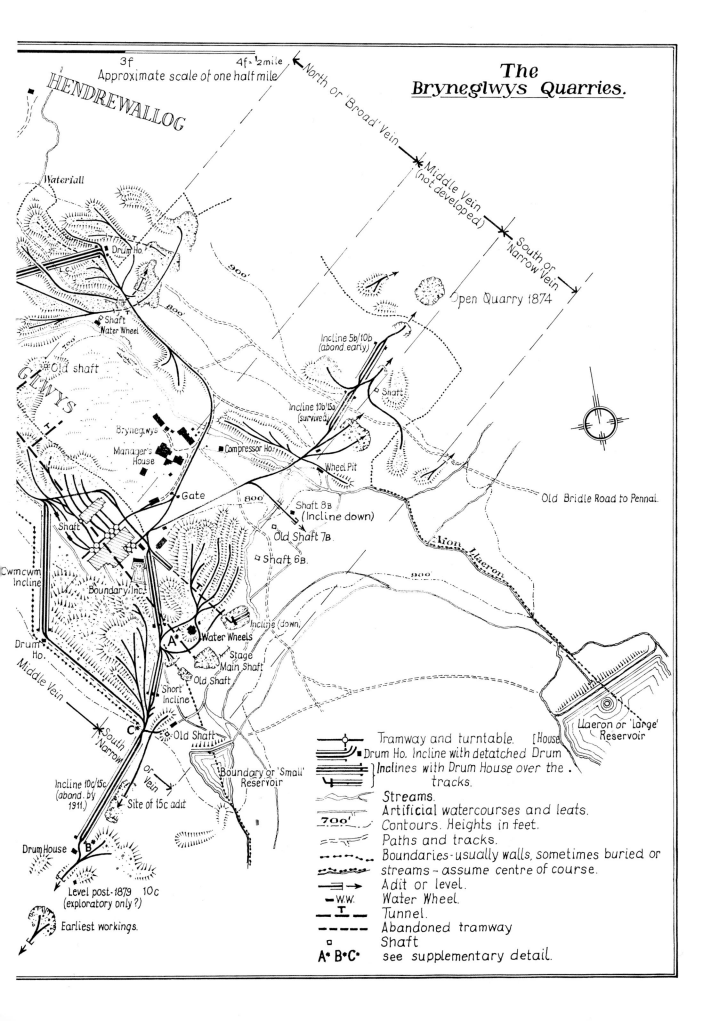

The Bryneglwys Quarries.

HENDREWALLOG

Waterfall

3f   4f = ½mile
Approximate scale of one half mile

North or 'Broad' Vein
Middle Vein (not developed)
South of 'Narrow' Vein

Drum Ho.
L.C.
Shaft
Water Wheel

GLWYS

Old shaft

900'
800'
700'

Open Quarry 1874

Incline 5b/10b (abond. early)

Incline 10b/15a (survived)

Shaft

Bryneglwys
Manager's House

Compressor Ho.

Wheel Pit

Old Bridle Road to Pennal.

Afon Llaeron

Gate

Shaft 8ʙ (Incline down)
Old Shaft 7ʙ
Shaft 6ʙ

800'

900'

Shaft

Cwmcwm Incline

Boundary Inc.

Drum Ho.

Middle Vein

Incline (down)

A*
Water Wheels

Stage Main Shaft

Old Shaft

Short Incline

C*

South Narrow or Vein

Old Shaft

Boundary or 'Small' Reservoir

Llaeron or 'Large' Reservoir

Incline 10c/15c (abond. by 1911.)
Site of 15c adit

Drum House   B*

Level post-1879   10c (exploratory only?)

Earliest workings.

Tramway and turntable.   [House
Drum Ho. Incline with detatched Drum
Inclines with Drum House over the tracks.

Streams.
Artificial watercourses and leats.
700'   Contours. Heights in feet.
Paths and tracks.
Boundaries-usually walls, sometimes buried or streams - assume centre of course.
Adit or level.
W.W.   Water Wheel.
T   Tunnel.
Abandoned tramway
Shaft
A* B* C*   see supplementary detail.

The caption to this locally-sold postcard reads ENTRANCE TO
SLATE MINE, NEAR TOWYN and may be at Bryneglwys.
                                    BURRELL'S SERIES

but the working of the Talyllyn Railway also, and the
position of that statutory undertaking and McConnel's
obligations to it were being feverishly investigated by
his solicitors as well, for it was of no use to Haydn
Jones if he took up the Quarry only to find he had no
railway by which to remove its products! Hence the
pith of the instructions from Carter Vincent & Co.

(Pugh's lawyers) to Thomas Jones (Civil Engineer)
' . . . that he should see that the Rails in question are
in good [word missing] and capable of performing the
obligations of the Lessee . . . and . . . that the rails are
left on the premises . . . also asked to advise as to the
Lessees obligations under the Talyllyn Railway Act so
far as they refer to the requirements of the Lessors for
the purpose of carrying merchandise from the Talyllyn
Railway to Towyn'. In particular, the object was to
satisfy their client, Rev. Pugh, that the last McConnel
had carried out all the maintenance provisions of the
1866 lease and as it was shown that in some regards
he had not, Pugh was in a difficult position if he wished
to re-let the property to Haydn Jones. Pugh would
have to be undemanding in his terms as Haydn Jones
was not only a lukewarm contender but the only one!

A few new points emerge from the foregoing: that
three-fifths of the total Quarry output arose on the
Cantrybedd property and the remaining two-fifths on
Bryneglwys; that the watershed providing water power
for machinery was partly on Ruck and partly on
Bryneglwys Estates, and stored in the Llaeron
Reservoir on the boundary of the two properties. From
this large reservoir the water was taken to a smaller reservoir but this was partly on Cantrybedd and partly
on Bryneglwys Estates.

It is significant that due to the three estates involved
hereabouts, with the tangled skein of ownership and
letting which had been pursued for over a century, the
whole complex position was then – and would continue

One of a number of similar groups posed in front of the Old Mill before World War I.
                                    GWYNEDD ARCHIVES

to be – a carcase on which generations of lawyers had feasted.

Haydn Jones faced a most difficult task. The slate trade was not prosperous and the Quarry had been worked beyond the point where development in The Narrow Vein was almost hopeless. Only by paying wages less than could be found in other places in the industry (but having in mind that he would be introducing 'social benefits' down in the village) could the business be kept alive. Soon the men found they had a running battle on their hands with him, which only the First War interrupted.

After a period when the labour force was seriously depleted by wartime needs, the men returning from that war expected a place where heroes might live. This seemed to have taken on an element of exception ... 'but not in Abergynolwyn'. The fruit of resentment was in the form of a Union in the Quarry, a development which could not have angered Haydn Jones more. However, after quarrels and then negotiations, the men agreed not to press for higher wages until business improved; some men did not return at all, but followed the trend which had begun in

A 1930s view of a wagon appearing at the head of Shaft 8B incline. GWYNEDD ARCHIVES

McConnel's time, for over 100 had left the premises since the turn of the century, and many of these had gone to the United States, South America and Mexico to work in slate quarries there. The New Mill was closed down (and may even have never worked in Haydn's time). It was later to become a barn or warehouse, and a place for concerts!

There was but a scant market for slates during World War I, and even the low productivity of that period failed to find a sale. With so little stacking room down at the Wharf station, slates were piled up in front of Cantrybedd Mill where 200,000 were alleged to be waiting for a buyer. However, the return of peace brought a short-lived demand which lasted until the mid-1920s, the creation of the post-war house building programme – but many new houses were being roofed in other materials. During these improved times, there were 'three runs a day from the quarry, eight loaded wagons being called a run'. This meant that 24 wagonloads were going down the Railway each day, and much of this found its way to Aberdovey for shipment to the Continent to rebuild the devastated areas of the war.

A group at the Quarry about 1930. GWYNEDD ARCHIVES

A slab-loaded trolley emerges at the mouth of 15C Adit.
GWYNEDD ARCHIVES

Employees numbered over 150 men and boys for a time; orders at this juncture might have been met more easily had not McConnel removed machinery in 1910. Haydn Jones decided to drive a sloping shaft at about 60° into chamber 8B on The Narrow Vein, hauling being by water wheel driven from the Llaeron near the exit tramway river bridge. This shaft and incline was dubbed the Haydn Jones Incline. Regrettably, a rockfall in chamber 11 diverted much water into the workings there to the effect that in time many men refused to work in its foul conditions and went elsewhere for the better wages in other mines. Another innovation by Haydn Jones was the use of compressed air drills in Bryneglwys – but not in Cantrybedd which continued to be hand-operated – which were supplied with air from a compressor driven off the same new water wheel, and housed nearby. This wheel was also

A view underground along the access tunnel on Floor 10C; there are entrances to chambers on the left.   R. THOMAS

used to drain a new sink below the existing Broad Vein workings.

The resurgence was short-lived. Some work was continued on The Broad Vein which was more economically worked in the open, but the sale for its hard, thick roofing slates was very slow; even these workings became increasingly unsafe. † Competition now came in a demand for coloured slates which Bryneglwys could not supply; orders for these were met from Caernarvonshire quarries which had blue-green or red-hued material to offer. Then came the influx of even cheaper tiles. By 1938 only 57 were at work, and these dwindled to less than 10 during the Second War and by 1946 only five men were left to mark the end of the Bryneglwys Quarry venture.

† There are adits from The Long Tunnel into The Broad Vein but being blocked, their extent is not known.

Part of the worked-out chamber on Floor 10 with access tunnel outside the slate vein on the left.

R. THOMAS

A neatly-executed piece of graffito found on the haulage wheel wall slab. There were many such, but seldom of this quality.

ALAN HOLMES

SEVEN BROTHERS

It is opportune to look more closely at the ship which had such near ties with the Bryneglwys Quarry, *Seven Brothers*. She was built on the Dovey in 1853 by 'Mr. Roland Evans' and carried the official number 20507 when first appearing in *Lloyds Register of British & Foreign Ships* in 1854 and also the Signal Code Letters NBLD. She was a smack,* of wooden construction with 'iron bolts' and dimensions of 48 ft. 4 ins. length, 14 ft. 8 ins. breadth, 8 ft. 3 ins. depth and of 43 tons. Initially her owners are given as Davies & Co. and her port of registration as Aberdovey; she was classified as an 'Aberystwyth Coaster' and rated A1 for ten years. It is conjectured that her name was chosen after the seven Davies brothers (William c. 1819, William, 1832, Thomas, 1833, David 1835, Edward c. 1837, John 1839, Evan 1842).

Certificate 24/1853 of the Bristol Registry stated that William Davies was the Master; he had, with 'William Williams Jones, shopkeeper of Towyn, and Humphrey Owen of Aberdovey, joiner (subscribed the Declaration required by Law), together with Edward Davies of Gwyndy, Daniel of Penllyn, farmer †, John Davies, Master Mariner and Edward Jones, shopkeeper's assistant, both of Aberdovey and all in the Parish of Towyn ... Mary Breese, spinster, John Meredith and John Jones, shopkeepers and Thomas Llewelyn, shopman, all of Machynlleth ... and William Lloyd of the City of Hereford, shopkeeper ... sole owners (in the proportions specified) ...'.

The same states that the ship was built at Derwenlas (on the R. Dovey) by Rowland Evans whose certificate was dated 15th August 1853. It seems strange therefore that the builder on Lloyd's Register is given as 'Lewis'. The ship had one deck, one mast, a running bowsprit, a square stern, and was of carvel construction with wooden planking. Ownership was divided into sixty-four shares as follows:

	1853		1870
William Davies	14	which by	24
William Williams Jones	4	8 July 1870	4
Humphrey Owen	4	had become	4
Edward Davies	4		4
Owen Daniel	4		4
John Davies	4		0 (sold 26.1.1861 to Wm. Davies, Towyn, Master Mariner.)
Edward Jones	4		0 (as for John Davies)
Mary Breese	8		0 (died 3.11.1866: to Nicholas Bennett)

	1853	1870
John Meredith	4	4
John Jones	4	4
Thomas Llewelyn	8	8
William Lloyd	2	0 (as for John Davies)
Nicholas Bennett		8 (ex Mary Breese)

On 21st July 1864, when the new owners of the Quarry were setting to work, the Master became Thomas Davies, and on 27th January 1870 James Morgan.‡ At some later date William Roberts took command and was succeeded by David Bowen on 12th May 1877. Curiously, David Davies' name appears as Master on 20th May 1875 following the above entries – perhaps 1875 is 1878? The last four registrations are at Aberystwyth whilst the next is at Workington on 2nd July 1880 when John Davies became master. The last entry is 'Caernarvon 9 September 1880, David Davies'.

By 1863 Lloyd's Register was much as that of 1853 but the classification was now 'Swansea Coaster' and the ten years A1 rating had expired. In the interim she was described as 'Trades: Aberystwyth and Swansea' suggesting she was plying between Derwenlas and the South Wales smelters carrying ore from the Dylife area mines and this idea is supported by Jones & Morgan's accounts at Derwenlas with their references to Dyfyngwm Mining Co. loadings on 28th November and 20th December 1862,§ and to the ship lying up at Aberdovey at this period.

In 1859 there was a new survey and another at Aberystwyth in January 1871. By 1873 the owners were McDonald, Aberdovey (which may be an error for McConnel) and the Master, J. Morgans. Some repairs had been carried out in 1871. The same entries appear for 1874–6 but then there is nothing until the register of 1880/1, with Master D. Davies and 'new deck and large repairs 1879', the Master by then appearing to be the owner also. The Aberystwyth survey of 1879 adds 'Restored 1879'. There is no entry for the following four years.

Once again the story of the intermediate years can only be read from the surviving records; on 6th July 1870 she was sold to T.H. McConnel 'of Manchester, county Lancaster, merchant', all 64 shares thus passing to him. Though he himself was dead, his name still appears as owner in 1875 but the registers are incomplete and by 1879 the owner is David Davies,

---

* lengthened into a Schooner in the 1860s.
† Haydn Jones' mother's family.
‡ See *Brief Glory* p. 193 onwards.
§ The last lead ore cargo to leave Derwenlas.

probably the same as is registered in 'Carnarvon' 9th September the following year, as Master.

(Confusingly, another *Seven Brothers* appears in 1871, a sloop of 53 tons, registered at Beaumaris and owned by John Hughes, of Llansantffraid, Denbighshire.)

T.H. McConnel died on 13th October 1873 and he appointed Frederick McConnel of Edinburgh and Thomas Robert Storey Cannan of Prestwich, Manchester, his executors; they now held the 64 shares in the vessel, jointly. On a Bill of Sale 8th June 1876, the ship was transferred to William McConnel of Prestwich, 'cotton spinner', who was now the sole owner, but on 4th May 1878 – and perhaps in the year before the Quarry business was first auctioned – McConnel sold to David Davies of Borth (near Aberystwyth), a Master Mariner. The latter promptly mortgaged the 64 shares to secure £322 with interest at 5% in favour of 'Griffith Jones, of Aberystwyth in the county of Cardigan, gentleman'. This sale had been advertised in the *Carnarvon & Denbigh Herald* the previous month headed 'The well-known and fast sailing smack ... built by an eminent builder at Derwenlas ... carries 70 tons ... recently thoroughly overhauled and fitted with new sails ... lying at Aberdovey ...'.

Not all the voyages were for the carriage of slate; a typical voyage in 1853 was Aberdovey–London–Liverpool – Bangor – Letterkenny (Co. Donegal) – Liverpool–Aberdovey. On this we may assume that slates were carried from Aberdovey and again from Bangor with general cargoes in between.

Another voyage in 1854 was Aberdovey–Gloucester – Portsmouth – London – Aberdovey – Aberdeen – Gloucester – Newnham – Newry (Co. Down) – Skerries (Dublin) – Aberdovey and later voyages all show that the first port of call was often Gloucester, which would be by way of the Ship Canal from Sharpness.

It is easy to follow the widening travels of the vessel by adding in to the ports of call over and above those already listed, thus:

1855	Hastings, Rye, Birkenhead, Ballyshannon (Co. Donegal), Ballysodare (Co. Sligo), Glasgow, Conway, Southampton, Poole, Runcorn.
1856	Dublin, Dungarvan, (Co. Waterford), Cahirciveen (Co. Kerry), Tralee (Co. Kerry), Falmouth.
1857	Chester, Swansea, Neath, Cork, Carmarthen, Milford, Aberystwyth, Caernarvon, Dumfries, Whitehaven, Porthcawl, Pembrey.
1858	Greenock, Plymouth, Greenore (Co. Louth), Cardiff, Portsmouth.
1859	Ellesmere, Gosport, Charlestown.
1860	Shoreham, Teignmouth.
1862	Bagillt, Greenfield (and at this period regular sailings to and from Chester, Deeside and Merseyside ports) lying-up at Aberdovey at end of year.
1868	Barmouth, Larne (Co. Antrim).
1869	Portmadoc, Ramelton (Co. Donegal), Dundalk (Co. Louth), (and frequent sailings to Liverpool and Chester).

A more detailed example is:

5 January	1877	Aberdovey–Cardiff with slates. Newport–Fishguard with coal.
6 April	1877	Cardiff –Waterford with coal.
30 May	1877	Aberdovey – Gloucester with slates.
15 June	1877	Gloucester – Newport with flour.

A small vessel of this type would handle well in the restricted water of the Gloucester Canal and the awkward waters of the Dee above Queen's Ferry. The above records mask a tragedy which occurred on 21st April 1877 when off the Tusker Rock (Co. Wexford), the Master, William Roberts aged 31 of Towyn, was 'hooked overboard by the boom and lost'.

Such records show how young were the men who manned these ships; we may take the crew of early 1854:

William Davies	aged 34	Towyn	Master
Thomas Davies	25	Towyn	Mate
Griffith Edwards	26	Llanlyfni	Seaman
Hugh Morris	18	Aberdovey	Boy

Sometimes the ship sailed without a boy and crews would be picked up at any port including those in Ireland; in early 1868 it was sailing with a crew of five, the boy being aged but 11 and this his first vessel (Robert Williams of Aberdovey).

The ship was ultimately lost (but all hands were saved) in the Irish Sea on 12th August 1880; the vessel sprang a leak and foundered about 12 miles south of the Calf of Man.

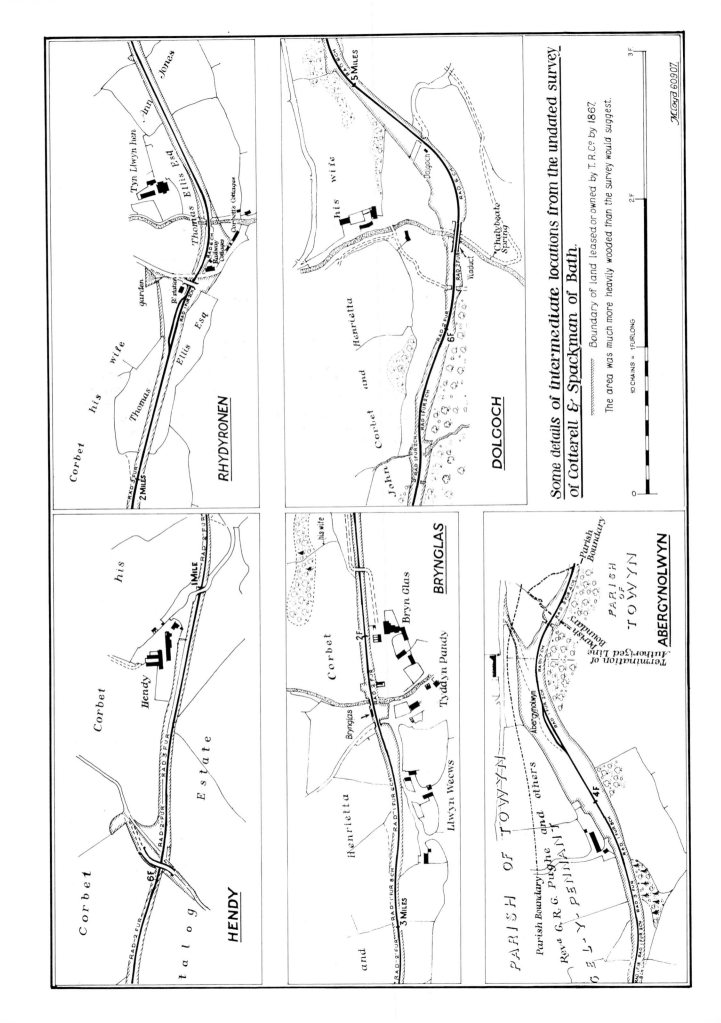

Some details of intermediate locations from the undated survey of Cotterell & Spackman of Bath.

— — — — Boundary of land leased or owned by T.R.C° by 1867

The area was much more heavily wooded than the survey would suggest.

10 CHAINS = 1 FURLONG

M.Loyd 6090Z

RHYDYRONEN

Corbet · his · wife

Thomas · Ellis · Esq

Thomas Ellis Esq

Ann · Jonas

Tyn Llwyn hen

garden

R. station

Railway Cottages

Cottett's Cottages

RAD 6 CH

RAD 1 FUR 8 CH

RAD 3 FUR

2 MILES

DOLGOCH

his · wife

Henrietta · and

John Corbet · and

Dolgoch

Viaduct

Chalybeate Spring

5 MILES

6F

RAD 2 FUR

RAD 6 CH

RAD 1 FUR 2 CH

RAD 2 FUR 2 CH

HENDY

Corbet · his

Corbet · Estate

Talog

Hendy

1 MILE

6F

RAD 2 FUR

RAD 3 FUR

RAD 2 FUR 8 CH

RAD 2 FUR

BRYNGLAS

Corbet

Henrietta · and

...his wife

Bryn Glas

Brynglas

Tyddyn Pandy

Llwyn Wecws

2F

3 MILES

RAD 6 CH

RAD 1 FUR 2 CH

RAD 2 FUR

RAD 1 FUR 6 CH

ABERGYNOLWYN

PARISH OF TOWYN

PARISH OF TOWYN

GELLI·Y·PENNANT

Rev° G.R.G. Pughe and others

Parish Boundary

Termination of Authorised Line

Parish Boundary

Abergynolwyn

4F

RAD 7 CH

RAD 2 FUR 2 CH

RAD 2 FUR

RAD 3 CH

RAD 1 FUR 8 CH

RAD 1 FUR 2 CH

CHAPTER FOUR
THE TALYLLYN RAILWAY

MANY questions have been asked about the early days of the Talyllyn Railway for they came in a period when little has survived to enlighten us about its purpose and extent. Certainly there was the intention to link the Quarry with the outside world, but as this could have been done without the official duties necessitated by the acquisition of an Act of Parliament, and the adopting of a title, the ambitions which lay behind these formalities have never been disclosed! And what of that title? Does it imply that the promoters had some territorial ambitions beyond that of simply linking Quarry and coast by rail? Did they mean to reach Talyllyn itself or even link with Corris? Perhaps it was but a simple title taken from the district at the upper end of the line (as 'Festiniog' or 'Corris')?

The earliest tangible plan of an intended line of rails is not much help as it bears no date; it may have been a proposal for a railway or perhaps a record of the railway as then already built. It does not bear a title but on the linen back has been inked 'Railway Ynys'. The condition of the tracing (once firmly attached to the linen) is such that every time it is unrolled, something flakes off and parts of the tracing have been lost in consequence. The drawing only covers that part of route extending from Towyn to a point just east of the present day Quarry Siding, and possibly there was a second sheet which showed the remainder of the railway right into the Quarry? The scale is 8 chains to the inch and the plan may have originated in the desire to show the course as it passed through the Ynysymaengwyn Estate; the title inked onto the reverse of the roll has not been added by the draughtsman responsible for the tracing itself – it is in a different style and unprofessional.

The next Plan by estimated date was prepared by Messrs. Cotterell & Spackman of Bath, who were agents for the Ynysymaengwyn Estate at the time the railway was built and who ceased to practise 1889–90, (apparently begun under Jacob Henry Cotterell of Broad Quay, a land surveyor, in 1826, who was joined by Henry Spackman in 1854. The firm was involved as surveyors, estate agents, architects etc.). They were connected with the Midland Railway line Bath–Bristol in 1865–70, and Cotterell, writing in the *Bath Chronicle* 2nd May 1865, states: 'I have had great experience as a land agent and surveyor and in laying out railways'. Again the plan is not dated. Luckily it was discovered in the Wharf office in 1967 and as Rhydyronen station has been added in pencil, it must pre-date February 1867; Edward Thomas (Manager) always insisted it was prepared

in 1866. Jacob Cotterell and Thomas Savin (contractor to the Aberystwyth & Welsh Coast Railway which had been building in the early 1860s) were both members of the Towyn Board of Health in the same period and each must have been chosen for what they represented rather than as local residents.

Recently the Plan was submitted to John L. H. Bate, Engineer to the Talyllyn Railway who conjectured:

1. Its purpose was to determine the exact extent of the land taken for the railway.
2. It shows the position of the line in relation to the then land boundaries; its predecessor, the Deposited Plans, would not show the eventual course taken and the plan is the result of a survey made from the finished work and shows the radii of curves precisely (etc.).
3. As to date of preparation, the bridges at Ty Mawr and Rhydyronen have been added; they were level crossings at the time of the survey. It is known that when Capt. Tyler visited in September 1866, all bridges were complete; they may have been built in the year commencing July 1865. As work on the project began about early 1864 (the exact date is not known) and the rails had been laid before July 1865, the survey could not be made earlier until the track was down and boundary fences established. The estimated date is summer 1865, somewhat earlier than the traditional one.

Comments on the Plan included:

1. The large area of land taken in north of Neptune Road which might have been suitable for an interchange passenger station, and the area south of Wharf for enlargement of the stock and exchange sidings.
2. The outline of the Pendre building (loco. shed and workshop) is the original length of about 25 ft. and there are no sidings.
3. Near Ty Mawr the line keeps as closely as possible on Corbet land and to field boundaries. A possible diversion of the access road to Hendy Farm on the north side of the line, was not carried out.
4. The Fachgoch embankment, built from a borrow pit on the south side of Corbet land, is dug exactly to the boundary of Roberts' land – and no further! There is a curiously curved hedge on the north side corresponding to the edge of the old road prior to its diversion.
5. Schedule amendments made in red ink (the Schedule itself being made after amendments to the plan) are of later date than the Plan itself.
6. The east end of loop points at Rhydyronen was closer to the overbridge than the later siding points there.
7. There was no siding or level crossing at Brynglas.
8. Many farm crossings and cattle creeps; these are indicated accurately including crossings long since abandoned or now hardly visible. Some crossings which exist today are not shown and must have been of post-1865 period.

(Most of the above, and others in addition, receive passing mention when describing the route of the Railway. Spellings on the Plan may disagree with the form used herein, or with Ordnance Survey maps.)

None of the foregoing has any formal bearing on the railway becoming a statutory undertaking (that is, a line which is backed by an Act of Parliament), but each is accurate enough to portray the line as built and existing before an Act was obtained. In fact these plans, though of different style and date, may both be linked to Ynysymaengwyn Estate purposes.

The third set of plans, however, is quite different, being the Deposited Plans for a railway which would go before Parliament for approval before an Act formally giving it statutory status would receive the Royal Assent. In most cases this meant that work would then begin on constructing the line but in the case of the existing railway between Quarry and Towyn, it would place that status on *an already-built and operating line* – or at least the greater part of it! This state of affairs was not unique to the situation, as several very old railways went to Parliament, for one reason or another, even years after they had first opened.

Apart from the cost of obtaining an Act, which was considerable, the ownership of one gave any undertaking certain rights which were laid down in that Act. One of the most difficult issues in the present instance is that, as mentioned already, the purpose of the Talyllyn Railway Act which received the Royal Assent on 5th July 1865 has never been made known. When Plans are deposited prior to an Act being sought, a Book of Reference must accompany them showing a list of all the landowners affected by the building of a railway. By warning of impending construction over land (to which a landowner could bring objections), an Act might be necessary in order to acquire it compulsorily from some objector. However, this surely cannot be the case, for the railway was already complete and carrying slate traffic before it obtained an Act. Perhaps an Act would make easier negotiation with the Coast Railway?

Deposited Plans were always prepared *before* the building of a line for which an Act of Parliament was sought; they would show the course of the intended route and give 'limits of deviation' from that course beyond which the route would be unable to go without further legislation. The Plans would be accompanied by a Register of landowners who would be affected by the building and a surveyor would prepare the Plans; in the present case they were carried out by James Swinton Spooner who was appointed 'Surveyor and Engineer' to a 'Tal-y-Llyn Railway' in late 1863.

James Swinton's plans were prepared for the Parliamentary Session of 1865 and were presented in November 1864 along with the announcements in the local press and *The London Gazette* of 25th November 1864. (Bearing in mind that railway construction had probably begun in the March/April period *before* this (!) suitably emphasises that a railway was built without an Act).

In the instance of the Talyllyn Railway, if Spooner began work in late 1863 (and his survey would take him but a few weeks), we must assume that he had finished both surveying and the Plans by early 1864

when building began. It is also interesting to speculate whether he was instructed by John Lloyd Jones or the McConnels, as the Aberdovey Slate Co. was not registered before late January 1864. In but a few places is Spooner's survey and Cotterell & Spackman's plan on the same course; for instance, the existing gradient of 1 in 60 up from Wharf station; here Spooner's plans show this grade reduced to 1 in 451 which would have required greater and more expensive earthworks. It could be that the owners of the Railway were unworried about the steep fall to Wharf, as they did not envisage passenger-working over it. Such arrangement was upheld for some years. (A present-day theory is that the 1 in 60 may have been an afterthought.)

The standard gauge railway had already reached Towyn on 24th October 1863 at what must have been a temporary station for a new one was built in 1870. This would bring a large number of navvies into the district, most of whom would be engaged on pressing northward with the Aberystwyth & Welsh Coast line towards Barmouth. It could be that a pool of men was available for the building of what would seem a small undertaking in the shape of the line from Bryneglwys Quarry to Towyn (they may have been 'encouraged' by an offer of higher wages than Savin was paying). On 5th December 1863 *The Merionethshire Herald* read:

> 'Ynysymaengwyn Rent Audit & Dinner ... took place ... on 3 December ... J. J. Cotterell Esq. of Bath, Agent* ... Mr. Edward Morgan, Solicitor, informed the meeting that there was an intention to make a railway from Towyn to Bryneglwys and put steam power on it. This, he was sure, would give the farmers a great advantage by getting their lime and coal, and other things cheaper than they could now. He was sure the district would be greatly benefitted by it, and the Quarries that would be opened would bring wealth to the country.'

(Cotterell was, as just said, on the Board of Health, would shortly become a member of the Drainage Board of 1864 and, of course involved with the Ynysymaengwyn Estate; Morgan was a partner in Howell & Morgan, solicitors of Machynlleth.)

It should be mentioned that at that time, the Bryneglwys Quarry was in the last stage of sale by John Lloyd Jones to the The Aberdovey Slate Co.

If there is a hint that some preparatory railway work was being done it is confirmed that James Spooner was at work at the turn of the year, for on 30th January 1864 the *Carnarvon & Denbigh Herald* says:

> 'Proposed Tramroad to Bryn yr Eglwys Slate Quarries. Mr. Spooner, Civil Engineer, is surveying for a tramway between this town and Bryn yr Eglwys Slate Quarries. Should the owners of the land through which the road is to pass and the Company come to amicable arrangements, the works will commence in March or April next which we trust will be the case as it may ultimately lead to there being steam power placed upon the road.'

Two suggestions arise from this article: firstly, that a 'tramroad' is envisaged which might mean that

---

* Whom it will be noted had in October 1862 been involved in the sale of the Quarry from Mrs. Pughe to John Lloyd Jones.

initially horse power would be adequate with steam to follow, and secondly, that no statutory measures were then contemplated, it being mooted that wayleaves could be arranged with the landowners to enable the line to be built. In the latter instance, this seems to have been satisfactorily achieved.

Whether Spooner applied himself in person to the work is not known, but it was 28th December 1864 before he submitted his Estimate of Expense (for building the railway) amounting to £15,000 and covered 'the expense of the undertaking under a Bill intended to be applied for in the next Session under the abovementioned name or short title at the sum of Fifteen thousand pounds including the purchase of lands and all contingencies.' Attached is a list of property owners affected, the list of Assenting & Dissenting Owners, lodged in Parliament with the Estate. The cost per mile of the line £2,143 (6 miles 5 furlongs in length) proves to be substantially lower than certain other narrow gauge railways of that time and shortly afterwards: for example (Board of Trade figures):

Corris Railway (1859)	£1,814
(An inexpensive horse tramway largely on the roadside)	
Festiniog Railway (1836)	£10,727
Glyn Valley Tramway (1870)	£7,311
North Wales Narrow Gauge Railways (1877)	£10,434

Furthermore, it can be borne in mind that the Company never had to take up its rights to borrow additional capital on loan as permitted under its Act; this non-event has its mysteries also! This estimate conveniently ties in with the notice in *The London Gazette* of the previous month.

Let us return to early 1864, when the newspapers allow glimpses of the progress of the scheme. On 9th April 1864 the *Carnarvon & Denbigh Herald* gives more news:

'The proposed Bryn yr Eglwys Railway. At a Meeting held last week at the Corbet Arms Hotel, arrangements were made for commencing the rail and tramway between Tywyn [it was occasionally spelled thus] and Bryn yr Eglwys forthwith. The proprietors of the land through which the line passes have agreed to sell the land at a moderate price. We also understand *the line will be extended to Talyllyn and even further to meet the Corris Tramroad.** A locomotive 2 ft. 10 in. gauge, the same as the Festiniog, is to be put upon the road with carriages attached for the accommodation of passengers, thus affording parties staying at Tywyn an opportunity of visiting the celebrated Tal-y-Llyn Lake and Cader Idris. There is no engineering difficulty in the construction of the line worth noticing. There will be a deep cutting on the southeast side of the town on the top of Penbryn near the British School and a bridge will be placed over the road, leading to Aberdovey. It is expected that the works will be completed by the end of this year.'

The error in the gauge of the Festiniog Railway is curious (or a misprint), as no other railway in Wales

was exciting so much press attention at this time. As to the tourist traffic, if the provision by the Company of only one passenger carriage at the outset (and allowing that the cause might be due to delay), this hardly reflected optimism for tourist traffic, and the paucity of potential passengers would be alluded to by the Board of Trade's Inspector when he made his Report. The proposed link with the 'Corris Tramway' (a horse-worked statutory undertaking of 2 ft. 3 in. gauge linking slate quarries in the Corris district to the Dovey riverside on its south bank at Derwenlas) may have been aimed at bringing out materials from quarries in the Upper Corris district – it would be hard to imagine there was any serious intent to go further in that direction. As it was, there would have been a climb of some 400 feet from the level of the Talyllyn Railway above Abergynolwyn, to the col above Upper Corris (664 feet) where the quarries were developing; this might have been achieved by a gradient of 1 in 100 over the 8 mile distance.

We may assume that James Swinton Spooner had finished his survey at this time; there follows four months of unbroken silence, when on 13th August 1864 the *Herald* announces:

'The tramroad between this town and the extensive slate quarries belonging to Mr. McConnel at Bryn yr Eglwys is progressing very favourably. The course is from the south side of Newtown Bridge and the Railway Company intend putting in a siding for the loading of their tram trucks into waggons made for the purpose to save the expense of loading and unloading. It seems at present the level is too low for this purpose. It is rumoured that an Act will be obtained to enable the Company to carry passengers from hence to Tal-y-Llyn. The gauge, being so narrow (2 ft. 4 ins.), we doubt whether a steam engine of that gauge will have the power to carry many passengers with anything like convenience.'

The article lifts the veil on several issues. Newtown Bridge is that beside the Wharf station where the Coast Line passes under Neptune Road. It is locally Trenewydd Bridge. The 'siding' would be the whole length of the mixed gauge interchange line involving a trans-shipment wharf and extending into the Coast Line's goods shed shown on plans of that time. As to the levels 'too low' to run slate wagons onto standard gauge transporters, this would be so, as the site of the Wharf station was a borrow pit which had been excavated for material for building the standard gauge embankment north of Towyn and it was not brought up to a convenient level until many tons of earth from Pendre cutting had been tipped into it and topped up with quarry waste; in this respect this is several years ahead of the time under review.

In a letter to the Cambrian Railways (into which the A & WCR had been absorbed by Act of 5th July 1865) on 25th June 1866 from Cotterell & Spackman on behalf of the Aberdovey Slate Co., the Cambrian was reminded of their earlier letter on the same subject applying for permission to allow the Slate Co. to build

---

* The italics are those of the Author. Would this be a deciding factor in adopting a gauge of 2 ft. 3 in., the same as the Corris? (There is a suggestion that the Corris was of 2 ft. gauge before locomotives were introduced.)

a wharf and siding east of Aberdovey ('between the railway and the turnpike road to which Mr. Corbet has the right of pre-emption') and to emphasise that this second letter was to prompt the Cambrian into making reply, which cannot be traced. Clearly, the Slate Co. intended to use such Aberdovey facilities in connection with loading of sea-going vessels.

A useful contemporary reference to the matter comes in a letter from W. Roberts, Secretary to the A & WCR to T. H. McConnel, Secetary of the AS Co. at 30 Pall Mall, Manchester, dated 3rd March 1864, confirming that this scheme to take loaded slate wagons direct for shipment without unloading into main line wagons at Towyn, was the original conception of the Quarry proprietors:

> 'There can be no objection to the trucks from your tramway being taken on the large trucks, but with respect to the wharfage at Aberdovey it is not in the power of this Company to enter into any arrangements as they have no wharfage ground. I have no doubt however, that you could make satisfactory arrangements with Mr. Savin, who will have wharfage ground at Aberdovey.
> 'My directors would be glad to receive a proposition from you specifying fully the terms which you can offer for the conveyance of your traffic from Towyn to Aberdovey.'

Throughout all the foregoing it is difficult to see any solid grounds for finding in the promise of potential passenger traffic, the necessity for the McConnels to use their resources to convert what was for them an exclusive private mineral railway into something which, when achieved at some cost, was to prove outwardly no different than what had been obtained before, namely a Statutory Railway Company with additional powers which its Act gave it. Whatever dreams that Act would enable to come true, are not revealed as they had no fruition, save perhaps in the purchase of some extra passenger carriages and possibly the safeguard of a second steam locomotive. Of course, the influence of J. S. Spooner (and what was currently happening on the Festiniog Railway further to the north) would be strong enough to encourage the McConnels to show that they too could initiate the first narrow gauge railway operated by steam power and carrying passengers from inception – and they did!

There is a suggestion contained in all these preliminaries that the McConnels intended to bypass Westminster involvement by floating a Railway Company on the same basis as had the promoters of the Festiniog & Blaenau Railway (Company Limited) which was registered on 7th August 1862 as a physical extension of the existing Festiniog Railway beyond Blaenau Ffestiniog. This would have enabled them to carry passengers and dispense with an Act of Parliament; in the event, however, this did not come about – again, the reasons are not clear. The customary need for an Act does not appear to fit this case where

satisfactory arrangements seem to have been made with the landowners involved.

Newspaper accounts continue to be of value. On 26th November 1864 the *Carnarvon & Denbigh Herald* writes:

> 'Tywyn–Bryn yr Eglwys Tramroad. The excavations ... are now fast approaching completion, the deep cutting at Tywyn is through, and the bridges are now in course of erection. The little locomotive is expected to be seen smoking up and down the line early next year.'

It is a pity we know so little about the actual building of the line; maybe 100–200 men, some of whom had come with the building of the Coast Railway, stayed on to help. Perhaps one quarter of them would be employed on Pendre cutting. Maybe quarrymen from nearby found it more profitable to use their skills on railway construction? One would have thought there would be but a limited amount of resident local labour as most people were tied to the farms of the tenant farmers and the duration of the work would be comparatively short. It would seem that the earthworks were in the hands of 'outsiders'. There is an oblique reference to a 'contractor' (a building contractor?) thirty years after the event, and this expression, not only coming so long after the railway was complete, might not convey the same meaning. The account comes from *The Cambrian News* (27th April 1894):

> 'On Sunday evening last Mr. Evan Humphreys, 1, Pier Villa, died after a lingering illness ... had been for many years contractor on the Talyllyn Railway, he also carried out some important works at the quarry of Bryneglwys ... He was 72 years of age and was a native of Caernarvonshire, but had resided in Towyn for many years.'

If the mention does nothing else, it certainly strengthens the impression that the Quarry and Railway owed much to men who originated in Caernarvonshire.

An earlier mention has been made of the formal Notices which were first put out on 12 November 1864; that in *The Merionethshire Herald* was typical:

> 'Talyllyn Railway. (Railways from Towyn to Hendre Abergynolwyn near Talyllyn. Powers of construction and maintenance to a new Company and Aberdovey Slate Co. Ltd. or one of them. Use of Towyn station. Further powers of the said Slate Company. Powers to make agreement with the Aberystwyth & Welsh Coast Railway Company. Power to lay down a mixed gauge line over the A & WCR and Running Powers over the same portion. Amendment of Act). Nov. 1st 1864 Howell & Morgan, Solrs., Machynlleth. Pitt, Sherwood, Venable & Grubble, 7, Great George Street, Manchester, Parliamentary Agents.'

There was a lot more in *The London Gazette* Notice thirteen days later, with reference to Railways Nos. 1 & 2, especially the former, and to places right off the ultimate route of the line.

Part of the remainder of the Notice was made up of the conventional clauses which always accompanied such fare, and in simplified form the most interesting parts were:

1. that the right to build the line would evolve upon a new Company 'incorporated for that purpose', the Aberdovey Slate Company (Limited).
2. that the gauge of the line should 'be upon such gauge as the proprietors thereof think proper'.
3. that the A & WCR and the new Company might 'lay down a mixed gauge of the A & WCR between a point of junction of the intended Railway No. 1, with the A & WCR in the said Parish of Towyn and the Towyn station on the last-mentioned railway, with power to the new Company ... to run over and use with their engines and carriages ... upon such terms and conditions ...'
4. that the new Company and the A & WCR would use 'the Towyn station of the A & WCR Company jointly, or to have the separate use of a portion of such station ...'

There will appear to be some contradiction in all this. If the new Company was given authority to lay its track to any gauge it thought fit, then clearly a mixed gauge line would only be required if the new Railway, i.e. the Talyllyn, was ultimately laid to narrow gauge. However, such clauses were useful to the promoters as they offered scope for a change of gauge at later date, if that proved wise. The whole exercise must be viewed against the likelihood that the Coast Line station's situation was a temporary one; it was likely to have been south of Trenewydd Bridge when first the line (in October) terminated at Towyn, and moved to the north side (opposite Plevna Terrace?) when the route extended to Llwyngwril in November 1863. The station was renewed in 1870, probably on the site used today; the Foundation Stone was laid on 1st April!

In February 1865 the Bill had its first reading, noted in *The Merionethshire Herald* on the 18th; the *House of Commons Journal* Vol. 120 p. 17 tells us that the Bill was brought in by William Wynne and Charles Watkyn Wynne.

'Mr. Dodson reported from the Committee on The Talyllyn Railway Bill that they had examined the allegations contained in the preamble of the Bill and amended the same by striking out the Recital as to the expendiency of laying down an additional line of rails upon the Aberystwyth & Welsh Coast Railway and also so much as regards the expediency of running powers over and the use of Town [sic] Station of that Railway.'

The original petition of the Bill of 1865 has not survived and 'it would appear that the Bill was unopposed in both Houses and consequently no evidence was taken before the Committees on the Bill ...'

The foregoing leaves us no wiser than before about the Talyllyn Railway's conception of a mixed gauge link into the A & WCR station with suitable running powers over it. The form of words and the intention certainly produced an objection by the Coast Company but the removal of the offending intention allowed that Company to withdraw objection. It will be noted, however, that the Talyllyn Act *permitted* such an arrangement – a somewhat different approach!

In summary therefore:

1865		
15th February	Bill receives Second Reading	Commons
9th May	Mr. Dodson reported ... (as above)	Commons
18th May	Third Reading	,,
30th June	Lords Amendment, and agreement to it	Lords
3rd July	Bill read twice, and Lords amendments agreed to. Bill returns to Lords	Commons
5th July	Royal Assent	

During May 1865 there are several press references and *The Merionethshire Herald*'s article on 6th May confirms the railway was already a fatal attraction:

'... On Friday last a woman named Roberts was run over by some small trucks on the Towyn and Talyllin [sic] Railway near this town. It appears she was riding in one of the trucks and alighting whilst it was in motion, her foot slipped and she fell across the rails. Fortunately the trucks were empty and no locomotive was attached. She is much bruised, but no bones are broken. Strict orders have now been given to prohibit persons from riding in the trucks.'

The important issue of that month (May) seems to have escaped notice for all the evidence points to a completion of the line sufficiently to carry mineral traffic.

To put the Talyllyn Railway in historical context, a selection of other railways obtaining authority in July 1865 makes interesting reading:

Formation of the Cheshire Lines Committee
Formation of the Potteries, Shrewsbury & North Wales Railway
Alexandra (Newport & South Wales) Docks & Railway Company
Ross & Monmouth Rly.
Mawddwy Rly.
Croesor & Portmadoc Rly.

There was good news in the paper on 13th May 1865 when it was given that the Bill, now unopposed

'... was passed by Mr. Dodson's Committee ... the first in which a Committee of the House of Commons has sanctioned the use of steam power for the carrying passengers on a line constructed on a gauge of less than the ordinary 4 ft. 8½ ins. The gauge proposed in the present Bill is 2 ft. 3 ins.'

Thus the Talyllyn Railway Company ensured itself an unique place in the annals of railway history. This was not all, for the same newspaper inserts: 'The Towyn and Talyllyn Railway. The locomotive is now at work on this line conveying slates from the Quarry to the station here.' But it was to be another eighteen months before the public would be carried, and during this time the line was simply a servant of the Quarry, and remained so thereafter whilst the Quarry remained in business. In passing it is important to note that in the following August the Quarry undertaking's capital was increased, though this does not necessarily reflect increased costs on the railway.

Still in May 1865, *The Merionethshire Herald* said on the 20th:

> 'We are given to understand that the Aberdovey Slate Co. Ltd. are about to erect an enamel works on the ground near the Old Malt House, at the east end of Towyn, where a siding will be laid down to run in materials etc. . . .'

and later

> 'We heartily congratulate the promoters . . . we expect to see this line opened for public traffic in July. Doubtless great demonstrations will take place in this town on the opening day.'

Unfortunately the position of the Old Malt House seems to have been forgotten.

The *Carnarvon & Denbigh Herald*'s reporter wrote on 20th May, headed 'Narrow Escape':

> 'One of the most silly and foolish tricks which a man in his proper senses could possibly do was attempted by a navvy on Wednesday.
>
> He was riding on one of the ballast wagons which was going at full speed, his hat was blown off and he leaped off the trucks after it and as might have been expected he got very much bruised about the face and hands but he escaped without having any bones broken.'

Trains were certainly running by the late summer and the concern had made at least one enemy for on 9th September 1865 *The Merionethshire Herald* records:

> 'Diabolical attempt to upset a train. A man named James Humphreys, a mason and native of Penllwyn near Aberystwyth (who had been working on the new buildings at Abergynolwyn, the present terminus of the Talyllyn and Towyn Railway) was brought before their worships charged with having, on 26 August last, attempted to overthrow the engine and trucks which now run to Towyn with slates, slabs etc. The prisoner . . . was prevented through some misconduct from riding in the empty trucks to Towyn and out of revenge placed a sledge across the rails near Brynerwast [*sic*] farm . . . On the following day he drove a stake into the centre of the line near Dolgoch Bridge, so as just to catch the engine. Fortunately, in the first instance the sledge was discovered just in time to put the brakes on and prevent disaster and in the second . . . the post . . . broke with the force of the engine otherwise many lives must have been sacrificed by the fall down a depth of fifty feet. A reward of £20 having been offered by Mr. McConnell [*sic*] several witnesses soon made their appearance . . . Humphreys was apprehended . . .'

From this we learn that workmen were using the train and Humphreys was probably engaged on building houses in Abergynolwyn village.

The newspapers again fall silent until on 20th January 1866 the *Merionethshire Standard & Mid Wales Herald* has:

> 'New carriage for the Towyn and Talyllyn Railway. On Saturday evening a passenger carriage for this line of railway arrived and on Tuesday was safely got onto the metals. It is of very neat construction and capable of seating from 18 to 20 passengers. We hope soon to see more arrive and the line opened for 'passenger traffic'.'

The last remark may hide some frustration at what would seem unnecessary delay, for the Act had received Royal Assent on 5th July previously, and to the uninformed, as the line had been carrying slate traffic for (probably) over half a year, there would seem to be no impediment to that end. The vehicle referred to was a four-wheeled, three-compartment 3rd class carriage, built by Brown, Marshalls & Co. Ltd. and is likely to have been transferred from a Cambrian Railways truck at the interchange wharf. It still survives as No. 3 and is the only one precisely of this type.

There followed an awesome silence as regards an opening for the public and doubtless this was due to the necessity to bring the railway up to a standard where the Government's Inspector of Railways might visit it with a reasonable assumption that he would find things to his satisfaction and allow public trains to commence. Was there delay in bringing Dolgoch Viaduct to the necessary calibre as opposed to one in which it would suffice for mineral traffic? It must have seemed that the carriage delivered in late January 1866 was somewhat premature, for the newspapers have nothing to report until 1st September following. However, it could be that the carriage was but a vehicle for the occasional use of the Quarry Manager and the type of customer who likes to know that, should he place an order, the slate is coming from a quarry to which he has made a personal visit. Such links would certainly be encouraged by the McConnels.

On 1st September the *Carnarvon & Denbigh Herald* stated:

> 'The bridges etc. on this line are now nearly completed, the stations are in building and we hope soon to be in a position to name the day of opening.'

We are not told which bridges are incomplete but they are likely to have included Ty Mawr and Rhydyronen where level crossings already existed but where, on second thoughts, overbridges to a higher standard of construction than the others, were provided in lieu. This was probably to avoid the necessity of furnishing some sort of accommodation at these crossings to house gatekeepers, as the Railway Clauses Consolidation Act required gates and a person in attendance at such crossings. Even as a mineral railway operated by a private company, this would have applied.

The substitution of overbridges for the two level crossings would conveniently explain the sale of semaphore signals to the Mawddwy Railway, referred to later. Such signals would be a requirement to ensure safety at the road intersection, but elsewhere signals could be dispensed with.

At last developments had reached the stage when the Board of Trade Inspector could be sent for; the newspaper account says of his visit on 25th September 1866 that he 'expressed himself well satisfied'. It continues 'there are a few alterations to be made and we expect in about a fortnight it will be opened to traffic'.

It was 8th November before Capt. H. W. Tyler returned again and the local correspondent could write:

> 'Captain Tyler . . . passed over this railway, minutely examined all the bridges and principal approaches, signals and stations and considered everything perfect.
> 'We expect the line will not be open for 'passenger traffic' until January.'

However, things proved to be better than forecast for the edition of 22nd December had:

> '. . . we are glad to notice that this line . . . has been opened for 'passenger traffic'. From the timetables which have been issued for December we see that two trains are running, each was leaving Abergynolwyn at 8 a.m. and 3 p.m. and returning from Pendre station at Towyn at 9 a.m. and 4 p.m.'

Initially, therefore, the service was based on Abergynolwyn where it is known one of the first drivers lived, and there was an engine shed at Ty Dwr above the village and east of the statutory limit of line. What is not known is where the carriage was left overnight, and if it was taken up and down with the slate wagons to the foot of Alltwyllt Incline each journey, and housed in the small fan of sidings there? This was done because accommodation at Pendre was then unfinished. The train service did not originate from Towyn until 17th February 1867.

Looking ahead, it seems hardly possible that more than one or two carriages would be needed during the winter months, and perhaps in view of this the newspaper continues:

> 'No doubt during the summer months extra trains will run for the accommodation of tourists and visitors to enable them to visit the far-famed Talyllyn Lake, the old Caerberllan Castle and the ancient church of Llanfihangel as well as Cader Idris which is only a short distance from the latter place or lake.'

The demonstrations which the local paper had forecast when the line opened are nowhere recorded; in fact, the actual opening date has been lost, though M. E. Vignes and *The Railway Magazine** quote a date of 1st October 1866. In this instance Tyler gave no written dispensation to the Company to begin a passenger service subject to his being able to find all items to his acceptance on a later visit.

An unofficial passenger traffic had already passed over the line in late August 1866 when members of the Cambrian Archaeological Association travelled to Abergynolwyn and back, using the one carriage available. The Cambrian Archaeological Association was founded in 1846 and in the 19th Century was in the habit of holding an annual summer meeting, lasting nearly a week, in some part of what it regarded as its territory. Thus it came about that the 20th annual meeting was held in Machynlleth in 1866, commencing on Monday 27th August and extending over

* Issue 1938 (ii) p. 197

a period of five days. A local committee had been formed, amongst whom were well-known names like Edmund Buckley, promoter of the Mawddwy Railway; David Davies of Corris, who was connected with both the Talyllyn Railway and the Corris; David Howell of Machynlleth, the Solicitor to the Talyllyn Railway; and Thomas Houldsworth McConnel of Towyn, a director of the Talyllyn Railway.

A prospectus of the meeting was sent to the members. The proceedings were to commence on Monday evening with the formal business of the annual meeting and a lecture on ancient camps in Cardiganshire. The members were informed that they could reach Machynlleth by rail from Shrewsbury and timings from Dolgelley were also given. As a specimen, the following was quoted: –

> 'Depart Dolgelley 11.10 a.m.
> Depart Barmouth Ferry 12.25
> Depart Towyn 12.51
> Arrive Aberdovey 1.00 p.m.
> Arrive Machynlleth 2.16 p.m.'

Much elaborate preparatory work for the week's entertainment was undertaken by David Howell and amongst the visits which had been arranged was one to Castell y Bere. In this connection David Howell evidently wrote to T. H. McConnel to seek permission to use the Talyllyn Railway for he received the following reply: –

> Brynhyfryd,
> Towyn,
> August 21st 1866.
>
> My Dear Sir,
> I shall be most happy to take up the line to Abergynolwyn just as many members of the Archaeological Society as we can find trucks for. Of course we can only take about eighteen in a closed carriage as we have only one, holding just that number of seats, but the slate wagons are pleasant in fine weather.
> Can you say how many there are likely to be and at what hour they will wish to start from our station, and at what hour to return from Abergynolwyn?
> Including the closed carriage I think we could take 70 or 80.
> It would take about three quarters of an hour each way, the distance being seven miles. Of course we can make no charge, nor should we think of such a thing.
> I fancy it is about $2\frac{1}{2}$ miles to Castell y Bere, a beautiful walk.
> By arrangement with the Cambrian Co, no doubt the members could be deposited at our station at Towyn to save a walk at this end.
> Yours truly,
> T. H. McConnel.

Evidently the arrangements were satisfactorily concluded for at about 9.30 a.m. on Tuesday 28th August 1866, the party started from Machynlleth Station for Ynyslas and their day's outing was reported in *The Merionethshire Standard* of 1st September 1866.

> About half past nine the party started from Machynlleth station for Ynyslas, where, as the tide was high, the steam-boat was waiting up the river to embark her cargo, and a walk of a few hundred yards brought us to the spot. There a large contingent from the Borth Hotel joined us, and the boat was very fully freighted as we steamed away across the beautiful Estuary of the Dovey, where the sea sparkling in the sunlight on the one side,

and one of the most picturesque of mountain landscapes on the other, made up a scene of perfect loveliness. Such a bright and genial introduction to the pleasures of the day put all the party in the highest spirits for the pleasant work which lay before them.

The short voyage was all too soon over, and then another short journey by train brought the party to Towyn, where the Talyllyn Railway Company had kindly provided a train on their beautiful little line to convey us to Abergynolwyn. Such a railway ride, we suppose, few of us had ever taken before. The Talyllyn Railway, as your readers know, is one of those two-foot lines constructed for the purpose of carrying slates, but also used to convey passengers. As the passenger traffic on the Talyllyn Railway is not expected to be very extensive, the coach accommodation was only just sufficient for the ladies, and most of the party were stowed away in slate trucks.

A jerk, which painfully reminded one of the absence of buffers, and off we went towards the beautiful valley, or rather series of valleys, where every turn reveals fresh lines of beauty, the mimic line creeps along the side of the hill, higher and higher, till at last we look down from a considerable eminence to the vale below, and back far away over the "happy autumn fields" to the shining sea. As the train, with its unwonted human freight, runs further and further up into the hills, the country grows in grandeur, and brave old Cader, looking like a familiar friend amongst the surrounding mountains, lifts his stately head above them. The only stopping place was Dolgoch, and there the train just halted for a moment on a bridge which spans the mountain stream, that the party might better enjoy the beauty of the waterfall. Then higher and higher, above the happy valleys full of harvest and bright with honeysuckle and ash berries, to the station at Abergynolwyn. To such a height had the train climbed by this time, that a long and precipitous descent led to the little hamlet below, where the slate company, represented on this occasion by Mr M'Connell who courteously accompanied the train, has provided such excellent cottages for the workmen.

When, with some difficulty, the ladies had accomplished this descent, the merry party started across the hills for Castell-y-bere. A walk of indescribable loveliness led over one branch of the Dysini at Pont-y-cwrt, and then, turning to the left, over the side of Moel Caerberllan, to that ancient castle, and though the way was steep and rugged, every difficulty was repaid a hundredfold by the beauty and grandeur of the scene, which culminated when we began to descend and looked down the valley of the Dysini to the curiously shaped Craig Aderyn (Bird Rock), and up towards the frowning steeps of Cader. A walk of some two miles or so brought the party to the foot of Castell-y-bere, where we were met by Mr Wynne, of Peniarth, who acted as guide over those interesting remains.

Castell-y-bere, the Castle of the Falcon, situated on a precipitous rock a short distance from Llanfihangel-y-Pennant, is the remains of the largest castle in North Wales, except Carnarvon, and perhaps, Beaumaris, its extent being about 500 feet by 100 feet broad. It is supposed to have been built in the eleventh century by Lupus, an Earl of Chester, who had captured a Welsh Prince. Edward I visited it, and from it dated some of his proclamations. He also granted a charter to the "Township of Bere," about the same time, and in similar terms to that granted to Carnarvon. The castle was doubtless destroyed by fire, as the remains fully showed, and the destruction probably took place about the end of the reign of Edward I, subsequently to which time there are no reliable documents concerning it.

It was as recently as 1850 that Mr Wynne (the property of whose brother-in-law, Mr Scott, the castle is) began to excavate the ruins. Before that time, says the *Cambrian Archæological Journal*, the ruins were so overgrown with trees and brushwood, and covered with the debris of the fallen building, that in several parts the plan could be little more than conjectured. The researches of Mr Wynne brought to light fragments of beautiful 'dog-tooth' moulding, highly-ornamented capitals, and a very remarkable lancet window, with a circular moulding, not only on the arch and jambs, but also on the sill. The labour of building such a structure on the summit of the rock, with stone brought perhaps from Cheshire or Bristol, must have been stupendous. A great number of arrow heads, one of them barbed, pottery, fragments of chain armour, and other interesting relics, were also discovered, and in one part of the building human remains were

exhumed. Altogether the ruins are of the most interesting character, and well repaid the members of the society for visiting them – by their great picturesqueness as well as the antiquarian interest which attaches to them.

Up the ascent to this ancient fortress, and over the mouldering walls, which were adorned with ferns, some of them of rare species, the excursionists gallantly charged, the ladies exhibiting, if possible, greater pluck than the gentlemen, in scaling the battlements. Mr Wynne explained the various portions of the building very fully, and an exceedingly pleasant time was spent at Castell-y-bere. Then the whistle was blown for another march, and the party followed Mr Howell, who carried the standard – a patent overcoat on a stick – down to the plain, where carriages soon arrived to convey to Towyn those of the ladies who chose to adopt that method of locomotion. The rest of the party made their way back to the railway station, to which some of them were wound up in the slate trucks, and half an hour's ride brought us back to Towyn.

A little information about the Inspecting Officer is timely. Henry Whatley Tyler was one of the Board of Trade's Inspecting Officers of Railways. His father was a Deputy Lieutenant of Gloucestershire but he himself was born in London in 1827; he received a commission in the Royal Engineers in 1844. Between 1853 and 1877 he worked on behalf of the Board of Trade, though not exclusively on the railway scene. His inspections were regarded by those with whom he worked as utterly exhausting; he went through an enormous amount of work in the shortest time, often completing Reports to the Board whilst night-time travelling between inspections. In 1868 he retired (without pension) from the Royal Engineers but, after being made Lt. Colonel, he continued with the Board of Trade, becoming their Chief Inspector in 1871. He was knighted when, on leaving the Board in 1877, he became chairman of the Westinghouse Brake Company. He continued to lead a very active life long after this, and died on 30th January 1908.*

The content of Henry Whatley Tyler's Reports follows.

Aberystwith,
25th September, 1866.

Sir,
I have the honor to report for the information of the Lords of the Committee of Privy Council for Trade, that in compliance with the instructions contained in your minute of the 8th instant I have inspected the Talyllyn Railway.

This is a single line 6 miles and 50.75 chains long, constructed on a gauge of 2'3" between the Rails. The steepest gradient is 1 in 60. The sharpest curve has a radius of 6 chains. There are only 2 stations namely Towyn at one end and Abergynolwyn at the other.

The permanent way is laid with rails of the ℒ section weighing 44 lbs. per lineal yard, and in lengths of 21 ft. There are cast iron chairs weighing $20\frac{1}{2}$ lbs each at the joints of the rails, and $17\frac{1}{4}$ lbs each for two intermediate chairs under each side. The sleepers are laid transversely 3 feet apart and are stated to average 4'9" long by 7" × 5". The chairs are secured to the sleepers by iron spikes, and the intermediate portions of the rails between the chairs by dog spikes. I recommend that locked chock blocks be added to the sidings and duplicate connecting rods to the switches.

The fences are principally of post and rail with five rails, and in some places of hedges. They require raising or improvement

---

* See also *The Engineer* August 1877 p. 117, and *Festiniog Railway Magazine* No. 30, p. 18.

and the hedges to be repaired, in some places, as I have pointed out in going over the line.

There are 7 Bridges over and 15 under the Railway, besides a viaduct 51 feet high, and 38 yards long, At a bridge $3\frac{1}{2}$ miles from Towyn the wall plate under the beams should be better secured and the beams should in this and other instances be bolted together towards each end. Two brick arches one at $1\frac{1}{4}$ mile and the other at $\frac{3}{4}$ mile from Talyllyn should be rebuilt.

The Bridges over the line have a span on the square of only $9'1''$ or $9'1\frac{1}{2}''$ and the only passenger carriage which has yet been purchased is $5'3\frac{1}{2}''$ wide outside measurement. This leaves but $1'11''$ between the outside of the carriage and the abutments, instead of $2'6''$ which there ought to be. Mr. McConnel the Chairman of the Company proposes to obviate this difficulty by permanently fastening the door and barring the windows on one side of his carriages and slewing the rails so as to allow sufficient space between the other side and the abutment. The objection to this course is that if a carriage was turned over on the unbarred side, with the barred side uppermost, the passengers would be unable to escape from it. But it must be admitted that this objection has not the same force in the case of a line of this description, on which only one engine will be employed for passengers and minerals at a speed intended to be not greater than 10 miles an hour and on which the passenger traffic will be so limited that it would not be worth while for the Company to carry passengers at all if much extra expense was to be incurred in the works as on lines of higher speed and greater traffic. It is necessary that other carriages should be provided.

The company has only two engines of which the heaviest is said to weigh 8 tons in working order – one of them is at work and the other under repair. It is desirable, that some alteration should be made in them, with a view to check the vertical motion to which the one is liable from its short wheel base, and the horizontal oscillation which is caused by the other by the action of outside cylinders upon a crank pin of excessive length in proportion to the diameter of the driving wheels.

Pending the completion of the various improvements which I have indicated I am obliged to report my opinion that this little line cannot be opened by reason of the incompleteness of the works without danger to the Public using it.

I have, etc.
(Sgd) H. W. Tyler

Aberdovey,
8th November, 1866

Sir,

I have the honor to report, for the information of the Lords of the Committee of Privy Council for Trade, that in compliance with the instructions contained in your minute of the 15th ulto: I have re-inspected the Talyllyn Railway.

I find that the fencing has been approved, the 3 Bridges to which I referred in my report of the 25th September last have been rebuilt, chockblocks have been added to the sidings, and indicators and duplicate connecting rods to the switches. I recommended that some gates which were being put up near the Towyn Station should be placed further from the rails. There is still only one passenger carriage on the line, but another has been constructed and is on its way. Mr. McConnel, the Chairman of the Company, informs me that he expects only 3 or 4 passengers for each train except on Saturdays, when he expects 30 or 40. It is desirable that extra carriages should be provided, before next spring.

The Engine which was working during my previous visit, is still at work, but with some slight alterations, which have tended to make it more steady; and Mr. McConnel informs me he has now determined to add trailing wheels to the other Engine as I have recommended. He will also shorten the crank pins on the driving wheels of the working Engine as soon as the other has been got ready to take its place. I travelled on the line today at a speed of 20 miles an hour with the working engine, and found it steadier than I expected at that speed, and Mr. McConnel does not propose in the course of working to exceed 10 miles per hour.

The safety of the single line will be secured by the employment of only one engine at a time as provided for in the certificate of the 6th September.

Subject to the above conditions, and to the precautions referred to in my report of the 25th September in regard to narrow works, I am, of opinion that this little line may be opened without danger to the public using it.

I have etc.,
(sgd) H. W. TYLER.

Whilst the building, opening and inspection of the Railway has now been covered, it is convenient to go back to 5th July 1865 to look at the Act of Incorporation more closely, and say something of the first directors of the Company. The Act said:

'... commencing near the ... Coast Railway in the Parish of Towyn ... terminating in a field called Cefncoch in the township of Maestrefnant in the same Parish, and a Railway therefrom to the Towyn station on the Coast Railway in the same Parish ...:'

The promoters and first six directors included two of the McConnels, a Manchester accountant and three other Mancunians; in fact the whole enterprise (Railway and Quarry) reflected connections with that city and all stationery supplies, from passenger tickets to account books and share certificates, were supplied by firms in that region. Engineering materials came from a wider spread of manufacturers. The first Registered Office was at 30 Pall Mall, Manchester where also the Company's solicitors were found in a nearby street. This was the partnership of Orford & Milne, originally Earle Son Orford Earle & Milne, William Orford then being senior partner connected with the formation of the Statutory Company. The first subscribers to be named are Thomas Houldsworth McConnel, James Murray, Thomas Swanwick, Murray Gladstone, James McConnel and Samuel Holker Norris. The capital was £15,000, the face value of shares being £20 each, and the aforementioned gentlemen, holding a qualifying number of shares, were appointed the first directors. There were borrowing powers of up to £5,000 which could not be taken up until all the £15,000 had been subscribed and issued (etc).

There were to be two Railways:

1. Railway No. 1 forms the Talyllyn Railway system as it exists today (terminating at a point east of Abergynolwyn station shown on the map on p.40). The railway (or Mineral Extension as it has been unofficially termed in recent years) from this point up to the Quarry was a private undertaking and not covered by the Act; its status was clear enough at the time of the Act but rapidly became unclear as the Quarry Company did not make an annual charge for its use by the Railway Company as it should have done. In consequence the ownership of that section of railway was placed in doubt after 1951, and required much legal investigation to establish. This issue is considered on p. 230.

2. Railway No. 2 was for a spur line linking a junction immediately east of the Aberdovey road overbridge at the present Wharf station (at first known as King's) and running west, south and then north, and south, entering the Cambrian (ex Coast Line's) goods yard at the Cambrian station by a reversal junction. This line was planned to be of mixed gauge and involved the transfer of slate wagons onto the floors of standard gauge wagons. It was never built, and power to do so lapsed in 1870.

The gauge of the new railway might be 4 ft 8½ in. but no less than 2 ft. 3 in. The latter dimension was adopted, probably because of existing tramways in the Quarry. [A further factor was likely to have been the influence of Thomas Savin '... a line, 16 m. long, for which he had given £20,000, was laid on the gauge of 2 ft. 3 ins....'. This was the Corris Railway. (Proceedings of The Institute of Civil Engineers, 11th April 1865)] In the event of narrow gauge being chosen, the speed limit would be 15 mph. Time for completion was five years. There were extensive sections concerning rates for goods, minerals and passenger charges. Such was 'The Talyllyn Railway Act, 1865' 28 & 29 Victoriae Cap. cccxv.

The directors were friends and even close friends of each other, and like those of the Quarry, would be somewhat competitive in their Manchester business interests but chosen for their commercial intelligence.

It is now opportune to refer to the Inspector's Reports; in that of 25th September there is a drawing of flat-bottomed rail section in the opening line of paragraph 3. The fourth word in the last sentence of the fifth paragraph should read 'Abergynolwyn' and not 'Talyllyn'. In the penultimate paragraph, we may speculate which engine was under repair. *Talyllyn* was first to be delivered (in September 1864) and *Dolgoch* followed (in Summer 1866). Was *Talyllyn* being overhauled after carrying out duty on its own, or was the same engine out of service awaiting return to the makers at Whitehaven for the alterations which would fit it with a rear axle? Or was Tyler recording what he would have been told – 'we work the line with one engine whilst the other may be under repair' – a frequent expression used on small railways which operated on the 'One Engine in Steam' principle and saved a little on the expense of providing safeguards against collisions when two or more engines might be out on the line at the same time? The second Report confirms that *Dolgoch is* the 'working engine'.

Between Tyler's Reports, on the south side the doors of the carriages were secured, the droplight openings fitted with bars; probably the track was slewed slightly off-centre under overbridges. Possibly impatient at waiting for Tyler to come again, the unofficial service began on 1st October, perhaps without charge and at traveller's own risk. Monsieur M. E. Vignes, who was touring the narrow gauge railways of these islands for his publication of *Etude technique sur le chemin de fer de Festiniog et quelques autres chemins de fer de l'Angleterre* was told of this date; Tyler probably wasn't! We have only Vignes' figure to inform us.

One wonders if some of the fitments noted by Tyler on his second visit survived for very long? 'Chock blocks have been added to the sidings, and indicators and duplicate connecting rods to the switches. I recommended that some gates which were put up near the Towyn station should be placed further from the rails'. This would be Pendre. Chock blocks and the like? No evidence remains.

Finally it will be noted that at the end of it all, only one passenger coach was available as yet, and it should be stressed once again that Tyler himself was breaking new ground – this was the first narrow gauge railway to operate with steam power and a public passenger service from inception. In that respect it made older horse-tramway lines like the Festiniog and Corris look like relics of the Iron Age.

As has been said, at the end of 1866 and until mid-February the following year, the morning train originated at Abergynolwyn. Tradition has it that a second driver lived in Towyn and walked to Abergynolwyn each Monday morning, but that he was given a trolley on which he might return at night; more likely he found accommodation in Abergynolwyn during the week. The tale does not end there for that same driver is said to have lost his job by driving over the end of the slate wharf at King's and ending up on Cambrian metals! It is said he promptly went round to the Corris and obtained a post as a driver there. The tale has imperfections as locomotives did not replace horses on that railway until February 1879 but it could be true. The man served on the Corris until he retired. The same legend is told in Corris also!

When the Talyllyn Railway opened, public passenger stations were Towyn Pendre (usually written as Pendref by the office staff) and Abergynolwyn. By February 1867 Rhydyronen had appeared, as did Brynglas and Dolgoch in 1873. The initial existence of the Village Incline might be doubted, but on balance it could have existed from the outset to provide a rail link from Quarry to village during the enlargement of Abergynolwyn as a residence for the Quarry employees. Not unnaturally, the Incline is added later in pencil on Spooner's Deposited Plans, because it was built off a part of the line not affected by the Parliamentary Bill.

The Railway may be said to have settled in to a low, slowly-paced lifestyle, geared basically to the life of the Quarry and a growing traffic in summer visitors which provided it with some problems during those months. Its personnel changed but slowly, it was provided with the minimal financial means for survival by its owners, and its original equipment, despite its existence on the edge of the industrial perimeter of these islands, was to serve it throughout the period of this narrative. This was achieved through the mixed fortunes of a Quarry which could not spare any more money, a weight of traffic which at no time put the equipment under severe pressure, and a gradually slackening demand for the line's services. However, man-made objects are prone, like nature's, not to last

Possibly one of the earliest views of a Talyllyn train known to exist — a cabless TALYLLYN with open-balconied Luggage Van stands on Dolgoch viaduct, a vista unrepeatable today due to the growth of trees which fill the gorge.
NATIONAL LIBRARY OF WALES

for ever, and the slow but visible run-down of the Railway which began from the opening day, was to continue until the death of its then owner Sir Henry Haydn Jones in July 1950. Unlike present times, changing external circumstances affected the Towyn area but lightly. Two world wars, new ownership of the Quarry, economic factors – none affected the Talyllyn Railway, in the same way as, for instance, its neighbour the Corris Railway, which was absorbed into the Great Western Railway and then closed when its route was eaten away by a river, or the Festiniog Railway whose slate-manufacturing customers boycotted it during the Second World War so that, without a peace time injection of tourist traffic, it was forced to close by those to whom it owed money. There is a host of reasons why the Talyllyn survived but without doubt it was the stubbornness of its owner, Henry Haydn Jones which – though that character had some dubious qualities in other circumstances – kept the Railway operational. Its obscurity grew; from about 1910 when he took the reins, no Official Returns were made, and the entry 'No returns available' is commonplace.

It must be explained that a Statutory Undertaking like the Talyllyn cannot be terminated summarily; born of an Act of Parliament, it can only succumb with another Act of Parliament but, as there is nothing in the Company's Act which obliges it to offer a train service (a point which was of importance when ownership passed from McConnel to Haydn Jones in 1911) it can continue without carrying out loss-making features. For some years the Festiniog Railway ran no trains but had an income from rents. Other companies have closed their railways and run road services instead. Haydn Jones' sense of duty was that he continued to provide a railway for his tenants, admitting the while that no one used it and even fewer thanked him for it!

To pick up the story again, the 'milestones' of those days form a convenient peg on which to hang the occasional happening. Detail of engines, carriages, wagons, the operation of trains, a journey along the route right into the Quarry, something of the timetables provided, the difficulties of dealing with sudden demands to carry passengers, a typical day in the lives of the staff and something of the men who kept the Railway going, have been extracted and given a place elsewhere herein.

In considering construction rather than operation of the line, the absence of evidence as to who took charge of the work and the form of labour employed is still unclear. One suggestion is that Thomas Savin, approaching a personal financial crisis which resulted in his bankruptcy on 5th February 1866, may have been attracted to overseeing the venture as a 'cash job'; evidence for this idea is based on similarity in style

and construction of certain brick and stone overbridges on the Coast Line, with those on the Talyllyn. Rough stone in bridges is not a local product and may have come from Aberdovey.

Another feature of the Towyn development period (in which the railway was one of several schemes, others being the building of a pier, an embankment and a Dysynni drainage project) would be the consequence of the influx of men into a district of comparatively peaceful agriculture. The effect on the lives of a rural community isolated from the pace of life even in those times, would be traumatic. Firstly, to be placed in contact with London, to have to adopt Greenwich Time, to be linked by railway telegraph to other points on the existing railway system, and to find uniformed men in charge of the station, would bring in a whole new dimension to life, and it must have been received with considerable fear as well as welcomed. Each day a Coast Line train would arrive in Towyn and the guard would check that the station clocks were set to the Company's time; surely Towyn was being brought into a world which many would reject and not all would see as the dawn of a new age? The district would be torn by heavy road traffic coming down from Bryneglwys and ruining the poor surfaces, and the old parish road between Ty Mawr and Rhydyronen (and on to Brynglas) would be completely mutilated by the building of the Quarry rail link.

There were several features in the newspapers about the state of the highways at this time; as the Railway route cut through the parish road in four places, its builders were obliged to construct a new one, traces of which can be seen from the train from time to time.

In order to build a suitable terminal interchange, and with the abandonment of the idea of building Railway No. 2 which would have brought their system to its western interchange on the north side of Trenewydd Bridge, the Talyllyn Railway (through Cotterell & Spackman) made application through George Owen, Engineer of the Cambrian Railways, to purchase a plot of land which they already leased. This was part of an area beside the Coast Railway where Savin's men had dug pits beside the line in order to obtain 'fill' from the glacial deposits available there. On this site, King's station came into being. Owen wrote to his Board on 25th July 1866, passing on the request and saying: '... now partially filled up by Talyllyn company and used for wharfage purposes'.

The Cambrian agreed to sell and a year later the Cambrian Board was reminded both of this and that the Talyllyn had (on 25th June 1866) applied for an easement 'for carrying the Talyllyn Railway under the Township Road so as to form a physical junction with your line ... at a point mid-way between the existing wharf and Towyn station ...', to which the Cambrian reply was that they were ready to give it 'subject to land being required by [their Engineer] for a double line ... wharves and other necessary accommodation.'

Owen referred to the plan which accompanied the proposal and the existence of a group of dwellings which are considered on p. 71 in the description of Wharf station. He wrote of them: 'I observe that the houses shown on the plan are the commonest sort of mud huts and would of course, have to be pulled down.'

If this formed part of the Railway No. 2 proposal, the land (according to a pencil note on C & S) was later disposed of as unwanted. The same would apply if Owen's letter implied the Talyllyn was considering a new junction from under the King's station road bridge, passing under the approach road to Trenewydd Bridge, and via a west and north curve into an interchange yard so avoiding the reversal of Railway No. 2.

The land in question had been part of the Ynysymaengwyn Estate, rented by the A & WCR Company. In the event, the site of the former ballast hole did become the Talyllyn terminal, but the interchange scheme was not prosecuted. In the matter of the purchase matters must have stalled for a time, but Cotterell & Spackman continued to act for the Railway Company to acquire it, being but partially successful on 31st July 1871. (This firm was still handling all Quarry and Railway conveyancing, probably because of their existing connection with the Ynysymaengwyn Estate; their surveyors in such cases were Messrs. Henry Spackman and Richard Gillart.) At that date only a lease was available @ £7 5s. 3d. per annum and so things remained until December 1879 when McConnel bought the land outright from A. J. S. Corbet's executors.

Under the terms of the Talyllyn Act the Company was permitted to buy certain lands which up to a time it had only leased. On 6th June 1868 Henrietta Corbet Corbet died leaving her eldest surviving son, a minor, as heir: he was Athelstan John Soden Corbet who became owner of the Ynysymaengwyn Estate. It was then possible to convey much of the course of the line between King's and a point east of Dolgoch to the Company; the total was only 27 acres and 12 perches, but much of it was the long narrow route of the track itself. There were considerable 'aprons' of adjoining land at King's, near the British School, at Pendre, Hendy and Rhydyronen, most of which had been sold off before Sir Haydn died. This conveyance was carried out in 1879.

Reverting to the year 1866, two events occurred which, though having no direct bearing on the Railway Company, had effect on all and sundry in the first case, and clearly sharpened local thinking about railways in the second. The first was the failure of Overend & Gurney's Bank. The second was a Bill by which

the Cambrian Railways intended to vest the Carnarvonshire Railway (then building between Afon Wen and Pen-y-Groes), the Nantlle Railway (a very active slate carrier between the Nantlle quarries and the port of Caernarvon), the Beddgelert Railway (a proposed line between Portmadoc and Llyn Gwynant, of 1865, termed The Beddgelert Railway as it passed through there!) and the Corris Railway (then linking the river Dovey at Derwenlas with the slate quarries in the Corris district). One may ask if the Talyllyn Railway was seen to be a competitor, a feeder or insignificant by the Cambrian special meeting held at 4 Westminster Chambers, on 26th April 1866? Would the TR have – bearing in mind its special link with Bryneglwys Quarry – entertained an approach by the Cambrian? The Bill however, was dropped. It might have been a serious event for the TR if the Corris ('it is a tramway but we have power to work it with locomotives' said the Cambrian Secretary) had gone into the Cambrian empire, for Corris slate was a commercial competitor with Bryneglwys.

Sunday was The Lord's Day and given that special observance which, though still obtaining in a few places today, was then of the strictest pattern. Nothing but essential work, such as feeding livestock on farms, was acceptable. Naturally, no train turned a wheel in this part of Wales and it was an inviting opportunity for a break-in. 'Between 7 p.m. Saturday and 8 a.m. Monday last the office of the Talyllyn Railway at King's station, Towyn, was burglariously entered'. This was done by breaking a window on the north side; the objective was the drawer where cash was kept during the day, and this was forced open. 'The door of the safe was tampered with to no avail'. There was said to be nothing worth taking, and that the culprit had also entered the station at Pendre 'to no purpose'. So the *North Wales Chronicle* of 28th January 1871 informed its readers.

There was further trouble in November 1876 when Hugh Griffiths and Owen Pughe of Abergynolwyn appeared at the Petty Sessions in Aberdovey (*The Cambrian News* 10th November 1876) and were summoned on a complaint by John Roberts, then Railway Manager and charged with being drunk and interfering with the comfort of other passengers on the said Railway on 7th October. They were respectively fined 40/– including costs.

This introduces an interesting issue; there is to this day a *Railway Inn/Hotel* at Abergynolwyn. Did this exist before the Talyllyn and if so, under what name. It appears on the 1871, but not the 1861, Census. Did men prefer to come down by train into Towyn and return home the worse for their visit?

To comply with the Explosives Act of 1875, James Stevens (the Secretary) had a notice inserted in *The Cambrian News* (8th December 1876) stating that the

Company's by-laws under the above Act might be inspected at the Company's offices, Towyn. Objectors would have to make their complaints known to the Board of Trade in London.

In June 1877 Mr. I. Hughes Jones of Messrs. Jones & Griffiths, Timber Merchants of Machynlleth, wrote to the Cambrian Railways from Aberdovey on the 15th, asking for a siding to be put in 'to the old ballast hole at Towyn (lately bought from your Company by me) for the following purposes: (1) I intend opening a timber yard and saw mill there (2) I have a stone quarry at this place out of which I can supply stone for about 1/- a ton less than they sell them now from the Aberganolwyn Quarry [sic] which will be very encouraging to builders as well as bringing traffic to our lines'.

George Lewis informed his directors:

> 'The granting of this application will involve the placing of another pair of facing points upon the main line, there already being two pairs close to this place, the third would form an additional element of danger unless rodded up and all placed inside a proper signal box in which case the Aberllynolwyn Company [sic] and Mr. Jones should each contribute ⅓ part of the expenses'.

The site of this application is not clear, but may have been opposite King's station and on the west side of the Coast Line. It seems a little hard that the Quarry Company should be asked to pay a part of the main line alterations and then lose stone orders to a competitor into the bargain – Jones' quarry was possibly that near the Trefeddian Hotel, Aberdovey. It appears the scheme did not proceed.

In 1886 there were but seven Ordinary Shareholders, their individual holdings being of nominal value £2,143. There were no Debenture or Preference Shareholders, none having been authorised.

The tentacles of Mother Parliament reaching out were to be felt by every statutory railway carrying passengers in 1889, and the Talyllyn was no exception. This was the outcome of The Regulation of Railways Act (52 & 53 Vict. c.57) of 30th August 1889 which amended a similarly-named Act of 1840 and others which followed it. The 1889 Act was concerned immediately with public safety, although it contained other matters. As to safety, the Board of Trade might require a company to carry out specified work within a given time, thus the Talyllyn was notified by circular dated 24th October 1889. Basically the BoT wished the Company to:

1. Adopt the Block System of signalling on all lines on which the public was carried
2. To have points and signals interlocked so as to prevent contrary movements
3. To fit a continuous brake to passenger trains, capable of being applied by driver or guard and coming into effect if the train divided (etc.) by self-application

4. The brake must be in daily use, of durable character and easily maintained

However, a clause added that the BoT would have regard 'to the nature and extent of the traffic of the railway ...' and would 'hear any company or person [who] ... may be entitled to be heard'. Under this clause the Talyllyn was to shelter.

Almost all impecunious railways sent up their individual 'bleats' to the Assistant Secretary of the Railway Department; their plea to be excepted was always the same, 'Poverty'. In the Welsh narrow gauge field, Festiniog and North Wales Narrow Gauge Companies were among complainants, but several concerns escaped the strictures of the Act by some good fortune (for instance) the Glyn Valley by coming into the 'Tramway' class, and the Isle of Man by coming under Island legislation, not that of Westminster.

The Talyllyn reply was dated 19th December 1889:

> 'Dear Sir,
> With reference to the circular marked R12521 issued by the Board of Trade to the railway companies on October 24th last and with special reference to clause (c) in that circular I am instructed to make the following representations for the consideration of the Board of Trade. The trains of the Talyllyn Railway are with few exceptions mixed trains. The usual load is two passenger carriages, one brake van and six to ten wagons loaded or unloaded. The average speed for the whole length of the line is about ten miles per hour while the maximum speed is not more than twelve or thirteen miles per hour. The line never has more than one engine in steam on it at one time and the present brakes are sufficient to stop the train under any conditions in a very short distance. For these reasons I plead before the Board of Trade that the proposed regulations for continuous brakes might reasonably be waived in our special case.
> I am sir, your obedient servant,
>
> W. H. McConnel,
> Secretary

According to the Board of Trade file, a précis of this letter was sent to Mr. Courtney Boyle and seen by the Inspecting Officers.

The next item is a draft order which is a printed document expressed to be made under The Regulation of Railways Act 1889 which has been filled in by W. H. McConnel. It is suggested that the railway has one year in which to adopt the block system, eighteen months in which to adopt interlocking of points and signals and eighteen months to fix continuous brakes. It is suggested that the block system be modified as only one engine is in use on the line at one time and it is stated that the line being a single line with no connections and only one engine in use at a time there are no signals.

The Second Schedule Part III is provided for exceptions of modifications of the requirement to install continuous brakes and McConnel filled this in as follows:

'Proposes that this order should not apply to the Talyllyn Railway for the following reasons:
'The traffic is extremely small and the expense of continuous brakes would be a heavy burden on the railway
'The trains are all mixed trains and the application of the order would necessitate the separation into goods and passenger trains and would curtail the passenger train accommodation
'The speed of the trains is low and nowhere exceeds twelve to fifteen miles per hour
'The trains are short, three passenger carriages and ten or twelve waggons being the limit, the trains can always be stopped within a very short distance
'The line is always clear as only one engine is in use on the line at one time.

W. H. McConnel,
Secretary, Talyllyn Railway.'

The Inspecting Officers made their comments on McConnel's points as follows:

'The block system is not required as traffic is worked with only one engine.
'Interlocking: it is stated that there are no connections. This seems incredible and is not consistent with the return of 1889. Any connections which there are should be locked with the staff which the engine should carry. Exceptions: none. Extensions of time: none.
'Continuous brakes: Exceptions: none: Extensions of time: twelve months.
'Mixed trains: the train morning and evening in each direction might be allowed on similar conditions to those proposed in the case of the Belfast and County Down Railway for mixed trains.

F. H. Rich, F. S. Hawthorn(?),
F. A. Marindin.'

The Board of Trade then overwhelmed the Talyllyn Company by sending them a copy of the full Order on 4th November 1890!
In due course a reply was made:

'17th January 1891
Sir,
I have to acknowledge receipt of your communication of 24th November marked R10912. I have to point out that the order of the Board of Trade throws a very serious burden upon this Company, a burden so out of proportion to any result it will achieve and so heavy when compared with the total takings of the Company that if enforced must cause the working of the line for passenger traffic to be given up. I may refer you to my letter of December 19th 1889. The present brakes in use would under the worst conditions suffice to stop the train in 60 or 70 yards and as only one engine is in use the danger of a collision is practically nil. I therefore contend that we are now in a much more satisfactory condition as regards safety than the large railways with the best continuous brakes and I ask in consequence that in our case the order as to continuous brakes may be altogether waived.

I am, Sir, Your obedient servant,
W. H. McConnel
Secretary'

The first Civil Servant to see this letter, Mr. Mackenzie, stated:

'The line is a narrow gauge line and should perhaps have the scale for reckoning engines and vehicles granted to the Festiniog Railway, pointing out that the Board of Trade cannot exempt the Company from continuous brakes.'

The Inspecting Officers appeared to agree with this. They suggested that details of the rolling stock be obtained. The enquiry seems to have been made for McConnel wrote to the Board of Trade as follows:

'12th March 1891
Sir,
In reply to your letter of 2nd inst. the weights of the rolling stock are:
1. Engines about 8 tons*
2. Passenger carriages empty 2 tons 11 cwts. 3 qtrs. These hold about 18 passengers.
3. Van weight about 2 tons 15 cwts. 2 qtrs.
4. Slate waggons weight about 12 cwts. 3 qtrs.
5. Normal load of slate waggons 1 ton 14 cwts. 0 qtrs.
The trains usually consist of 2 passenger carriages, a van and 10 slate waggons.
Yours faithfully,
W. H. McConnel'

The Inspecting Officers' comments on this letter were:

'The weight of the rolling stock is much the same as the Festiniog Railway except that there are no heavy engines, none apparently exceeding 8 tons and there are no quarrymens carriages.
The gradients on the line are not so severe as on the Festiniog Railway but there are gradients varying between 1 in 77 and 1 in 100 amounting to about one sixth of the whole length of the railway which is 6⅝ miles long. We cannot see our way to recommend the Board of Trade to dispense with continuous brakes and we think the following scale might be adopted:
Engine to count as two vehicles, carriage as one, van as a half and slate waggons as a half.
The wording of the Ravenglass & Eskdale Order might be adopted with the necessary alterations.'

The Board of Trade then wrote to McConnel as follows:

'7th April 1891
Sir,
With reference to your letter of 17th January touching the order made by the Board of Trade upon your company under The Regulation of Railways Act 1889 I am directed to inform you that as at present advised they do not see their way to dispensing with continuous brakes on the Talyllyn Railway. The Board of Trade have however taken into consideration the description and weight of the rolling stock in use and having modified the Order now issue the same. A duplicate is enclosed on which you are requested to endorse acceptance of service and return it to this Department.
I am etc.'

McConnell took some time to consider this letter and then wrote to the Board of Trade as follows:

'19th June 1891
Sir,
I have to acknowledge receipt of your letter of 7th April R825 with enclosures. I am still hopeful that the Board of Trade may decide to relieve us entirely from the burden of providing continuous brakes. I may again point out that they are not necessary in any way. The speed of our trains is limited under our Act to 15 m.p.h. and we have no desire to run at 25 m.p.h. as mentioned in the Order. I find that on our worst gradient of 1 in 77 the train with full load is stopped when running at its ordinary speed in 45 yards with our present brakes. On a less gradient the stoppage could be effected in half the above distance. I should be quite willing to agree that our speed should not exceed 12 m.p.h. if we were exempted from the Order as to continuous brakes.

_____

* There was no means of weighing the engines accurately; other vehicles could be put on a weighing-table.

An immaculate PRETORIA and train stands at Wharf in the early years of this century. John Rowlands is on the engine with Tommy Lloyd (slate loader) standing in front of the carriage. The two little girls have Jacob Rowlands (guard) in uniform behind them. Note the slabs stacked near the wharf edge.

C. H. YOUNG

Another view of a train at Wharf about ninety years ago; note the timber parapet on the road bridge. Jacob Rowlands stands in front of the first carriage. The middle figure before the second carriage is believed to be R. B. Yates, with Hugh Thomas at his left side.

TALYLLYN RAILWAY CO.

I must urge very strongly that the safety of the public will be in no way improved by the adoption of the Order of the Board of Trade. I must also point out that it is impossible for us, with our small passenger traffic to accept the Order and the stopping of the passenger service which must ensue if the Order is enforced will cause great inconvenience in the district. I am not aware that any brake yet in use can stop an ordinary express train on our main lines running down a gradient of 1 in 77 at 60 m.p.h. in anything like 45 yards. I hope the Board of Trade will from the above facts decide that continuous brakes are not necessary in our case.

Yours etc.,
W. H. McConnel'

C. S. Hutchinson, Inspecting Officer, noted on the file:

'As the speed of this railway is limited by Act of Parliament to 15 m.p.h. which speed the Company is willing to be further limited to 12 m.p.h. provided the adoption of continuous brakes is not made compulsory, and as there is only one public road level crossing which is approached on easy gradients and as the traffic is worked with only one engine so that there can be no danger from trains colliding with one another the Board of Trade might perhaps see their way to waive in this case the Order on the adoption of continuous brakes provided the company undertake to limit the speed of their trains to 12 m.p.h. the adoption of which speed will practically bring this railway under the category of a tramroad.   C.S.H. 2/7/91.'

The Board of Trade file has then a series of notes as follows:

This would appear to involve a point of importance and possible legal difficulty.
I think we may act as the Inspectors recommend. *Sir H. Calcraft.*
Yes. *Courtney Boyle.*

The Board of Trade accordingly wrote to McConnel in the following terms:

'Sir,
I am etc., of 19th ult. with reference to the Order under the Regulation of Railways Act 1889 and requesting that in the circumstances stated the Talyllyn Railway Company be relieved from the necessity of providing continuous brakes. In reply I am to report that the Board of Trade as at present advised are prepared to accept an undertaking duly signed and under the seal of the Company that the speed of their trains shall not exceed 12 m.p.h. and to state they are of the opinion that so long as this limit is adhered to the Company may be exempted from providing continuous brakes.
I am etc.'

The years move on and modern inventions begin to find their way into rural Wales. So the *Towyn on Sea and Merioneth County Times* [21st October 1897] says:

'After years of talk telegraphic communication between Towyn and Llanegryn and Abergynolwyn will soon be an accomplished fact. This will undoubtedly prove a boon to all, especially to the quarrymen. At present when an accident occurs at the quarries the only means of summoning medical aid is with a truck which runs along the Talyllyn line to Towyn, and even this mode of conveyance is not available if the wind is from the sea for it cannot come down except when the wind is favourable.'

Of course, this new feature was a public telegraph and nothing to do with the Railway Company which never went to the expense of a telegraph line of its own along the system. The public installation was sufficient throughout the years covered herein. When a train left a terminus, no report of its progress could ever be made; there was no speaking link between (for

A special train for the McConnel family has worked its way to the foot of Alltwyllt Incline in the 1890s; driver Bob Thomas (deputising for Jonathan Rowlands who was off sick with rheumatic fever) stands with oil feeder in hand, and the three children are told to 'Stand still' by their mother, Mrs. W. H. McConnel.

W. R. McCONNEL

instance) the Company's office at King's and the Works at Pendre, and the stations had no need of a telephone system for they had no personnel to use one!

A tide in the affairs of Railway and Quarry occurred on 17th October 1902 with the death of William McConnel, aged 95, at his Ayrshire home, the man who had saved Railway, Quarry and the village from the effects of the collapse of the initial foundings. Newspapers, which are not given to colourful obituaries when they are not deserved, called him a model employer and praised him and his Manager (Meyrick Roberts) that there had never been a strike at the Quarry (the strike at Penrhyn Quarry was then current). Although not resident in Towyn, he followed local affairs very closely and with a keen mind to the end, Meyrick Roberts sending monthly returns to him. Both Meyrick Roberts and Hugh Thomas (entitled 'Chief Accountant of the Company' by the paper) 'were summoned to attend the funeral . . .'.

There is no doubt that McConnel, with a Unitarian background and a Liberal upbringing, was, by some standards of those times, a considerate employer with a good relationship among those whose livelihood depended on him. Even the Welsh papers, accepting that he 'came in Wales', thought well of him, his prompt payments to his workers and his concern for the well-being of Abergynolwyn, as he considered that those who came from good homes also gave good service in return. He made provision for quarrymen to have small plots of land for their personal use – 'he brought more money into Wales than any man during the past 23 years' (which is doubtful, but the sentiment is there).

In the latter days of William McConnel's ownership, when Meyrick Roberts was managing the Quarry business, he had brought in R. B. Yates to be both Railway Manager and Quarry Chief. Titles do not seem to have been a strong point of definition in this small enterprise, and though in the late 1890s Hugh Thomas was Slate Wharf Manager and sometimes given as Railway Manager, McConnel had engaged Yates (a Scot) to be overall Manager about 1897. It could be that Hugh Thomas did not quite fit the post. Yates was a retired Civil Servant from India and is said to have known the McConnels, who found him a suitable person to send to Towyn and take charge of affairs. In the changeover period from McConnel to Haydn Jones in 1911 he was an important link-man in negotiations and made frequent calls on Daniel's shop or the farm at Pantyneuadd to discuss matters with the Daniel and Jones families. He made numerous small improvements on the Railway in the name of economy but the railway of the new century was still the railway of the 1860s!

The news of McConnel's death cast a great shadow over the village, Quarry and Railway, for he was the personification of them all, and almost all the population local to the Quarry was tied to that occupation. We may imagine the uneasy state of minds thereabouts until news came through that he would be succeeded by his son, William Houldsworth McConnel. There is evidence that before 1909 Yates had had plenty of indication by McConnel that he intended to pull out of the Quarry and close down the Railway at the same time. We find on 20th April 1909 Yates is writing to the Board of Trade on the prospect of the line being closed by its 'owner', so he must have had warning of that eventuality.

'Dear Sir, It is more than likely that our railway will be closed for traffic early next year. Is it necessary to advertise this probability beforehand or to take any steps say 5 or 6 months before the proposed closure? I would be grateful for any information you can give me. R. B. Yates, Secretary & Manager'

The Board's usual reluctance to pontificate was apparent, as it declined to advise 'as to the steps he should take but would call his attention to the Abandonment of Railways Act 1850 as amended by the Railway Cos' Act 1867'. So not for the first time Yates wanted for advice, and worked in isolation.

There is little or nothing surviving to show what anxieties were felt in the district as rumours, no doubt, took a hold. Whatever they were, they were not confined to Abergynolwyn for Towyn traders must have relied on custom from that village whose own retail outlets were limited. So we find Samuel Edmunds, owner of a 'General and Household Drapery; Ladies & Gents outfitters: Specialities – Dress-making, Millinery. Agent for Perth Dye Works' writing to the Board from his shop immediately opposite St. Cadvan's Church'.

A neat and trimmed Dolgoch station about 1894 showing evidence of John Jones' work on the rustic seating, and slabs on hand to improve the platform edging. Ballasting is taken well up beside the rails and the water tower has its earlier wooden tank on top.

H. S. BRISTOWE

'The quarries and the railway were worked originally by a company but eventually the Lessee of the quarries and the owner of the Railway became one and the same person – Wm McConnel, Knockdolian Ayrshire – He died in December 1902 and bequeathed the railway and his interest in the quarries between his four sons – who have taken but very little interest in the concern. In December last year the quarry lease expired and as a consequence the quarries closed down and as the lessees have no intention of renewing the leases the prospects of reopening them are very remote. It is rumoured (although no official notice has been given) that the railway will also close down the end of next month – now this is a very serious matter to the district generally especially as it is an agricultural one and something must be done to try to keep it going – But before moving in the matter I should like to know if it is necessary for the owner to give notice to the district of his intention to close down the Railway and if so what notice must he give. If you would kindly favour me with a reply to these questions I should feel very thankful.

I remain Sir your ff Servant
Samuel Edmunds
Manchester House,
Towyn Merionethshire 19/8/10'

The gist of the Board's reply was:

'Not aware of any general regulations – such a notice would however be issued if application were made by the TR Co. to this Dept.'

Yates submitted figures for 1907: Passengers carried 22,233. Goods carried 5,000 tons (of which 4,547 tons were minerals). Gross receipts were £1,264, working expenses £1,500, showing a loss of £236.

One of several aspects of McConnel's threats to abandon the Quarry and ceasing to operate the Talyllyn Railway as a consequence, was the right of Rev. Pugh (owner of the Cantrybedd Estate) to use tramways within and from the Quarry for his own purpose under the terms of the lease given to the Aberdovey Slate Company Limited. Such rights, if upheld, would, in the opinion of Pugh's solicitors, ensure that the Quarry Tramway and Talyllyn Railway were protected. However, Tapp Jones & Sons, reporting on the condition of Quarry etc. on behalf of these solicitors in May 1910, were cautious – 'covenant between the Slate Quarry Co. with the Rev. G. R. G. Pugh is open to grave doubt as to whether the company or Talyllyn Railway Co. is compellable to maintain a tramway . . .' along the Nant Gwernol valley's Quarry Tramway section to the top of Alltwyllt Incline. Nor did they feel his Reverence could demand a right of way along it for his goods etc. They felt that McConnel was the sole owner of the Talyllyn Railway and this connecting Tramway.*

'I understand (and he can, I believe, legally do so) that it is his intention to entirely stop the working of Traffic along the Talyllyn Railway and if he does so, it will be a serious impediment to any future working of the Abergynolwyn Quarries . . . it is a case for Counsel as to whether Mr McConnel can cease working the Talyllyn Railway . . . but I take it that the Act does not compel continuing maintenance of traffic facilities . . . it is

not to be expected that he *will* continue to work this railway at a dead loss and even if it were put into the hands of a Receiver he would probably stop all traffic, if he could not make a profit upon its working . . . the alternative . . . for the Talyllyn Railway and connecting link . . . to be left undisturbed for (say) three years at least to enable Mr. Pughe . . . see if they can let their property as a Slate Quarry with the liability to work their own traffic along the Talyllyn Railway to and from Towyn at their own cost and pay Mr. McConnel or other owner, a wayleave for such traffic . . . based upon a reasonable tonnage rate . . . the position . . . with . . . Railway and connecting tramway is a complicated one . . . an arrangement should be [made] with Mr. McConnel for acquiring the tramway up to Talyllyn Station [*sic*] to give access to the High Road at that point in the event of the Talyllyn Railway being discontinued to be worked'.

Had this come about, only the Quarry Tramway would have survived eastwards from Abergynolwyn; the statutory railway company was clearly not only in danger of ceasing to operate a service (as when the Quarry closed, there would be no reason for continuing any service whatsoever) but of realisation of its assets by taking up and selling the railway track, machinery, stock, etc.; McConnel's belief was that there was no requirement upon him to run a railway nor, indeed, did the demise of the Company itself seem necessary (for which, of course, an expensive and time-consuming Act of Parliament would have been required). Not surprisingly, Carter Vincent & Co. acting for Pugh, did not support this belief, understanding that McConnel had a statutory obligation to continue to run trains at tolls fixed by the Railway's Act and also that under its provisions he must convey slate thereby and not sell its rails or part with its land. Fortunately, the matter of the Railway never came to the test, as Haydn Jones' purchase of Quarry, Railway *et al.* took the heat out of the situation. As the Quarry was virtually at a standstill for twelve months from December 1910 until The Abergynolwyn Slate & Slab Co. Ltd. was formed in November 1911, there was no official output registered in 1910 and 1911, but the Railway continued to clear away McConnel's stock in 1910 to the tune of 2,221 tons, and the residue the following year of only 332 tons. With but six men each above and below ground when Haydn Jones began, the trains only carried 353 tons in 1912, Returns thereafter being suspended for the duration of the First War.

One other lucky break for all parties during this period of change-over was that Pugh's legal position as to whether he might re-possess the Quarry Tramway in consequence of the land reverting to his ownership, was not settled to the detriment of the railway link before Haydn Jones appeared on the scene. Fortunately all were agreed that the original Pugh deed was very vague!

Whilst there was no outward change to the Railway or its employees through all these foregoing years – save in the visual evidence that all were growing older! – the hidden aspects of the Railway Company (which had never been in evidence to the onlooker)

---

*This family of Pugh is rendered Pugh or Pughe in the records; the form Pugh is used here to differentiate from John Pughe.

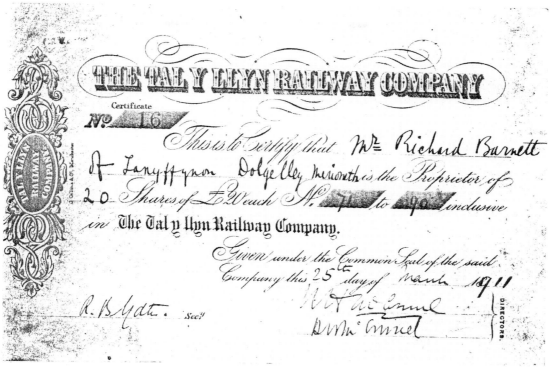

The Share Certificate of one of Haydn Jones' nominee shareholders, 1911.   AUTHOR'S COLLECTION

became more confused. The status of owners, share-holders and much of the background to the Company's formation, which had been carefully and properly managed during the lifetime of the McConnel régime, was, with a change of ownership, lost. Not only had the Statutory Returns ceased during McConnel's time, but worse was to follow when the legal advisers to Haydn Jones were either unaware of the requirements and the necessity to comply with the Company's Acts and their provisions as regards Statutory Under-takings (or were happy to disregard them), to the effect that activities took place which were inappropriate, and activities which should have taken place, did not do so!

It is generally true that that side of a railway company which is not reflected in its physical aspects actually on the ground, has been of little interest to those whose superficial interest lies solely in visual reaction; what a lot such people miss! The Talyllyn Company is an excellent example, for its timeless appearance long belied what lay beneath the surface so that when McConnel left the stage and Haydn Jones took it, the proper handing-over of records (which surely took place!) was not followed by such essential custodianship that, by Haydn Jones' death in 1950, they were available to his successors. Many were not! In consequence partly of this, and more largely in the personality of the man himself, the affairs of Quarry, Railway and Estate and his own personal affairs

became inexorably confused. This arose in the first place when he became the buyer (and therefore sole owner) of the Railway (disregarding his other pur-chases).

In order to comply with Parliamentary legislation he was advised by his solicitors Ellis Davies Bros. of Caernarvon (William Ellis Davies was then Member for Caernarvon – then 'Carnarvon' and a close friend of Haydn's) that he must transfer five lots of 20 shares to each of five nominees. In the event these were:

William Ellis Davies (solicitor)	Caernarvon
Thomas Jones (schoolmaster)	County School, Towyn
Richard Barnett	Dolgelley
Owen Lawrence Jones	Aberdovey
Owen Daniel Jones	Aelybryn, Towyn

This was done to meet the provision that to hold a General or Extraordinary General Meeting of the Railway Company there must be a certain number of shareholders in proportion to the capital of the Company.

Unfortunately, neither Haydn Jones nor his legal advisers 'differentiated between the Railway Company and himself' and when at his death there was a hurried cremation of his papers, it left an awkward vacuum for those who had to follow up his affairs, into which some true and some false suggestions were inevitably sucked. No trace has been found of Annual Meetings

A much later view of Dolgoch viaduct with DOLGOCH and train; by now the trees have begun to close in on the scene.

Another posed scene at the Wharf; the overbridge parapet has been rebuilt, the Gunpowder Shed with dovecote has been erected, but Edward Thomas' house 'Trefri' has not been commenced. The neat rhododendron-dominated garden on the left survived to the 1950s.
TALYLLYN RAILWAY CO.

or Minutes of the Railway Company which should have been kept in the period 1911–50 and there are no official announcements in the newspapers giving notice of such meetings. It must be concluded they were never held, and that the nominee shareholders were unconcerned. There was never any money in it for them, anyway! During this period, Haydn Jones (considering himself entirely within his rights as owner of the Railway) sold land, for instance, in his own name which was the property of the Railway Company! The precise ownership of ground east of the Statutory Limits of the Company and up to the Quarry required many years of tortuous investigation to establish in the years to come.

Against such a background, it is hardly surprising that details of day-to-day goings-on, (the keeping of records of locomotive boiler inspections is an example) and other desirable data are missing. Possibly the only 'records' available about the rolling stock kept at Pendre were to be found in pencilled graffiti on the walls of the workshops as to where urgent help might be obtained from outside firms. It is absence of written notes which emphasises the day-by-day nature of problems which were overcome among the few who had passed their experience down through the generations. Nothing that ever went awry after the time of Haydn's death, was new. Old, retired employees would wander into the workshops and tut-tutting through their moustaches, would recall when this happened to so-and-so about 1916 . . .

Something of Haydn Jones' problems with the Quarry and the periods when work ceased have been

told and at these times slate traffic would cease. But all the while and especially after the First War, the holiday traffic grew and made the Railway viable, bearing in mind that its owner hardly ever spent anything on it, a policy he pursued to the end. Slate wagons were brought into service to hold extra passengers, trains followed each other only yards apart in order to cater for additional crowds, maintenance of the track by a faithful few became less and less successful, and the state of locos and rolling stock was, at best, a tribute to the workmanship of the 1860s. Throughout a long, long period, it was the devotion and primitive skills of the men which kept the wheels in motion.

Haydn also failed to complete the Annual Returns to the Board of Trade which every undertaking was bound to do. Such Returns showed numbers of locomotives etc., mileages run, tonnages and other useful statistics, no less giving a certificate signed by the Railway's Engineer concerning the condition of the rolling stock and the state of the permanent way. Why the Board of Trade and its successors, (who should have been in receipt of these Returns) failed to carry out their duty of ensuring the Returns were duly received (and if they did put pressure to bear on Haydn Jones, how he slipped through the net) is not on record. Nor can it be assessed by how much this influenced the situation when in the early 1920s under the Railways Act of 1921, most railway companies were 'grouped', the most likely to swallow up the Talyllyn being the Great Western Railway, the only one of the 'Big Four' to retain its former title. True, certain other

TAL-Y-LLYN RAILWAY.

(NARROW GAUGE, 2ft. 3in.)

Time Table, Oct., 192   , and until further notice.

THE terminus of the Railway, Abergynolwyn, forms a convenient starting-point for the ascent of Cader Idris, and is only 3¼ miles from Tynycornel Hotel and Penybont Hotel, Talyllyn Lake, thus bringing the visitor a mile nearer than any other route.

Other objects of interest in the immediate neighbourhood:—The Bryneglwys Slate Quarries, the village of Llanfihangel-y-Pennant, most picturesque in its antiquity, with the celebrated Bird Rock and the ancient Castell-y-Bere (Bere Castle) close by. Conveyances for Talyllyn Lake can be hired at Abergynolwyn.

The times shown on this bill are the times at which the trains are intended to leave and arrive at the several stations, but the Company cannot guarantee these times being kept under any circumstances, nor will they be responsible for delay.

PASSENGERS' LUGGAGE.—The Company are not responsible unless it is booked and paid for according to its value. Each passenger is allowed 60 lbs. weight of personal luggage free of charge, the same not being merchandise. Any excess above this weight will be charged.

The Company will not be responsible for any articles left in any of their offices for the convenience of owners, unless deposited in the Booking-office and the fixed charge of 2d. per package paid.

It is requested that all Goods and Parcels be delivered at the Wharf Station, Towyn.

UP TRAINS.	†Mondays only.	Daily.	Every other Sat. starting Oct.	Daily.	†Fridays only	DOWN TRAINS.	†Mondays only.	Daily.	Daily.	†Fridays only	Every other Sat. starting Oct.
	a.m.	a.m.	p.m.	p.m.	p.m.		a.m.	a.m.	p.m.	p.m.	p.m.
Towyn (Wharf) dep.		9-25		3-15		Abergynolwyn dep.	7-0	11-20	4-35	6-45	1-5
,, (Pendref) ...	6-15	9-30	12-20	3-20	6-0	Dolgoch ...	7-15	11-35	4-50	7-0	1-20
Rhydyronen ...	6-25	9-40	12-30	3-30	6-10	Brynglas ...	7-25	11-45	5-0	7-10	1-25
Brynglas ...	6-30	9-45	12-35	3-35	6-15	Rhydyronen ...	7-30	11-50	5-5	7-15	1-30
Dolgoch ...	6-40	9-55	12-45	3-45	6-25	Towyn (Pendre) ...	7-40	12-0	5-15	7-25	1-40
Abergynolwyn arr.	6-55	10-10	1-0	4-0	6-40	,, (Wharf) arr.		12-5	5-20	7-30	

†These trains will not run when any stoppage occurs at Bryneglwys Quarries.
The 6-15 a.m. and 6-0 p.m. trains from Towyn start from Pendre and not from the Wharf.

N.B.--NO SUNDAY TRAINS.

H. HAYDN JONES,
General Manager.

J. Wynn Williams, Printer, Towyn.

One of the winter timetables of the early 1920s, an economy version which intended no change in train timings and allowed the year to be filled in by hand.
TALYLLYN RAILWAY CO.

similar small railways evaded take-over and there must have been guidelines as to small companies – especially of narrow gauge – which were omitted. Suffice to say that like the Corris, Glyn Valley, North Wales Narrow Gauge, Festiniog, and Welsh Highland, it remained independent. Several of the aforementioned companies put up a good fight to stave off being engulfed (the Festiniog/Welsh Highland making a case that to put them either in the Great Western or London Midland & Scottish would make a nonsense of the FR/WHR scheme of providing a through route between Caernarvon and Blaenau Ffestiniog), with ultimate success.

By the late 1920s the Quarry and Railway had each become a gerontocracy. Haydn himself had suffered periods of illness and threatened not to stand again for Parliament, but he recovered. The Railway was but a small feature in his life; he provided it solely for the convenience of his tenants. If they did not use it, that was their loss – clearly they did not appreciate his gesture. So it was with this conception of the railway

Dolgoch station in the mid-1920s, with an elderly but still nimble Jacob Rowlands — now without uniform — checking tickets.   H. G. W. HOUSEHOLD

A family group poses in front of DOLGOCH at Pendre in the late 1920s. One of the few pictures which shows a Gunpowder Van — possibly by then used to carry sand?
COLLECTION G. D. BRAITHWAITE

Another 'timeless' view at Dolgoch. Only the dress of the people affords an estimate of date. Two of the notoriously bad rail joints in front of the locomotive also confirm things are showing shortage of maintenance.

L. T. CATCHPOLE

A not-so-common event; TALYLLYN takes water at Dolgoch with a Down train, which has come to rest some distance before the station.   REAL PHOTOGRAPHS

Dolgoch again, but the former smart appearance is now a little tarnished; the rustic furniture is not that of the earlier picture and the water tank tower is rebuilt with tapering sides and a new wooden tank atop.

L. T. CATCHPOLE

This evocative glimpse of the Mineral Line beyond Abergynolwyn must have seemed to be the encapsulation of the pre-1950 Railway; entitled 'Road to Adventure', it appeared in L. T. C. Rolt's book, RAILWAY ADVENTURE, as a charming frontispiece.

BRIAN GOODCHILD

Sunday, and nothing stirs down at the Wharf station. There is an air of disuse about the place, though some stock of virtually unsaleable slates still lies around. On the previous day, some of Towyn's youth had pushed three wheelsets down the slope from Pendre and they feature prominently where they came to rest.   AUTHOR

he owned, that although he was not prepared to put any money into it, he felt constrained, perhaps for his public image, to keep it operative until his death.

To conclude this account to the point in time when Haydn Jones' executors came to handle his ownership of the Company, we must pass to February 1951 when his widow, Lady Barbara, handed over the operation of the line to a Preservation Society, Messrs. W. Trinder, P. J. Garland, L. T. C. Rolt representing the latter, and with Edward Thomas, then Manager, present, all together in the office of Arthur & Co., of Machynlleth, solicitors to the Railway Company.

Agreement was reached whereby the Society would operate the Railway for a trial period of three years (later extended to five). If the Society failed, Lady Barbara would receive £1,350 being the value placed on the Railway by Edward Thomas at the time of the take-over. In this we must not overlook Edward Thomas' continuous and stimulating enthusiasm for the continuance of the Railway, which did much to encourage Lady Barbara to allow the arrangement to take place – and no less the spirited gesture of Lady Barbara herself.

In the same year such shares as could then be traced, mainly those which had passed to Lady Barbara herself, were placed with Talyllyn Holdings Ltd., a Company limited by Guarantee formed solely for that

purpose, and after many years of search, the shares of the nominees (all of whom were dead) were traced and also placed in the same Holdings Company. Nothing had ever been paid by way of dividend during Hadyn Jones' period, and possibly none before that – there is no means of knowing. The shares, though by now historic documents, were financially worthless.

Also, it was agreed that two directors of the Railway Company would henceforth be nominated by the Jones family, and two by the Preservation Society, the latter also appointing its Chairman.

And so one 'Act' of the Talyllyn Railway Company was rung down by a curtain and with once more, no outward sign immediately visible, a new 'Act' commenced as the curtain lifted on another season. Many of the former actors had survived and many of the new ones did not expect the play to run for much longer.

Now, in 1988, the Railway has become the only surviving Welsh narrow gauge passenger railway which never fully closed down. One is frequently asked what Spooner, the McConnels and Haydn Jones would have made of it all had they returned to their place of business today? Unreserved approval? Probably not, (unless good profit was being shown) but would show surprise that today we value what to them was simply a means to an end.

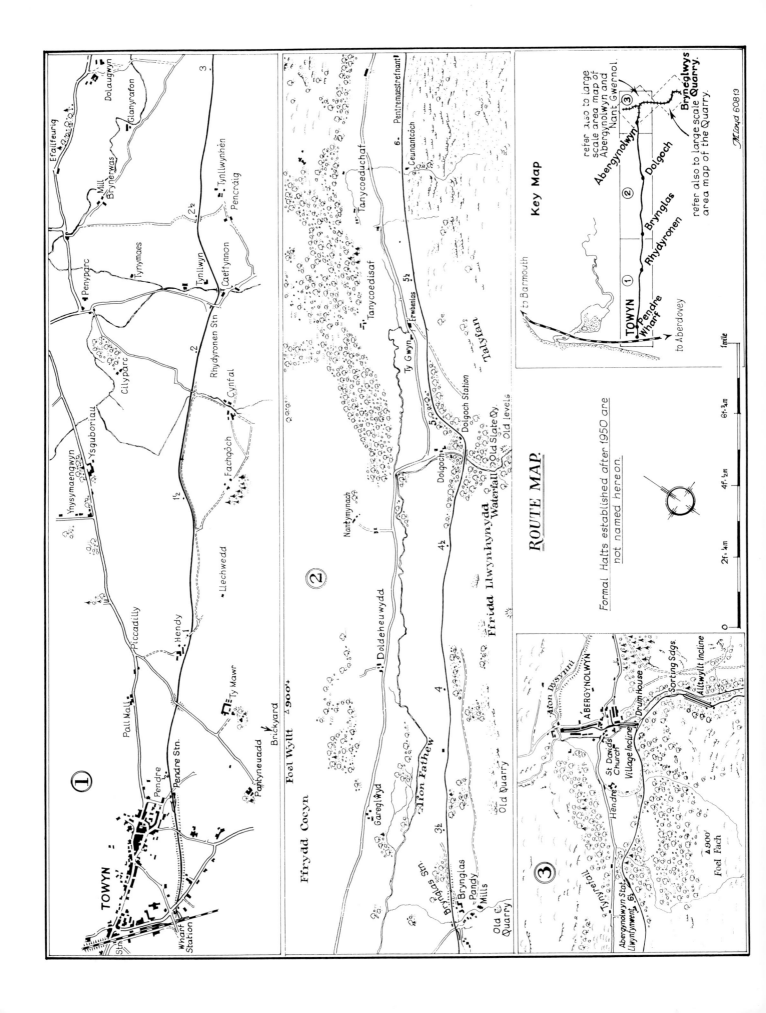

ROUTE MAP.

Formal Halts established after 1950 are not named hereon.

Key Map

to Barmouth

TOWYN

Pendre Wharf

to Aberdovey

① Rhydyronen Brynglas

② Dolgoch Abergynolwyn

③ Bryneglwys Quarry

refer also to large scale area map of Abergynolwyn and Nant Gwernol.

refer also to large scale area map of the Quarry.

T.Lloyd 6.08.13

1 mile

0   2f.4m   4f.5m   6f.8m

① TOWYN

Wharf Station

Stn.

Pendre Stn.

Pendre

Pall Mall

Piccadilly

Hendy

Ynysymaengwyn

Ysguboriau

Cilyparc

Penyparc

Tynymaes

Tynymaenguyn

Rhydyronen Stn

Caeffynnon

Tynllwyn

Tynllwynhên

Pencrâig

Efailfeurig

Dolaugwyn

Glanyrafon

Mill

Brynerwas

Parkyneuadd

Brickyard

Ty Mawr

Fachgôch

Cynfal

Llechwedd

2

1½

2½

3

② Ffrydd Cocyn   Foel Wyllt △900+

Nantymynach

Doldeheuwydd

Garegl Wyd

Afon Fathew

Brynglas Stn

Pandy Mills

Old Quarry

Tanycoeduchaf

Tanycoedisaf

Ty Gwyn

Erwbenlas

Dolgoch Station

Dolgoch

Talyfan

Ceunantcôch

Pentremaestrefnant

Ffridd Llwynhynydd   Waterfall

Dolgoch Slate Qy.

Old levels

Old Quarry

3½   4   4½   5   5½   6

③

Afon Dysynni

ABERGYNOLWYN

St David's Church

Hendre

Tynyrefail

Abergynolwyn Stat

Llwynywnwynt 6½

Village Incline

Drum House

Sorting Sdgs.

Alltwyllt Incline

Foel Fach   △900'

CHAPTER FIVE

THE ROUTE FROM WHARF TO QUARRY

(The Railway Scene before 1950)

[Landowners mentioned are those of 1867. As no official gradient
figures are available before 1953, those quoted are official for the
period 1953–59. It must be emphasised that many of the following
features had been altered or destroyed by 1986. Loop lines were not
passing places as the system was worked with one engine/train only.]

IT would be more correct to describe the rail link
from the Quarry end of the line but as most
visitors commence their acquaintance with it at
Towyn, the route is unfolded therefrom.

Seen from the town (or on a summer's day, from
the shallow waters of the sea whilst swimming) the
range of hills and mountains which form the backdrop
to the coast is a feast for the eye. The curve of the
hilltops against the sky, the folds of valleys which
merge indistinctly one into the other, perhaps a wisp
of cloud hugging the summit of Cader Idris and above
all the varied hues of green and brown, leave a pictorial
impression which lingers in the memory. From such
a vantage point on the shoreline, the flat, somewhat
uninteresting ground which separates the town from
the foothills is completely hidden. It is as though the
hills start to rise from the eastern outskirts of the
community. The valley up which runs the Railway,
the course of the line therein and any detail whatsoever
is lost in an almost half-circle, one of nature's most
lovely backdrops.

Between the sea and the present town was once a
largely wet tract of grassland where previously the sea
had washed, coming right up to the edge of what
was hardly more than a village and was frequently
described as such. Had we walked from the shore
towards that village in the first half of the last century
we should have been struck by the small size of Towyn
as it then was, and of the existence of a community to
the west and slightly south of it of which there is
no evidence today. The two places were linked by a
country lane. The building of the Coast Railway drove
its metals right through the middle of that satellite
hamlet, Trenewydd or Newtown. The name is still
used and more modern housing stands on a part of the
site, but rude and unsavoury mud huts clustered on
the place where the standard gauge goods yard is now.
Beside what is these days called the Wharf station,
Neptune Road is carried over the Coast Line by
Trenewydd Bridge. Just south of here was the likely
site of the Coast Line's first Towyn 'station', with a
life of only a few weeks.

The Talyllyn station, now known as Wharf (and
shown as such on Cotterell & Spackman's Plan) and
previously as King's (said to have been the name of a
previous occupier, or perhaps the vernacular for the
ballast pit once there, or the name of its leading navvy,
but this cannot be proven) for many years was simply
the place where that Railway terminated at right angles
and somewhat above the main line track. It never
enjoyed the status accorded to the Railway's other
stations; there was no platform, no waiting shelter and
if enquiry had been made, passenger trains did not
officially serve it until the late 1890s. Guide Books and
timetables made it clear that if you were warm and
breathed, you caught the train at the next station
(Pendre or Pentref); here there were the customary
trappings – a platform, somewhere to sit and shelter,
a booking office and store-room. On the other hand, if
you were, for instance, a parcel or a slate, the King's
station would be the place for you, for all the Company's trains initially worked down there, (and indeed,
later the passenger carriages worked between the
two places on every advertised train, even though they
travelled empty on that section). The real business of
the Railway was evident from the loaded slate wagons
attached to the rear of carriages on King's-bound
trains, and the empty wagons hung on the rear when
they returned.

King's was different in other ways: the main office
building of the Company (but not at first the Registered
Office) was there – it was not finished in time for
the opening and the parlour at Brynhyfryd was used
instead. A large wagon weighing machine by Avery
had its most delicate portions inside the goods store of
the new building, which was built in brick and,
although some features at this end of the line, such as
bridges, were also in brick, the other initial buildings
were in timber and later ones in stone. Use of brick
(rather than stone from the Quarry which may then
not have been connected by rail) at King's was dictated
by urgency, for though paper work was being done at
Brynhyfryd, accommodation had to be found urgently
for the weighing machine – a vital item.

In the corner of the King's yard, under the lee of
Trenewydd Bridge, was a brick bothy or 'caban' where
the slate loaders might shelter. Also hereabouts, and
alongside the earthen embankment carrying the road
over that bridge, was a slab-walled and wooden-gated
yard into which coal delivered by the main line was

71

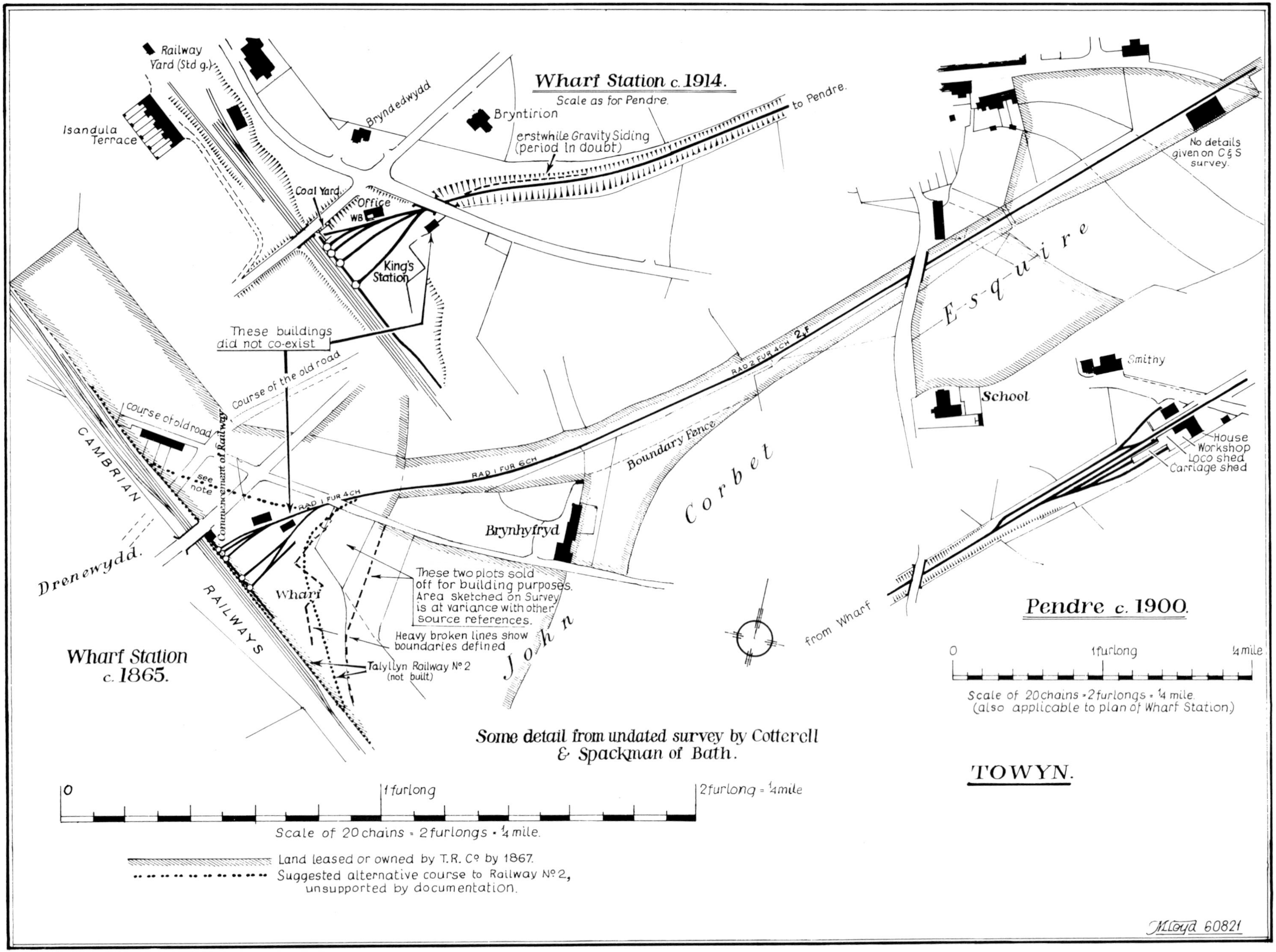

TOWYN.

Pendre c. 1900.

No details given on C&S survey.

House
Workshop
Loco shed
Carriage shed

Smithy

Esquire

School

Corbet

from Wharf

Scale of 20 chains = 2 furlongs = ¼ mile
(also applicable to plan of Wharf Station)

0   1 furlong   ¼ mile

Wharf Station c. 1914.

Scale as for Pendre.

to Pendre.

Bryntirion

erstwhile Gravity Siding
(period in doubt)

RAD. 92 FUR. 13 CH.

Corbet

Boundary fence

Penybrynau

Isandula Terrace

Railway Yard (Std g.)

Coal Yard
Office
W&

King's Station

These buildings did not co-exist

course of the old road

RAD. 1 FUR. 6 CH.

Brynhyfryd

These two plots sold off for building purposes. Area sketched on Survey is at variance with other source references.

Heavy broken lines show boundaries defined

Talyllyn Railway Nº 2 (not built)

of Nov

Some detail from undated survey by Cottrell & Spackman of Bath.

2 furlong = ¼ mile

Scale of 20 chains = 2 furlongs = ¼ mile.

1 furlong

Land leased or owned by T.R. Cº by 1867.

Suggested alternative course to Railway Nº 2, unsupported by documentation.

Wharf Station c. 1865.

Wharf

RAD. 1 FUR. 4 CH.

RAILWAYS

CAMBRIAN

Drenewydd

course of old road

course of old road

Commencement of Railway

see note

The Wharf in the years after the First War, showing small stocks of slates to the left and larger slabs nearer the office. The walled coal yard peeps out from behind the office, whilst in front of it a weighted point lever is held over by a short length of rail to jam it, so allowing wagons to pass over the weighbridge and to the coal siding. Evidence of rustic work around the garden is prominent too.

AUTHOR'S COLLECTION

stacked, and locked up. This was used on the loco-motives and also taken up for use at Bryneglwys Hall, in various working premises in the Quarry, and also down into Abergynolwyn village by an incline which led up from the village to the level of the Railway on the adjacent hillside.

In summer when it was the practice to cut the hay beside the Railway, a stack would be made at every station; at this one it was built up in the coal yard. The hay was used to pack between slates in main line wagons, to protect them.

The west end of the station area was bounded by the main line wharf, and to the east the Talyllyn tracks funnelled smartly to pass under Brynhyfryd road bridge carrying the 'Township Road' (in 1865 being the responsibility of 'The Local Board of Health for the District of Towyn'). This did not become the main road until 1955; before then the main artery left the town opposite St. Cadfan's Church and made its way out of it past The British School, and passed over the Talyllyn Railway by a skewed bridge, where the Railway was in deep cutting.

Back at King's, there was another rough clapboard building, demolished by about 1900 to make way for a gunpowder storage shed, connected with the Quarry business. Railway matters were dealt with in the brick premises previously mentioned; this dates from the

building of the Railway and its windows and doors have been moved around e.g. the main door was pre-viously at the west end. Inside the timber window lintels is branded

A D
S Co.

Along the top edge of the wharf, and by means of four 5 ft. diameter wagon turntables, supplied by Thomas Dunn & Co., Manchester;* slate wagons could be run alongside waiting standard gauge wagons at a lower level, thus facilitating exchange of slate and slab by hand. It will be remembered that there had been an intention to run the Talyllyn wagons bodily onto the larger. From under the road bridge at the far end of the station the single line fanned out into four tracks (though Cotterell & Spackman show five with turntables), each ending with its wagon turntable. A fifth siding branched out to serve the walled coal yard and crossed the weigh table *en route*. When built, the gunpowder shed was given a siding at a later date into which a van could be locked. Over the years there were

* Thomas Dunn & Co. Engineers, Boiler Makers, Manufacturers, Traders in mills, machines, tools, engines and railway plant and exporters and valuers. Herculanean Boiler & Windsor Bridge Iron-works, 3 Corporation Street, Manchester. (1861)

A picture of Wharf taken about 1905 shows many of the types of van, slate wagon and goods wagon in use. Most of these varieties did not survive to 1950. There is a haystack in the coal yard and the office poster advertises the Corris Railway 'Grand Tour'.   F. MOORE

modest alterations in the track layout, but there was never a release road and run-round for the locomotive, and it was usual to propel stock down from Pendre, with the occasional result that vehicles 'got away' down the gradient and ended up on the main line. So trackage in 1866 was very similar to 1950, save that the sidings were re-aligned when a large shed between them was demolished.

When Quarry business was slack or for other convenience, the Slate Company utilised an unusual piece of their ground to the south of the station and laid a temporary siding into it† – this was used as a stock yard until new orders cleared it. Otherwise the whole of the station area (known locally as 'Iard Fach': The Little Yard) was itself the principal storage yard for slates which were laid out on the ground in rows set on angled edge, size by size ('Duchesses', 'Countesses' and suchlike in the vernacular of the trade).

The accommodation at this place was limited from the start but sandwiched between the road and Coast Railway as it was, there was little scope for enlargement. For a Railway whose principal purpose was the transport of slate, it was no more than an interchange yard, but it was probably forty years later when R. B. Yates who, coming onto the scene with the eye of one

who had a wider experience than his predecessors, appreciated that whilst the slate business was falling away, passenger figures could be increased if visitors coming by main line train could use the nearest Talyllyn station and not be directed across the town to Pendre. Yates had the idea of making a portion of the four-wheeled luggage van into a booking office which could travel up with the train and dispense with using the small offices at each station ... clearly manned by the guard who would leave the train for the purpose ... but the Wharf (as it had become by then) was given no Booking Office before 1910. From earliest times passengers had been taken to and from King's unofficially, and spasmodic notices appeared at the foot of timetables from 1899 to this effect! 'Trains leave King's station (Wharf) five minutes before leaving Towyn (Pendre) station'. Although *Bradshaw's Guide* is not an absolute authority, the late M. D. Greville – who certainly *was* an authority on *Bradshaw* – maintained that the name 'Wharf' first appeared in October 1906 as a footnote 'Trains leave King's Station (Wharf) ...' and this continued until July 1911, though from July 1909 it became 'Slate Wharf Station'. From August 1911 to September 1912 it was simply 'Wharf' but a change of operational policy must have followed for *Bradshaw* makes it clear that during 1913 and 1914 it was used by passenger trains only July–September:

† Now Tynyrardd Nurseries.

In the Goods Office adjacent to the Traffic Office at Wharf, Hugh Jones purports to weigh an empty barrel, so posed for the purpose of a magazine article.

A neat and tidy Wharf station with an Up train standing on the line more commonly used for departures after the First War. The road overbridge now has stone parapet walls but the dovecote has been removed from the Gunpowder Shed.   F. FRITH & CO.

This similar scene, c.1930, shows the wealth of homespun seats below the garden, and the well-trodden path between the rails where the men pushed wagons to and from the loading wharf.   REAL PHOTOGRAPHS CO.

In the summer of 1936 the coal yard seems no longer to be in use. Locomotive coal is stacked outside the Caban. Behind the loaded coal wagon is a flat wagon of unknown parentage.
S. W. BAKER

In 1930 the rustic fencing and home-made seats were a feature of the Wharf station.   L & GRP
Cty. DAVID & CHARLES

it appeared every month August–August 1915–16 only to disappear again until November 1918 when it achieved a permanent, monthly insertion. As the Company's own timetables had, as just mentioned, used the phrase first appearing in *Bradshaw* in October 1906 in 1899, the foregoing is curious as the leading national timetable publication appears to be seven years late! Incidentally, Wharf was still shown as 'King's Station' on the Railway Clearing House map dated 1926.

Oddly, although passengers were taken up at King's, returning passengers were decanted at Pendre, and to prove this, even if one continued to sit in the carriage after arrival at Pendre, the engine crew would ignore one, screw down the engine handbrake and begin an exaggerated ritual of taking on water and coal. This pantomime was always sufficient! Passengers who were good friends of, or relatives of the train crew, were, of course, treated differently.

A letter sent by the Company to the Board of Trade on 5th November 1895* read:

'Sir,

    We are much obliged by your letter of the 4th inst. There are five stations on this line and we have a signboard at each with the name of the station painted in large letters so that the name can readily be seen by the passengers.
    We have no advertisements in any of our stations.

                    I am etc.,
            Signed pro. W. H. McConnel
                            Secretary
                                (A. B.)

[More recently, the Company received an enquiry from a Welsh language-biased source asking if the names on the station were bi-lingual? The answer sent was that they were almost entirely in Welsh and did

That same year DOLGOCH stands in front of that part of the station garden which was first to disappear.   L & GRP
Cty. DAVID & CHARLES

they wish the Company to add the names in English and charge up the cost to the enquirer?]

It was in the 1920s that the Wharf station was emblazoned in a rash of rustic work, the product of John Jones who kept the paths, fences and seats in repair at the Dolgoch Ravine, and whose efforts also adorned Dolgoch station.

The Talyllyn Company's original intention was to have an exchange siding on the north side of Trenewydd Bridge; this would have been served by Railway No. 2 in the T.R. Act and enabled T.R. slate wagons to run onto standard gauge wagons bodily, by means of a high level T.R. interchange wharf. There was already an established shipping point at Aberdovey and suitably adapted standard gauge wagons could have carried slate (loaded in Bryneglwys Quarry mills), to reach a ship's side without further handling. No doubt the Cambrian Railways preferred to have slate loaded into their own wagons and have it consigned to

_____
* It is probable that 'King's' was not included.

any station in the Kingdom, rather than having a few specially adapted wagons for a brief run with all the necessary shunting. It is not clear as to why the pick-a-back idea was not carried through but as it was not, probably the whole conception of Railway No. 2 lost its meaning and the project was abandoned. The. Cambrian did in fact enjoy the carriage of all slates in its own wagons from King's and the endorsement of this arrangement (from which time nothing more is heard of Railway No. 2) comes with the formal conveyance of the King's land to the Talyllyn Company.

It will not pass unnoticed that the largest nearby surviving building ('Llechfan') is a domestic one now screened from the rest of the area by a hedge, 'The Wharf Bungalow', as it is unofficially termed. Its existence stemmed from Haydn Jones' desire to accommodate a 'caretaker' to safeguard stocks on the Wharf from theft. The building was erected c. 1914 and originally had no bathroom as its tenant had no confidence in water heating systems. The bungalow stood on part of an area taken over by the Quarry for additional stocking of finished slates/slabs when the order book was slack; in due course it was let off for horticulture as a Nursery. After Meyrick Roberts had shown disinclination to take residence there, it was taken by Harvey, Haydn's head gardener, and later by Mr. Yeomans. The land on which the bungalow stands was obviously Railway land, but the bungalow itself was erected at Haydn Jones' own expense, and left to his widow – yet another example of the perplexing property position which faced his successors at his death! Today, the bungalow has no links with the Railway Company but has to be entered through the station premises – a somewhat historic nuisance for all parties!

A fine vista of the Wharf area in July 1936 with a wide sweep of hinterland beyond, as yet unaffected by the housing which was to smother it later.

S. W. BAKER

The Wharf stock yard seen from the Neptune Road bridge; three loaded slate wagons await emptying and in the left corner a wagon-load of locomotive coal is ready to be drawn up to Pendre.

L. T. CATCHPOLE

Mainline wagons stand at the exchange wharf ready to receive slate and slab cargoes. Almost everything produced at Bryneglwys left Towyn by rail.

TALYLLYN RAILWAY CO.

The station stands on a falling grade of 1 in 220 and is 40 ft. above sea level; the measuring datum is taken from a point in the north-west corner of the site. Before the arrival of the Coast Line, the landowners were John and Henrietta Corbet.* The Corbet land to the north side of Trenewydd Bridge and extending for some distance towards the present station, was also acquired in anticipation of Railway No. 2 but afterwards sold (in fact throughout the length of the line Corbet land was utilised where possible). It will be seen that the 'Township Road' made its way across this site before the main line was made, and the road deviated eastwards. Also, the land to the south of King's was 'McConnel' (i.e. Slate Co.) property up until 1910.

Perhaps from the foregoing we may deduce the dreams of the Slate Quarry Company; the line would approach Wharf station from the east, and passenger trains, along with other stock intended for interchange at the Coast Line station, would have terminated at a site almost opposite Plevna Terrace, taking the northerly course from a set of points possibly located on the inland side of the Brynhyfryd road bridge. Business connected with the slate trade would be conducted by the 'south curve' of such a junction, this taking wagons to and from the slate stockyard and the intended transfer point whereby the pick-a-back wagon service was schemed using standard gauge wagons. The 'compromise' outcome of a station lying physically between these two sites can only have been the result of the Quarry business failing to create the tonnages to support these ambitions.

Before leaving the station, let us mark the former existence of three features: a wooden shed approximately where the gunpowder shed now stands was a somewhat homespun affair, resembling in some ways the 'temporary' carriage shed at Pendre save that the sides were enclosed by clapboarding. Was it a very temporary residence for the locomotive at this end of the system during construction? The Cotterell & Spackman Plan shows a building of similar size (and almost as big as the brick office block!) between the tracks as they fanned out west of the road bridge – this could well be the same building which had been moved to the edge of the yard. It is possible that a track entered the building at a later date; it appears on a photograph of March 1900 and had been replaced by the new neat gunpowder shed in slab in 1902. This later shed was shortly given a dovecote on its west gable. In more recent times Haydn Jones used it for housing an old lawn mower, a repository for a large redundant safe from his shop, and other bric-a-brac.

When in use as an explosives warehouse, the loaded gunpowder van might sit alongside the gunpowder kegs therein until a journey to the Quarry was made.

Along the rear edge of the track which traversed the wharf was a long hoarding reading ABERGYNOLWYN SLATE CO. LTD. (with other advertising details not recalled). The local gag is that at the Wharf the slates were always counted in threes 'two for the lessee and one for the landowner's royalty'!

Next, the skewed road overbridge under which the Railway starts its route has been rebuilt in recent times; originally it was of brick walling and supported the road with wrought iron riveted beams. The parapet walls were made in vertical timber planking, originally supported by diagonal X framing on their outer faces. Early this century this was replaced by rectangularly-shaped frames, and, later still, brickwork was substituted. The original appearance was notable for its sloped timber parapets which fell sharply from either side of the central section.

By this time grass was creeping over the little-used portions of the Wharf; here the slateloaders' Caban, its roof now unable to resist the weather, stands behind a slate wagon used for carrying locomotive coal.
P. D. HANCOCK

---

* John Soden of Bath and Rt. Hon. George Henry Robert Charles Vane Tempest (Earl Vane) were Trustees of the Will of Athelstan Corbet. John Soden had changed his name to Corbet on inheriting.

A neat shrubbery grew on the slope which carried the road. There was an orderly chestnut paling around its foot with several seats for waiting passengers in front of it; this paling continued up the road sides over the Trenewydd Bridge as well, presumably hereabouts erected by the Cambrian Railways. Most of the shrubbery was of rhododendron bushes which thrive especially well in this area; in May they were an annual delight. One especially large boulder brought out of the Quarry (and many others) served further to enhance the 'rockery' effect of this station garden. The large specimen survives – sent down for a lady who wanted 'a large rockery stone' and whose instructions were faithfully followed and who then changed her mind! The wagon carrying it was tipped on its side to remove it.

Up the cutting under the public road bridge the line reverse curves steeply up at 1 in 60 and provides a heavy start for trains, especially on a damp day, for large trees on the slopes above make the rails greasy. In past times a siding on the north side was driven up into the bank to form a 40 yard storage road for loaded slate wagons; these would be brought down by the engine from Pendre after the carriages had been detached from them and pushed into the loop there. The wagons would trundle down behind the locomotive; having passed under the road bridge and with the last wagon clear of the points – which were about 100 yards east of the road bridge – these would be changed and the rake pushed up into the siding. Here they could be braked or spragged until, in ones or twos, the slate loaders would drop them down in the yard as required – all of which made good reason why passenger working on this section was discouraged! The dates of the existence or photographs of this feature are a 'missing link' in this narrative.

After about 60 yards the gradient eases to 1 in 200. Though passing round the edge of the town, the cutting is so deep that nothing can be seen of it; c. 13,000 cu. yds. of material are calculated to have been removed – the biggest earthworks on the Railway. The top of the gradient is reached and a slight downward drop of 1 in 236 ensues. The road bridge now approaching (known from earliest times as School Bridge) carries the historic turnpike road from north to south through the town. Railway-owned land

G. H. W. Clifford visited the Railway on several occasions, firstly before 1914; this picture of TALYLLYN leaving Wharf is believed to be of that early date.

G. H. W. CLIFFORD

In 1949 the periodical 'Picture Post', together with 'Emmett' the cartoonist, featured the Railway, and numerous illustrations taken from that article will appear in the following pages. Here, DOLGOCH charges up the foot of the bank below the Wharf overbridge.

BBC HULTON PICTURE LIBRARY

extended on either side of the line here, fanning out from a narrow neck and spreading out in a sweeping area to reach the edge of Frankwell Street on the west side, and in a similarly shaped piece diagonally opposite. Most of this land was sold in later years. Beyond the fringe of it on the east side was Towyn British School,* the site for which was agreed in July 1860. On the west side of the line again and close beside the road bridge is shown a cottage; a house (Pen-y-Maes) was developed from it. A footbridge hereabouts does not appear on the Deposited Plans, but only on Cotterell & Spackman's, suggesting it was a temporary route during railway building.

The line is now quarter of a mile from its start; the School Bridge is built in common brick and supported the highway with the same type of wrought ironwork as the Wharf bridge. The parapet walls in brick have limestone coping slabs (imported perhaps from Llanymenach) to decorate the cappings. The bridge is skewed and 36 ft. long, and beyond it the cutting ends, the land widens out on each side and Pendre station ('Stesion Fach' – the Little Station) is reached (43½ ft.

a.s.l.). The station itself is not shown on the Cotterell Plan though the area of the stopping point is there; at the time of the Plan the building may not have been erected – there was no actual platform here nor anywhere else at first, the coaches having footboards in

At some date in the late 1930s, DOLGOCH slumbers in the cutting above Wharf overbridge. The train is empty, the foot-plate deserted, and a slate has been put over the chimney to dampen the fire.   G. F. PARKER

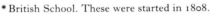

* British School. These were started in 1808.

Near the summit of the climb from Wharf comes School Bridge, formerly carrying the main coast road south and out of Towyn. This photograph was taken in August 1948.
H. C. CASSERLEY

Tal-y-Llyn Railway, Towyn.

77782

Looking east over the limestone parapet of School Bridge, there is activity in Pendre yard with TALYLLYN bringing passenger stock out from the loop.
F. FRITH & CO.

lieu – much cheaper! The Plan suggests that initially, only the loco shed was erected here – yard and station came later.

When the building was put up, it had a small store and booking office at the east end; the remainder is a shelter, and all is of timber with slated roof. The cottage and engine shed are not distinguished separately but appear on Cotterell; no other building is shown there, so the crude carriage shed, which has the appearance of an afterthought, must have followed later. Spooner's Deposited Plans show that the bridle way Ty Mawr Lane (now Frankwell Street) at the side of Pendre was intended to be a level crossing from the start.

In later days a barn was put up, possibly by Haydn Jones, adjacent to the station, clad in corrugated iron. In times recalled it was purely for agricultural purposes; at one time a donkey and cart operated to link the Cambrian station with Pendre, and hay from this barn fed the motive power for that service.

In the above period, the north side land had been raised to its present height and the south side of the land featured the cottage (still standing) where the driver lived. The adjacent locomotive shed which has been extended at some period, possibly to hold the second engine (the window frames were slightly

different) had a wooden water tank in the north-west corner: this was kept warmer than an outside tank would be, by heat from the engine alongside. (The Corris Railway had a similar tank in the roof but it was in slab.) There is a sump near the outside corner of the building formed by a slab-walled chamber; above it on the wall within the shed a vertical pumping engine took water from there up into the tank. The sump is fed from the stream beside the level crossing.

The cottage (now no longer a dwelling) chimneys were built of bricks, some from a small brickyard at nearby Caethle. (There was another small yard at adjacent Bron Prys). Behind the engine shed was the workshop, a shorter building and originally making a common frontage with the unextended engine shed, in part of whose slab floor was included two large gravestones placed face-downwards (rejected by the stone engraver after making errors in lettering). The workshop's contents included:

8 ft. bed × 8 ins. back-geared non-screw cutting lathe
Drilling machine up to $\frac{3}{4}$ ins. capacity
Screwing machine to 2 ins. (Gas) capacity
Sandstone grinding wheel
Smith's hearth
8 h.p. oil engine of 1906

[The compiler of this list in the mid-1930s was told that there were certain jobs beyond the capacity of this

A short distance beyond School Bridge comes Pendre (or Pendref) station, the 'Crewe' of the Talyllyn Railway. August 1948.

H. C. CASSERLEY

Looking seawards from Pendre, a train approaches from Wharf; the appalling state of the track is evident and there are only three weeks before The Old Regime ends. Sir Haydn was now dead.

R. K. COPE

The seat of operations — Pendre. The barn to the left, the passenger station in the centre, the engine shed right of centre and the 'temporary' carriage shed with Works behind on the right. Off right, out of the picture, was a jumble of pig sties, hen runs and discarded wagonry.

J. C. WILKINS

A closer look at Pendre in 1937; TALYLLYN is just entering the station on a Down train. The barn (extreme left) housed bracken, hay and the donkey and cart; at one period many of the Quarry workers came from South Wales and would return home at weekends, and the donkey and cart carried their luggage to and from the mainline station.   B. ROBERTS

The station building was largely of timber and matched the original one at Abergynolwyn. Behind the engine shed was — at this time — the cottage occupied by Peter Williams and his wife. The tall chimney on the engine shed assisted steam-raising. To the right the half-open carriage shelter (though said to be awaiting replacement by something more permanent), was quite a substantial affair, roofed, of course, in Bryneglwys slate. Note the mainline points are set for the loop . . . but Talyllyn drivers were always ready for this kind of situation!
AUTHOR

August 1935 and steam has been raised in TALYLLYN which is just leaving the shed. Hugh 'Gas', her driver, is allowing the fireman to shunt the yard and hook up to the carriages.
H. F. WHEELLER

One might be excused for thinking that all trains for the season had ceased after noting the wagon left on the running line and the barbed wire entanglement at the opening of the carriage shed. But no, the season (though it was September 1949) had still some little time to go. The Talyllyn Railway was never exactly what it appeared to be.   R. K. COPE

equipment such as wheel turning, and for this work, for instance, wheel sets were sent to W. G. Bagnall Ltd., Castle Engine Works, Stafford. Oddly, there is no reference to this in *Bagnalls of Stafford* (Oakwood Press 1973). There were once earlier machines and a steam engine to drive them.]

A wooden open-sided and slate-roofed shelter extended westwards from the workshop end to hold the carriage stock; this was usually dubbed a temporary building but clearly it was sufficient unto the day for Talyllyn purposes. Behind, and up on the adjacent bank was a motley collection of piggeries, sheds, sties, poultry pens and suchlike; the conveyance of animals was not usual on the Railway but when done, pigs for instance, were put into open wagons and sacking netting tied down over them. Nonetheless some of the more nimble would frequently make good their escape. They were all part of the 'amenities' of the cottage which has always been occupied by persons employed on the line, and it was the duty of the wife to attend to the crossing gates.

Although the foregoing description of Pendre in general terms will allow readers without a thirst for detail to read on and ignore the following, there were many other small features of the place which are sufficient for more than passing attention, and some may still be seen.

Prominent on the station were two large lamp cases, one on the shelter and the other on the rear wall near the road crossing; these contained gas lamps. Just

'Closed for lunch'? Or closed for good? Not much sign of life and the doors to the Works hang limply on their sagging hinges.
R. H. G. SIMPSON

when these fell into disuse is not clear, but they were fed from the gas main which was passing up the road to Ty Mawr: it would seem that the cottage and Works, even in days gone by, did not enjoy the facility. Wharf station – at least the office – once had gas also, but, owing to a difference of opinion between Haydn Jones and the gas undertaking, it was cut off from both Wharf and Pendre.

The mention of these services would not be complete without referring to water; there had been at one time a water supply from the local main to Wharf, but

June 1950, and this time-stilling scene will soon be no more. Ranged round the Workshops are the lathe, grindstone, drilling machine, a collection of locomotive spares, bellows and forge, brass furnace and bench. The pit with track materials of 1866 is revealed . . . TALYLLYN must have been moved off it. Veritably a museum of the industrial past.
                                                                                    I. L. WRIGHT

With no apparent future, TALYLLYN rests over the pit. The quenching tub near the forge might be some vessel from a dairy; on the wall hang various bits and pieces; some are mementoes of trial and error. September 1948.   R. K. COPE

Dawn breaks over Pendre. To save time, the carriages have been left in the open. Once again, the mainline points are set for the loop.
J. H. RUSSELL

Pendre station in close-up. The engine shed wall on the extreme right becomes the wall of the cottage further along. September 1948.
R. K. COPE

the pipes became corroded and the sink (or washbasin) there was never used again. There is a tradition that during Haydn Jones' time, when it became necessary for the Towyn water supply pipework to be passed under the Railway, he permitted this to be done without an annual charge in exchange for free water in perpetuity. The water main passed under the line near Rhydyronen station; at Pendre there was also a very basic supply in the form of a tap in the cottage and one in the engine shed. The latter was used to fill the engine-supply tank (and superseded the steam water pump on the wall) but a ball-cock had been omitted so if the tap was left running, the tank over-flowed.

Continuing at Pendre – which incidentally is more correct as Pendref, 'The Head of the Town' – the observant will note on the north wall of the engine shed the 'join' in the slabwork where a decision was made to extend the building about another 20 ft.; immediately below the wallplate the stonework is con-tinuous, as is the timberwork of, and the roof itself.

An Up morning train with TALYLLYN stands at Pendre awaiting the opening of the crossing gates. August 1935.

H. F. WHEELLER

Another contrived set-piece for the 'Picture Post' article. The small bracket on the corner of the near coach once carried a candle lamp. 'Emmett' leans from a window, old Mr. William Rowlands is helped into a compartment by Will Pugh and someone has robbed the Properties Department of a harp to load into the van.

BBC HULTON PICTURE LIBRARY

The Way Ahead. Though there may have been other gated crossings, that at Pendre outlived them for eighty years. 1949.
R. H. G. SIMPSON

Mrs. Peter Williams opens the gates for the 'Picture Post Special'.

With a soft blast from the chimney, DOLGOCH begins the journey up Parry's bank.　　　BBC HULTON PICTURE LIBRARY

Formerly there was a tall salt-glaze-pipe chimney poking above the ridge: this assisted steam-raising and also the draught for the fire when the engine was connected by flexible steam pipe to either the water pump or the stationary engine; the base of the chimney was supported on two old rails.

Remains of the position of the cooling tank for the oil engine are also visible inside the north wall of the shed, as are the supporting walls of the water tank. The precise details of that engine have not survived, but it was probably by Ruston, Proctor & Co. Ltd. of Lincoln and possibly of their 'hot bulb' type; it is known that Haydn Jones installed a similar one at Pantyneuadd to drive a generator, and kept the machine running by removing parts from the one at Pendre! Along the ridge of the engine shed roof was a long, wooden, louvred ventilator for clearing the place of smoke.

In the Works' portion of the establishment, the stationary engine is said to have stood in the middle of the building (where the heating stove now stands),

and the pit in the workshop track dates from earliest times; rails over it are supported by lengths of the original chaired track.

Just beyond the crossing was a stream and legend has it that engines were at first obliged to take on the brackish water by hose in traction engine tradition. For this reason, the temporary Ty Dwr engine shed on The Mineral Line to the Quarry, being copiously supplied with clear water adjacently, was preferred. The Pendre stream (now actually quite clear!) in due course became the source of locomotive water which was fed by cast iron pipe into the aforementioned sump; as for the workshop machinery, the waterlifter from this well was also steamed by a connection from the working locomotive. There was, of course, no mains water when the line was built.

Once over the crossing ($3\frac{1}{2}$ furlongs) the 'stream' (which once fed into the town drain) is crossed: its source is in Ty Mawr woods and it runs past the smithy and the back of the Corbet Arms Hotel, and into the flood dyke on the Morfa behind the town.

A bleak prospect to the east. The foot of Parry's bank about 1900. The valley of the Afon Fathew is to the right.   F. FRITH & CO.

The occupants of the carriage include Llew (or 'Tarzan') Evans (left), William Rowlands (centre), and 'Genfronydd' Jones, the Bard (right). Jones lived near Woodlands and was an enthusiastic cyclist even in his 80s. 'They went round the town looking for people to be filmstars'!
                                                      BBC HULTON PICTURE LIBRARY

DOLGOCH with all the passenger stock approaches Ty Mawr bridge. 5th April 1926.
K. A. C. R. NUNN

The line is raised on a low embankment ('Parry's bank' is the local name) for some distance using material brought out of the Wharf – Pendre cutting; the course follows the boundary of Corbet land closely and now takes on a long gentle curve to the right; the road overbridge at Ty Mawr comes into sight, especially notable for its lengthy slab-sided, curving approaches carrying the road. Reference has already been made to the origins of this work, and just beyond it may be seen traces of the level crossing it replaced and how the boundary of the line delineates the would-be arrangement. The road over the bridge (a typical Talyllyn Railway construction) is carried on cast iron T-section beams having a 10 in. wide foot, supporting a slab floor. There is some interesting graffiti cut in the walls.

Ty Mawr bridge from the west. The intended level crossing which it usurped would have been just beyond. 1949.
AUTHOR

Looking up-line from Ty Mawr bridge, Hendy farm on the left.   AUTHOR

The land on the north side of the track was on the Corbet Estate and part of the other side belonged to Bodtalog: there is a stiffish climb up through this section. Hendy farm* appears on the left and from first times trains would make a stop here if required (57 ft.). Whereas Ty Mawr bridge carried the Turnpike Road, the next bridge – Hendy, 1 m. from Wharf – carries the Parish Road which starts near Hendy farm. The replacement 'Parish Road', the original of which was being so cut about by the railway contractors, begins at the foot of Cynfal bank and ends at Rhydyronen, and is the one the contractors were legally obliged to substitute as the new railway cut through the old one in four places.

Unlike the three previous overbridges, Hendy is arched, and like the first two of them, is on the skew. The materials used are slab and brick and the parapet cappings are made of large sawn slabs which repay close attention as once again they have some nicely-cut graffiti on them, the earliest date being 1898 (was the parapet renewed about then?) Someone with strong nationalistic feelings has carved EIN GWLAD

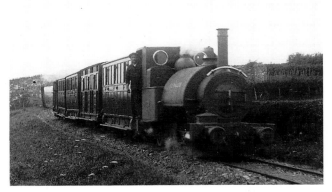

An Up train leaves Ty Mawr bridge; TALYLLYN has an unusual chimney cap. 14th August 1913.   K. A. C. R. NUNN

EIN HIAITH EIN CENEDL with a degree of professional skill, whilst another with time to spare but less skill has engraved 'D. C. JONES PENCADER 1898'.

From the top of the bridge it will be noticed how low hills have ranged up on either side of the line and are enfolding it as it makes its way eastwards and climbing all the time. The route ahead indeed, appears to be a wall of hills which bar further progress.

---

*The newer (present) farmhouse was built about 1910 – the old one is a ruin.

Hendy was an unofficial stopping place — not that there was any visible sign of it, save for the stile in the hedge on the left.   AUTHOR

To the north and now somewhat behind stretches towards the sea Talygareg Beacon with its navigation marker on the summit. To the south, with its foothills running almost to the lineside, begins with Graig Fachgoch the long line of the divide, up to 2,000 ft. high in places, which separates the valley of the Mathew (Afon Fathew) from the more impressive valley of the Dovey which parallels it to the south. This long range of mountains reaches far into the hinterland, and seen from the train peak succeeds peak in a series of summits and valleys. Slowly ever higher, so the flanks of this divide fall down steeply to threaten the little railway, with overhanging steeps and rocks – 'unenclosed sheep walks' as they are known – but this feature is yet to come.

A cutting ensues after Hendy bridge (1 m.) but then comes a length of almost straight line. Looking out of a train to the north, the village of Bryncrug can be seen distantly at the foot of Foel Wyllt. By looking directly behind, can be seen Towyn and the sea (often highlighted by sunshine even on gloomy days inland) sparkling in a silvery band which suitably diffuses the horizon with the Lleyn Peninsula and Bardsey Island on the skyline. How markedly is Towyn with its

Hendy overbridge carried the old Parish Road. It was a structure dating from the building of the Railway and, in the centre of the arch, was the highest above track level on the line.   AUTHOR

Hitching a lift . . . . . the dog has no ticket either!

At the top of Cynfal bank, Cynfal stream is crossed and then comes the bridge carrying the lane to Cynfal farm. September 1949.
R. K. COPE

marshy surrounds separated from this utterly different highland country into which the Railway is now entering, for geographically the line serves two quite different environments. Here come reverse curves of 1 fur. 8 ch. and 1 fur. 4 ch. radii in shallow cutting (created so it is held, by the presence of an enormous boulder and a smallholder's cottage – Brynglas-Bach – which were not removed), and across the fields may be picked out the fine gateway to Ynysymaengwyn, though the house itself is no longer. Perhaps as some recognition of the Corbets at the time the railway was built, there seem to have been proposals for something of an ornate stopping place, for the Cotterell & Spackman Plan has a wall and gates with the word 'Ynys' pencilled in on it here: it could be from this use of that place-name that the 'Railway Ynys' plan derives its title?

Something of the way in which the railway is climbing is now appropriate. Up as far as Ty Mawr bridge the climb steepens from 1 in 360, 147, 71, 97, and then 72 under the bridge itself; there follows a longer pull

at 1 in 94 to and beyond Hendy bridge: before this the climb eases to 1 in 252 and then falls at 1 in 555. The site of the Ynys proposal – always treated as a stopping place even if it was never made more ornate – is still a Halt (now Fachgoch: 70 ft.) preceded by a resumed climb of 1 in 207 and 548 (1 m. 34 ch.).

Now comes a length through open fields as momentarily the hills to the south have fallen back somewhat and the climb steepens from 1 in 259 to 79; near the top of the climb the only portion of original track to be replaced was found – this was a length of Glyn Valley Tramway rail put in in 1936–1939. There is another small 'summit' (105 ft. a.s.l.) ahead and the arch of Cynfal overbridge stands beyond it where the slope eases to 1 in 146. The line crosses Cynfal stream (making its way to join the Dysynni) immediately preceding this overbridge which carries a road leading to Cynfal farm. The bridge over the stream is only of 4 ft. span on the skew and rests on timber sills, and is made in pairs of old TR rails bolted together with tie rods.

The east side of Cynfal bridge, with a portion of the little platform down on the right. This bridge had the widest arch of any, but had tight vertical clearance; the 'halt' was provided by Haydn Jones for the convenience of the Roberts family at the farm.

Parallelism was not a characteristic of the rails, as each here makes its uncertain course between Cynfal and Rhydyronen. April 1949.
AUTHOR

When the stream was in spate it would frequently extinguish part of the engine's fire as the locomotive drove through the flood water!

On the east side of the overbridge (2 m.: 91 ft. a.s.l.) is a small slab platform on the north side of the line – as are all platforms – installed after the Roberts' family of Cynfal persuaded Haydn Jones to provide it for them. The adjacent bridge is built in slab and brick. After a short level length the climb resumes at 1 in 114 and, with a noticeable right-hand curve, enters Rhydyronen (2 m. 13 ch.: $100\frac{1}{2}$ ft. a.s.l.). The station was built and open by February 1867. Here the old Parish Road in the course substituted by the railway contractors, comes to an end. The line reaches the attractively-sited stopping place with its copse of trees and the sharp-eyed may notice a bluff to the south which is Brynycastell, an ancient castle-mound fortification 350 ft. high.

This station has several points of interest including that it was on an island of the property of Thomas Ellis which the Railway cut in half. The line swings round in something of a part-circle to regain its former direction beyond the station. This may have been due to opposition from the same Thomas Ellis, the land-owner at Tynllwyn on the north side, which obliged McConnel to make a circling movement – in fact, this

Still surviving in 1988, this neat cast-iron finger-post gives equal importance to both station and town! AUTHOR

Rhydyronen station was noted, pre-1914 in this picture, for its floral garden, the work of Dafydd Jones.   G. H. W. CLIFFORD

again is one of the Railway's mysteries. The station was the first intermediate one to be opened and the first to be given 'station' on the Cotterell & Spackman Plan. It is perhaps the most typical of them all and has a building in slab incorporating waiting shelter and booking office – not unlike that at Pendre save that it is not of timber. There was formerly in 1867 a loop siding and it is noticeable that the station is served by a short lane which connects to the road: the boundary with the Corbet property follows this lane and an area of surplus land about the station was sold by the Railway Company to the McConnels about 1883 and was conveyed to Haydn Jones in March 1911.

As at Ty Mawr bridge, the road overbridge which marks the further boundary of the station was built as an afterthought to replace a level crossing which can still be traced just beyond it. The line rises steeply under the bridge, and climbing, also curves onto the bridge crossing the Braichyrhiw stream which runs at the rear of the hamlet of Rhydyronen with the house, Plas Goch, of Dafydd Jones and his family (a property

of the Slate Co. in times past) being immediately adjacent to the railway. An old sailor once lived in one part of the house for at some time past it was two dwellings.

The road which crosses the line here, heavily used before the present coast road through Aberdovey was constructed, is an ancient packhorse road which makes its way over the Bryn Dinas ridge and carries on down to the Happy Valley at Pantyron, taking in *en route* several small slate quarries – and lead mines – together with a manganese mine, the existence of which, together with the delivery of building stone for the Peniarth Estate, was said to have collectively created the need for the loop line at the station. Further up this side valley was the largest slate mine, Caerffynnon. Carts were used to carry the output to Rhydyronen station: in the case of Caerffynnon (or more commonly Brynhyfrwyn) hopes were expressed that this would develop, and a branch railway was pegged out and remained in abeyance for some time before an accident in the quarry resulted in closure.

The old manganese mine was close by Caerffynon farm and the adit had struck a source of iron-bearing water which early guide books extolled as a chalybeate spring, maintaining it was 'of great efficacy in cases of nervous exhaustion, dyspepsia and nervous debility'. Even as recently as the 1920s the spring drew travellers to it – 'One of the most powerful in the Kingdom'. The adit was converted into a *bijou* spa with the help of some tiling but still surrounded by rocky outcrops – a curious place indeed. [At my only visit a faded notice informed me that a cup of water cost 2d. and indeed a cracked cup was there for

the purpose. I took a sampling drink from the cupped hand (rather more sanitary) and was off colour for a day or so afterwards!] The well was the scarcely-disguised entrance to the mine and the farm shows evidence of being once the stamping mill. There are signs of smelting and traces of the course of a tramway.

From the platform end there is a short steep climb at 1 in 91 and a 6 chain curve to Braichyrhiw stream bridge, marking the place where the venerable pack-horse road forded the stream – hence Rhydyronen means 'Ashford'. At this point the hills have fallen away to either side and the situation is one of gentle

A similar view, but in 1936, shows little change but there is an ugly rail joint in the left foreground, leading to the storage siding.

L. T. CATCHPOLE

Rhydyronen bridge from the east, taken from the site of the intended level crossing. In the boscage on the right, there lurks the remains of the last covered van. 1949.
R. K. COPE

countryside with upward slopes set back. For a short distance the line actually falls at 1 in 115 and 252, being the second of three descents on the eastbound journey. Ann Jones' and John Foulkes' lands were here traversed.

Rhydyronen deserves more than a simple description, for it comes upon the rail traveller as does an oasis in the desert; suddenly, on a route somewhat harsh with naked hill, field, and swept by winds off the sea, there comes this unexpected hamlet, nestling in a fold of the hills to the south. From Cynfal the seclusion of the cutting along the fall from Cynfal bridge brings him, quite unprepared for such change, to the little station, hidden coyly in its grouping of fir trees. Up to here, trees have seemed to be apart from the line and their appearance softens the scene. In past days the station (today rather a bare, functional building) was clothed in climbing nasturtiums, reached by a small driveway hedged by broom and nurtured by Dafydd Jones of adjacent Plas Goch, who also leased the little plot of land beyond the road bridge on the other side of the track from his house. He beautified the station with plants; the plot was a utilitarian vegetable garden.

Plas Goch, a large stone-built cottage beside the line and formerly standing close to the roadway before it

was diverted to the railway bridge, is apart from the row of cottages which straggles down the road beyond it to form the rest of the hamlet. Most buildings have been whitewashed in their time; local building materials are evident, including great boulders brought down by the stream in days past and used in the walls. The hedges are very old as witnessed by their great mixture of content, and a cluster of sycamores overhangs the community whilst the Railway passes behind the terrace of cottages in the cutting; passengers have but a brief glimpse of backyards and domesticity, coal sheds and outside privies. Slate roofs, and smoke from coal fires lead the eye upwards to the hills beyond, ever at some distance. The stream babbles under the railway bridge, a place where the local children have always played – for them the beach and seaside paddling at Towyn was a world away and almost unknown. Now and then a passing train denoted the passage of time. Mondays would produce lines of washing on both sides of the line, not overlooking that done for Pantyneuadd which was hung out to dry in the vegetable garden, carried on a washline supported rather obviously by two old rails.

As the train emerges from this rural haven, bare hills dotted to their very outlines with sheep come into view once more, and black Welsh cattle graze in fields nearer the line. The oasis has come and gone: orchards, gardens, washtubs and sheds fade away behind . . . and are forgotten.

For the inhabitants the Railway was a lifeline; with their nearest dwelling standing within 10 yards of the track and the convenience of a siding beside the little station, movement up and down the valley was by rail – but not necessarily by train: wagons would always be left in the siding and, of course, Arthur Pugh's permanent way trolley. High days and emergencies saw wagons brought into use and, if necessary, gravitated down to Towyn. Special occasions such as Sunday School outings from Towyn, festival, fairs and other gatherings at times unsuited to the railway timetables, would see more than one family *en route* to Pendre, with the prospect of pushing the wagon back at the end of the day! In cases of accident, the trolley would carry the victim down to the doctor in Towyn.

In the tiny station yard the annual haystack would be set up; using materials obtained from the lineside, it was roped with plaited hay. If there was sufficient,

there would be a pile of bracken too; this was collected from hillsides above on horsedrawn car-llysg (sledge) or cart, and brought down as bedding for the pigs – every household kept them. The surplus was stacked in the station and might be used to implement that cut from the lineside.

A passing train might drop off a wagon of coal as it went by, and it would be left standing on the main line until attacked by villagers with buckets to carry the contents away – as soon as it was empty it would be pushed into the siding to clear the line. This business was later lost to the lorry of the local Co-operative Society. Occasionally a wagon-load of bricks (or such-like) for local use would be left in the siding, for by then, the one-time loop had long lost its western end and the finish of the resultant siding was in the form of a curious twist in the rails as if it was making-off to the north-west.

An event of some note would be family picnics to Dolgoch – not by regular train of course, but by the redoubtable wagon from the siding. A word to Arthur

Another scene devised by 'Picture Post'; William Pugh (undertaker and co-owner of Pugh's Garage) together with Hugh Jones carry out a piece of emergency trackwork at the rear of Plas Goch, by the Braichyrhiw stream bridge. 'Emmett' looks on. (Pugh had never worked on the Railway at any time!)

BBC HULTON PICTURE LIBRARY

With Tynllwynhen to the left, the line makes eastwards towards Brynglas. Iron fencing was uncommon. Between Rhydyronen and Brynglas the Railway was a well-used footpath for all and sundry.   AUTHOR

Pugh would make all these parochial journeys 'all right' with the management!

The Railway now enters a strange valley, not because of its appearance (which at first sight looks like any other valley in these mountains) as now the hills begin to close in on either side of the line. At first shyly hidden but, as the line climbs steadily higher, the little river Mathew shows itself from time to time. In the next mile or two the fields will gradually change from places where things are grown to bleaker pastures where cattle and sheep graze.

For any reader disinterested in the curiosity and nature of this valley the following will be of little interest! Firstly, one must go to the lake of Talyllyn from which the Railway takes its name but does not reach. It is sited in the great Bala Fault, superbly between sweeping flanks, a typical glacial feature: despite its apparent aspect of being 'bottomless', it is said to have an average depth of but six feet but it is the glacial moraine at its seaward end which accounts for the features through which the Talyllyn Railway runs. Although the view from the Railway looking ahead suggests this is a conventional river valley, this is not so for the river which leaves the west end of the lake is not the one which the Railway follows to

Abergynolwyn! It is the Dysynni which flows from the lake and after successfully threading the 'moraine' around the hamlet of Talyllyn, reaches Abergynolwyn where it is faced with a second 'moraine'. This it does not succeed in penetrating and instead swings off to the north-west, cutting through the dividing range and finding its way to the sea in a parallel valley to the north of that of the Mathew. The Mathew rises between Dolgoch and Abergynolwyn and its main tributary is the considerable stream which flows down the Dolgoch gorge. Rivers beyond this point, with which the Railway had close associations to its ultimate end, all flow into the Dysynni; consequently, the Mathew (mutated, this becomes Fathew as in Afon Fathew) is never a large waterway; it finds its way through Bryncrug into the Dysynni just below Pont Dysynni, augmented by the Braichyrhiw or Nant Rhydyronen stream. Receiving so much glacial deposit has choked the mouth of the Dysynni with silt and cobble banks so that what might have become 'Aber Dysynni' never developed.

Secondly, as the line rises up the valley, when approaching Dolgoch a 'Hanging Valley' opposite comes into view on the north flank; this leads over the ridge through Llanerchgoediog to the Dysynni valley and is left 'hanging' above the floors of its adjacent valleys on each end.

The railway track between Rhydyronen and Brynglas, so far from the main road, became a well-used link between these points. It was commonplace to find people on horseback, on foot, farmers taking the cow to the bull, the postman (or postwoman) on bicycle, making regular sorties along here in the days before motor vehicles became prevalent. Wheeled vehicles were not suited to the site, however! The cow (or sometimes the bull) was the first to disappear from it – 'The Bull in the Bowler Hat' (artificial insemination) took its place.

Vegetation will now become more scarce but the woodland which grows on the steep slopes on the north side of the valley gives way to that of the Forestry Commission as the Railway goes eastwards. (L. T. C. Rolt maintained the valley was once thickly wooded and in the ownership of the Kirkbys, who, however, sold it to their tenants, who cut down all the woodlands probably for oak bark.) To the south side of the line

the hills come closer until the line takes up a feature which becomes more prominent for the whole of the remainder of the journey – and nowhere more so than at its termination.

But to the curious valley itself (which gave the construction of the Railway every help from its geological inheritance), after a couple of straightish sections it becomes narrower and more steeply-sided as the Railway nears the next station, Brynglas. The line ambles between the hedgerows at first, past a little stopping place, Tynllwynhen ($2\frac{1}{2}$ m.) which was recognised (but not advertised) many years ago. In winter this is one of the sections most likely to be affected by driving snow and in spring is one of the most delightful, with primroses in profusion on its banks and bluebells as spring turns into summer. The views ahead of the train are best seen from here, with summits and escarpments breaking the skyline. Gradients still climb at 1 in 179, 104, and 143 until Brynglas is reached, having originally two simple sidings laid out on the south side of the track for use by the nearby

Brynglas, a station used almost exclusively by the local people rather than visitors. The bridge in the foreground carried the line over a cattle creep. 1936.
L. T. CATCHPOLE

hamlet of Pandy, and weaving and fulling mills there, together with the flour mill some way down the road to the north. The unloading of Abergynolwyn's night soil into the neighbouring field was done hereabouts from the running line. The road, which goes no further than Pandy, crosses the line on the level here. There survives, however, an original feature in the cattle creep under the line just beyond it, and clearly an item which dates back to the start of the Railway (it is shown on the Cotterell & Spackman Plan) so the level crossing must have replaced it. The creep is only 10 ft wide and perhaps 6 ft high and was a very restrictive factor to Pandy access. As to the two mills, the lower was driven by a large overshot waterwheel and was latterly a weaving mill making blankets etc. The smaller, upper mill was used for fulling woven cloth.

Brynglas (124 ft.), like Rhydyronen, is not the simple little station it appears to be on first acquaintance. It is sited immediately on the east side of the level crossing and the platform and building are of slab and resemble those at Rhydyronen in many respects. On the Cotterell & Spackman Plan the station name has been added in pencil but with no detail; it is 3 m. 15 ch. from Wharf, the name meaning 'Blue Hill' and derived from the nearby farm; the reason for this is not known unless it was the farm which created the stopping place rather than the hamlet. The local stream is the Afon Cwmpandy and formerly noted for its trout. Up in the small cwm above there are trial levels for slate, and from there Trumgelli (1793 ft.) was accessible to the walker, but there is no proper route in this instance. From the train the observant

Westward from Brynglas. In early days, the course of the line was to the right behind the building. 1949.   R. K. COPE

The little hamlet of Pandy (or Brynglas) seen from the Railway, lying in a fold in the hills. Peeping through a break in the middle ground, the launder carrying water to the wheel at the Woollen Mill may be seen. GWYNEDD ARCHIVES

will see on the north side the roof and chimneys of Dolaugwyn, a notable 17th-century manor house associated with the Corbets and Wynnes.

One of the nicest features of the whole journey up the line is the variety in station surroundings. On the map, for instance, Rhydyronen and Brynglas might appear to be similar, but in reality they are very dissimilar. Here at Pandy (the local name is more often used) the hills are more bold for they have conquered their disquiet about the Railway and come forward much more closely to see what it is all about! Almost from the lineside the slopes begin; they grow more steep with every yard and soar to such heights as to close in the view to the south. The little roadway quickly disappears into a cwm, and from the train is lost to sight by the crown of a small rise in it. Farm buildings on either side add a sense of theatre and of

the beyond which, in fact, never comes to pass, for, unlike Rhydyronen, the roadway (apart from taking a sharp left turn at the top to serve the woollen mills) peters out quite quickly in a ford, with accompanying footbridge. The walker hereabouts must be prepared for some rough going and negligible pathways.

Behind the station platform the fields stretch across the valley floor in abundance of hedge and tree to end in the low range which bounds the valley on the north side. How different the scene from here on the opposite side! The hills thrust up, stone walls clinging improbably to their flanks, and here and there rocky outcrops break up the smooth outlines of those hilly slopes; the narrow defile which divides them is hardly visible, and the farm buildings which create this small community are partially hidden by a coppice of fir, sycamore and ash. There is a forthrightness about

The approach to Brynglas; the level crossing was not at first intended but is believed to have been gated and signalled before the Railway opened to passengers — these fittings were sold to the Mawddwy Railway almost immediately. The cattle creep under the line (beyond the crossing) was an original feature and its existence probably allowed the Railway Company to avoid gating and signalling the crossing which they could maintain was 'out of use' in favour of the creep! Ultimately the creep became disused and the crossing took over. 1949.
R. K. COPE

A wet summer's day in 1949; DOLGOCH waits at Brynglas while a passenger takes his time capturing the scene. The driver was considerate of everyone's needs.
AUTHOR

Leaving Brynglas, the line makes for the slopes of the mountain and so continues, hugging the mountainside all the way to Bryneglwys Quarry.
R. K. COPE

Pandy which distinguishes it from the more sylvan Rhydyronen – the traveller must decide which has the more appeal.

At the end of the platform the line crosses the Cwmpandy and heads into a cutting, climbing at 1 in 94 initially. It is possible to trace that the present line actually runs on a later course about 12 ft. south of the old throughout the length of the section and at this point the alignment of the original can clearly be determined when looking back to the west. Why was this replacement line built? The reason would appear to be a weakness in the supporting arch brickwork of the Railway's bridge over the stream, and maybe to create space for the platform.

The line passes under a 'typical' accommodation road overbridge (built in slab and brick) and, after following the cutting to its end, the straight section which ensues after Brynglas emerges at much higher altitude above the surrounding fields than up to now. The climb here is at 1 in 164 and now a series of reverse curves occur, with the river quite some way below the Railway and meandering through a marshy

The first overbridge east of Brynglas simply linked the fields which had been divided by the building of the Railway. It was the last overbridge on the Up journey. April 1949.   AUTHOR

A series of curves in the line ensues some way beyond Brynglas. This is the first of them, the '26th Curve'. 1940.   J. W. SPARROWE

and somewhat drab valley bottom. Above the line to the south the mountainside rises steeply from the trackside and continues in this unbroken fashion right up to the end of the system. In the distance the eye-catching summit of Cader Idris is often visible (2,927 ft.).

There now follow what are today dubbed 'The Six Bends' but are shown on Cotterell & Spackman as '26th Curve', the four miles from Wharf being completed at the 30th Curve. Hereafter the line weaves slightly from one curve to the next, each of about 1 fur. 5 ch. radius, passing out of Corbet lands into those of the Wynnes of Dolaugwyn. So the woodland approaching Dolgoch (said to be haunted) is gained and Corbet property once more. There are delightful

views from the route now as the track climbs even higher above the valley floor, which in turn has returned to fields of better drainage.

On entering the attractive woodland there is a short stretch where the line is carried on a 20 ft. embankment. It is the place where, having some advantage in height and possibly with the thought that the trees kept the operation out of sight, D. & J. Daniel's shop (and probably others) were wont to unload their rubbish and throw it down the embankment. The problems of more recent times had their origins in the period under review, when the embankment was gradually being waterlogged due to blockage of its culvert. The present-day track is carried on a course which is slightly different to the older. At 4 m. 5 fur.

The Down afternoon train trundles softly through the Dolgoch woods with father and son (Hugh and Herbert Jones) on the footplate. April 1949. 'After dark, we hang a lighted oil lamp on the engine bracket.' AUTHOR

The Up 9.25 a.m. ex Wharf enters the Dolgoch woodland with empty slate wagons behind. 26th May 1941.
W. A. CAMWELL

a stream passes under the embankment, a site where it was said engines would take water in the first decade – it would be intriguing to know more.

Another cattle creep passes under the line when suddenly, and without warning, the surroundings of the line change completely though still passing through the woodlands. The ground falls away and the viaduct at Dolgoch gorge with its small river is crossed, approaching it by the '40th Curve' and with the viaduct 4 m. 6½ fur. from Wharf. Up to now the curves on the line have been relatively gentle (excepting that on the east side of Rhydyronen) but, on

The sylvan setting on the approach to Dolgoch viaduct emphasises the variety of countryside which embraces the route.   R. K. COPE

Yet another artifice of 'Picture Post'. Here 'Emmett' purports to be sketching the train; it was later, and hereabouts that DOLGOCH's frame was cracked and the service suspended.

Only from the footplate can the top of Dolgoch viaduct be anticipated.   R. K. COPE

The viaduct, now almost hidden by trees; it is the largest piece of similar engineering on the journey. 1936.   L. T. CATCHPOLE

The 'Picture Post Special' is halted on the viaduct and the early sun casts deep shadows as it climbs over the ridge beyond.

Then comes Dolgoch station; between trains the place would be almost deserted. The Second War has begun but here, in September 1940, the world seems still at peace.
J. W. SPARROWE

coming off the viaduct, there is a sharper bend to the left (6 chains radius) into Dolgoch station (187 ft.). This curve passes through a considerable rock cutting. The station building is similar to that at Brynglas, and opposite the platform was a tower carrying a slab-built tank, both replaced in the 1920s, the new tank being of wood on a similar tower but not precisely in the same position.

Dolgoch, no matter how attractive for the visitor, was no convenience to the few local people who used it. Goods of the type which came and went into Rhydyronen and Brynglas were also exchanged on a more limited scale at Dolgoch, but without the advantage of either a siding or a roadway up to the platform, the work was heavy labour. Sacks of the various commodities were left on the station platform and had to be humped down or up a rough path from the level of the gorge below; worse, until the 1940s there was no proper path over the rocky slope up to the station, and it was treacherous walking in frosty weather.

The gorge and two farmsteads (one now The Dolgoch Falls Hotel) were given access from the valley road by a side track which ran beside the stream. Behind the buildings, this track entered the defile (and passed under the viaduct in due course) and was firmly

gated before entering the gorge proper. Locally this is the Ffordd Degwm (The Tithe Road) but the origin of the name is not clear; the ownership of the land around had no connections with the Church. Certain it is that the local roadman never did his work beyond that gate.

The rhododendrons were a feature of the Dolgoch Estate but how they first came to be there is another mystery. Whilst there was the Ponticum (or common) variety in goodly number, there were also plenty of species and it is suggested that the local landowners vied with each other to relate how they had been to the fore in planting newly-imported shrubs onto their lands.

The station was not among the original ones, had not opened by February 1867 but was in use by 1st August of that year. Early Guide Books encouraged the ambitious to alight here – 'Dolgoch is the nearest station for Bird Rock (2 miles)', a fact which the unwary who attempted it would agree must have been far less strenuous for the bird on the wing than the casual passenger who left the train in search of a gentle stroll; Bird Rock is a renowned landlocked seabird site in the adjacent Dysynni valley.

Return must be made to say something about the Dolgoch Ravine; the gorge was the property of R. J. Roberts, a chemist in Towyn High Street, and had been investigated as a source of slate from the time when Bryneglwys opened. There was one main adit and several trial levels there: each had its own tramway which brought out rubbish, carried it over the stream and dumped it on the farther bank. There was, in 1865, a chalybeate spring and, in view of the preponderance of such a century ago, we may wonder if every issue of water from these hills which contained a noticeable amount of iron ore in it, was dubbed thus? Perhaps it was hoped every one would prove to offer a cure?!

Roberts, in his own lifetime, set about not only making a gift of the Dolgoch Estate, 'The Roberts'

Charity' (which he had bought from the Corbet executors) to the people of Towyn, but set to work with his own hands to build a series of paths, bridges, seats and steps to give access to the upper parts of the gorge which is notable for its succession of waterfalls. As has been mentioned, John Jones was also engaged on this work and broadened it to make rustic fences and seats for Wharf and Dolgoch stations. Roberts spent long hours each summer in improving the facilities, leaving the running of the shop to an assistant. In this attractive gift, Roberts may be thought today to have been a far more generous benefactor to Towyn than the wealthy John Corbett.

The writer's early memories of the Talyllyn Railway and the intimacy of Dolgoch have long been overlaid by countless visits since. Take for instance, a war-time

DOLGOCH clanks into Dolgoch, a haven of light and shade. The water tank spouts wastefully, and that nasty joint in the rails has several more years before it! 1949.

Without the use of the Brake Van (which at that time was unfit for traffic) Edward Thomas walks smartly to the separate compartment in the First Class Coach which he used instead of the Van. Worse, there were no brakes on the engine just then either, so Hugh must stop the train by putting the engine into reverse. August 1948.
H. C. CASSERLEY

The remainder of the train on the foregoing day was made up of slate wagons fitted up with plank seats on which the overflow of passengers sat. It would be the following April before the Van's wheels left Towyn for repair.
H. C. CASSERLEY

journey; two days earlier I had come from the harsh reality of an Army barrack block; though on this occasion my leave was but a break into what would prove to be almost six years away from civilian life, the experience of the Railway would have been equally incredible against a peacetime, home-living background. It was a double-act; firstly a railway train which, by the sheer forces of built-in obsolescence, should have survived against all that my young experience had taught me, and secondly, it ran through a world that was itself Elysium, a place set apart from the political greed of an Adolf Hitler, and surely not within a day's journey of cities such as Liverpool and Manchester, where only weeks before I had watched the bombs fall and destroy by fire and explosion. It seemed impossible, in the silence of the woodland approaching the viaduct, that this was not a dream which would shatter suddenly.

That delicious mixture of smells, often described as a compound of hot oil and the smoke from steam coal, came intermittently to the nostrils as the engine nudged its way between the trees. It was not the best of days. I cannot write of shafts of sunlight piercing the umbrella of boughs, nor of butterflies in the clearings, the smell of wild garlic or any of the usual ingredients designed to complete the word-picture. The ground under my feet (the footplate of *Talyllyn*) swayed under me, the overhanging branches of trees swept the side of the cab and threatened my face, the carriage and wagons fought each other's progress behind us as they lurched first one way and then that. The open hillside had changed for the intimacy of the woodland and we groped between the trees like a man-made caterpillar, somehow unsure that those unlikely, grass-covered rails beneath us could guide us safely into the open again. Even the beat from the chimney was muted as if not to disturb the wild life in the undergrowth which had not then awoken to the spring. Would the war last until spring? Should I ever come through it? Why was I here at all, after an

Yet another of the angles of the Railway concocted for 'Picture Post'; DOLGOCH takes water from the gushing tank at Dolgoch. 1949.
BBC HULTON PICTURE LIBRARY

In the early 1920s, TALYLLYN, still carrying its second saddle tank, is watered at Dolgoch to the interest of those leaving the train.

F. FRITH & CO.

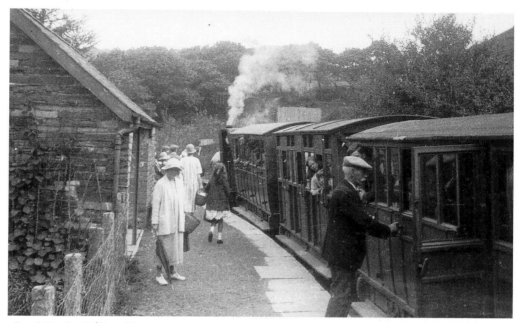

Jacob Rowlands (his uniform now worn out and unwearable?) checks tickets on an Up train in 1923.
B. EDGINGTON

A second photograph taken by Frith's man in the early '20s; in those times visitors were smartly dressed to a degree which makes today's average holiday-maker look a disgrace.
F. FRITH & CO.

The gorge at Dolgoch was always a mecca for many pursuits. In this and the above record, the viaduct has mellowed into the woodland as if part of nature's bounty; in the glen above it a series of waterfalls may be followed up the mountainside and past the abandoned slate mines.   R. K. COPE (upper)
                    L. T. CATCHPOLE (lower)

overnight journey on the mail train from Crewe to Machynlleth – and the rest of the discomfort? How I wished I had brought my wife from whom I had separated myself for one of those precious seven days of leave!

One of the two men on the engine had come across and pointed out the approaching viaduct, so waking me from such thoughts. The engine was slowed almost to walking-pace – I believed for my delectation but more likely in the interests of our survival – and at tree-top height we trundled over that unexpected structure. It would be some years before I would see it from below.

We drew up at Dolgoch and the drizzle came on again. The routine of filling the tank took place and the wooden trough was edged carefully into position on the filler-opening, using a fire-iron shaped like a billiard cue rest to judge it to a nicety. Some of the water went down the trough but much of it went over the side, the engine got a considerable wetting, and the injector, turned on to fill the boiler meanwhile, whistled its little tune. The woodland smelled damp and wet and I ventured away as I knew the men would wait ... what a place this was! Hidden away up its cwm, the epitome of the Victorian Guide Books' 'Faery Glen', tall mature trees such as could only be found occasionally between these bare rounded slopes. Rhododendron bushes, their buds just beginning to open, and introduced into the British Isles from the

The knowledge that Sir Haydn has gone seems almost tangible at lonely Dolgoch. Overgrown, track appalling, its seat without a top, the place seems to have been reclaimed by an invading jungle.
R. K. COPE

Himalayas about 1800, were, like the train, brought by man into surroundings where others might accept them as native.

Not surprisingly, although this was a timetabled stop, there was no sign of life. The only passenger was snug on the engine and he checked to see that his rucksack, tidily seated in the corner of the First Class compartment which he had been bidden to use, had not fallen over. 'Thermos' flasks were a part of wartime living and almost irreplaceable if broken – the warning of our earlier disaster in this wise on the Welshpool narrow gauge line was fresh in mind! Everywhere there

There is an end-of-season feel here too; autumn is approaching. It is the last week of the timetable and passengers are few. Edward Thomas awaits the photographer's pleasure before he waves off the train. 4th October 1950.
R. K. COPE

was water – under the boots, down the track, dripping off the trees. I stood under the bare platform shelter and listened to the roar of the river and wished there was time to see the falls which must have been in spate. I must hold this moment against the odds ...

The whistle blew to say we were ready to start again; two smiling faces drew back into the cab as they made way for me to climb up. The driver stood back, waved his hand towards the controls and invited me to proceed. Heaven must pale before this!

Beyond the station platform, and coming out of the curve, the line crosses a more generous cattle creep, a slender arch of 12 ft. span built entirely of stone. Leaving Dolgoch ('Red Meadow') and 4 m. 72 ch. from the start there comes an easing of the 1 in 118 and 201 climb into the station and there follows a straight length, still threading the woodland. At the 5th mile there was intended to be a branch railway junction to serve the slate mines in the Dolgoch gorge which would have made a trailing connection on the south side of the route. Tradition has it that some blasting of rock had also taken place in the cutting at the west end of the station to prepare the site for a siding. But the only extra piece of trackage proved to

Leaving Dolgoch the line threads the woods for a little way; looking at the track one may ask, 'Do trains really pass this way?'
R. K. COPE

Beneath the embankment of the previous picture, a wide cattle creep leads up from the farm at Dolgoch to the slopes of Talyfan.
AUTHOR

Restored to working order again at The Atlas Foundry, DOLGOCH forges through the boscage above Dolgoch. AUTHOR

This was a favourite viewpoint for early photographers as it was one of the few places where the light might be helpful . . . but not in this instance! Erwbenlas lies below the line.

F. FRITH & CO.

Tancoed, with its siding to the 'quarry'; a hurdle has been placed across the line to prevent straying sheep which had penetrated the insufficient hedges, from wandering too far along the Railway.
J. H. RUSSELL

be a short spur not physically connected with the running line some way beyond the station on which the track gang could park its maintenance trolley; this has long disappeared.

The line falls slightly (due to subsidence), passing through the trees as Dolgoch is left behind; there comes a second (and final for this section) 6 ch. curve (5 m.) and the line emerges from the wood with evidence of its now considerable height above the valley floor beneath. Almost immediately comes an accommodation road, Erwbenlas or Tancoed, which crosses the line acutely on the level and heads up southward into the bare hills. There is a small coppice on the upland side. Though not an original installation, there was a short sharply-curved siding here – facing east – on the south side to take wagons into an end-loading bank. There had been also another short spur to stable a permanent way trolley. Both here and at the trolley siding east of Dolgoch, track connections were of the 'spoon type', that is a loose rail was dropped onto each running rail; their other ends were linked to the pair of fixed rails alongside the main line. This simple system enabled light vehicles to be run on and off the main line without having to install a traditional turnout. The writer recalls the parlous condition of

the 'spoons' and trackwork generally at this place, and that the train crew carried a pocketful of spikes which they took with a hammer to the track where it required their attention and before the train passed over it. This spur and that at Dolgoch had been removed before 1948: it could be that the one at Tancoed replaced that at Dolgoch.

The adjacent quarry, which was, in fact, only a face in the hillside where shale had long been obtained to 'ballast' the line (and was probably used to that end when the line was first built), was 202 ft. above sea level and was the *raison d'être* for a long siding running parallel to the main line here, entered from the Abergynolwyn end, and which might have been used to stable wagons from earliest times. The later shorter siding clearly gave closer contact between wagon and the quarry face, which would no longer be adjacent to the original siding due to removal of shale.

Ahead now reaches a long straight length. Firstly, a cattle creep is crossed (construction is slab with arch in brick) and the bareness and wildness of the countryside on either hand accentuates the fact that the railway forms a boundary between the cultivated lowlands and the upper mountain, though a few trees do line the route in a number of places. This is sheep-farming

Beyond Tancoed there comes a straightish length which resembled by 1949, a country lane and was in fact used as such.   R. K. COPE

country and the farms on the other side of the valley stand under the steep slopes, of which some parts are covered by dwarf woodland.

In the neighbourhood of the aforementioned siding and its short successor into the 'ballast' quarry, the land was owned by John Nanney, and it is important to note that where his estate ended, just east of the accommodation level crossing, so did also the railway shown on the 'Ynys Plan'. Also, the boundary was recognised in times up to the Second War by the placing of a fence across the tracks, marking the pre-serve of adjacent farmers' land and preventing the roaming of sheep which would escape through the by-then inadequate fences onto the line and walk into the adjoining property. The boundary between these properties passes between two buildings on the road-side below, the venerable Ty Gwyn (still standing) and the more modern Erwbenlas (which was demolished in 1985) on the railway side of the road. Shortly after this, on the north side, was Tynymaes, all trace of which is lost; this was a smallholder's dwelling. On the trackside was formerly a Benchmark (224 ft. a.s.l.).

At 5 m. 7 fur. there is another small cattle creep, built in the usual manner of rough stone with a three-course brick arch, a crossing of a tumbling mountain stream and, in a small dell hollowed out of the steep hillside to the south, is the remnant of a building known locally as The Agent's House, or Ceunantcoch. Having been on Corbet land again, the line now passes through that of 'Rev. Wynne and John Nanney', and

One of TALYLLYN's two older saddle tanks was used to make this welcoming bothy for trackmen at Tancoed; the large hole in the top where the water-filler lid had rusted away, was covered by a convenient slab.   J. W. SPARROWE

DOLGOCH on a Down working see-saws gently in all directions as Hugh Jones (alone on the footplate) negotiates the familiar irregularities in the track near Tynymaes.
AUTHOR

There was another small cattle creep at Ceunantcoch.
AUTHOR

This scenario on the line approaching Abergynolwyn was what the 'Picture Post' thought — with some truth — was a regular happening on the line. Hugh Jones on DOLGOCH holds up the train whilst Will Pugh drives a cow off the verge . . .

BBC HULTON PICTURE LIBRARY

. . . a contretemps then ensues as Morgan ('Mog') Roberts (Tancoed Ucha) drives the same beast back again for the delectation of 'Picture Post' readers.

BBC HULTON PICTURE LIBRARY

The memory of this picture is that it was posed for the purpose at Pentremaestrefnant; the driver is William Lewis on a purely passenger train, and TALYLLYN carries its second water tank.
VALENTINE & CO.

on a similarly ecclesiastical note had passed out of the Parish of Towyn into that of Talyllyn, and from this place is in Llanfihangel until Abergynolwyn woodland is reached. The north side of the track, with its grassy enclosed pastures, is frowned-upon by a fine upward sweep of Mynydd Pentre's open mountain uplands; rocks and scree threaten from above to the south. Below the shelf on which the route now runs, the ground falls steeply away to arching curves of fields and the roadway beyond. Remnants of once-extensive woodlands which recent centuries ago clothed all these hills, can be seen. Some of the fencing along here – and probably much more at one time – is done by inserting slate upright into the ground and wiring it along the upper part to keep the slabs at regular distance from each other. Looking up in the direction of progress, the narrow defile at the head of the Afon Fathew Valley, where stands the terminal passenger station, Abergynolwyn, (242 ft.) is prominent. Though today almost disappeared, there were two farmsteads on the lower side of the embankment here, Pentremaestrefnant followed almost at once by Llwynfynwent, upon passing which the line enters woodland again, rounding a slight reverse curve, and approaches Abergynolwyn station (6 m. 45 ch.). Now for the first time the Railway was on land owned by 'Rev. G. R. G. Pughe & Others', ('Daddy Pughe of Mellor') the party who appear regularly in connection

A very young Herbert Jones leans from the fireman's side, and his father from the other. The train has stopped for the benefit of the photographer. Luckily it was a Saturday, and Master Herbert could be away from school to assist with the engine . . . lucky lad! September 1947.
S. W. BAKER

This is the way the Up train has come, and the line is now surrounded by close-fitting woodland as it nears Abergynolwyn. June 1932.
H. C. CASSERLEY

with the Quarry. There are considerable variations in the curves here as between the Deposited Plans and Cotterell & Spackman.

In early 1867 there was no station here, but Cotterell & Spackman show a short passing loop and the word 'station' has been pencilled in at a later date. A lane linking the road comes up at the side of the loop and the line then curves to the right at 7 ch. radius. The access lane down to the road also being Railway property, the Cotterell & Spackman Plan reveals the 'finger' of roadway going off in one direction and the 'finger' of railway in the other, forming with the line from Towyn, the letter Y on the Plan; in the fork is marked 'Termination of Authorized Railway'.

The station, when built, must have occupied part of the road interchange alongside the loop, for the position and length of the loop remained throughout the period herein. There was at first a wooden building similar in style and design to that at Pendre, being 'reincarnated' in 1936–8 with an entirely new smaller one in slab, 20 ft. long × 12 ft. wide, 7 ft. from eaves to ground. (A photograph taken in 1926 shows a dilapidated wooden structure much rotted at ground level. One of 1936 shows piles of slab on hand ready for substitution.) There was in the former's east end a sash window, similar to that at Pendre: it was partially blocked in before being replaced, only to be altered again to make it into a Block Post for the Home Guard during the Second War.

Approaching from the Towyn end, the first set of points led to a short siding behind the platform, at the west end. The date of its installation is not known but it existed before the turn of the century and was taken out again before the First War. It was reinstated during that war for the purpose of loading round timber into TR wagons for carriage to Towyn. The timber came from a Forestry Plantation on the east side of Abergynolwyn near the graveyard, and arrived by

Track like this would make even the most sober locomotive roll drunkenly; pointwork at the entrance to Abergynolwyn.　　R. K. COPE

The Up morning train reaches Abergynolwyn in late May 1941; the usual favoured passengers are permitted onto the footplate for pictorial mementoes of the trip. Here David Tipper, then with the Great Western Railway at Wolverhampton's Stafford Road Works (and later to become a priest), leans from the engine.

W. A. CAMWELL

The building in 1936 was wholly of timber and virtually a twin of that at Pendre; materials for rebuilding are stacked on the platform.
H. B. TOURS

After rebuilding in stone, it gave evidence that the Railway Company was looking ahead to a more prosperous future; at the further end the wall was provided with apertures for firearms when it became a Block Post for the local Home Guard and there were Tank Traps on the nearby highway. September 1948.
R. K. COPE

About 1930 Abergynolwyn still harboured the occasional wagon in the short spur line behind the platform. Perhaps this one was retained for gravity working by those visitors who found the last afternoon Down working was too early for their purposes?

REAL PHOTOGRAPHS

No one about. The engine has gone up to Ty Dwr for water, and the passengers down to Abergynolwyn for something stronger.
LENS OF SUTTON

The engine has returned, bringing some loaded slate wagons with it from Alltwyllt. Hugh Jones gives them a drop of oil before starting; he will push the carriages onto them and couple up at departure time. 1937.
B. ROBERTS

Another aspect of that quiet lull when the carriages were left to themselves. The end window is not worth repair as the whole building is due for renewal.

LENS OF SUTTON

Beyond Abergynolwyn stretched another railway which visitors seldom knew. Here The Mineral Line begins its way to the Quarry.
L & GRP courtesy DAVID & CHARLES

Some years after the last slate had been carried down to Towyn, The Mineral Line curves tantalisingly away and beckons the curious to follow it.
AUTHOR

A little further on towards the Quarry, the track looks decidedly better than much of it on the passenger section!   H. C. CASSERLEY

TALYLLYN returns to pick up the coaches, rounding the ultimate bend on The Mineral Line, into Abergynolwyn station. Hugh 'Gas' is the driver. 1935.
H. F. WHEELLER

horse-hauled timber drags. Over £10,000-worth of timber is said to have been put onto trains here. The siding survived until the early 1950s.

Beyond this station no passenger trains were worked, though occasionally the McConnel family (or) would be taken up to the end of the line in a single coach. There was a fine piece of dry supporting stonework to retain The Mineral Line eastwards of here, and this may still be seen. Shortly there came a gate across the track which seems to have had no other purpose than to prevent sheep straying along the line;

it does not mark the end of the statutory line as this comes a few yards to the west of it. Beyond the gate a short embankment carries the track over another cattle creep and then a stream. From here for a few yards the line is in Towyn Parish again.

Further comment about the gate just mentioned will not be out of place. It was clearly an authorised feature as it was mounted on a stout gatepost. It was not the only one across the line, there being another at the Tancoed occupation crossing near the shale quarry; the latter, however, was more of a hurdle than a gate.

'The Gate' of the earlier picture, but now a little more dilapidated and overgrown, invites the adventurous to see further; for to be open suggests a welcome.

R. K. COPE

Careless investigators beware, for The Mineral Line carries trains too and leaves little room for the thoughtless pedestrian to remove himself from the path of the train; TALYLLYN trundles towards Abergynolwyn, slate wagons in tow. 1937.

B. ROBERTS

No end in sight but the track leads ever towards the Quarry.

N. FIELDS

It seems that to avoid the expense of new fencing, Haydn Jones did not discourage farmers in property adjacent to the Railway from allowing their sheep to push their way through worn fencing and dilapidated hedging, and graze on the lineside. This was an acceptable *quid pro quo* for not repairing the boundaries, though an occasional sheep was run down by the train and the farmer's practice of claiming it was a special beast when a price was named, was as rife here as in any other part of the country – even to the point of substituting a corpse for a fatter one.

Both these gates were positioned at the boundaries of certain farms, and were left in place in winter for the train crew to open them. In summer they were removed completely in the case of the Tancoed example, and fastened open at Abergynolwyn.

THE MINERAL LINE

For the remainder of the trackage, (which it is out of order to style The Talyllyn Railway but is more exactly The Mineral Line), the system can conveniently be divided into six sections.

No.	Style	Length	Notes
1	Abergynolwyn to foot of Alltwyllt Incline	= c.8 acres.	Land never the property of the Railway: property of Quarry Co. before purchase by McConnels c. 1883. Conveyed to Haydn Jones 1911.
2	Alltwyllt Incline		(As for 1.)
3	Galltymoelfre Tramway. Top Alltwyllt Incline to foot Cantrybedd Incline.		Forming part of Hendre Estate lease to Quarry Co.: expired c. 1907 and not renewed although Quarry Co. continued to use and occupy it without payment.
4	Cantrybedd Incline		Land leased to 1912 and renewed to 1942. Thereafter on day to day basis.
5	Quarry tramways		(As for 4.)
6	Village Incline and branch		Local property of Quarry Co. etc. (As for 1.)

The Forestry Commission crossing above Hendre created problems when the occasional train was forced to plough its way through the mud churned up by forestry tractors. Here, Morris Lewis busies himself with the fireman's shovel to clear the rails. TALYLLYN is propelling a wagon for the Quarry and is pulling (out of sight) wagons destined to be lowered down the Village Incline, March 1943.

W. H. TATE

Ty Dwr, site of a former engine shed and watering point for locomotives. 1941.
W. A. CAMWELL

The construction of this mineral line is about as minimal as would suffice for the needs of a quarry outlet; the earthworks are of lesser scale than on the Railway proper. Scenically, passengers who had had, of course, to alight, were here deprived of one of the most expansive views of the valley, with the village extending below and the Dysynni Vale, with its steeply rising sides, disappearing into the distance. The line continues upon its mountain shelf over an occupation crossing above Hendre, and draws level with the village and its nearer church (St. David's, its foundation stone laid by Mary Cornelia, Marchioness of Londonderry* on 6th November 1879) with every yard. So to Ty Dwr, with a mountain stream rushing down from the cliffs above to feed a wooden trough upheld by a slab tower beside the line. The locomotive, with or without slate wagons attached, left its coaches at Abergynolwyn and ran up here to take water; it was a basic process, utilising one movable wooden trough stuck into the stream at one extreme and a second which stretched from the slab tower and directed the flow into the engine's tank filler. Much spillage resulted, but water was plentiful and without charge!

---

*i.e. Lady Vane Tempest of Plas Machynlleth.

Many an anxious engine crew has reached Ty Dwr with an empty tank and much relief. On a summer's day an idyllic spot; in heavy rain and low mist in winter, a place to leave as soon as possible. 1948.

H. C. CASSERLEY

The operation itself. The portable wooden trough connecting the engine with the fixed section of the launder, which led into a mountain stream, has duly filled the engine's tank and has been pushed out from under the deluge whilst the engine crew enjoy a moment's peace before returning to Abergynolwyn and the coaches.   AUTHOR

Ty Dwr again. During the watering process, opportunity is taken to oil around the engine.   R. K. COPE

Now beyond the watering point, the line reaches the head of the Village Incline . . .

Round the next curve a large slab-built building (261 ft.) comes into view, apparently blocking the line completely until it is seen that the rails actually pass underneath it, and that there is an acute-angle crossing of tracks on the level inside the building. On the uphill side there is a loop with a 6 ft. diameter turntable behind the structure and used only as access to the incline head. The building's purpose is to support a huge wooden drum, on and around which the incline's wire rope passes; there is an opening in the downhill wall of the building and through it the village track metals pass after crossing the main line on the level! It then bifurcates and, by means of some very acute curvature to take the rails over the edge, drops down in double track to a bridge over the Gwernol river below, and then is swallowed up within the walls of the village. We shall return to this (p.173).

. . . and the track bifurcates, one line leading through the winding drum house and the other passing behind. AUTHOR

The drum house is built in random stone and somewhere under the grass those uncertain rails lead through it. The drum brake lever is prominent to the left; the Incline itself leads down to the left.
R. K. COPE

Seen from a point in the west and looking over the roofs of Abergynolwyn, the Incline (centre right) falls down into the village. In the centre is Nant Gwernol gorge and the road to the Quarry climbs steeply in the left of the picture. The village was almost exclusively occupied by employees of the Quarry; accommodation could only be rented to those in the Quarry-owner's employ. The title mistakenly reads 'from north'.   F. FRITH & CO.

ABERGYNOLW

ROM NORTH. 1300.

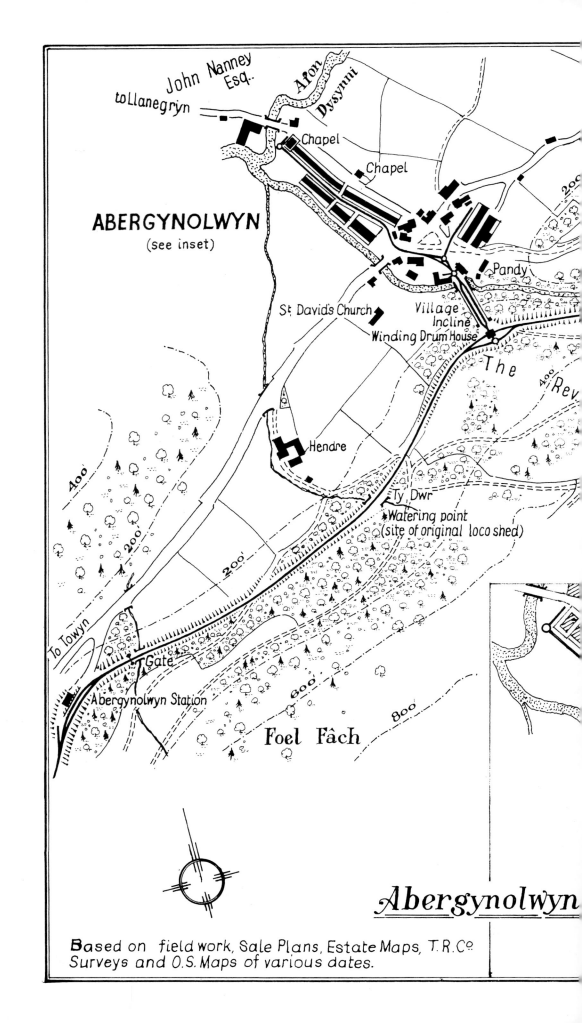

John Nanney Esq..

to Llanegryn

Afon Dysynni

Chapel

Chapel

ABERGYNOLWYN
(see inset)

Pandy

St. David's Church

Village
Incline

Winding Drum House

The Rev

Hendre

400

200

Ty Dwr

Watering point
(site of original loco shed)

To Towyn

Gate

200

600

800

Abergynolwyn Station

Foel Fâch

Abergynolwyn

Based on field work, Sale Plans, Estate Maps, T.R.Cº.
Surveys and O.S. Maps of various dates.

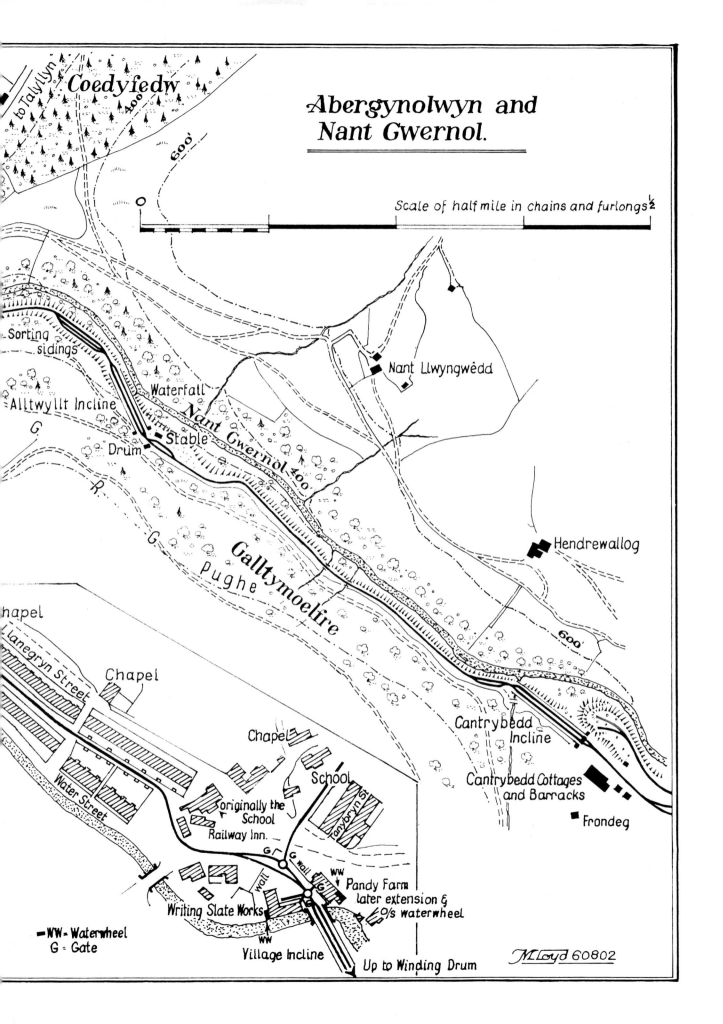

Abergynolwyn and Nant Gwernol.

Coedyfedw

to Talyllyn

400

600'

Scale of half mile in chains and furlongs ½

O

Sorting sidings

Waterfall

Nant Llwyngwêdd

Alltwyllt Incline

G

Drum

Stable

Nant Gwernol 400

Galltymoelfre

Pughe

R

G

Hendrewallog

600'

Chapel

Llanegryn Street

Chapel

Chapel

School

Cantrybedd Incline

Water Street

originally the School
Railway Inn.

Tanybryn St

Cantrybedd Cottages
and Barracks

Frondeg

G

G wall

wall

ww

School

Pandy Farm
later extension &
o/s waterwheel

Writing Slate Works

ww

- WW - Waterwheel
G = Gate

Village Incline

Up to Winding Drum

M. Loyd 60802

Back up behind the winding drum again, TALYLLYN approaches pushing empty wagons bound for Alltwyllt Incline foot. The acute-angled rail level crossing in the drum house can be seen.
L. T. CATCHPOLE

Beyond the Village Incline head, the line curved round an escarpment on a narrow ledge which it shared at this time with the feedpipe for a water turbine at the village Generating Station. Derailments here were to be avoided at all costs – the fall into the gorge on the left hand would be spectacular if nothing else.
AUTHOR

Beyond this drumhouse The Mineral Line takes a sharp curve into the gorge of the Gwernol and the valley and village are lost to sight. Trees envelop the route, the course is carried on a narrow shelf with retaining walls and clings to the rockface in a manner not encountered previously. Turning even further, the shelf gives little clearance between vehicles and the rock wall on the one side; the unfenced edge falls precipitously down to the river below, which can be heard roaring through the trees which fill the gorge.

So with a final curve – ever to the right – the line comes to an apparent end in a small yard of three sidings (but two originally?) sandwiched between the afforested crags above and the sharp rocky edge of gorge – just sufficient room for a man to pass between wagons and the brink. Beyond these sidings the tracks come together again on an even further curve, and a single line reaches out to the foot of a double-tracked balanced incline, Alltwyllt by name (270 ft.). With a similar sharp upward twist, the rails rise abruptly, still carried on a shelf with the river booming away in the canyon below. This place could be miles from anywhere – in no distance at all the site has become remote and it is hard to believe that passenger trains

actually come to within $\frac{3}{4}$ mile of this situation, so great is the change in surroundings.

Without much effort, upturned and broken slate wagons can be seen among the whirlpools and rocks in the river below, with water spewing through the spokes of jettisoned wagon wheels and creating a stream of sticky bubbles. There was plenty of opportunity to lose wagons in spectacular fashion in a place like this!

In the time of Haydn Jones an electricity power station was installed in Abergynolwyn to supply the village and sawmill (the latter one of Haydn's interests). It was operated by water turbine supplied by a pipeline which took water from the Gwernol near the foot of Alltwyllt Incline. The pipeline kept company with the rails, between them and the rock wall on the south side of the ledge. The latterday condition of the pipe was so poor that to traverse its length between the drumhouse and Alltwyllt was to pass through a perpetual morass.

It should be added that as regards legal ownership of land on The Mineral Line, the description has been slightly simplified to make it more acceptable! Strictly, ownership as tabulated covered only about three-

An evocative reminder of what the Railway was all about. Wagons are shunted at the foot of Alltwyllt Incline, the nearer one is loaded. Lying on one side behind the train are the remains of a wagon which has run amok. 1941.

W. A. CAMWELL

A much earlier scene (August 1925) at the same spot, looking away from the Incline foot. Certain Incline Wagons feature in the train.
How different the surroundings today; have we lost or gained in the ensuing years? H. G. W. HOUSEHOLD

quarters of the distance and this was the portion ultimately conveyed to Haydn Jones. An Opinion given in the early 1960s was that he was 'on the face of it, the owner of the fee simple in the land. Subsequent researches revealed that although this was so, the Talyllyn Railway had exercised absolute control of this land for over 90 years without, so far as is known, ever having paid any rent or given any account to the owner of the freehold, and therefore had possessory title . . .' In May 1964 the same legal source maintained that 'The Talyllyn Railway had possessory title to the land at Nant Gwernol and has had it for many years, and all that is on it particularly the rails which were laid about 1865 . . .'

The opening for passenger trains from Abergynolwyn to Nant Gwernol in recent years has divested the line of its last veils of secrecy. Like a strip-tease dancer, her last claim to modesty undone by the invitable *coup-de-grace*, all mystery and wonder ceases to exist. So it was when Nant Gwernol was 'opened up', and perhaps the choicest section of the old under-

taking, virtually unchanged since the middle 1860s, fell prey to the objectives of those who strangely did not appreciate that of all their brief, this was the one unspoiled example of the lonely, part-inaccessible and characteristic Welsh narrow gauge railway which might claim to be the ideal subject for being left alone . . .

In the time of our story, the line beyond Abergynolwyn was a road to adventure – and mis-adventure. It ran through a riot of vegetation; it was carried on one of the most exciting ledges above the ravine and its track threatened to pitch vehicles spec-tacularly into the gorge below. The trains which used it were unlike most others; with an engine in the middle and wagons at either end, they would puff their way under an umbrella of overhanging branches, take water at Ty Dwr from archaic but adequate apparatus, stop to operate the Village Incline and then, puff gin-gerly onward again, lurching round the awesome curves with the tops of trees growing in the ravine below reaching level with the line as if to emphasise

The approach to the little fan of sidings at Alltwyllt marked the end of the narrow ledge between here and the Village Incline. AUTHOR

the finality of a derailment. By the time the foot of Alltwyllt was reached, the visitor would sense a mixture of relief, wonder and isolation. Surely the jungles of the Amazon could produce nothing more wondrous than to survive that piece of railway – and yet it was not 'The End', for the onlooker would then witness the Incline in operation. Incredulity piled upon incredulity!

Alltwyllt Incline This work is also supported by walling and embankment where it stands on the south face of the gorge: the track materials throughout are of Talyllyn standard pattern, but these alter at the top.

The winding drum at the summit is unusual in that it was perched on a rocky shelf about 20 ft. above the track, due to the change in direction of the tramway, which was 633 ft. long with an average slope of 1 in 3.53. A feature of this slope is the considerable increase

Accidents on Alltwyllt Incline would all end in this manner; dry weather reveals three smashed vehicles in the bed of the river. AUTHOR

The Incline became more steep as it rose; it was the cause of more runaways than any other. TALYLLYN RAILWAY CO.

Owing to the configuration of the surroundings the winding drum had to be perched on a rock ledge above the tracks.
G. D. BRAITHWAITE

There was a quietness about the length of the Galltymoelfre Tramway section, broken only by the occasional passing of the horse drawing the wagons.
                                                                    D. COZENS

of inclination towards the top. There was a small stable building nearby, but not used overnight.

Galltymoelfre Tramway ('The High Hilly Place') This takes the line from the summit of Alltwyllt Incline to the foot of Cantrybedd Incline. It is about half a mile long and formed part of Rev. G. R. G. Pugh's Estate. It was leased to the 'Railway Company' [*sic*] in or about 1862 'for building the line to the Quarry'. The lease expired in 1907 and was not renewed, though the Railway operators continued to use it. In 1940 the greater part of the Estate was sold to the Crown but the Commissioners of Crown Lands refused to take land occupied and worked by the owner of Quarry or Railway. The land remained the property

of the personal representatives of the descendants of Rev. G. R. G. Pugh until more than a decade after the period of this narrative. The track, in light bridge rails, was carried on a narrow ledge in the wooded gorge and had two shunting loops, one at Alltwyllt summit, the other at the far end. It was worked originally by horses stabled at the head of Alltwyllt Incline.

Cantrybedd Incline Under somewhat like circumstances of the Village Incline, Cantrybedd is obliged to cross Moelfre stream at its foot: a bridge is provided just after level ground is left and this is preceded by a shunting loop. The wooded gorge which confronts the course of the tramway is the Nant Gwernol and a separate footbridge catered for those

At the end of Galltymoelfre, the foot of Cantrybedd Incline was reached. After the closure of the Quarry, wagons left scattered like a child's toys abandoned at bedtime, lie at the foot. The cable had broken again.

G. D. BRAITHWAITE

From the summit of Cantrybedd there was a superb view of the wooded gorge below.   D. COZENS

Behind the photographer of the previous picture was the drum house and the first of the cottages on the Cantrybedd level . . .
W. G. TRINDER

on foot and Quarry horses which were brought down from there to haul on Galltymoelfre. The Incline drum was worked by 'Lewis Hendre-Wallog'.

It will be noted that since the Village Incline summit was left behind, the direction of The Mineral Line is now wholly to the south-east, being the only section where, since Towyn, the track has run in this direction. Cantrybedd Incline continues this orientation and at its summit the Line comes to an end (612 ft. a.s.l.): this place marks the beginning of the Quarry tramway system. This feature is also built on a ledge on the mountainside and brings the tramway to a spectacular terminus high above the gorge. The peace of this remote fastness is accompanied by the constant sound of falling water in the river below. The Incline was of average grade, 1 in 2.75, and 440 ft. long, the winding drum at the top being of conventional pattern, housed in a slab-walled erection with slated roof. Unusually, the side walls taper as they rise.

. . . the drum house having somewhat different features from most in the Principality. The tenants of these cottages spent their lives within the sound of constantly falling water.
D. COZENS

The whole of the Cantrybedd level spreads out before the viewer, as seen from the cottages' windows. The tramway winds its way through the empty stockyards and the Lower Mill has done no business for the previous two decades. 1935.   L. T. CATCHPOLE

Quarry Tramways Unlike some of the bigger quarry systems in North Wales, the basic layout of tramlines in the Quarry, though extended over the years, has remained unaltered since the Railway opened. Though there were some lengths of track, notably underground, where Talyllyn Railway-type 40 lbs./yd. iron rails were in use, most of the tracks were laid in c. 20 lbs./yd. bridge rails on wooden sleepers, spiked thereto and joined on common sleepers.

From the head of Cantrybedd there first come the cottages of that name, and Frondeg, where several families lived. Frondeg was a barracks divided into two small sections, 'Aberdovey' and 'Machine', the names given by Aberdovey men who lodged there. Their gardens were on the opposite side of the tramway which passed the front door. The tramway continues into Cantrybedd yard with a large tipping area between it and the gorge; the line turns more eastward and there is a stockyard similar to that at

Wharf, served by numerous tracks which pass through doors on the north face of the Cantrybedd Mill, a long slab-built building on the right, known locally as Shed Isaf (Lower Shed). In the busy times, several horses were employed here to shunt wagons.

The site is surrounded by bleak mountain flanks and the river, now much smaller, flows out of sight behind rubbish tips to the left, and similar tips loom down from above on the right. The tramway has no option but to rise sharply as the head of the valley is near. Just across the stream to the left is Beudynewydd and to the right of an incline which reaches upwards ahead, was its smaller 'partner', Beudybach, long buried by rubbish. Both these farms were used to lodge Quarry employees.

The tramway, now facing due east and in single track, becomes double line to ascend the next incline, Beudynewydd, and again, it is necessary to cross the much-diminished river at its foot; the incline is built

Cantrybedd level as seen from part-way up the next Incline, Beudynewydd. 1936.

D. COZENS

both with earth and slab to carry it to a height of c. 760 ft., passing over a tributary of the Gwernol *en route*; in latter days most of its flanks were surrounded by rubbish tips. The incline in 710 ft. long with an average slope of 1 in 4.9.

Concentrating on ascending this incline, an important feature might easily be missed for just beyond the end of the Cantrybedd Mill, a tramway curves away and, passing into a short cutting, disappears into the bowels of the hillside. This is the entrance to The Long Tunnel.

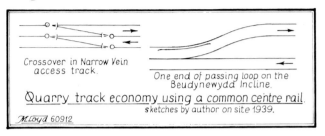

Returning to the route of Beudynewydd Incline, in more recent times a junction was made at about 674 ft. and a tramway led off south-west to enter an adit marked by a water wheel just outside. This is a Broad Vein entrance opened up by Haydn Jones: the wheel was overshot, 18 ft. diameter, and by Williams & White of Aberystwyth.

Meanwhile, at the summit of Beudynewydd, the tramway turns sharply right along the contour, and almost due south. Note how the winding drum is perched away from the track in a niche on the hillside above – a common arrangement in slate quarries where an incline comes up a hill in the shortest steepest manner, only to turn off abruptly and follow the contours on a ledge instead; drumhouses straddling the tracks were the more frequent form, however, but they were erected on a quarry level.

The sweep of Bryneglwys with its attendant mills, hall, and barracks, lies laid out to the right; up to the left the tramway passes some of the Broad Vein

Though taken in 1951, little has changed; L. T. C. Rolt's 'Alvis' makes a fitting foreground to the Haulage & Compressor House with its waterwheel and launder.

J. B. SNELL

Working scenes in the Quarry are virtually non-existent but the overall view of Bryneglwys level shows the Old Mill (bottom left), Barracks (foreground), the Large Magazine or Gunpowder Shed (centre right), Carpenter's Shop (lower right) and Bryneglwys Farm and Hall above the Gunpowder Shed. In the centre distance the workings on the hillside are those of the Broad Vein near the summit of the Beudynewydd Incline.   G. D. BRAITHWAITE

workings. The tram line has now reached 766 ft. a.s.l. and the rough road which comes up from Abergynolwyn has also attained it. Shortly the track sweeps south-westward, crosses the Llaeron on a girder bridge (769 ft.) and passes through a shallow cutting and a gate in a wall to reach the stacking area between the Old and New Mills (The Upper Mill) on the Bryneglwys level. By means of a 'back shunt' a tramway with its ultimate incline (un-named) runs eastwards to serve the workings on the east side of the river Llaeron, which it crosses on its journey.

Back at the Old Mill the gunpowder magazine, served by a siding, will be noted, also the tramway entering The Daylight Adit and the incline coming down from the tips above on the east side of the mill, being the foot of the Boundary Incline, with the 'Short' Incline above it, and even yet another (also un-named) above that again. At the foot of this last one (879 ft.

a.s.l.) a line comes up from the west side of the Old and New Mills; this was built to avoid the Boundary and Short Inclines and comes off sidings in front of (north of) the New Mill: by means of the Cwm Cwm Incline it climbed south-west-south to a contour line and so to reach the short level stretch between the top of Short Incline and the final incline. Many of these internal quarry-like 'junctions' are perhaps somewhat boastfully thus termed, for connection was usually made by wagon turntable for, where tramways intersected on the level, it was often convenient to place a turntable rather than a plain crossing, and so increase the flexibility of operation.

Off to the east of the Boundary Incline, tramways led off to serve the main shaft and, with the growth of rubbish tipping, there have been many similar changes among the access tramways; these may be more easily followed in the diagram on p.32-3.

The village, seen from the head of the Village Incline in 1903. The gated yard at the foot and the tramways setting off across the village are discernible.

H. FAYLE

The Village Incline and gated yard.

COLLECTION E. D. CHAMBERS

The Village Incline & Branch At the point of 7 m. 10 ch. from Wharf and 261 ft. a.s.l. the winding drumhouse for the double tracked Village Incline – which was 363 ft. long and inclined at 1 in 2.58 – stood about 150 ft. above the village itself, and separated from it by the Gwernol. The only connection to the main line was by the 6 ft. diameter turntable at the rear of the house, taking one vehicle at a time. A band brake was provided to control the speed of the drum (with its control handle placed with a good view down the Incline), though by careful balancing of the vehicles passing up and down, it was possible to regulate the pace without excessive need for it. At the Incline foot the tracks passed over the river by a girder bridge, through a double gate and then became single. Thence over a wagon turntable which gave access eastwards to a smithy and yard (complementary to the one at Wharf) wherein coal etc. might be locked.

The other side of the turntable (the west) served the carpenter's yard (formerly a writing slate factory).* There followed a wagon storage loop which was formerly walled-in and had a second pair of gates: next (outside the walling) came a second turntable on the

Under the Village Incline drum house, the essential turntable was the only access to the Incline from The Mineral Line. The tracks crossed each other within the drum house (top right).
G. S. HOOKHAM

* Both sawmill and smithy each had a water wheel.

loop's east side: this led off into a siding which went some distance to the north-east as far as the school. At the far end of the storage loop, a single track passed northward, crossed the village main street on the level, passed the frontage of the Railway Hotel and, by means of a reverse curve, ran along a narrow alley between the backs of two rows of houses, these having their frontages in Llanegryn and Water Streets; tracks on the further side of the level crossing had been lifted by 1945. Here came a third turntable and a short spur ran off as far as Capel Jerusalem at the top of Llanegryn Street. Some of these village lines were on a considerable gradient and provided Young Abergynolwyn with after-school joy rides; perhaps the walled yard to contain stock also helped to prevent this form of gamesmanship? The layout provided an almost door-to-door system; coal could be emptied into backyards and the cess pits of privies emptied through those intriguing little iron doors which caused we towns-children so much perplexity. Empty wagons were man-handled or horse-hauled back to the storage loop. Abergynolwyn was not unique in this private railway system; they existed, for instance, in North-East England, and North and South Wales. Some were of narrow gauge.

The track used on the system was of the same materials as used on the Talyllyn Railway.

The Winding Drumhouses Whilst rollers/drums and their attendant brake gear were common to all the drumhouses, the houses themselves were each different to suit the individual sites they occupied. Each drum was built up using three cast-iron spoked rings; these

Wagons wait patiently in the village yard. 1936.
S. W. BAKER

Along such narrow back alleys as this one, trundled the wagons which collected the 'Night Soil' from this 'Sanitary Village', lifted it onto the Railway and hurried it away elsewhere. By this date, however, village tramways were buried almost out of sight.   AUTHOR

Back in the Quarry again, the drum house at the top of Beudynewydd was, as that at Alltwyllt, set back above the tramway. The long rod to the left works the band brake on the drum.

G. D. BRAITHWAITE

were keyed to a square section rolled wrought iron bar. The outside of the drum was planked longitudinally. At one end, and supported by extensions of the spokes, a segmented iron ring provided the rubbing surface for the handbrake, which was brought into play through suitable linkage by pulling on a long handle. Brakesmen would be positioned at the summit of each incline to operate these brakes and attach etc. wagons to the cable. In later days the train crew had to do this on the Village Incline. The brakesmen were given a small recess in the wall of the drumhouse (where practicable) as a shelter.

The drum had two cables, wound in opposite directions: one cable served each track. It was not possible to balance wagons travelling up and down exactly, and the length of the brake lever gave considerable leverage and braking power when necessary. It was the custom to keep a small pile of slabs etc. at the top of each incline so as to give descending wagons power to overcome the weight of those ascending, and that of the rope itself.

Clearly the use of balanced working on inclines was not always practicable, and a horse was often used to start the 'run', besides other tramway work which included loaded coal wagons making their way along the Galltymoelfre section towards the Quarry. An irresistible account is given by Holmes (p. 91):

'I was on the slates, loading trucks, I was an incline operator they called it, taking the slates down to meet the train. We loaded six or perhaps eight wagons – two of us working together – you needed the horse just to start them moving but once they were going the gradient was enough to keep them moving. The worse thing the horse was doing was taking the empties back again. There were three inclines and we sent the wagons down two by two – two loaded ones going down, two empties coming up. Sometimes there would be coal coming up and the horse would have to haul it up the gradient above the incline.'

Of course this quotation is strictly about working the Galltymoelfre, but other men have spoken of using the horse on this section to assist unbalanced loads on both Alltwyllt and Cantrybedd Inclines.

As regards overbridges on the main line (there were none elsewhere), the basis of size was related to the cab on *Talyllyn* which, of course, did not possess one when the line was built. In accordance with Tyler's Report, there was a vertical clearance of 9 ft. and a horizontal one of 9 ft. 1 in. The exception was the later bridge at Cynfal which was wider.

(Post-1950, the track below School and Hendy bridges has been lowered to suit stock brought in for use on the line since that date.)

The Village Incline was latterly operated by the train crew, but attachment (or) of wagons at its foot was left to the village carpenter, James Davies, or someone else in authority 'who knew about these things'. The

Wagons were attached to the incline cables by a somewhat complicated and ingenious hitch — see drawing on the opposite page.
J. M. LLOYD

There was a second form of hitch, much simpler than the one above. This example was found in the Quarry but its sphere of operation is not recalled.   AUTHOR

Incline equipment declined somewhat in maintenance as the years passed – as did Peter Williams, who, with Hugh Jones as engine crew, was called upon to work it. The trick was to let the wagons run until they passed each other, and then to apply the drum brake, gently at first and more strongly later. Peter Williams was as erratic with the drum brake as he was with the regulator of the steam locomotive. On one occasion he failed to enhance his leverage on the brake, and the up-coming wagon, passing its fellow on the way down, put on speed and shot clear of the top of the Incline and into the drumhouse. Operators all yelled and ran for shelter – and their lives. When it was quiet again, the errant wagon was found swinging from its coupling, upright under the drum.

As the iron ropes which formed the incline cables grew older and more rusted, they lost their 'nature' and became life-expired. The weakest point was where the end of the rope was formed into a loop round a thimble and brought back on itself, secured by heating and given a long riveted collar; it would break there under tension. Incline operators were given slight forewarning by the sudden cessation of movement of an upward-climbing wagon, and those at the incline foot would dash for cover both from the empty wagon(s) going up, and the risk that those coming down might not be held sufficiently by the drum brake. At Alltwyllt, wagons would literally fly off the foot of the Incline, over the top of the storage sidings and leap into the gorge below. There would be a sound akin to a loud explosion as the whole wagon disintegrated, often so violently as to shatter the axles completely. The 'hitch' – that piece of linkage which connected the wagon to the rope – was seldom damaged and would still be down there among the debris with the broken end of the rope attached to it, so the first job was to send a lad down into the valley and poke around among the trees and river bed until the hitch was found. When recovered, the blacksmith would bring the broken rope end to the foot of the incline and build a fire in the open to heat it (there was no portable forge) and so remake the loop with its thimble, open up the collar and try to re-use it again in the repair. Thus the rope grew shorter.

The hitch was contrived from a J-shaped piece of steel attached at one end to the thimble in the rope's loop by a short chain. The other end was secured to the shackle (not the hook) of the wagon coupling by means of a very long split pin device; the split pin prevented the J-piece from leaving the wagon shackle; a means of opening up the split sides and keeping them thus was to force a piece of stone between them and leave it wedged there! The split portion was actually so long that there was no fear of the pin falling from the J-piece. (See diagram opposite).

The slate wagons left here at the foot of Beudynewydd Incline are still hitched to the cable; note the position of the wagon link. AUTHOR

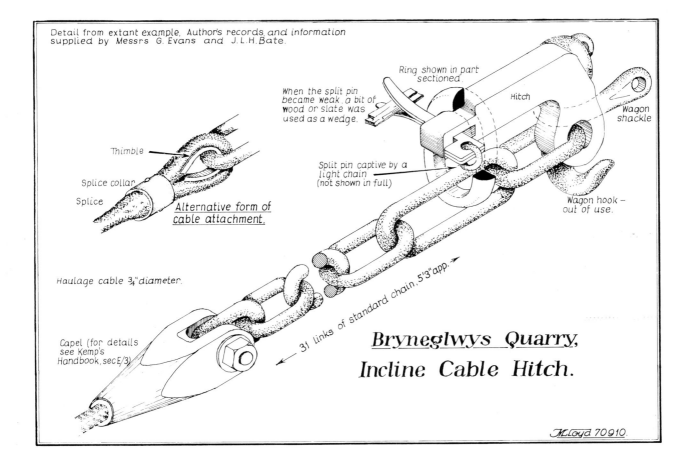

Detail from extant example, Author's records, and information supplied by Messrs G. Evans and J.L.H. Bate.

Ring shown in part sectioned.

Hitch

When the split pin became weak, a bit of wood or slate was used as a wedge.

Wagon shackle

Thimble

Splice collar

Splice

Split pin captive by a light chain (not shown in full)

Wagon hook – out of use.

Alternative form of cable attachment.

Haulage cable 3¼" diameter.

31 links of standard chain, 5'3" app.

Capel (for details see Kemp's Handbook, sec E/3)

Bryneglwys Quarry, Incline Cable Hitch.

M. Lloyd 70910.

TAL-Y-LLYN

RAILWAY.

TIME TABLE

FOR

AUGUST 1ST, 1867,

And until further Notice.

Passengers to ensure being booked should be at the Station five minutes before the time fixed for the departure of the Trains.   The times shown on this Bill are the times at which the Trains are intended to leave and arrive at the several Stations, but the Company cannot guarantee these times being kept under any circumstances, nor will they be responsible for delay.

PASSENGERS' LUGGAGE.—The Company are not responsible unless it is booked and paid for according to its value.   Each Passenger is allowed 60lbs weight of personal Luggage free of charge, the same not being Merchandise.   Any excess above this weight will be charged.

For the protection of their Luggage in the Van, Passengers are requested to have their names and destinations clearly stated upon, and properly fastened to each article.

The Company will not be responsible for any articles left in any of their offices for the convenience of Owners, unless deposited in the Booking Office, and the fixed charge of 2d. per Package paid.

It is requested that all Goods and Parcels be delivered at King's Station, Towyn, *(and not at Pendre Station)*, at least half an hour before the time fixed for starting, so that they may be Booked and Signed for.

UP TRAINS.	a.m.	a.m.	p.m.	DOWN TRAINS.	a.m.	Except on Saturday. p.m.	Saturdays only. p.m.	p.m.
Towyn (Pendre Station)..leave	8.0	11.0	3.45	ABERGYNOLWYN........leave	9.30	12.30	1.30	5.10
Rhydyronen	8.10	11.10	3.55	Dolgoch....................	9.45	12.45	1.45	5.25
Dolgoch....................	8.25	11.25	4.10	Rhydyronen	10.0	1.0	2.0	5.40
ABERGYNOLWYN ...... arrive	8.40	11.40	4.25	Towyn ....arrive	10.10	1.10	2.10	5.50

TAL-Y-LLYN RAILWAY.—This Railway runs up a narrow valley east of Towyn to Abergynolwyn, the privacy of which has been seldom intruded upon, and the inhabitants left unmolested to pursue the noiseless tenor of their way, until the Iron Horse with breath of Steam and Smoke startled with its echoes the quiet ravines.   The scenery is all that can be desired, the mountains on both sides are majestically grand.   The Waterfall and Railway Bridge at Dolgoch are to be seen to advantage, and are objects of romantic beauty, which require the Painter or the Poet's touch to vividly pourtray.   Reaching Abergynolwyn, the Visitor can either pursue his journey to Tal-y-llyn Lake or Caerberllan Castle, called in history *Castell y Bere*.   The latter is most interesting to archæologists, and its architectural features surpass any of the old Welsh Castles, as many fragments have been found amongst the ruins, which have been carefully preserved.   Tal-y-llyn Lake is about two miles distant from Abergynolwyn, and is celebrated for its Trout fishing.   The lake is 1¼ mile in length, ⅓ mile in breadth, and 3 miles in circumference.   This Lake fills the head of the Valley, with the exception of a road on each side.   The Scenery from its position at the Southern base of Cader Idris is strikingly romantic, at the upper end the hills almost meet, and present a rugged aspect, and are broken into numberless crags, of which some are vertical and sharply pointed, but the greater part project horizontally and impend with threating gloom over the vale beneath.   Cader Idris can easily be ascended from Tal-y-llyn, and the neighbourhood abounds with rich and numberless objects of romantic beauty, including mountains of different forms and elevations, valleys, lakes, &c., which combined form a picturesque and diversified landscape, rarely excelled for richness and variety.

N.B.—Trains do not run on Sunday.

BY ORDER.

PRINTED BY D. EDWARDS, "ST. CADVAN'S OFFICE," CORBET SQUARE, TOWYN.

CHAPTER SIX
OPERATING THE RAILWAY

CONCERNING Towyn, Black's *Picturesque Guide Through Wales* published in 1860 has this to say:

'... is a small town, situated near the mouth of the Dysynni. The mountains in the neighbourhood are lofty and noble and the roads to Tal-y-Llyn, Dolgelley and Machynlleth pass through much grand and beautiful scenery. The beach, which is nearly one mile distant, consists of remarkably hard, smooth sand, extending nearly five miles, favourable for bathing, walking and riding. Great numbers of country people resort to these sands for bathing. The church, dedicated to St. Cadfan ... A small but picturesque waterfall may be seen at Dolgoch. At about a mile from the town is Ynys-y-Maengwyn, the noble mansion of the family of Corbet, now unoccupied ... the celebrated fishing lake Tal-y-Llyn is within reach ...'

Baddeley's *Thorough Guide* of 1895 thought the place:

'... a well-built little town greatly improved of late years, and possessed of a well-earned reputation for healthiness. As a seaside resort its weakness is that from the town the sea, $\frac{3}{4}$ m. distant, is hardly if at all visible, while the number of lodging houses overlooking the water, though increasing, is very limited ... A fine promenade and carriage-drive extends along (the beach) ... There is no shelter for boats ... for boating you must repair to Aberdovey or to landlocked Dysynni. Lodgings are comparatively cheap.'

The map in the *Guide* shows clearly the old trackway from Bryneglwys Quarries over the ridge and down to both Machynlleth and Pennal. Once again a footnote confirms that passenger trains started from Pendre:

'N.B. The station for the narrow-gauge line to Abergynolwyn is at the east end of the town, $\frac{3}{4}$ mile from the Cambrian Station.'

In another section of the same *Guide* the journey is made westward:

'... to Abergynolwyn. Here the main valley strikes away to the right, but it is only a few yards ascent to another which forms a direct continuation of the one we have been descending. ABERGYNOLWYN STATION is 10 minutes' walk beyond the village, and from it Towyn is reached by a gradual descent of 7 miles. The line affords peeps of one or two pretty waterfalls on the left. Its passenger terminus is nearly a mile from the Cambrian station of the same name.'

In these days this would certainly be found 'off-putting' but the Victorians were made of sterner stuff! The 1915 edition of the same *Guide* emphasised the Talyllyn Railway as running between Pendre and Abergynolwyn only and by means of a bold black line on the map. Nothing whatsover was shown to indicate a railway east of Abergynolwyn and the Pendre – Wharf section is shown in a delicate hatched manner, implying 'goods only'! The section headed TOWYN has an unfortunate opening sentence: 'TOWYN (rhymes with "Cow-in").' The later edition tells of four passenger trains a day '(and an extra early one on Mondays 6 a.m.)'. The morning train was 'generally 9.25'. The

last reference to the line recommends it only to 'save uninteresting miles of walking' and 'hitherto the last train to Towyn has left about 4.30 (later Fri. and Sat.)'

So much for the flavour of the old guide books! More recent ones have been kinder.

The timetable poster for 1st August 1867 had the rather nice footnote:

'This railway runs up a narrow valley east of Towyn to Abergynolwyn, the privacy of which has seldom been intruded upon, and the inhabitants left unmolested to pursue the noiseless tenor of their way, until the Iron Horse with breath of Steam and Smoke startled with its echoes, the quiet ravines. The scenery is all that could be desired, the mountains on both sides are majestically grand. The Waterfall and Railway Bridge at Dolgoch are to be seen to advantage, and are objects of romantic beauty, which require the Painter or Poet's touch to vividly portray. Reaching Abergynolwyn, the Visitor can either pursue his journey to Tal-y-Llyn Lake or Caerberllan Castle, called in history Castell y Bere. The latter is most interesting to archaeologists, and its architectural features surpass any of the old Welsh Castles, as many fragments have been found amongst the ruins, which have been carefully preserved. Tal-y-Llyn Lake is about 2 miles distant from Abergynolwyn, and is celebrated for its Trout fishing. The lake is $1\frac{1}{4}$ miles in length, $\frac{1}{2}$ mile in breadth and 5 miles in circumference. The Lake fills the head of the Valley, except for a road on each side. The Scenery from its position at the Southern base of Cader Idris is strikingly romantic, at the upper end the hills almost meet, and present a rugged aspect, and are broken into numberless crags, of which some are vertical and sharply pointed, but the greater part project horizontally and impend with threatening gloom over the vale beneath. Cader Idris can easily be ascended from Tal-y-Llyn and the neighbourhood abounds in rich and numberless objects of romantic beauty, including mountains of different forms and elevations, valleys, lakes etc. which combined formed a picturesque and diversified landscape, rarely excelled for richness and variety.
N.B. Trains do not run on Sunday.'

Whew!

The *Gossiping Guide* for 1881, (published in Oswestry and widely used) had added the Railway to its pages:

'A 2 ft. 6 ins. gauge railroad now runs from Towyn to Abergynolwyn which, though made chiefly for the conveyance of slates, accommodates passengers as well. Tourists wishing to enjoy a day at Talyllyn can travel the greater part of the distance by rail ... if he is lazy he will probably find a donkey cart plying for hire at the station.'

As to Towyn itself ...

'... perhaps of all the watering places in Wales, Towyn is likely to become the most popular with the large class who want to take their families for a fortnight to the sea at moderate cost ... there are bathing machines ...'

How these guides extolled such destinations ... how they coerced, cajoled, comforted in order to assure the visitor that the most outrageous pastime was as cosy as taking a stroll in the roadway back at home – for confidence in untried pursuits had to be won among a great population for whom even one night away from home was the height of adventure! No less were the exploits which they were enticed to sample: horse-riding, carriage driving, journeys by horse bus, sails on river steamers, the promise of a pier – not to say tennis, bowls, golf – the list was endless and Towyn could provide them all. Further, it had that extra feature, a railway

'of Toy Gauge – a little wider than the Festiniog ... three passenger trains a day save some seven miles of tiresome walking or hiring ... Except for here and there a pretty streamlet tumbling down from the hills on the right, as at Dolgoch, and the summit of Cader, seen on the left, there is nothing noteworthy during the railway journey, or at Abergynolwyn itself, which is simply a straggling collection of quarrymen's houses ...'

so wrote *The Thorough Guide to North Wales* in 1895, one of the few which did not extol all it saw.

One of the earliest informed railway travellers wrote of his findings at the turn of the century; before that time accounts were usually whimsical or tending to the vacuous. Harold Fayle, then a student at Owen's College, Manchester (later the University), writing in 1904 had made comment on the availability of booking tickets on the train or otherwise, and says:

'... the Wharf station is used for goods traffic, but passengers are permitted to join the train here on the Up journey, obtaining their tickets at Pendre station, as there is no booking office at the Wharf.'

Fayle goes on to stress the unpretentious nature of the Towyn stations and the fourfold duties of R. B. Yates; he probably overlooked that at that time Yates was also running the Registered Office of the Quarry Company, but accurately described the Wharf as the place where Yates had his 'offices', continuing: 'but beyond this there is no other accommodation.'

He confirms the then-existence of the booking office and waiting room at Pendre and entirely misses the point as to why the carriage doors open only on one side:

'... as never more than one train is on the line at once, the carriage doors are only made to open on one side.'

At this time too, the guard performed the work of guard, porter, ticket collector and booking clerk at each station. The engine ex-*Dolgoch* was then carrying the name *Pretoria*.

'... she was receiving a fresh coat of paint as the British army was entering Pretoria, she was re-named PRETORIA in honour of the event.'

As to the make-up of the train, Fayle comments:

'usually consists of two carriages and a brake van and about a dozen empty wagons on the Up journey, unless it be that a few wagons are filled with coal; on the Down journey most of the wagons are filled with slates. Through the courtesy of Mr. Yates the author was permitted to make the journey in one of the empty slate wagons, and the experience was a novel one.'

The journey as described leans heavily on the current guide books, as the Towyn water supply, old Bryn Castell Farm with mound and watchtower, not forgetting 'the most powerful chalybeate springs within the United Kingdom' faithfully receive mention, also remembering the 'old Welsh woollen mills at Brynglas, the trout stream and ravine at Dolgoch affording fair sport ... and the old disused slate mines are also worth a visit'. Fayle clearly thought of Abergynolwyn station as most convenient for Talyllyn Lake and ascending Cader Idris – emphasised as the most southerly of the ancient extinct Welsh volcanoes, now stripped to their roots – and obviously quoting once more from his ever-informative Guide Book:

'Cars meet the trains during the season and convey passengers to and from the lake at 1/– single and 1/6d. return; the traveller can, however, return by means of the Corris Railway by driving 4½ miles from Talyllyn to Corris station ... the latter is the route taken by most tourists and four-horse brakes ply regularly during the season.'

Oddly, Fayle comments that round tickets were only available via Corris to Abergynolwyn and not vice versa; clearly the enterprise was Corris Railway inspired! The wagons of coal on his train were lowered down the Village Incline and Fayle inspected the three

'self-acting inclines the trucks are worked by horses between the bottoms of the inclines ... The scenery around here is magnificent and the quarries themselves are worth a visit. Unfortunately time did not permit of the author looking over them as in order to do so the visitor must travel up by the first train from Towyn at 9.30 a.m. and cannot get back until 5.15 p.m. The passenger traffic is as yet very small and for the greater part of the year two trains in each direction amply suffice ... This summer, Mr. Yates has been putting on two extra trains running during August and September only, leaving Towyn at 1.30 and 5.45 p.m., and Abergynolwyn at 2.15 and 6.30 p.m. There are no Sunday trains.
Single tickets only are issued; a third class ticket from Towyn to Abergynolwyn costs 6½d; the third class tickets are coloured purple and the second class green.'

The change in the Company's attitude towards passengers joining the Talyllyn train at Towyn was already seeping into publicity before 1910 was over; we read:

'The Towyn Station (Pen-dre) is at the other end of the town from the Cambrian railway, but the trains can also be joined at a siding, which is much nearer, and for which we turn to the right on leaving the Cambrian station.'

Recommended was the Bryn Castell hill-top fortress by leaving the train at Rhydyronen, the waterfalls from Dolgoch station ('property bequeathed by the late Mr. R. J. Roberts to the people of Towyn') and for the hardy:

'The walk from Abergynolwyn to TALYLLYN LAKE is three miles ... A public conveyance may perhaps be found in the summer meeting the trains at Abergynolwyn and conveyances run between Tal-y-Llyn and Corris in connection with the Corris Railway. It is a delightful round to go to Corris and return by the railway to Towyn. The walking distance from Abergynolwyn to Corris is 7 miles.'

Emphasis usually alights on the same landmarks but the 17th century manor house of Dolaugwyn and the standing stone at Croes-Faen where the old coast

'The Grand Tour' passes Talyllyn Lake en route for Abergynolwyn. 'I remember standing at the end of Talyllyn Lake in 1912 . . . and seeing horse-drawn carts and charabancs slowly moving down towards the Lake . . .'   F. FRITH & CO.

road turns shyly behind the town of Towyn, are among items often overlooked, whilst Bird Rock, Llanfihangel-y-Pennant, Castell-y-Bere feature frequently. Ynysymaengwyn is usually well described with its 18th century 'Hanoverian' entrance front to the east sandwiched between two wings of Elizabethan character. There was a garden front to the west, 'reminding one of an old French Chateau'.*

The attractive mountain slopes to the south of the Talyllyn Railway were largely overlooked by the greater attractions of Cader Idris and we may wonder how many travellers on the Railway actually were *en route* for the summit in those – or in present – times? However,

> '. . . some fine mountain walks can be enjoyed on the range lying to the east of the Tal-y-Llyn Railway. To climb the highest summit TAREN-y-GESAIL in Abergynolwyn take the road on the right and ascend until you pass some slate works on the road. The summit for which you are bound is on the left . . . and so reach the cairn 2,187 ft. – 1½ hour from Abergynolwyn.'

* Now all of this is razed to the ground. Athelstan Corbet was the last of his line to occupy the house; the following line of Corbetts was not descended from him. The difference in spelling is clear. In 1935 Ynysymaengwyn's owner was Roger J. Corbett 'the son of Towyn's benefactor'.

The account recommends extending the walk by following the ridge and returning down to Brynglas station; this would be quite an exercise if the train was used from Towyn, having in mind the usual timetable, but by using the Quarrymen's Train on a Monday it could be done.

The 1935 *Ward Lock Guide* continues to recommend the Railway to reach Abergynolwyn:

> 'the village from which ascents of Cader Idris may be commenced [shades of the Himalayan Base Camp] . . . The terminus is Pendre . . . but is a siding [The Wharf] where passengers are allowed to join the train. The trains are not very frequent but . . . allows return journey to be made in the same morning or afternoon if a prolonged stay is not desired.'

If in our own generation we have remembered the Railway as a remarkable survivor from earlier days and ways, how much more surprising is that a visitor in 1913 found it even then to be so non-conformist:

> '. . . we advise a visit to the little narrow-gauge Tal-y-Llyn Railway . . . to see what our railways were like 45 years ago . . . line was constructed in 1866 and was no doubt built in accordance with the standard practice of that time, being modified to meet the requirements of a 2 ft. 3 ins. gauge railway . . . unfitted with continuous break the pigmy goods trucks are coupled by means of a D-link, and when trucks have to be coupled to a passenger coach a spare long link is made use of to effect connection . . . TALYLLYN was recently working the whole of the traffic as

DOLGOCH, the other locomotive (0–4–0 rear tank) was at the makers for a thorough overhaul . . .

> . . . the passenger rolling stock consists of a 4-wheel second class carriage with three compartments, body measures about 5 ft. wide, 13 ft. long and 5 ft. 6 ins. high. The seats are stuffed, as is also a portion of the back, just where the shoulders touch it; the partitions between the compartments are carried up about halfway between the seat and the roof.'

(It was in those times not common to find anything but complete partitions between compartments, from floor to roof. Present day 'open carriages' are a reversion to earliest practices.) Continuing:

> 'There is a three compartment third class coach of approx. similar dimensions, the seats of which are not stuffed. This coach had larger wheels than the others; they project through the floors, but are boxed in similar to some of the coaches running on the Great Western Railway twenty years ago. The composite coach has three compartments – two thirds at the end and a second class compartment in the centre. The accommodation on the railway is second and third class only. The guard's break is the most interesting vehicle, as it is also the booking office. The break portion has sliding doors; one end is partitioned off, and entered by means of a door in the partition. This portion is the booking office. The projecting wing on the platform side of the vehicle has a rather small aperture with half-circular top of regulation Booking Office type, and is lettered 'Booking Office' on the outside of the vehicle. At the intermediate stations the guard stands within the travelling 'booking office' and issues tickets to the passengers, who pay their money and receive tickets through the window.
> 'The guard is provided with printed tickets and a regulation dating press.'
> 'The major portion is a light blue colour the part on the left of the dotted line is white. The train usually starts from the wharf adjoining the Cambrian Railways at Towyn . . . the guard issues tickets at the Booking Office here, as he also does at Abergynolwyn the other terminus . . . As the termini are 'open' stations, the guard collects the tickets at the previous station; he also collects tickets from passengers as they leave the train at intermediate stations . . . difference from standard practice is that the guard nodded to the engine-driver as the right-away signal instead of using a flag or whistle . . .
> '. . . There is a break on the wheels of the guard's van, actuated by a horizontal bar with a handle at top and screw gear at the bottom; the break is outside the end of the van . . . actuated through the window.
> 'The trucks are quite small and inside the wheels, so are about 2 ft. wide and 6 ft. long; they are provided with a lever break on one side, which operates on the wheels of both axles . . .
> '. . . line is continued . . . to the slate quarries; on this section are two inclined planes at right-angles to the railway, connection being made by turntables. Although the railway is single, the planes have double lines. At their foot are villages inhabited by the quarrymen, and we were told the inclines were built to supply the villages with coal which is brought up from Towyn in the small trucks. These trucks have a wire rope attached to them when descending the inclines . . . The railway is in a cutting on embankments etc. and is properly fenced (with slates) and has hedges . . . The tanks for supplying the locomotive obtain their water from streams let into them, the water overflowing and rejoining the stream, much in the same fashion as mill streams, only on a much smaller scale.'

The odd feature of this pleasant (though in places inaccurate) account, is that it is clear that the author saw no slate traffic and he does not mention clearly that the Railway was built for that purpose; it was perhaps of insufficient prominence as to have been overlooked! It might be that work at the Quarry had been temporarily suspended? The date of the child's half-fare third class ticket (Brynglas to Rhydyronen) is 1st September 1913 (Ticket No. 59).

Commenting on railways which had been hard-hit by the First World War, and respecting those which only had two trains per day, a correspondent writes (incorrectly, incidentally):

> 'Another Welsh line contributes $6\frac{1}{2}$ miles to the total of the 'two-train' lines . . . the Talyllyn Railway . . . narrow-gauge tracks are run up against those of the standard-gauge system to facilitate the transhipment of the immense quantities of slate brought down from the . . . quarries . . . The headquarters of this railway are at Pendref station . . . and this is the terminating point of all passenger trains coming down from Abergynolwyn.'

A visitor the previous year (1916) refers to a visit to Towyn:

> '. . . a growing seaside resort with a resident populaton of about 2,000 . . . a favourite resort for golfers . . .'

Naturally the Talyllyn Railway is

> 'a "toy" line . . . to a mining village . . . after leaving Towyn . . . crosses the low-lying valley and strikes the mountains on the south side of the river, continuing thence on high ground the whole of the distance. Originally constructed for slate and mineral traffic, but some years ago was adapted for passengers . . . The locomotives and rolling stock are of the usual type used on toy railways.'

In the summer of 1925 two well-known names went to the Railway and set down their account; Messrs. H. G. W. Household and Oscar Elsdon. Like all preceding articles, the authors' visit was fairly brief and they probably never climbed above the foot of Alltwyllt Incline due to the time factor; at the time Bryneglwys Quarry was employing 160 men (the short post-war boom was ending) and we read that a motor charabanc did the journey to the lake and back between trains. Presumably this waited at the foot of the lane leading to Abergynolwyn station? Some nice descriptions include:

> '. . . The permanent way seems to be more or less heterogeneous, rails of Vignoles, Bridge and Bull-head sections being laid, the first and last of about 40 lbs. per yard . . . only one engine is allowed to work at once . . . speed is limited to 10 m.p.h. . . . The journey takes about 35 minutes, including stops. A shuttle service suffices to work the railway, so there are no passing places, the track being single throughout . . . trucks conveying the slate are brought down on the passenger train.'

Emphasis is placed on Wharf having a waiting shed but no platform.

> 'Almost all trains arrive and depart from this station as Pendref, the main station of the Company, is at the other end of the town of Towyn. Pendref station has a waiting shed, booking office and platform, and here the offices of the Company, the locomotive and carriage sheds and repair sheds are situated.'

Even in the 1920s the Railway was bounded by hedges which had grown wildly to the detriment of any passenger catching much more than passing images between them; this was an early problem when the Preservation Society came onto the scene. Fayle comments on the line 'running between thick and high

TALYLLYN has drawn up at Abergynolwyn; at this time it carried a 'dished' smokebox door. August 1925.   H. G. W. HOUSEHOLD

hedges', and buying tickets at intermediate stations through 'a pigeon-hole window in the guard's van'. Clearly Dolgoch viaduct was too much of a passing feature for he describes it as 'a steel bridge'. Beyond Abergynolwyn:

'... the line to the slate quarries, very picturesque all the way, continues winding along the side of the valley through the woods to a point ... near where the bottom of the first incline there is a waterfall in a deep and narrow gorge into which more than once, runaway trucks from the incline have crashed!'

Of the carriage colours he says '... recently been smartly painted crimson with yellow lining and lettering' and by this date the second class had become first for in contrast with the third's 'plain wooden seats ... the first class have a blue covering.* [The *Locomotive Magazine* 7/1920 says 'now painted in bright vermilion with yellow lining and "Talyllyn Railway Company" in gilt letters along the cornices.'†]

Regarding the mineral wagons:

'... mainly four-wheeled open-sided slate wagons, with a few ordinary open trucks for coal etc. A small cattle wagon to carry sheep was also seen by the writer at Pendre station'.

---

* Later it became fawn.
† Clearly Middleton's recent work!

(This last remark removes room for speculation!)

A wartime journey in 1944

'Found the line extremely busy. During the summer a passenger train made the return journey over the line twice on Wednesdays and Fridays ... on this day ... reached the Pendref station ... already full which was not surprising as the formation of no more than one passenger coach and two open wagons, both filled with passengers ... additional accommodation was provided by the attachment of two further wagons, each thoughtfully lined with straw. The driver then opened the booking office and issued tickets to all but a few faint-hearted tourists who decided that this alfresco type of transport was not in their line. Conversation with the driver revealed that five or six coaches stored at Towyn could not be used for strengthening the train, as their weight would be too much for his engine; the real reason was probably that of excessive weight in relation to the brake power, as no continuous brake is in use. The characteristic rolling and pitching on the narrow gauge ... gave the 'outside' passengers the usual occasional alarms ... the coach which is provided with springs, presents the spectacle of 'a small boat riding at anchor on choppy water' but the wagons, with no springs, merely jolt the passengers. The first class coach still retains its bright red livery ... no other locomotive than the green-painted *Dolgoch* was seen on the journey.'

The foregoing comprise some of the major descriptions of the line which have come under notice; they cover the 1890s to 1920s interval and enjoy certain common features. None of the travellers was entirely correct in his facts; few received the impression that this was a slate-carrying railway with passenger over-tones – rather that it was a little-known passenger carrying railway with mineral traffic undertones. Each writer had noticed certain features such as the absence of doors on one side of the carriages, platforms to the north side and the issue of tickets from the van; most had noted the availability of transport from Abergynolwyn to the Lake, but none wrote as if they had sampled it (nor the onward journey to Corris). Whatever their individual impressions, one factor emerges in them all – the Railway was a singular insti-tution and the journey made sufficient irrepressible impression that they were impelled to record their experience on paper. Similar journeys on other Welsh narrow gauge railways (for instance the North Wales Narrow Gauge, Festiniog or Corris lines) were fre-quently chronicled but accounts of Talyllyn journeys are comparatively rare; the few imply that it struck a chord within the writer because of its unsophisticated qualities.

Now to say something of timetables, trains and oper-ation of the line. The exploration of what appears to be the timetables of a simple, short railway less than eight miles in length soon leads into a labyrinth of circumstance and conditions, perhaps only suggested by the essential footnotes which appeared on its every public timetable – 'Does not run when any stoppage occurs at Bryneglwys Quarries', or 'Passengers may join the train at King's station five minutes earlier than the times shown for Pendref', and so on. No wonder timetables are not favourite reading and more people are put off railway travel by them than has ever been discovered – so much for exploration! Pity the just-come visitor, taking an evening stroll and arriving at King's station hopeful of a train by which to enjoy a holiday journey on the morrow, desperately searching for someone to inform him if in fact this *is* King's station (for there is no nameboard) and if by some unseen means, news has yet reached Towyn that there is/is not a stoppage at Bryneglwys Quarry – wherever that may be? And why should Bryneglwys Quarry apparently have some controlling influence on the first train on a Monday and the last on a Friday . . . Friday, the very day he wished to enjoy a journey . . .? And so on.

The cult of timetable study is a peculiar pastime and not given to most who have read thus far, but like the Talyllyn Railway in general, the Company's table of train times gave a respectable face to an institution which became more bizarre as the years passed by, and the chapter of mishaps and the ends to which the Company was put in order to honour a timetable which its equipment became less able to perform, is a story in itself. Firstly, to underline that public trains were of secondary importance. Attached to them were the

loaded slate (or) wagons which were hung on the rear of Down (Towyn-bound) trains, or the empty slate – plus any loaded goods wagons engaged in business for places up the line towards the Quarry – which were hooked onto the back of Up (literally) trains returning to the Quarry. These loaded wagons carried the main-stay of the Company's business; they conveyed Quarry products beyond Pendre, the Towyn terminus of pas-senger trains, and ended up at the slate wharf there. Similarly, empty slate and loaded merchandise wagons continued eastwards beyond Abergynolwyn where passenger trains terminated and where the carriages were left in splendid isolation whilst their locomotive continued about its business over the remainder of the line! It must have been quite confusing to the intelligent passenger experienced only in main line travel.

Then there was the subtle difference of times between winter and summer, for virtually all the time the Railway provided public trains, the basic pattern was for a departure at a comfortable hour in the morning bound for Abergynolwyn, returning to Towyn before lunch. The same rake of carriages would trundle once more eastwards after lunch, and return in good time for tea. Obscured by these cosy times, which gave those starting from Towyn a fair oppor-tunity to enjoy an outing in the Abergynolwyn district, but little opportunity for Abergynolwyn people (who did not much need it anyway) to savour the delights of Towyn, was the slate train requirement. Looked at more closely, one may follow the hours of a typical Monday–Friday weekday (Saturday was not a working day in the Quarry and Sunday, railway-wise, was a *dies non est*) starting with the departure of empty slate wagons behind the first passenger train from Pendre, the emptied slate wagons having been brought up by the engine after taking the loaded down to King's on the previous evening. On arrival at Abergynolwyn and detaching, the engine would run forward and then back down the loop to pick up the wagons, so pro-pelling them out of sight up The Mineral Line to the consternation of many passengers who perceived they were being abandoned in a foreign land.

The engine would frequently take water at Ty Dwr – as this was preferred to the Pendre supply – and if required, the crew would interrupt their journey to work any wagons up or down the Village Incline. This done, they would proceed to the sorting sidings at the foot of Alltwyllt Incline and the engine would propel the wagons, one or more at a time, to the foot to be attached to the rope, the number depending on the balancing rake coming, loaded, down the Incline. Often, this work, time allowing, had been done by men before the train arrived, but this was in the days of plenty when men other than the train crew were sent

Prominent beside the line out of the engine shed at Pendre lie piles of coal and clinker. PRETORIA approaches with a mixed train whilst a well-dressed gentlemen (R. B. Yates?) looks on. One of the Gunpowder Vans stands in the loop c.1911.   G. M. PERKINS

down from the Quarry to the sidings to prepare the wagons into trains. (It is Hugh Jones' boast he had driven an engine further along the Railway than anyone else. The problem of coupling a wagon onto the shortened rope – due to repaired breakages – at Alltwyllt was the cause. He would drive the locomotive up the foot of the Incline to achieve this but the brake gear would jam on the rails at the rear of the engine and he had to lift it with jacks and release it a bit at a time!)

So in due course anxious passengers would heave a sigh of relief as the engine hove into sight (replenished with water at some stage), leave its wagons in the passing loop and drop back onto the carriages. The 'right away' would prove not to be exactly just that, for the train would stop beyond the Abergynolwyn loop and set back onto the wagons before the whole equipage departed for Towyn; 35–70 minutes was allowed for the Abergynolwyn – Alltwyllt – Abergynolwyn performance, sans passengers.

Arriving at Pendre, the coaches would be put into the loop and then, leading the wagons, the engine would slip down into King's, stop before the road bridge and push the wagons up into the gravity siding after which they could roll into the Wharf sidings to the convenience of the slate loaders. Picking up the

empties, the engine would propel them to Pendre, ready to pick up on the next passenger train. So the day passed, and so to bed.

All this was relatively nice and simple, but to the unwary would-be passenger the issue was not as easy, for in the spacious days and in high season, the time-table for July–September 1909 would be typical of his consternation. What appeared to be a choice of six Up trains and even seven Down trains ('NB No Sunday trains,' in heavy type) was, footnotes being interpreted, such that his optimism might turn to despair as he read:

'+	These trains will not run when any stoppage occurs at Bryneglwys Quarries.
Mo	Mondays only.
S	Saturdays only.
D	Does not run on Saturdays.
C	Daily from July 12 to September 18 inclusive.
A	Thursdays only during July: daily except Saturdays during August and to September 17.
B	Saturdays only during July, August and to September 18 inclusive.

Passengers can get into trains marked thus X at the Slate Wharf Station, providing they are there 5 minutes before the above times. The times shown are the times of departure from Pendre Station.'

The above appears on a little pink folding card vest pocket-size timetable, the inside of which has a brief guide to the railway. It was published at a time when

An Up train chuffs out of Dolgoch with passengers and workmen in the wagons at the rear. The last wagon carries a gate in a 2·3 plank open wagon. The rhododendrons are kept in check and there is a sturdy rustic fence. 1923.

B. EDGINGTON

It was the custom to slide planks between side members of slate wagons to provide seats for the 'overflow'; however, in this prospect, school benches seem to have been brought in to do that duty. Pendre in the early 1930s.   E. D. CHAMBERS

the slate trade was winding down but holiday traffic was becoming more important to the business; McConnel was coming to the end of his lease and within months there would be no slate trains at all. When McConnel quit the Quarry, only passenger trains were run until Haydn Jones began to work slate again.

So over the years the backbone of the timetable was for two published public passenger workings, one outward and returning before lunchtime and another similar return working in the afternoon. This required the use of one steam locomotive which was as laid down in the Board of Trade instructions. In practice most of such trains would run – as just described – 'mixed' with wagons attached to the rear. Over and above this basic skeleton, extra trains were run for quarrymen or workmen (both titles have been used) to suit the months and hours of the Quarry pay system; these workings involved early morning trains on Mondays and early afternoon workings on Saturdays until 1889 when Saturday Quarry work ceased and the train ran on Friday evenings: the public could use these trains – 'subject to stoppages etc.'! There were no special vehicles for the quarrymen as on some other Welsh lines.

In summer the Company would add extra trains to cope with holiday traffic; assuming intending passengers could make something of the footnotes, it could be established that trains ran thrice daily to and from Abergynolwyn, again using but the one engine and the available carriages. Such days were heavy work for the train crew and guard; 'while we were waiting for the train the driver and fireman pushed the coaches along the line and then backed the engine ... and coupled it to the carriages'. (This was at Pendre.) In peak times the Company's carriage stock was insufficient to carry all those offering, and passengers were not discouraged from travelling up the line in a rake of empty wagons (temporarily removed from Quarry duties) standing in the siding nearest the office – the usual practice – and Edward Thomas would suggest that adventurous passengers could use them. When the empty stock came down from Pendre, they were often full already! The management thoughtfully provided planks which slid between the side slats of the slate wagons, for them to sit on. The matter of safety and what would happen if anyone reported this highly irregular practice to the Board of Trade was a risk the Company was quite happy to take. Similarly, the passengers, tempted by this unusual mode of

The first wagon is loaded with sacks; in the second passengers seem to be sitting on the floor and in the third, on the side rails. 'We mostly (from 1912) went to Dolgoch to see the falls and pick the bilberries high up there year after year . . . always stayed in Towyn for a week in 'Apartments' and a week on a farm at Llanegryn . . . there was always a few slate trucks available at the end of the train . . . a doubtful privilege'. 1919.
C. P. BAINES

travel, loved it – but only on fine days. This sort of informality caused the same people to come back to enjoy a journey over Talyllyn metals, year after year. Occasionally empty stock had to be propelled from Towyn to Dolgoch (where most people detrained) to collect those who had been unable to find accommodation in the last down train.

> 'Our usual load for a winter train before the First War was with one passenger coach and about thirty drams but at holiday times we would have all the coaches on, with twenty drams behind – not empty but brimming with passengers, about twelve people in each. One day we counted about 400 on the train as we left Dolgoch for the last return to Towyn.'

The Company met this problem quite easily; the slate trade being ever less plentiful, a number of slate wagons became superfluous for the traffic and these were kept in fair repair and clean, and used solely for the summer 'overflow' business, and attached to the rear of trains in both directions. It was a popular facility.

> 'Conveyances are always in attendance at Abergynolwyn station to take passengers, returning in time for the trains . . .'

says *Darlingtons Handbook Advertiser 1895*, but if they failed to do so then there was always a gravity wagon which 'happened to be there', in the short siding at Abergynolwyn. Incidentally, if a doctor was needed urgently in the village, he would be sent for by sending someone down in a wagon to Towyn.

That side of the business which allowed visitors to remain behind after the last Down train had left Abergynolwyn by keeping ('by chance' or as Company policy) the odd wagon in the small siding there, so that they might gravitate back to Towyn in their own time (in a strong headwind, this was almost impossible) must, in terms of the Railway's safety, have been highly risky; although the Company did not disapprove of the habit, and made an appropriate charge for the wagon, the scheme was 'undercut' by guard Jacob Rowlands who made his own private arrangements to hire out such wagons, making himself a nice sideline. The last such official journey in the Train Book is 29th June 1942 'Miss Evans, by wagon, from Abergynolwyn: 7 @ 6d.' In practice, not all the line was suited to downhill running, and though such wagons were oiled more frequently than usual(!), there were several cases of the first Up train the next day meeting a solitary unattended wagon between stations; its earlier occupants having become tired of pushing and had made their own way home across the fields. Poachers also took these wagons to shoot what they could *en route* and some 'sportsmen' found it amusing to fire from a moving wagon.

As a result of the timetable being based on Towyn and linked, of course, to alterations in the Cambrian timetable, passenger traffic was expected (and did of course) originate there, whilst those who wished to go down to Towyn from Abergynolwyn and return were naturally at some disadvantage. However, it was this village which created almost all the special trains which were yet another category of business and will be described later.

The early days of the Workmen's/Quarrymen's Trains are obscure: the working first appears in *Bradshaw's* Timetable in the mid-1870s. There would appear to be no call for it in early times as a survey of the Census Returns shows there were virtually no quarrymen living outside the Abergynolwyn area such as would require transport from the Towyn direction, but by 1881 almost 20 persons employed in the slate quarries were living in Towyn and Bryncrug.

It has not proved possible to obtain many details of the working before World War I; departure times

A lone gravity-waggoning party halts (perhaps for further strength?) for a snapshot to record the unusual experience.
                                                    DR. N. A. MOULSON

included 5.40 a.m. (June 1913) and 6.30 a.m. at times during 1916–18. Usually it was 6 a.m. After then, this Monday and Friday train began and ended its journey at Pendre, whilst certain other 'passenger' workings used Wharf. This fact may not agree with the reference in *Bradshaw* but the Talyllyn Railway was ever a nonconformist! At the month end, (and after 1899) when the Quarry closed and stocks were taken, and Bargains made therein between men and management, the train returned to Pendre early on a Friday afternoon. At times this would form an extra working. As recalled on p. 15, the Quarry had worked a five-day week since 1889 and was well in advance of its day when compared with Saturday Workmen's Trains such as ran on the Penrhyn and Padarn Railways! Odd return workings include Wednesdays in May and June 1909 and Thursday in July 1909, probably due to short-time being worked in the Quarry. It must also be emphasised that Monday and Friday Workmen's Trains ran in connection with a 'balancing traffic' of schoolchildren which again seems to have been a feature peculiar to the Talyllyn.

There must have been several eras of the Workmen's Train. Vignes (p. 118) refers to it, saying the quarrymen are 'carried almost exclusively in open slate or coal wagons'; his book was published in 1878. Does this suggest that wagons formed the customary train but that carriages might be added if numbers increased? Certainly from the year when the train was put into the public timetable, proper carriages would have to be available for public use, even if workmen used them or goods stock. Vignes' remark may imply that there had been a train dating back to an earlier date and, being composed of goods stock, it was not advertised in the public timetable; however, the contemporary Census Returns mentioned do not encourage this line of thought.

The Workmen's Train remained of almost constant composition during the time of Haydn Jones' ownership. It was simply the customary form of mixed train having sufficient coaches to carry back the schoolchildren, and enough empty wagons at the rear to carry the men. As far as Abergynolwyn the men rode in the coaches and only then transferred to the slate wagons to travel along The Mineral Line, crowding into them if necessary; the number of wagons dropped to four when, following World War I, only about six men were travelling. [There was still a father and son walking weekly from Pennal (winter and summer alike) at this time.] The coaches were left at Abergynolwyn, the wagons taken off the back and propelled along The Mineral Line and through the Village Incline winding house. Once clear of the top points of the loop behind the house, the train would stop and the engine run back. The wagons were held on the brake and, after changing the top points, those destined for the village ran back with the aid of gravity, into the loop. Here the men would alight and take the path through the woodland which led directly into Cantrybedd level, and the engine would propel the slate empties onwards. This path was used by those living on Cantrybedd to reach Abergynolwyn village; they walked down the path at the side of the Village Incline. Men using the Workmen's Train never walked up Alltwyllt Incline as this did not provide a convenient route. People living on Bryneglwys level could walk over to the west side of the river, having a convenient footbridge to cross the Gwernol higher up; this facility was not available to those on Cantrybedd.

Passenger coaches would only work through to the foot of Alltwyllt 'to fetch the bosses down'. This was invariably the first class vehicle; it was usual to propel the coach. Haydn Jones used this coach, but his working terminated at the Village Incline head, and he used the path to Cantrybedd, too.

An accident-prone place on The Mineral Line was the road level crossing above Hendre and derailments due to 'moraine' building up over the track in bad weather, were very frequent.

The procedure for using the Village Incline was similar to that employed for the Workmen's Train. With wagons for the Quarry propelled in front, wagons for the village were hauled behind and beyond the winding house loop, and let back by gravity onto it and the turntable there.

Whilst musing on this subject, it is interesting that when William Rowlands, a Brecon-born man who had migrated to Towyn, had made the big skylight frames for the initial mill at Bryneglwys, he was obliged to cart them – and glass – from Towyn to the Quarry as there was no other means of conveying them. There was no Talyllyn Railway then, of course.

The return working of the Workmen's Train on a Monday from Abergynolwyn (about 6.50 a.m. or later, an exception being June 1913 when it was 6.35 a.m.) was always advertised as a Workmen's Train even though it had emptied of them. As will be seen, it now contained – during term time at least – schoolchildren; the working always ended at Pendre. If there are doubts about the exact starting date and sufficient demand for the Monday and Friday Workmen's Train, there are none about the return and outward (respectively) content of *this* train. Those who could afford to send their children to attend the County School (opened in 1894 – in the former Brynarfor Academy, a Boarding School for boys – and from that date a mixed school) at Towyn were not numerous in the surrounding districts, but it was the ambition of

all parents to send their children there. Those who lived away from Towyn were therefore obliged to board by the week in the town, and premises linked with the school (e.g. the school premises themselves, 'Brynarfor' for the boys and at 'Bryntirion' and 'Trefeddyg' for the girls) were boarding houses by the week. Those houses soon filled, but additional children could be accommodated in the cottages of the men who had gone up to the Quarry barracks for the week. Thus on Mondays and Fridays the Workmen's Train was also a school children's train in one direction, though the Company never officially gave it that name. Early on a Monday morning children would gather at Abergynolwyn from the outlying districts at the borders of Merionethshire (this would include that part of Corris lying therein), many having had a weary walk over the hills at an early hour, and obliged to carry a week's food and clothing with them; one may imagine it was hard to stay awake over the books on a Monday afternoon. These same children would return to Abergynolwyn on the Friday train which went to collect the quarrymen. How fortunate the pampered child of today who seldom walks anywhere, let alone to school!

'This school was established owing principally to the liberality of John Corbett Esq. JP, DL, CA, of Ynys-y-Maengwyn, Towyn and Chateau Impney, Droitwich, and was opened by him on May 17th 1894' – so reads the inscription over the door of the former 'County School'.

Like the Workmen's Train, the numbers of children using this service fell over the years; first not to do so were those from Upper Corris whose walk from home to Abergynolwyn involved the steep little road above Dolffanog beyond the east end of Talyllyn Lake and known as The Black Staircase. To be in Abergynolwyn by 7 a.m. they would risk limb down this treacherous slope when the surface was ice or snow covered. Other children from beyond the Lake would come in combinations of boat, horseback, or pony and trap. In later years, bicycles were to the fore.

When these children travelled in the latter days of the train, their destination had become The Grammar School. Whilst Welsh was the native tongue of all the local children, those at The Grammar School were taught to speak English, whereas the unlucky ones who did not attend it, had to pick up English as best they could. So not unnaturally, children from The Grammar School were apt to tease other children who might be travelling on the same school train. This made the train unattractive to children who might be the butt of teasing and bullying from the regular Grammar School children, and Jacob Rowlands was

All ready for an excursion to the seaside; an Abergynolwyn Sunday School prepares to board with R. B. Yates looking on from the Van. Jacob Rowlands just to the fore as ever, beside the engine. The split railhead in the stub siding was a common weakness along the track.
BURRELL'S SERIES

constantly remonstrating with children who tried to ride in the van to avoid travelling with the Grammarians.

Continuing the subject of Workmen's Trains (and disregarding the double-act it carried out) an official Annual Statement had to be made: that for 1898 reads:

TALYLLYN RAILWAY

There are no sections in any of the Company's Acts which have any reference to workmen's trains.

Workmen's Trains
One train at 6 a.m. every Monday from Towyn to Abergynolwyn.
One train at 6.30 p.m. every Friday from Abergynolwyn to Towyn.

Fares charged to Workmen
From Abergynolwyn to Dolgoch, distance 2 miles, fare 1d.
From Abergynolwyn to Brynglas, distance 3½ miles, fare 1½d.
From Abergynolwyn to Rhydyronen, distance 4½ miles, fare 2d.
From Abergynolwyn to Towyn, distance 6½ miles, fare 3d.

The same charges are made for the reverse journey.

Composition of Trains
Each consists of three third class carriages and one brake van.
Number of workmen's tickets issued during 1899: 2,392.*

[perhaps about 24 men travelling.]

---

*The apparent error between heading date of 1898 and this date should be noted.

At the Merionethshire Slate Mines Enquiry in April 1894, these fares were described as 'We have a cheap train at half-fare . . .'

The Monday morning train, usually 6 a.m. from Pendre, has a long history and though, as already mentioned, first noted in 1878, may have run earlier. This working was suspended for periods in 1910 and 1912, and did not run in 1911 at all, thus overlapping the start of Haydn Jones' ownership and suggesting the Quarry could obtain employees from Abergynolwyn sufficient until about a year after his purchase. The train is noted as running in July 1934 but not in October, and never thereafter.

The Friday evening train (which usually started from Pendre), would contain mainly returning school-children bound for Abergynolwyn and beyond; it returned all the way to Wharf after 1918. It did not leave Pendre until between 5.25 and 6 p.m., which must have caused the children much waiting and a late return home for those whose walk began at Abergynolwyn. After 1924 it was shown intermittently in summers as an 'ordinary' train (did the Talyllyn really have any such?!) and usually as a Workmen's

TAL-Y-LLYN RAILWAY. 15310.

F. FRITH & CO.

Ready for the 'Right-away' at Abergynolwyn. The horse and cart are hardly waiting for passenger business and must have brought goods up from the village.

It all looks somewhat decrepit. And how did that wagon come to be at the rear of the engine? It appears that some irregular propelling is about to take place. The wagon contains a gate-post and perhaps a plank 'seat'. Jonathan Rowlands (driver) awaits the photographer's pleasure and the young lady placed alongside the engine refuses to show her face. 1923. B. EDGINGTON

Train in winters without a qualifying note and the working in summer ran at approximately the same time; it ran daily each summer until September 1939. Here again, as a Fridays only winter train it ceased in 1934.

At the risk of being tedious, and having described the general pattern of 'ordinary' trains publicised by the timetables and said something of the 'hidden extras' which made the Railway anything but the simple system which the timetable suggested, it is worth adding mention of some curiosities, the reason for which is not always clear.

The Railway was officially worked by 'One Engine in Steam' but the practice of catering for the passenger numbers well outside the capacity of the carriage stock by adding wagons to the train, often resulted in loadings beyond the power of the locomotive. In answering this problem the Talyllyn proved itself to be 'a line of character' for which it was notorious among the informed; a second engine would be steamed and, by dividing the available stock between the two steeds, the timetabled working would run in two parts, one train a few yards behind the other and driven by ... well, the most suitable persons available.

The summer timetable of 1904 is another instance where only five minutes was given for running round the train at Abergynolwyn. It is hard to see how slate traffic was hauled unless the second engine was also in use – this seems unlikely and other arrangements for slate must have been made.

In the Haydn Jones period and following the First War, train patterns were very consistent until the slump of the early 1930s; timings might vary 5–10 minutes, occasionally more. There was printed an 'Economy Timetable' in versions for winter and summer respectively in the 1920s when the dates were left blank and filled in by hand.

From at least 1878 (1895–97 excepted when the time was 9.35 a.m. from Wharf) the regular daily (Monday–Saturday) morning train was leaving Pendre in that year at 9.30; this was the 9.25 from Wharf (with all that entailed as to whether passengers were picked up there or not!) The afternoon train also started from Pendre (in fact the timetable often showed no other station in Towyn) at 2.15 but might vary to as late as 2.45 or even 3.20 p.m. The earlier start gave the trainmen less time to work wagons to and from the Wharf but as the Quarry business dwindled these

Taken on the same occasion as the previous picture, the lady in white features a second time. Shortly the engine will back the carriages onto the wagons waiting on The Mineral Line, one of which contains products from the village saw mill – did the post in the earlier view also come from there?
B. EDGINGTON

became fewer and it became less of a problem. A start at 2.25 p.m. in the summer would give passengers longer at their destinations – Dolgoch remained the most popular one.

Having said that Abergynolwyn was ill-served, perhaps a summer Saturdays Only train leaving Pendre between 7 p.m. and 7.45 p.m. was to allow return from shopping, football, drinking and visiting; from time to time it acquired a somewhat infamous character for the drunken state and the bawdy songs of its passengers, some of whom may have 'made a day of it'. There were years of suspension (1910–25) for so late a working, which ceased entirely in 1930.

Perhaps for the same purpose, and to satisfy Abergynolwyn that their Member of Parliament was conscious of their needs, a midday train was put on on alternate Saturdays in winter from 1918 to 1923: there was no corresponding daily train in summer.

The summer season was a short one, its height being from the third week in July (with August Bank Holiday then occurring at the first weekend of that month) until mid-September. Holiday habits were in those days far more concentrated into that brief period so it was worthwhile putting on an evening train from

Pendre (such workings would run 'passenger only' and not 'mixed') at about 5.40 p.m. – after High Tea – which returned however, to Wharf. Such extras ran each summer during the 1930s and ended with the Second War. A recent broadcast revealed that one family would take 'the 7 a.m. train up to the terminus ... when we set out to climb Cader Idris ... we explained to Jacob that we might be late for the 6.30 p.m. down, and he agreed not to let it start without us'.

Economies followed the slump which affected the whole nation in the early 1930s. After Workmen's Trains were taken off in 1934, the twice daily ordinary train only ran on Tuesdays, Thursdays and Saturdays in winter 1934/5, slate wagons being worked on Tuesdays and Thursdays. After 1935 this was altered to Mondays, Wednesdays and Fridays in winter, slate and goods being worked as offering, and with passengers of little consequence. During the short summer timetable daily Monday–Saturday services were resumed, starting early July to late September – a more extended season than when off-summer trains ran every day. Behind all these arrangements the tenor of Quarry business can be detected.

During the last decade of this account, it was the practice to issue timetables printed locally, but not all stations displayed them. Notice of times was often sent late to publishers such as *Bradshaw* with the result that their timetables might, in an October edition, show Talyllyn trains which had ceased to run in the previous month. The wise would confirm the times from Wharf beforehand. The writer was often informed by postcard that though *Bradshaw* might misleadingly imply, the Company, however, was not issuing timetables that year owing to the uncertain state of the locomotive (!): it was intended to run trains at ... and so on, usually ending up with a cheerful message 'looking forward to seeing you on ... With kindest regards ...'

The Railway had a Post Office contract to carry mail between Towyn and Abergynolwyn: until at least 1905 daily bags were made up at Towyn P.O. for both Abergynolwyn and Bryneglwys; these were taken by messenger to Pendre to be put aboard the 9.30 a.m. train in the charge of guard Rowlands (the only man on the railway in uniform, and with gold-braided cap). Another messenger would meet the train at Abergynolwyn to be given the bag for the village, and the other bag would travel on the footplate to the foot of Alltwyllt. The afternoon train returning to Pendre would bring back both bags which would leave (as the contents required) by evening train from the main line station.

Reference has been made more than once to the peculiar position of King's/Wharf both as to change of name and use as a passenger station. This can be summarised as regards usage:

	1899	Station first appears as footnote in timetable as departure point in summers only*
	1901	Continues as summer departure point but Down trains terminate at Pendre*
	1904	As before, but use continues to be intermittent*
October	1906	Name first appears as 'King's station, Wharf'†
July	1909	Name in footnote 'Slate Wharf Station'*
August	1911–	'Wharf'† No workmen's train for part of
September	1912	this period Jan. 1912 & April 1912– at least – basic service departs 'Towyn (Wharf)' but returns 'Towyn' though times suggest latter is Wharf. Towyn Pendre does not appear in these tables (*) but footnote shows 5.40 a.m. Monday Workmen's and 6 p.m. extra train in July–September 1912 table as departing from 'Pendre, not from the Wharf'; the corresponding return Workmen's journey as terminating at 'Towyn' (depart Abergynolwyn 6.35 a.m., arrive 'Towyn' 7.15 a.m.) the running time suggesting this is Pendre†
	1913–14	Used by passenger trains summers only*
August	1915–	Used by passenger trains *throughout year**
August	1916	(maybe insertion incorrect due to failure to notify Bradshaw!)

September	1916–	Station does not appear throughout this period i.e. World War I until Nov. 1918†
October	1918	
November	1918	Stations re-appear monthly† (This is the second occasion when winter trains commence at Wharf – see Jan. and April 1912 above – but return workings terminate Pendre)
July	1919	Most trains return to Wharf for first time in July*
Autumn	1939	After the summer season service ended, the service was reduced and all trains now ran to and fro from Wharf* (Workmen's Trains had been suspended from 1934 and had always started from Pendre)

* Company timetable reference.
† *Bradshaw's* timetable reference.

As to Pendre, this was spelt Pendref by both Company and *Bradshaw* from the time of World War I until 1950. Occasionally some printing errors appeared, and the name was shown as Pendre on the Up table and Pendref on the Down. An article written in 1909 emphasises that passengers who joined the train at Wharf had to 'alight at Pendre for the purpose of booking, as there is no booking office at the Wharf'.

The *passenger* service in force during the Second War and up to 1950 must have been conveniently based on the earlier experience of running trains only on certain days of the week.

PASSENGER SERVICES (1939–1950)

9 Sept.	1939	Last run of Sats. Only 5.40 p.m. ex Pendre. Thereafter: Mons., Weds., Fris. only Wharf dep. 9.25 a.m. and 2.45 p.m. Abergynolwyn dep. 11.20 a.m. and 4.5 p.m. i.e. in the same manner as previous winters – three days per week
14 Jan.	1942	Above timetable has continued to this date, but thereafter Monday train ceases
8 June	1942	Monday train reinstated
20 Jan.	1943	Monday train ceases
23 June	1943	All trains cease (incl. goods etc.)
20 July	1943	Weds., Fris. resumed
2 Aug.	1943	Mons., Weds., Fris. only
4 Nov.	1943	Last day of Mons., Weds., Fris. only
5 Nov.	1943	No passenger services, but goods carried on four dates only between this date and 30 Dec. 1943
31 Dec.	1943	Weds., Fris. resumed (with extra workings on Bank Holidays in 1944)
12 April	1944	No trains run
13 April	1944	Weds., Fris. resumed
24 Jan.	1945	All trains cease
3 Feb.	1945	Weds., Fris. resumed
9 and 14 March	1945	No trains run
16 March	1945	Service for this day only (i.e. one month before Easter) ... last passenger working until Easter holiday period 1946

(The passenger timetable was thereafter based on commencing services for Easter only, then resuming during May or June until the following October. There were no passenger workings at other times of the year.)

19 and 22 April	1946	Good Friday & Easter Monday only
15 May	1946	Whit Monday and Weds., & Fris. only
12 August	1946	Mons., Weds., Fris. only
5 October	1946	All trains cease
	1947	Easter & Whit Monday
28 May–18 July	1947	Weds., Fris. only
21 July–3 Oct.	1947	Mons., Weds., Fris. only
	1948	Easter & following Wed.: Whit Monday‡
19 May–9 July	1948	Weds., Fris. only
12 July – 8 Oct.	1948	Mons., Weds., Fris. only
	1949	Good Friday & Easter Monday
6 June	1949	Mons., Weds., Fris. Wharf dep. 9.25 a.m. and 2.15 p.m. Abergynolwyn dep. 11.20 a.m. and 4 p.m.
27 Aug.	1949	All trains cease§
19 Sept.	1949	Mons., Weds., Fris. resumed
7 Oct.	1949	Last day of service
	1950	Good Friday & Easter Monday
29 May	1950	Whit Monday only
5 June	1950	Mons., Weds., Fris.
6 Oct.	1950	Last day of service

[Running time for the full journey was always about 45 minutes in either direction, though slightly lesser times can be found.]

‡ Easter is Good Friday & Easter Monday throughout; Whit is Whit Monday only.
§ *Dolgoch* cracks frame. *Talyllyn* unserviceable.

Goods services for the use of the Quarry (whose output then was quite minimal) continued until it closed. Traffic for intermediate stations had been largely lost to the roads before the war began. There being no passenger trains in winter, goods trains were run as required in winter months 1946/47 and 1947/48, but after October 1948 they appear to have ceased.

After the Preservation Society took over the operating from 14th May (Whit Monday) 1951, various slogans were adopted to publicise the novelty and peculiar worth of its initiative; the Railway was accorded several tributes to which it had no claim but one was indisputable. The Railway was the oldest narrow gauge public passenger railway in England, Scotland or Wales which could claim it had operated a passenger service continuously since its opening. Temporary suspension of traffic it had certainly experienced, caused by circumstances beyond its control, but, unlike its Welsh neighbours, for instance, which the Second War caused to close completely to passengers, the Talyllyn Railway, unique from its opening day, remained and remains unique. A glance at some other Welsh passenger lines which lost their passenger trains either at the start of or during that War, (or had done so by complete closure or retention as goods-only lines many years before) will reinforce

the point. Alphabetically these were: Corris, Festiniog, Glyn Valley, Snowdon Mountain, Vale of Rheidol, Welsh Highland, and Welshpool & Llanfair.

Having looked at some of the timetables, considered the carriage of workmen and schoolchildren and the overall 'cause and effect' which Quarry traffic had on the line, an effect which grew less with the passing of years, there are other aspects of running the Railway which come to notice.

Firstly, down at Wharf, the place where most activity might be found (as opposed to Pendre where activity was spasmodic), slate loaders spent the first part of each day unloading wagons sent down the night before. On them depended a supply of empty wagons and the object was to keep the yard clear of them, siding room being limited. In good times wagons could be emptied on the wharfside, straight into open main line wagons, suitably observed by the checker who kept his record, naturally enough, on a slate. Slates were stacked on edge; they were removed from Talyllyn wagons and placed on edge once again in the larger ones; straw or hay was used not only to prevent abrasion and breakage, but also to break up different quantities and sizes. A large slate might be used as a 'marker' too. The object would be to pack the slate as tightly as possible inside the vehicle; this prevented movement and breakage.

In less good times, slate might be sent down to await orders; the purpose of Wharf yard was to stock slates on the ground in rows (like grim grey rows of playing cards) by size. When orders were received it was from this stock that main line wagons were loaded; wheelbarrows of design suited to carrying slate, with flat bed and end board and having no 'garden outlines', were used for this. As business fell away, the track gang was used for the first hour or so of each day and in due course they became part slate loaders and part railway men. If only a small number of wagons was to be unloaded, an early start would have emptied them ready for the morning train. In really bad times, slate would accumulate at the Wharf as the Quarry tried to keep its labour force in work for which orders were scarce; there was a limit to space at the Quarry and finished products had, perforce, to make their way to Towyn. Another problem was to find a market for slates which were of the wrong size for the builder, or unsuited to buildings then being erected, or worse, unfashionable to the current architectural whim. These were usually small sizes which, though of attractive appearance, required much additional work on the roof at a time when labour charges were mounting. J. L. H. Bate explains that much of the rock at Bryneglwys was too irregular for making large slates; the rock at the west end of Cantrybedd was 'very small' – that is to say, it would only make small slates. For this reason no attempt was made to develop the

No sign of life, no trains, no people – but business for 1949 is about to begin with the 'Easter rush' – a very gentle one. AUTHOR

Quarry further west. So of all slate stacked at Wharf, there was a nuisance value in the quantity of small sizes which had but limited demand. By 1939 there was an accumulation of stock here which was too thick for roofing and could not be sold. Some of it had lain there for up to a score of years, and was only shifted (with furious energy) in the 1940s when the London blitz called for anything which would repair bombed buildings. Because during the late 1930s the stocks grew beyond the confines of the Wharf area, it is said Quarry rubbish was thrown into part of the former Cambrian Railways ballast pits. There were no problems as Haydn Jones owned the land anyway, and temporary sidings were extended to serve yet more stock piles; Wharf edge siding may have been lengthened then. This practice might have begun when McConnel cleared his stocks.

The 'best days' of the Railway during Haydn Jones' time were the short boom years after the First War. In 1921 there were three slate runs a day (only two on Saturdays), the morning and afternoon being 'mixed' but the 1 p.m. Up having only empty slate wagons, about ten on a train. At the time, about 30 wagons came down the line each day and there were over 100 employees in the Quarry 'working on the blue and grey slates'. (In 1878 Vignes reckoned a mixed

train with all passenger stock and van included, might additionally have 20 empty slate wagons.)

Also, Abergynolwyn village business required that at least one wagon should be taken up the line every day, and duly lowered down the Village Incline. By 1943, the engine propelled wagons for the Quarry and pulled those for the Village Incline, when it proceeded beyond Abergynolwyn. Stopping past the Village Incline top, the latter were hand-shunted to the Incline head. Commodities included bricks, gravel, human and pig food of all kinds which could be packed into sacks (e.g. flour) or crates, clothing, beer in barrels, timber – an endless list of all items from soap to buttons which the community did not create itself. If there were insufficient empty wagons at the bottom of the Village Incline to balance the down-going load, the empties would be filled with slabs kept at hand for the purpose; the handbrake on the winding drum could then hold 'the run'. Empty beer barrels in a single wagon were considered to be of negligible weight which could be brought up without counterbalancing under control of the drum brake! The very last wagon down the Incline carried four barrels of beer. Perishable goods were carried in sacks in both incline wagons and the covered vans ... all forms of wagon found their way to the village, not only the incline wagons. The latter were essential for such items as loose coal (not in sacks) otherwise the load would be spilled.

Brynglas was known locally as Pandy or Tyddynypandy. It created a little business for the line; on the west side and some way down the road was Dolaugwyn Flour Mill which would deliver two sacks of flour to the station on Mondays, and these would be loaded into an empty wagon on the rear of the train by the fireman and guard. The wagon would be placed at the front of the engine at Abergynolwyn and propelled to the head of the Village Incline, then lowered. In former days Brynglas was given what appeared to be a loop line, but in reality was two sidings which did not 'connect' with each other.

The other business there was the fulling mill or 'Pandy' with its three cottages; here tweeds, woollen flannel and blankets were made and sewn up in hessian (or as parcels, respectively) for despatch by train. Latterday partners in this venture were brothers, Evan and Dick Jones, who would also sell locally, door to door from a suitcase. The mill survived to the 1930s. There was no doubting the main business of that little hamlet, for the products of the mill – blankets, socks and the like – would be stretched out on frames in the fields to dry after washing. Evan and Dick would spend much of their time going round the local farms for wool, and would pick clean every bit they found lying in fields or hung on barbed wire. Their mill was driven by an overshot water-wheel, supplied by an overhead wooden leat: it was one of the oldest woollen mills in Wales and fifteen years before the Railway opened it employed nineteen weavers and spinners. Of all the places on the line, there was no community which relied so heavily on the Railway as did Pandy. All coal and groceries came by it; Pandy passengers were regular users and when trains were suspended, it was Pandy which felt the loss the most.

The privies of Abergynolwyn were served by incline wagons which were taken round the village track system so that tenants might empty their 'night-soil' therein. Although it is suggested these wagons were made up into trains which moved after nightfall, this is highly unlikely; certainly they were carefully marshalled 'the correct way round' to ascend the Village Incline, and left on the track above the field at Brynglas siding, where the local farmer would cart and spread it on the surrounding ground. The carrots grown in this district were well known for their dimensions – of their flavour there is no complaint – human compost was widely used elsewhere in this manner.

A different form of rubbish conveyance came up the line from Towyn; most of it was dry and from the shop, but friends of Haydn Jones also availed themselves of

the service, but for a fee. The contents of these rubbish trains were simply thrown over the edge of an appropriate embankment somewhere up the line.

Seen from the engine, too, the Railway was quite a different place and every journey might be described as 'an individual experience'. In the mid-1930s a visitor's diary reads:

'I had several trips on TALYLLYN. Although the pressure was only 70 lbs., it was at all times master of its load.
'On one occasion it was four coaches, one brake van and nine partly-loaded slate wagons with merchandise, barrels of oil etc. ... On the return trip (6.25 p.m. ex Abergynolwyn) we encountered a large bull in a cutting which called for much opening of the cylinder drain cocks, waste water gear and so on to remove him from our path. Both engines are fitted with special low pressure injectors which function very well.'

In recent times water could be taken for the engine at Pendre, Dolgoch and Ty Dwr. Before water was made available at Dolgoch station, there was a source fed by a wooden lander (trough) near the small occupation bridge on the Towyn side of Dolgoch viaduct but there is now no trace of this. One of the highlights of Talyllyn operation would occur in high season when two passenger trains would sally forth from Towyn, each with an engine and each in charge of but one man (often no 'fireman' being available). Officially the working would be deemed to be one train, running in two separate parts. Hugh Jones, the senior driver, naturally took the engine he preferred, *Dolgoch*, but most other drivers liked *Talyllyn* as it carried more water. Old Peter Williams would therefore take 'The Black Tankie' and Hugh 'The Red Engine', the latter having more red in the lining than *Talyllyn*. The choice of which water stop to use would be determined on the Up journey, when Hugh, turning his back on the train in front (and separated by only a few yards at times), would roll up his shirt sleeves and dip his hand into the back tank of *Dolgoch*. If he could touch water he would forego the water stop at Dolgoch and run on to Ty Dwr. Sometimes it was such a near case of touch-and-go that by the time Abergynolwyn was reached, the engine tank was empty and the water had disappeared below the 'bottom nut' of the boiler gauge glass. Passengers getting off the train at Abergynolwyn would often walk in front of the engine, talk, and generally hamper the righting of the emergency, so he perfected the art of drawing up there, uncoupling and shooting off up the line towards Ty Dwr before passengers had left their seats.

On these occasions *Talyllyn* would take the brake van and two coaches; *Dolgoch* would have two coaches and all the acceptable slate wagons (very few in number!), filled with passengers. *Talyllyn* would lead, followed by *Dolgoch*, each driver also firing, working Pendre gates, changing points, coaling etc., and

Edward Thomas would endeavour to book tickets from the van in the first train, to passengers in both trains! (It is on record, however, that once when a passenger asked to have his ticket issued through the van window, 'he curtly refused to do so'!) By the time shunting and other work had been done by *Dolgoch* with its smaller tank on this and any other day, the engine was usually short of water on the Down run. After leaving Dolgoch on the Down journey, the engine would have to enter Pendre engine shed to take on water, if essential.

In recalling the early days of the Second War (1942) it was remarked on the 'inefficiency' of everything; a correspondent had been on the Abergynolwyn-bound passenger train when *Talyllyn* broke down 'and we had to return to Towyn in a slate wagon' – presumably by gravity? To this wagon was added a coal wagon at Rhydyronen. *Talyllyn* and train were subsequently hauled back to Towyn by *Dolgoch*. *En route*, in those times of food rationing, the driver stopped to collect some eggs, and the guard (no longer Jacob Rowlands, of course) carried a gun in case he saw any rabbits. 'All the track was overgrown … passenger services were never from the Wharf, only from Pendre … you had to have special permission of the guard to board at Wharf, or to go on to Wharf, and not all trains went through'.* (Perhaps another instance of adhering to personal convenience rather than to the public time-table!)

The same writer recalls slate trains coming down exclusively, and not as mixed trains 'although usually on days when the service trains did not run'.

The records give us some idea of when goods were carried, and it may be assumed that in almost every case they were only taken when a slate train was running. There is a prevalence of Wednesdays and Fridays in the dates but no record of slate train running has survived, so this is only surmise. The occasional appearance of Mondays, Tuesdays and, very rarely, Saturdays, may suggest a special working. Could this have been for use of the village, for at this period, road transport, with petrol, tyres etc. rationed, was at a nadir? There was goods traffic on 48 dates between 16th March 1945 and 19th April 1946. Between once and six times a month, wagons might be found attached to the rear of the slate empties, which, in the writer's experience, could contain building materials for urgent repairs in the village (no wartime building, save for essential work, was permitted), coal, potatoes, farming necessities such as animal foodstuffs in jute

The Railway carried a few regular, local worthies, mostly bound for market and similar business in Towyn. The staff could tell which day of the week it was by the human content of the train. Here a passenger joins at Brynglas; the Booking Office is 'open'.
O. ELSDEN

sacks. In certain weeks there might be two trains with goods, followed by three weeks with none. In October 1945 there were no less than seven such trains, possibly due to the return of *Dolgoch* the previous month.

If the critical war-time staff position has not already been made evident, Hugh Jones would make one further comment. Living at Rhydryonen, he would have to make his way down the track on his bicycle at an early hour each morning. He would light a fire in the engine before escaping from the smoke-filled shed. He might calculate he could return home again for a wash, shave and breakfast before going back to Pendre once more. He would build up the fire even further and then, in the carriage shed, oil the carriage bearings. Then, one by one, in order to save time until the engine had sufficient steam, he would push them out of the shed onto the main line. It was heavy work for the track was upgrade and the wheel flanges did not pass easily through the crossings.

Taking some of the 1930s figures, it has been calculated that assuming an average output per man in one year in the Welsh slate quarry trade as 20 tons,

---

* The Author's first journey was about this time; he confirms that special arrangements were made for him to pick up the train (one coach) at Wharf. No guard was provided on those wartime journeys; the driver (Hugh Jones) also issued tickets.

Bryneglwys was somewhat below that figure with 17.6 tons. In 1946 that Quarry employed five men but had employed 57 in 1937/8; in the late 1930s an average 1,003 tons were produced each year and all is assumed to have been taken down to Towyn by rail. Taking the payments made to the Railway, the Company's lawyer then based his negotiations on 10/– being received by the Railway for each ton of slate. Coal was taken to Abergynolwyn for 5/– per ton and the average income from all other forms of goods traffic was 7/– to 8/– per ton. It is likely that the Quarry had to bear the cost of taking wagons to and fro from the foot of the Alltwyllt Incline on The Mineral Line.

A prospectus issued by the Dolgoch Slate & Slab Co. Ltd. in 1876 gives the rates chargeable by the Railway under its Act as 2½d. per ton mile in Talyllyn Railway wagons. The prospectus suggested that if the Dolgoch Company provided its own wagons, this would be reduced to 2d. per ton mile; they maintained that in Talyllyn wagons a ton would cost 1/0½d. at Wharf or 10d. in their own wagons. To load a main line wagon would cost a further 1/– per ton 'while it can be contracted for 6d. per ton'.

Two intriguing thoughts arise from this. Firstly, did any privately-owned wagons operate over the Railway? It is unlikely. Secondly, Bryneglwys Quarry must have been unusually placed among slate quarries, being in the fortunate position of having to provide no wagons of its own and not being the target of the constant warfare which existed between, for instance, quarries served by the Festiniog Railway which, too, were supplied with wagons by that railway – but then, the Festiniog and its quarry customers were 'unrelated', so to speak! Talyllyn Railway wagons were maintained by the Quarry workshops.

It has been estimated that Quarry products accounted for about 85% of Talyllyn Railway mineral traffic. In the five years before the Railway opened, the output is likely to have been less than a total of 5,000 tons; in the period 1865–1909 during the McConnel era it was 255,000 tons, and during the Haydn Jones time up to 1946 was 52,000 tons.

Payments by the Quarry to the Railway Company for carriage of slates are available for 1924–1939 (not always agreeing with the figures in the Official Returns):

1924	£807	16s.	0d.	1932	301	18	7
1925	656	10	5	1933	349	15	9
1926	704	9	2	1934	330	11	3
1927	673	15	2	1935	429	16	1
1928	598	4	6	1936	426	3	2
1929	398	8	10	1937	469	5	0
1930	306	12	1	1938	513	15	0
1931	472	9	8	1939	358	7	6

In March 1948 were seen 'two old men . . . loading the very last wagon of slate' (it was apparently taken down by *Dolgoch* on the following day).

From time to time special trains were worked from Towyn for visits to the Lake; one such was mentioned in the *Montgomery & Cardigan County Times* for 24th July 1897:

'A TRIP TO TALYLLYN LAKE – On Friday, the Congregational Sunday School, numbering over 150, took a trip to the above lake. The weather being so fine many others availed themselves of the opportunity to visit that picturesque spot. At 9.30 a.m., the "Giant Coffee Pot" steamed into Pendre Station and in a short time the coaches were filled as well as about a dozen trams. A ride in a train on such a lovely day was quite a treat, and the journey in the toy railway to Abergynolwyn was very pleasant. At the terminus, Mr. J. R. Pughe had provided conveyances, and a start was again made, and the lake was reached by 12. On arrival, refreshments were freely partaken of. After a little rest, all went to seek enjoyment such as hill climbing, boating, fishing, paddling, cycling, &c. At about 2.30 p.m., close to the ancient church, tea was laid out on the grass, under fine shady trees. Sports were afterwards got up for the children. At 5.30 p.m. a start for home was made, Towyn being reached about 7.30 after a most enjoyable day. Great kindness was shown to the trippers by the Misses Jones (Tyn-y-cornel), Mr. and Mrs. D. M. Jones (Maes-y-Pandy), and Mrs. and Miss Richards.'

Local worthies were sometimes honoured by having special trains provided for them – but seldom in the form they could enjoy! – as in the case of Lewis Roberts, who died at Beudynewydd, Bryneglwys in September 1897 'at the ripe age of 70'. He was a native of Caernarvonshire (once again) though spending much of his life in Somerset, later becoming Manager of the Frongoch Quarry (near Panteidal), Aberdovey; he came to Bryneglwys as Weighing Clerk and Overlooker when Frongoch closed. Such was the esteem in which he was held that the Quarry closed for the day of his funeral in Towyn to enable the quarrymen to attend; a special train was provided to and from Abergynolwyn.

Another such is reported in *The Cambrian News* for 7th February 1902:

'Funeral – Mr. David Davies of Gwernol House, Abergynolwyn met, on the 27th of last month, with an accident in Bryneglwys Quarry, which ended fatally on the 28th. The funeral took place Saturday February 1st at Towyn Cemetery. The body was conveyed from Abergynolwyn to Towyn by a large special train and was met at the Pentref Station of the Talyllyn Railway by a large concourse of people. The funeral is considered to have been as largely attended as any which has taken place at Towyn for the last 20 years . . .'

There was formerly a thriving Male Voice Choir and a Brass Band in Abergynolwyn, and the Choir enjoyed nothing better than to support its favourite rugby football team, travelling often to South Wales for the match. A special train on the Talyllyn Railway would be organised and in the late hours of a Saturday, Towyn and Abergynolwyn would await the travellers' return. There was no need to enquire whether their favoured side had won, for was this so, both the Cambrian and Talyllyn trains would be full of song and drunken shouts. Had the team lost, there would be an eerie silence as each train reached its destination,

Arthur Pugh, though by now nearly blind, could make his way from home to Rhydyronen station by the instinct of his many faithful years in the Company's service. We may hazard his thoughts as, smartly dressed, he follows the train as it leaves for Abergynolwyn.

MRS. M. SPRATLEY-JONES

broken only by a few bars of discordant boozy crescendo from 'Y Mochy Du' (The Black Pig), rising from the rear carriage. On such occasions the Talyllyn manager would wait anxiously – even up to 2 a.m. on the Sunday – to ensure that the empty stock had returned intact to Pendre. This information was conveyed to him – whilst still abed – by a long whistle from the engine there.

If the above train (and there were many of the same kind) recalls the musical traditions of the Welsh, mention must be made not only of the annual Towyn Easter Fair originally held on a Good Friday, but also The Singing Festival held at the Towyn School at each Whitsuntide; special workings from Abergynolwyn were provided for each of these events and there being too many passengers for all the coaches, the children rode in slate wagons.

There were other musical dates in Towyn for which trains were run, and though the Railway enjoyed comparative immunity from incidents and accidents (and there was never a fatality), from time to time events occurred which perhaps gave rise to amusement rather than concern.

'AN EVENING ENTERTAINMENT' – so read the *Towyn-on-Sea and Merioneth County Times* on 10th December 1896 ...

'As the Narrow Gauge train for Abergynolwyn which arrived in Towyn at 5.15 p.m. on Monday was within two hundred yards of Towyn station, one of the springs broke and dropped on the axle trees breaking one of the sheaves and straps clean off. The train was to have returned after the Music Festival at 8.45 p.m. but owing to the breakdown was about forty minutes late. We are pleased to find that no-one was injured. Great praise is due to Mr. H.W. Griffiths, the locomotive superintendent and to Mr. Hugh Thomas, the General Manager of the Railway and the staff generally for the promptitude with which repairs were carried out.'

One of the most accident-prone workings was the Monday Workmen's Train, which would work in darkness in winter after perhaps the line had become obstructed by debris from storms over the weekend. On 6th February 1882 that train left the line east of Dolgoch (at the Tancoed occupation crossing) and ploughed down the embankment. The locomotive and

one coach fell on their sides but no-one was hurt. It is possible of course, that in those days this was the entire train, except that empty wagons might have been coupled on the rear of the coach. The cause was a landslide onto the track occasioned by heavy rain.

The Directors of the Cambrian Railways were informed that on 10th July 1896 . . .

> '. . .some narrow gauge trucks broke loose from a train on the Talyllyn Railway and ran back past the Talyllyn Company's station and through the Slate Yard and fell over the Wharf adjoining the Cambrian Company's Siding. Two of the trucks ran upon and knocked over a Cambrian wagon standing in the siding fouling the Main Line within twenty minutes of the time when a passenger train was due. The line was cleared as quickly as possible and the passenger train passed after a delay of nine minutes.
>
> 'I have asked the Talyllyn Railway Company to state what means they propose to adopt to prevent the recurrence of an accident of this kind which might lead to serious consequences if it happened in the dark or when a train was passing, but have not yet received a definite reply.'

From time to time slate wagons became derailed at the rear of a passenger train; they would be hauled for considerable distances before the attention of the train crew could be caught. Only then would driver and fireman dismount and rerail them – as to their success with loaded wagons we are left in doubt!

It looks as if the Monday train was again in trouble in 1905 when it was reported that an accident to one of the engines 'caused some inconvenience and necessitated the conveying of the mails to Abergynolwyn by road.' Smaller incidents were not invariably put on record for obvious reasons but the local newspaper reporter was not under the same duress as, for instance, was the person covering Lord Penrhyn's Estate where accidents affecting the Penrhyn Railway (etc.) were obviously suppressed. So only the least affair made news at Towyn – the fall of a large tree near Tynllwyn just after the morning Up train had passed in 1928, missing the last vehicle 'by only a few yards. It took two men all day to clear the line' ... the day *Talyllyn* broke an axle and one of Haydn Jones' horses went up to drag the engine back to Pendre ... and how the brake van became derailed in Wharf

cutting in 1948, and a man was trapped inside. He was extricated through the little trap door in the end ...

An unusual tale relates how during the Second War *Dolgoch* took some slate wagons up The Mineral Line after leaving the carriages at Abergynolwyn ... 'after a very long wait, the driver returned on foot to say that the engine had failed and he would not be able to take the train back to Towyn. Following a further long wait, the guard said he would take the train back ... by gravity.' The writer of this reminiscence travelled back in a slate wagon at the rear of the train which arrived at Wharf without further incident!

It was beyond Abergynolwyn and in the Quarry where most of the unconventional activities took place. There was naturally a great temptation for employees to ride within the workings and also between home and work; the latter might involve sneaking a trip on

The driver felt an unusual tugging at the coupling behind his engine and looking back he saw something was amiss. 'We're off the line I think', shouted a middle-aged lady, opening the carriage door and alighting quickly before worse befell. A small boy was examining things more closely: 'The wheels aren't on the rails at all', he cried. There were lots of willing young men on the train ready to emulate Sir Galahad and in no time at all they had lifted the errant carriage back onto the track. And a photographer was there to record it all .... 1936.   H. B. TOURS

the Village, Alltwyllt and Cantrybedd Inclines. The Inspector of Mines (from 1873) was to receive reports of accidents caused by this risky transport and Bryneglwys soon appeared on his desk. A man was killed going home from his work as in order to save himself the labour of walking home, he 'rode on trucks down the inclines'. He was standing at the bottom of one of them when a truck let loose in some unexplained manner came down at terrific speed and killed him instantly. It was added that it was forbidden 'to trespass on the lines of rail or riding in the wagons . . . but men were continually disobeying these orders.'

In July 1888 'an empty truck was pushed against an empty ''lorry'' at the top of an incline and knocked it down. It was broken in the fall and a piece of one of the wheels struck William Jones (below ground).' But he escaped with his life.

Some of the men showed more disregard for danger than others – a notable character would take many risks and one evening whilst riding down the Alltwyllt the cable broke; he and the wagon fell into the gorge below but whilst the wagon descended, his path was more of a trajectory into a Scots Pine on the far bank – thereafter he was known as 'Flying Dick'. His only injury was a sprained wrist.

The Village Incline saw its share of incidents too; the desirable balancing was to lower two loaded and raise two (or even three!) empty wagons, but the state of the frayed cable told its own tale. It was usual to leave rolling stock in the small yard at its foot and the state of crippled wagons lying around show that they formed a useful purpose as a buffer. Wagons of beer and packets of cigarettes were sometimes fatalities: the beer was soon lost to earth but the cigarettes found their way into other hands.

A typical example of this took place on 23rd July 1920:

> 'On Friday afternoon while goods were being lowered down the railway incline the wire rope broke and one of the wagons came plunging down at a terrific rate. When it reached fairly level ground, the wagon left the metals, ultimately coming to a standstill about 100 yards further down. The contents were scattered in all directions – coal, cigarettes and beer – three excellent materials for heat production, all being mixed together. The weekly bundle of *The Cambrian News* on its journey to the local distributor (Mr. G. R. Evans, Dysinni Stores) was in the debris and emerged therefrom plastered with coal and well saturated with beer. Miraculously, as it were, no one was injured as the spot is a favourite playing ground for children.'

According to David Evans, 'if riding on inclines, one kept alert for any jerk in the haulage cable; this frequently took place and sometimes the wagon hook disengaged from the cable as a result; the prudent would leap from the wagons immediately any pause was felt in the haulage, just in case!'

Perhaps one of the most publicised incidents involved the locally prominent Meyrick Roberts, reported in the paper for 24th November 1911. Just

as the district was congratulating itself on the acquisition of the railway, Quarry etc. by Haydn Jones – itself the subject of several newspaper articles with headlines 'It's on, It's off' portent we read:

> 'An accident which might have had fatal results took place at Bryneglwys on Monday morning. Three trucks, on the last of which was seated Mr. Meyrick Roberts the Manager of the Quarry [a fine example of the exception to the rule] were ascending the first incline, the higher portion of which is exceedingly steep. The first two trucks had reached the level at the top but before the third could follow the coupling snapped. Mr. Roberts . . . jumped free of the truck which made a headlong descent. Failing to negotiate the turn at the bottom of the incline the truck left the rails and taking a mighty leap over the river and breaking down a large tree in its flight, landed in a field on the other side, broken into pieces . . .'

More informal was the revelation by a tall, elderly and scholarly Welshman recalling his youth at Abergynolwyn; his sisters commonly rode down the Village Incline and were so doing on two occasions when the cable broke. 'Being Talyllyn-trained they took immediate and remedial action with the hand brake, but even so they shot right across the road before stopping.'

When the time came to dismantle the Quarry machinery the tramway and Railway could not be used as the incline cables were unsafe; road transport was substituted instead.

From time to time some not-so-common passengers and loads might be seen aboard the train. The Abergynolwyn policeman's journal (1879–1887) contains reflections on the pastimes of some villagers, of which salmon poaching was a frequent activity. Then there was the scourge of Sheepscab and the enforcement of the sale of bread by weight – perhaps just another chore? Occasionally some malefactor had to be escorted on the train, for instance a gentleman *en route* for Ruthin gaol.* The policeman himself had to make frequent journeys to Towyn not only to make contact with his superiors or collect his pay, but to deliver messages to the Coroner after accidents, mostly in the Quarry. No doubt the local village carpenter was also a coffin maker but whether by accident in the Quarry or through other causes, some villagers were buried in Towyn, so the brake van must have occasionally done duty as a hearse.

In the earlier days the Company sought to classify certain trains as 'Parliamentary' in order to avoid paying Passenger Duty Tax. This was levied on all persons not travelling in Workmen's Trains which were made compulsory by The Cheap Trains Act 1883 (46 & 47 Vic. Cap. 34); in fact, the circumstances of the Talyllyn Railway were such that it could not have been compelled by the Board of Trade to provide such

---

* Coincidentally, where some of the research for this material can be carried out in the 1980s!

trains 'between 6 o'clock in the evening and 8 o'clock in the morning' as appear to the Board of Trade to be feasible, but it was clearly financially advantageous to advertise trains as 'Parly' (the usual term for such workings) to avoid the Duty. It was not abolished until the Finance Act of 1929.

A limited number of Returns is available to inform us of the employee position at certain times. The designations given are taken from the records:

March 1884   *Secretary's Department*:
1 Secretary   1 Accountant
1 Clerk

                   Locomotive Department:
1 Driver   1 Fireman

                   Engineer's Department:
1 Engineer   1 Mechanic   4 Plate-layers

                   Traffic Department:
1 General Manager   1 Guard
1 Porter (etc.)
14 employees in all

December 1911   *Ways & Works Department*
4 employed @ £3 16. 0d. per week*

                   Locomotive Maintenance Department
1 employed @ £1 12. 0d. per week

                   Locomotive Operating Department
2 employed @ £2 2. 0d. per week†

1913   as 1911 but additionally listed:
1 Superintendent @ £1 15. 0d. per week
1 Guard @ £1 14. 0d. per week
1 'Collection & Delivery etc.'
@ £1 4. 0d. per week
1 Secretary/Manager/etc.
@ £1 0. 0d. per week

   * Probably 4 @ 19/– each.
   † Probably total for driver and fireman.

Comment on these must include that the driver (and fireman?) received £2 12. 0d. for one week and £1 12. 0d. for one three week period during 1911, and that he and all other employees received lesser rates of pay for much of this time, e.g. the guard was reduced to 18/– and it might be assumed this depended on the number of passenger trains (summer timetable etc.) but this is not borne out. More likely it was based on hours worked, a few statistics for which also survive. As to the Secretary/Manager's humble award in 1913, it is suggested he only spent part of his week attending to Railway business; possibly some was given to

Quarry affairs or even to those of D. & J. Daniel! (From the foregoing it will be deduced that the form in which the Returns were made makes particularisation difficult).

As to overtime and hours worked, in January 1887 some drivers worked over 14 hours per day on four occasions, but the guard did so only once. In the following July, drivers did 13 hours thrice, 14 hours four times and 16 hours once; but the guard did not work over 12 hours, the minimum time required for notification. Again, it can only be hinted that certain slate business required the services of drivers (there was more than one at times) and not the guard (there was never more than one). Driver's time would include lighting-up and disposal.

Finally, a brief reference in 1937 gives the employee position as 1 Driver/Fitter, 3 Platelayers, 2 General Labourers; no mention is given of office staff or guard, which there must have been.

Dolgoch station in September 1940.   J. W. SPARROWE

Goods traffic to and from the village was always a lifeline to that community – in times of heavy snow, volunteer parties from there would assemble to clear the line and re-open it to trains. Coal trains were especially important, and for a time there was a small village goods shed attached to the smithy (the former Pandy farm) which the village line served together with the coalyard opposite; the latter was complementary to that at the Wharf and was difficult to pilfer!

Over the Company's existence, three classes of passenger have been catered for in the modestly small collection of vehicles; according to the Board of Trade Returns these have been:

1866–72	1st	–	3rd (incl. Parly)
1873 only	1	2nd	3
1874–1911	–*	2	3
1911–31	1	–	3
1931 on	–	–	3

*[According to E. K. Stretch list: no 1st 1874–1912 but 2nd throughout]

In 1911 the Cambrian Railways abolished second class and in the same year the Talyllyn did the same by upgrading their seconds to first! There was but scant difference in the comfort.

The Company was indifferent to what appeared on the doors of its stock, and the lettering 'FIRST CLASS' or '1' seems to have survived at all times where there was some superior upholstery. Some changes in class were caused by working arrangements in summer between Corris and Cambrian Railways, and the working of The Grand Tour by the three companies. This was arranged so as to travel the coast line from Towyn to Machynlleth, change into a Corris train to Corris and thence by Corris horse-bus,* up through Upper Corris and, after dropping down to Minffordd, turn westwards again, skirt Talyllyn Lake and connect with a Towyn-bound Talyllyn train at Abergynolwyn. This was an extremely popular tour, in an age when travel by any means was far from universal, and came to an end only when the Great Western Railway purchased the Corris Railway in 1930.

What of mishaps? The derailment at Tancoed crossing appears to have been the most serious incident of them all. *Dolgoch* is said to have been involved and that every available man and boy from Abergynolwyn came along to re-rail the train; following this event the line was patrolled by an old Irishman on a ganger's trolley each Monday morning before the first train went up. There are tales, too, of whole rakes of wagons coming down the Pendre – Wharf cutting (sometimes from the gravity siding), out of control, and landing on Cambrian metals, a very likely happening. Two generations ago, two young gentlemen looking for a lark, watched *Dolgoch* and train disappear up the line

* Later, a motor-bus.

from Pendre; *Talyllyn* had been under repair and was being tested in steam, but the driver had gone up on the regular train. The miscreants took that engine out of the yard and drove up the line as far as Brynglas where either the engine or their courage failed and they parked the engine in the siding; unfortunately whilst traversing the points, the lever was not held over sufficiently and *Talyllyn* fell into the ballast and blocked the main line. When *Dolgoch* and train returned they found an engine with all its wheels off the line and no sign of the cause, but a certain backside, belonging to one who later became a well-known Towyn citizen, was in due course given full parental treatment for that offence.

Some of the young lads from Abergynolwyn would sometimes take an evening gravity trip down to Towyn in one of the slate wagons left at Abergynolwyn station – 'You had to push a little of the way, but it did no harm to anyone'. Edward Hughes, son of Daniel Hughes of Tynllwynhen, recalls that at the age of eight he used to push up the line the occasional slate wagon left in Rhydyronen station; he would free wheel back again for about 100 yards. When management heard of this they placed 'a padlocked wooden beam … across the entrance to the siding'. (This was before the turn of the century.)

Almost imperceptibly the centre of the Railway's business would pass from the eastern to its western extremity as the years passed.

An amusing exercise can be performed with the Annual Statistics by comparisons with various sets of figures. Simplest is, recalling that figures for September 1870, for instance, refer to operation during the previous months, to extract certain 'all-time highs'. These can be summarised:

Highest receipts for:	passenger traffic	1922	= £1050
	goods	1882–83	= £1501
	passenger and goods traffic	1876–77	= £1823
Year of highest:	expenditure	1872–73	= £2047*
	number of passengers carried	1897–98	= 30,918
	surplus (£545)	1879–80	
	deficit (£525)	1890–91	
	train mileage	1896–97	= 12,080
Year of lowest:	surplus (£7)	1903	

* Perhaps the year when the line at Brynglas deviated and a station building was built?

An interestingly high figure appears in 1883 when 7,641 tons of slate and 1,052 tons of other goods were carried. The cause of this sudden upsurge is not known and a first reaction might be, how did the railway cope with it? It will be seen that a twice-daily run of ten wagons each carrying 1 ton 14 cwt. of slate and operating on five days for fifty weeks would transport about 8,700 tons, so the railway would not be overtaxed.

A delightful vignette of TALYLLYN at Abergynolwyn. The wagons have been picked off the rear of the coaches and the engine is about to propel them to Alltwyllt. 1939.

H. B. TOURS

The engine has brought the wagons down to Aber (as it is usually known). The fireman drives and Hugh rides the footstep, ready to change the points at the west end of the station. 1940.   J. W. SPARROWE

The year of highest receipts reflects the big increase in inflation during World War I, showing nonetheless a deficit of £125 on the year 1922. (Returns made after 1920 are taken to 31st December).

Between 1867 and 1938 (allowing that there are no Returns 1913–18) there were only fifteen years when a surplus was shown; Returns for September 1875–September 1884 show an annual surplus and these may be taken at face value only as being the most profitable years for the Railway.

A more worthwhile calculation (among others) can be done, for instance, with passenger receipts; taking 1867, 1901 and 1930 at random, a train ran one mile to generate 9.9d., 11.822d., and 9.617d. respectively, a most consistent pattern. For the same years, taking the passenger receipts and the 'passengers carried' (i.e. not 'passenger journeys') the average receipt from each passenger was 6.807d., 4.73d., and 13.709d. In 1901 the single fare to Abergynolwyn was 6½d.; taking 1897–98 when the highest number of persons was carried and setting this against the timetables of the period,

there would only be an annual average of 19 passengers per train (and only a handful when the holiday season had gone). A similar figure for 1938 produces 5 passengers (and about 2½ tons of goods) per train – from 1921 the Returns include slate as 'goods traffic'. More than any other facts, these figures reveal the true nature of the Talyllyn Railway, no less the generous provision of four coaches for its average passenger train content!

A nice sidelight on the revised form of Returns which were made after 1920 is that calves, sheep, pigs and 'Misc.' are shown under 'Livestock'. So we find that for pigs: 1922/40, 1923/35, 1924/31, 1927/20 down to the late 1930s when there were only two or three per year. There were 11 sheep in 1922, then none to 1927; after that they came in twos and threes per year. Calves came in ones and twos, whilst 'miscellaneous' (which can't have been very large animals) was never more than five per year!

Statistics have been published for the Railway in other forms and in other reference works, and found to be fairly consistent with those given already. The accuracy of any of them is open to doubt – the existence or otherwise of first/second class passenger accommodation from 1911–1920 is a clear case in point.

So we may envisage a railway where the carriage of slate, slab and building stone was at the heart of its business; what had begun as a very small sideline in carrying holiday folk had developed by 1950 to the virtual extinction of the original purpose. Mixed in between these activities might be noticed the Monday and Friday Workmen's Trains, and their return workings carrying schoolchildren. Then there was the essential business of carrying the mail, supplying the quarrying communities at Abergynolwyn and Bryneglwys, and the smaller hamlets *en route*.

Goods traffic was recorded in large leather-bound ledgers and concerned the enormous variety of items which all railways then carried: so we find 'one duck (in box)', a bicycle wheel *en route* for Beudynewydd, 'four kilderkins* of ale' or (in the Second War years) 'five cases of jam'. Much of this was going to Abergynolwyn (the jam was from Gloucester, so not everyone made their own or were they just helping out the sugar ration?!)

Fish from Grimsby and beer from Wolverhampton were sent weekly in latter times but finally ceased 1945–46.

In general tonnages were falling, only to pick up during petrol rationing and tyre shortages of World War II, and decline sharply as fortunes of war went in our favour. In 1949 income from this source fell to an all-time low of 11/1d. though it rose to £1 6. 7d. in 1950.

---

* Holding 16–18 gallons each.

In the following year Arthur Camwell and his friends have the train and the Railway almost entirely to themselves.   W. A. CAMWELL

The news that Sir Haydn has died has reached the Railway staff but is not yet spread in the town. Fittingly, a full train with a wagon of coal for Pendre engine shed will shortly leave the Wharf. Sir Haydn has fulfilled his promise and the Railway has operated to the end of his life.   AUTHOR

Taken overall, the traffic of the Talyllyn was in many ways similar to any other carried by a Victorian railway save that ordinary passenger traffic must have been trifling and confined to those from Abergynolwyn who had business in Towyn and vice versa. Some of these have been noted – the policeman, the blacksmith, schoolteacher, carpenter, rector, pigbreeder and so on. It is almost impossible to visualise a form of life where over and above the speed and power of the horse, the railway formed the ultimate in transport creativity; how few Welsh villages could boast a railway station at all!

A little more will be said about livestock traffic and the conversions of vehicles made for it on p. 291; and there remains one other commodity which the average passenger might never see – gunpowder. This was stored in wooden kegs in Wharf powder shed, probably in one of the two converted slate wagons built for that purpose and which lived in that shed. The gable-roofed vans would be taken right up to the gunpowder store near the Manager's Office at Bryneglwys. The store was a curious building as the vans had to pass through the end where no explosive was kept at all, before reaching the gunpowder store; the other end was used to keep many forms of materials and equipment, much of it for the smithy and blacksmiths' shops – for instance, pickhandles, chains and ropes. The remainder of the building was timber-lined and here caps, gelignite and powder were kept, together

with the tapered wooden containers (each with carrying handle, nailed in copper and with a 'spout' having a wooden bung in the end) which the miners used to carry the powder. At a later time the powder kegs were carried in the brake compartment of the passenger van – no doubt a highly illegal practice. It is thought they were then transferred to wagons for onward transport to the Quarry.

At some unrecalled time, one of the gunpowder vans (some say there was but one) was brought up to Pendre, its running gear removed and the body used to store sand used on the locomotives to overcome wheelslip. Sea sand was unsuited but largely used for all that, the sanding gear on the engines being unsophisticated!

If in 1951 the group which formed the 'Preservation Society' had intended that the Railway (with all that this meant in terms of the past), should be so halted in time that besides such obvious features of trains and track, the actual *raison d'être* for the Railway being in existence at all would be retained, then theirs was A Lost Cause before it began. For to measure the Railway of the past in terms of the tourist business of today, is not only to fail to grasp a world-picture now wholly eradicated, but to miss the very lifestyle of our forebears; in that unfortunate event the Railway today can only be measured as 'just another tourist attraction'.

Composed for the pages of a magazine. 'Emmett' the cartoonist simulates the cleaning of DOLGOCH which is blowing off lustily in Pendre shed. Young Basil Jones sweeps up alongside.

Pictured at the same occasion, the rightful driver Idris Williams holds one of the famous teapots of oil which were carried on the engines. The unsavoury inspection pit, usually far from clean and dry in those times, is prominently in the foreground.

BBC HULTON PICTURE LIBRARY

More preparation scenes at Pendre; Basil Jones is probably looking for some workably-sized lumps among those huge boulders of coal . . . .
BBC HULTON PICTURE LIBRARY

. . . . . and the engine pulls away from the shed premises in search of some carriages.
BBC HULTON PICTURE LIBRARY

More of the same, and DOLGOCH pulls the rake from the carriage shed . . . .   BBC HULTON PICTURE LIBRARY

. . . . and runs round to head them at the Pendre loop. The condition of the track gives little reason for confidence.

L. T. CATCHPOLE

'Hugh Gas' with TALYLLYN at Brynglas in 1935.

CHAPTER SEVEN
PERSONALITIES
(involved with the District, the Quarry, the Railway 1864–1951)

INITIALLY, human enterprises have grown from seeds in the minds of creative men, no less the activities described herein which, like many ventures in Wales, were brought into that country by outsiders who had had no previous links with the Principality.

In the Towyn district there were already a few men, mainly the major landowners, who showed this form of zeal. In their wake the sea was pushed back, the land drained, pastures improved and mountain slopes put to cultivation. Other entrepreneurs dug for lead, iron ore, gold or slate in the area and on the coastal fringe men built small ports and shipyards to carry these geological winnings overseas.

However, this was essentially a pastoral district and the efforts of the most active men, both then and now, made relatively small impact on the community. So it was with Towyn. But the most momentous happening, both then and since, came in the early 1860s with the building of a railway which linked Towyn with the outside world and in due course changed the lives of everyone from that time forward. The existence of the main line railway has come to be accepted without remark by later generations who are no longer dependent on it, but it may be said in truth that of all men who made the greatest impact on Towyn and district it was the promoters and builders of the Aberystwyth & Welsh Coast Railway.

The existence of a small slate quarry in the hills behind the town would not be of great moment. Various workings on the hills around, some large and some small, were part of the lives of the local people in the mid-19th century. Some of these workings (many of which can be seen today) proved worthless, and a few, such as Bryneglwys, blossomed. The effect of an invasion of navvies and the fears and hopes they brought, would tend to overshadow the acquisition of a local slate working with, as an early result, the arrival of yet a second railway into the small town.

However, over the last century and with hindsight, we may see how landowners, quarryowners, property owners and railway owners have developed Towyn and district and made it what it is today. Behind these half-dozen men came a larger group – yet still small in number – of those on whom their enterprise depended: quarry and railway managers, Masters of ships, those in local authority . . . those who carried out the owners' wishes. Under them came (and even these were a chosen race) what we now know to be a loyal band of employees whose lives were very hard, whose rewards were small and yet who enjoyed a continuity of employment which even then was enviable. Let us consider some of these personalities in the following sequence:

Landowners	The Corbets and the Corbetts of Ynysymaengwyn
Quarryowners ⎱	The McConnels of Manchester and Henry
Railway owners ⎰	Haydn Jones of Towyn

Quarry and Railway Directors and their appointees
Railway operatives
Other personalities

YNYSYMAENGWYN AND THE MORETON CORBETS

For two and a half centuries Ynysymaengwyn was the family house of the Corbets which came into the family by marriage of Robert Corbet, 3rd son of Sir Richard Corbet of Moreton Corbet, Salop, to Bridget, daughter of Sir James Pryse of Gogerddan and Elizabeth, who was the daughter and heiress of Humphrey Wynn of Ynysymaengwyn. Robert Corbet was an ardent royalist and fervent for the cause; the house was burned down in 1645 during the civil wars – as was Moreton Corbet. Ultimately, the property passed to Anne, from her father Vincent Corbet (d. 1723: there is a memorial tablet to him in St. Cadfan's Church); she married Athelstan Owen of Rhiwsaeson, Montgoms. There is a massive monument to Anne and Athelstan in St. Cadfan's; Anne built the imposing central block of Ynysymaengwyn in 1758, and almshouses too. When she died in July 1760 aged 76, she had been a widow for more than 30 years. A descendant Athelstan Maurice (the Maurice family had succeeded to the Ynysymaengwyn Estate) had, like all other Maurices, changed his name to Corbet on inheriting; one Maurice had been Vicar of Towyn 1785–1803. The inheritance was frequently made through the female line with consequent changes of name – the Maurice connection followed the death of Edward Corbet (of whom more anon) and the Estate continued to pass in the female succession until 1874 when it was sold to John Corbett of Impney, [no relation].

Edward Corbet had become owner in 1782 and his influence on Towyn and district was considerable, mainly due to his inception of the Dysynni Drainage Scheme which he began in 1788, [the ditches were made wide enough to take boats] duly receiving the Gold Medal of the Society for the Encouragement of the Arts in 1794 to commemorate the progress he had made.* He was a somewhat eccentric character but had some liberal leanings, the poor being given the

---

* The precursor of a much larger work in 1863, q.v.

Ynysymaengwyn seen from the east, showed the influence of several periods and architectural styles.   GWYNEDD ARCHIVES

privilege of turbary on his waste lands. He acquired a sinister reputation, however, by his attitude to Methodists who were suspected of kindling revolutionary ideas and showing sympathy towards the French Revolution which had preceded the threat of Napoleon and culminated in the French invasion at Fishguard in 1797. Edward may be said to be the first creator of modern Towyn; he died in London in 1820 but he is buried in St. Cadfan's, the body lying in state at Dolgelley *en route*. In another sphere, which emphasised his patriotic leanings, he founded the only Corps in Merioneth under the Volunteer Act of 1782, being dubbed henceforth 'Captain Corbet'.

It is difficult to accept that a cell of much sophistication was to be found at Ynysymaengwyn even in the time of the marriage of Elizabeth Wynn, heir to the Estate through her father Humphrey Wynn, and the new Shropshire connection must have brought changes in its train over the years. Not that Elizabeth would be unfamiliar with the lifestyle but it would take a different form in Merionethshire. The Corbets had had a long pedigree in the area, owning the Aberdovey Ferry before the 15th century; their connections, the Gwyns and the Nanneys, lived at 'Dolau Gwyn' (Lewis Gwyn built 'Dolau Gwyn' pre-1620 and a stone commemorates the fact 'GNAN 1620' being Lewis and Ann Gwyn) whilst the Pryses were of Gogerddan, all of which underlines the intermarriages of the great families in that district. It is significant that the *Dictionary of Welsh Biography* down to the year 1940 shows the ancestry in this form: 'Wynn, Pryse and Corbet families'.

Many of the Corbets became High Sheriffs of Merionethshire, the last of the line also holding this

office; he was Athelstan John Soden who added the name Corbet in 1866 and whose work in Towyn is mentioned elsewhere.

YNYSYMAENGWYN AND JOHN CORBETT (1817–1901)

In *John Corbett – Pillar of Salt**, we read that the Moreton Corbets tended to be 'profligates who whored, gambled and drank away a fine inheritance', and it was no surprise that the Estate was put up for sale in 1878. The Estate being sold to John Corbett (who was no relation) in 1884, the situation changed at once to ownership by a man who simply wanted to provide himself with a title and crest but who had little interest in the Estate itself.

John Corbett was the son of a Staffordshire farmer who had become a canal carrier. He had helped his father with the boats from the age of 10 but, having a mechanical bent, he was apprenticed at the age of 23 to an ironworks. He left reluctantly to become his father's partner in 1846 and in due course Corbett & Son became a large business with a fleet of boats. The undertaking was sold in 1852, and, looking around for a fresh enterprise, John purchased Stoke Prior salt works which had been operative since 1828 when salt was discovered thereabouts. Corbett found the business in a troublesome state, both in methods and finance, but he designed and built new equipment to suit the local problems and built it up with 50 boats on the adjacent canal and canal branches into the works; he built a railway, a wagon works and brickyard etc. and sold out in 1899 to The Salt Union.

*(Barbara Middlemass and John Hunt) Droitwich 1985.

At Towyn his outstanding contribution was the building of the esplanade and the massive sea-wall, but his motive for doing this was not altruistic, for, having bought the necessary land and protected it from the ravages of the sea, he intended to develop the hinterland.

He was an associate of the Institute of Civil Engineers and had married, in Paris in April 1856, Anna Elizabeth O'Meara (1832–1914) of Tipperary but born in Paris; they had six children. Her family was in the Diplomatic Service and she a Roman Catholic ... 'if anything, he was Anglican'. He was to become JP for the counties of Worcester and Merioneth and, as a Liberal MP (1874–92), was the last representative for the Borough of Droitwich, and the first of the mid-division of Worcestershire. A relation of his, Sir Rupert Kettle (County Court Judge on the Midland Circuit), had built a summer residence at Towyn (Rhowniar) and mentioned to him that Ynysymaengwyn was for sale. John Corbett's marriage had failed and, thinking he might find the house a good place wherein to leave his estranged wife (and at the same time that the ownership of it would be good for his image), he purchased it.

In John Corbett Towyn saw something of what they did in Haydn Jones in later years. He was met at the Cambrian station and given a 'reception committee all the way to Ynysymaengwyn'. He and his wife were separated and she continued to live with her daughters secreted away at Ynysymaengwyn; he nonetheless continuing to shower the town with developments. He meanwhile spent most of his life at Impney, Droitwich, which had been built in French chateau style to dispel any homesickness in his then-new wife. They were formally separated in 1885 and Anna left Ynysymaengwyn, only to move back there in 1906; when she died in 1914 she was buried in a small corner of Towyn graveyard.

Whilst the Moreton Corbets (sometimes spelling their name Corbett, rather confusingly) still have links with their old Shropshire seat near Preston Brockhurst, there has been no lineage for the incomer. When he died the Estate was bought by his daughter Mary who found the place too big and left to live at Rhianfa, and later at Lluesty in Towyn, and is remembered for driving round in an old Rolls Royce motor car. When she died in 1951 the County Council was given the Estate and they presented it to Towyn Council. The house was by now fated as dry rot had obtained a strong hold on its timbers. During World War II the military made use of it and it was further damaged to the point where little could be done but to have the building demolished in 1965. The four foot thick walls defied conventional demolition and explosives had to be used.

Much more could be added about this strange and once beautiful place with its Swiss governess, cook, four maids, Lady's maid, coachman, gardeners and footman, but so far as this account is concerned only the Railway had strong links with it and none of the Estate owners had any influence on the course of events of Railway or Quarry. During the lifetime of the Quarry, the influence of the landed gentry in Towyn became less and less, and those who survive have become valuable members within the community rather than an untouchable clan without that community. Forestry Commission, Farmers' Unions, Drainage Boards, Tourist Boards and others have brought about a quiet revolution in the countryside which the Railway – so apparently unchanged – has seen come to pass.

Towyn has had its share of 'difficult men' and John Corbett – received with such great hopes – never spent much time there. A recent commentator, describing the men whose names have been at the forefront in Towyn over the years admitted that self-made men were not very popular locally and that John Corbett, despite his several attempts to memorialise himself thereabouts, 'was not missed'!

THE McCONNELS

The McConnels formerly spelt their name M'Connel; they were never McConnell; there are only four of the family concerned. In order of birth they are James (1803–79), William (1809–1902), Thomas Houldsworth (1816–73) [being the sons of James (1762–1831),] and lastly a son of William, William Houldsworth (1858–1943). These McConnels spanned the period 1863–1910: their interest is more simply expressed by the following table:

Name	Cotton Industry	Bryneglwys Quarry	Talyllyn Railway
James	1826–1861 (retires)	c.1863–1879	c.1865–1879
William	1831–1878	c.1863–1902	c.1865–1902
Thomas H.	—	c.1863–1873	c.1865–1873
William H.	—	1882–1910	1882–1910

James seems to have retired from business about the onset of the American Civil War which so hit the Lancashire cotton spinning trade that firms went out of business, due to the cessation of raw cotton imports into Liverpool as a result of the blockade of shipments. Messrs. McConnel & Kennedy comprised Henry and James, eldest sons of James McConnel senior, and John Kennedy, their friend and neighbour. Becoming McConnel & Co., the firm was one of those in

MCONNEL & KENNEDY'S COTTON MILL
From a drawing dated 1800

The dark satanic mills of Manchester and district from whence interest in the Quarry and the consequent building of the Railway would stem. Even today, a few of the older and more of the magnificently-built later ones (once so familiar to the author) have survived and are now part of a trend to attract visitors to the area for its Industrial Heritage.

FINE COTTON SPINNERS

Although in competition, the leading cotton spinners were often close friends, of the same religious and political persuasions and inter-married.

FINE COTTON SPINNERS

Lancashire to be least affected by the cotton famine*, and managed to keep in production whilst starvation hit the workless, and nationwide relief was set up to help the impoverished spinners and their families.

James had married Ann Morewood of Ashford, Derbyshire in 1842 but they had no children.

William was born at Ardwick, Manchester and married in 1852 Margaret Bradshaw Wanklyn from Gloucester; her family had come to Manchester in 1790. Their fourth child was William Houldsworth, born 1858. William leased Hengwrt House from 1869 to 1872; (Hengwrt was bequeathed to Mary, Jane and Harriet Lloyd, sisters of Lady Vaughan (deceased) when her husband died in 1859; he was Sir Robert

Williames Vaughan. They had no children. The estate later reverted to the Vaughans). *The Cambrian News* for 5th January 1872 says:

> 'RENT AUDIT, HENGWRT ESTATE. Was held at the Golden Lion, Dolgelley when the tenants were treated with a substantial dinner as usual ... Mr. McConnel is an enlightened employer ...'

The draft lease (25th May 1869) is of 'Hengwrt House and premises at Dolgelley ... with the right of shooting over lands belonging thereto ...' and was for the lifetime of the lessors from 30th June 1869 for a rent of £305 per annum.

William had obtained control of McConnel & Co. in 1861 and this probably enabled him to widen his interests. His solicitor was William Orford and when William moved to Brooklands, Prestwich, the Orfords were neighbours. Next door lived his elder brother, James. Orfords already had a house near Towyn and obviously would tell William – socially if in no other way – of their holidays here. How William came to rent Hengwrt, which was some miles away, is not known, but many Englishmen were then renting or building houses near the Welsh coast and travelling there in their own road carriages.

---

* Cotton Famine. Three quarters of England's raw cotton came from America; Civil War began in April 1861 and the Federal Navy cut off supplies to overseas. By November 1862 a quarter of a million people in Lancashire were on relief. The big Lancashire-held stocks had been depleted and the remainder sold off at inflated prices. An appeal for relief funds met with charity from all sources. By 1865 the worst was over but a fresh crisis arose in 1866 owing to failures in the banking system of this country. Of the cotton famine it could be said it covered the period 1861–70, the period due to Civil War was 1861–65, but that the peak of difficulty had been passed by the end of 1862.

William McConnel.   FINE COTTON SPINNERS

Something of the character of William can be read into *The Cambrian News* reporting his death on 17th October 1902:

'... proprietor of the Abergynolwyn Slate Quarry, Abergynolwyn Estate and Talyllyn Railway died on Friday at Knockdolia Mansion, Colmonell, Ayrshire ... 95 years old and retained his full faculties to the end ... when the Company (the Quarry) was wound up some 20 years ago he purchased the whole concern ... for all that time he worked ... on his own account and was a model employer. It is highly creditable to him and his Manager (Mr Meyrick Roberts) that there has never been a single strike. The deceased was a very strong personality and followed the working of his great undertaking most closely to the end of his days ... had monthly returns sent to him showing the result of working the quarry, railways etc. ... news caused a grave state of things in the minds of those directly and indirectly connected with the works ... Mr. Roberts and Mr. Hugh Thomas (chief accountant of the company) were summoned to attend the funeral ...'

The account also quotes a correspondent:

'... he was one of the best employers of labour who ever came into Wales ... he never failed to pay the men to the day and the hour and the very best feelings always existed ... he was always under the right impression that he could not expect the best out of his men unless they were made comfortable in their homes as well as in the quarry ... he divided his estate ... so that the men could keep a cow or two or grow potatoes ... for family use. He converted one field into plots for gardens, charging ½d. per yard rent ...'

The men could go to the gardens instead of the public houses in their free time, it added.

'He brought more money into Wales than any man during the last 23 years' [this was certainly true of the Towyn district]. '... in late years he was assisted at Towyn by Mr. Roberts and also Mr. Yates ... he leaves a son who takes an active interest in the quarry and will doubtless follow ...'

Thomas Houldsworth was also born at Ardwick but moved to fashionable Hale Carr, near Bowdon in Cheshire. He married Catherine, daughter of George Murray of Ancoats Hall, Manchester, and also of Clugston, Wigtownshire. Murray Bros. had begun as machine makers in Manchester in 1790 and for a time were in partnership with the Kennedys. It will be clear that this small Unitarian community from Scotland was close-knit, intermarried and the most energetic in business affairs and promotion.

During Thomas H.'s time as Managing Director and Secretary to the Railway, he lived (sometimes) at Brynhyfryd, Towyn, an attractive stone-built house a little way from Wharf station. Although his personal visits were short, the convenience of this residence was undoubted, and it became expedient to house the Railway management there (and possibly more of the Quarry paperwork) as there were sufficient rooms to accommodate it. Certainly before 1865 the parlour there was the office, and wages for the railwaymen were collected therefrom.

It is almost impossible to resist the impression that the answer to the many unknown features about the McConnels – their introduction to the Quarry and the building of the Railway – stemmed from their close family and business ties. Their appreciation of the business competitiveness of their colleagues in the cotton trade, and the expansion of such cotton-linked names as the Buckleys, who created the Mawddwy Railway at the same period as the Talyllyn Railway, seem a likely result of an interwoven commercial and social pattern of life among the immigrant industrial families to Lancashire of that period. Surely William Orford, already settled at Towyn, would perhaps in an off-hand conversation mention that nearby Bryneglwys Quarry was being offered for sale by John Lloyd Jones?

An unexplained aspect of T. H. McConnel's scene is the lease c. May 1869 of part of the foreshore 'on the north side of the River Dovey near Trefri between a small stream called Nantbach and the mouth of the tunnel on the Cambrian Railways westward of the said stream and having a width of 154 yards and a depth of 260 yards' granted by the Board of Trade. Was this for a pier or jetty? It was apparently connected with

Hengwrt Hall, ancestral home of the Williames Vaughan, was leased to William McConnel for a number of years. How different from the dark narrow streets of Ancoats on the north side of Manchester.   FINE COTTON SPINNERS

the Abergynolwyn Slate Co. for in a quite different locality relating to a lease of foreshore at Nevin there is reference to 'McConnel & Co. in arrear . . . rent due 1 January 1888, paid 30 July 1888'. As the Dovey location was over 2,000 yards upstream of the existing Aberdovey harbour works and on a very limited site, it would have been suitable only for rail access while the sea access would have needed much dredging to make it suitable. In short, it may have been considered that 'a bird in the hand was better than two in the bush' on the part of McConnel.

William Houldsworth was the last McConnel owner of Estate, Quarry and Railway, as his descendants had no interest in these matters. He married twice and had very wide business connections but was never involved in the Manchester end of the family business, living much of his life at Heathend House, Baughurst, near Basingstoke. His elder brother, John Wanklyn, however, continued to live in the family house Brooklands, 'having been settled in cotton by his father . . .'. John Wanklyn's interest 'in Welsh slate quarries and the Talyllyn Railway which serves the quarries . . .' were bought out by William Houldsworth.

Family sources suggest that William Houldsworth intended to confine himself to limited interests but whether for that reason or not, as prospects for the Quarry dimmed, he moved into other business spheres. Basically it is unlikely he would ever have

found himself linked with the undertaking for he was in business in India when his father bought the Quarry from the liquidator in 1882 and he returned from thence to join him in the venture. Incidentally, during World War I he was doing work on paravanes at the Admiralty.

The widening spread of interests of William and his son William Houldsworth is evidenced by the following extracts from *The Directory of Directors*.

1880 – McConnel, William, Prestwich, Manchester:
    Abergynolwyn Slate Co. Ltd.   Chairman
    Brennan & Co. Ltd.   Chairman
    Manchester & Salford Bank
    Talyllyn Railway Co. Ltd.   Chairman
    W. Connels Co. Ltd.   Chairman
1900 – McConnel, George*:
    Calico Printers Association,   Managing Director
  McConnel, J. W.†:
    Fine Spinners & Doublers Association Ltd.
  McConnel, W. H. Stretton House, Alfreton:
    Monmouthshire Steel & Tinplate Co. Ltd.
    Sheepbridge Coal & Iron Co. Ltd.
    Tinsley Park Colliery Co. Ltd.
1909 – McConnel, W. H., Heath End House, Baughurst, Basingstoke:
    Dinnington Main Coal Co. Ltd.
    Sheepbridge Coal & Iron Co. Ltd.
    Tinsley Park Colliery Co. Ltd.

Note: W. H. McConnel became a director of Dinnington Main Coal Co. Ltd. 1901 and was later a director of Williams Deacons Bank.
* Cousin.
† Elder brother of W. H. McConnel.

THE HENRY HAYDN JONES ERA (CYFIANDER)*

It was Henry Haydn Jones (27th December 1863–2nd July 1950 and often known as Harry) who stepped in to rescue Quarry, Railway, Abergynolwyn Estate† and supporting district from an inevitable death; in January 1911 he purchased the whole lot to add to his already vested interest in the locality. (The conveyance is dated 25th March 1911.) At the age of 47 he was now a force to be recognised, a strong personality with oft-declared views on the purchase which, in later years, his opponents linked with a desire for political muscle and vote-gathering.

To understand the man – without whom the present generation would know no Talyllyn Railway – we must understand his background, which was unusual. His father, Joseph David Jones (1827–70), has been called one of the 'Noble Trio' of Montgomeryshire, each of whose birth fell in 1827, while each was eminent in his own subject which covered music, railways and geology. The two foremost were aforementioned J. D. Jones, and Benjamin Piercy, the contractor (1827–88) who lived latterly at Marchwiel Hall, Wrexham; the third was David Christopher Davies (1827–85).

'J.D.', as musicians and historians recall him, came from a simple farmhouse background at Bryngrugog west of Llanfair Caereinion, the residence now only a fragment on the ground, moving with his parents (his father a farmer and Wesleyan preacher) to Pantgwyn-bach in 1832, a house now demolished but which stood near the Llanfair Caereinion–Llanerfyl road. His family had once owned land and properties but, owing to some misfortune, they had been lost. His parents could not afford to give him more than one year's education but the impulse to improve it was accelerated by his mother's death on 20th October 1847 and his father's intention to re-marry. This set J.D. out on the road for Y Golfa, near Welshpool, to receive the six months 'schooling' which set out his lifestyle. Whilst there he had occasion to visit Towyn, being put in charge of a fellow pupil who was being sent to school there for his health.

Even by the age of 14 he showed strong musical ability and at 20 had published a small book of Psalm Tunes, the proceeds from which went towards the cost of six months spent in a Teachers' Training College in Borough Road, Southwark in 1847. On leaving Borough Road he obtained a post in Towyn School, later moving to Bryncrug; at this time he had fallen in love with Catherine Daniel of Penllyn, a sister of Daniel, John and Owen. The Daniels considered a struggling schoolteacher too menial to marry into their family but the pair eloped one night in 1860 and married at once; the affair had come to a head with J.D.'s appointment as Headmaster of the British School, Ruthin. He and his new wife made their home there in Rhos Street, in the School House.‡ Here they had six sons, but Joseph Haydn (aged 9 months) and Edward Howard (aged 14 months) died and were buried in the Baptist Cemetery, Llanfwrog, Ruthin. The four remaining sons, of which Henry Haydn was now the second eldest, all survived and each achieved eminence in his own right. Longevity was a common factor of their lives.

At Ruthin J.D. developed his musical talents, continuing to compose and publish while his life-style was improved by the extra income. His contribution to Welsh hymn singing was to develop its harmony aspects, now such a strong feature; though born a Wesleyan he found their beliefs prevented him from exploiting his musical ideas and he became an Independent whilst at Towyn. Chapel and Church music flowed from his pen, and hymn tunes such as 'Gwalchmai', 'Noddfa' and others are still widely used by all denominations. In 1868, together with Rev. E. Stephen, he published the first Welsh Congregational Hymn Book to coincide with the Eisteddfod held at Ruthin that year.

Of his three years (probably 1848–51) at Towyn, J.D. wrote '. . . to Towyn . . . made friends who . . . persuaded me to open a day-school of my own . . . I remained there for three years . . . I never turned out better pupils than those under my care at Towyn.' He ran singing classes at Towyn, Aberdovey, Bryncrug and Llanegryn. 'On 18 October 1851 I left Towyn to take charge of the British School, Ruthin . . .' So it would seem that this remarkable young man had actually set up his own Towyn school after qualifying at Southwark and it is no surprise that the British School, Ruthin, did not fulfil his ambitions for '. . . in June 1865 I left . . . and opened a Private School at Clwyd Bank'. This was advertised as being 'in union with the College of Preceptors, Headmaster J. D. Jones, ARCP, Latin & Greek Rev. E. Jones, French Mr. D. M. Bynner, Pianoforte & Harmonium Mr. J. A. Davies.'

It was a 'boarding and day establishment for the sons of prosperous farmers and businessmen sent there for a sound English education', and was locally dubbed 'The Academy'. One colleague (Bynner) would become J.D.'s wife's second husband.

---

* 'CYFIANDER' – Haydn Jones' shop-pricing code (i.e. 1 2 3 4 5 6 7 8 9) used to retain the secrecy of his buying and selling prices.
† This Estate had been conveyed to the Talyllyn Railway Co. on 10 May 1869 and excluded the railway between Abergynolwyn station and Nant Gwernol.
‡ British Schools had been started in 1808 by a Quaker, James Lancaster, who was supported by many other non-conformist movements. These were a different group from the National Schools, started in 1811 by the 'National Society for the Education of the Poor in the Principles of the Established Church'.

Jones put music high on the curriculum, he pushed himself hard, rising at 3.30 a.m. for his musical creations, but his health declined. An outbreak of typhoid in the town in 1870 raised his doubts about the water supply to the School and he may have contracted the disease after making his own tests on its purity. He died age 43 leaving a penniless young widow and four small boys, after failing to appear on the podium at the Caernarvon Music Festival due to the suddenness of the fever.

Ruthin was hard hit by the outbreak, and J. D. Jones was one of its brightest sons; he was buried alongside his small children. In 1927 – his centenary – 1970 and again in 1973 he was not forgotten; the BBC gave two broadcasts in his name in 1970 and in August 1973 a plaque was put up on the house in Clwyd Bank, commemorating this 'Schoolmaster & Composer'.

His young widow, age 34, returned in 1870 to her parents' home at Towyn; they had moved to Penllyn in 1835 and purchased it in 1851, moving to Caethlle* in 1865 where her brothers Daniel and John also farmed there, whilst Owen, the youngest, had a draper's shop in High Street, later moving to Brynhyfryd (a former home of T.H. McConnel). (In 1869 Owen took out an auctioneer's licence and with rare ability created a large business selling such big estates as Ynysymaengwyn, Bodtalog, Caethlle, Dinas Mawddwy, Gogerddan etc. He served on the Towyn Board of Health and was involved in the formation of the Towyn Gas & Coke Company. He died suddenly at Brynhyfryd in November 1894 and is buried in the Old Cemetery. He had the reputation of being the 'Black Sheep' of the family.)

[Though having no direct bearing on this narrative, it is informative to look at the Census Returns for Towyn in the year 1871. At Caethlle (just mentioned) Owen Daniel (aged 66) and his wife Catherine (aged 68) farmed 500 acres, employing five labourers and two boys. Sons Daniel (aged 38) and John (aged 36) were Head Bailiff and Shepherd respectively, but young Owen (aged 32) was living at the draper's shop with his wife and young family; he also lodged a draper's apprentice there. This was just as well, for John Jones' widow (aged 34) had returned home the previous year (described as 'visitor'), with Owen D. Jones (11), Henry H. Jones (8), John R. Jones (6), and Daniel L. Jones (4) all 'visitors' and all 'scholars'! Five other servants, etc. lived under the same roof, some were Welsh, one from Ludlow and one from Cricklade.

(In Frankwell Street lived two railway porters and the booking clerk; in Ynys Street lived another railway clerk (aged 15) and in High Street (at the station?) was John Ceiriog Hughes (aged 37) Station Master, from Denbighshire, and his wife from Chirk, Annie Catherine. All the foregoing would have worked at the then new Cambrian Railways' station, not the Talyllyn.)]

Farmer brothers Daniel and John saw potential in their sister's second-eldest child and made formal adoption of him. In 1877 Catherine re-married a Mancunian, the Rev. D. M. Bynner, minister of St. George's Street Congregational Church, Chorley, whence she moved with her three remaining sons. Haydn had been attending firstly the Board School then The Academy† in Towyn but at 16, Catherine's brothers set him up in business, giving their own name to it as he was still a minor. Meanwhile Catherine and her husband gave every opportunity for Haydn's brothers to develop their education; they went to Chorley Grammar School and each gave great service to the community in later life. Much later she lost her husband and for a second time was to return to Towyn as a widow, leading a far from leisurely life there, and dying in 1928 aged 92.

The new business was styled 'D. and J. Daniel, (H. Haydn Jones Propr.) Hardware Merchants, 22 High Street, Towyn, Merionethshire' and it flourished. Ironmongery and building supplies were its foremost features, and customers supported the business from well outside the county. Haydn bought widely – for instance, 55 bags of cement from Ghent came into Aberdovey on the *Kindly Light* on 21st October 1901.

While the business was expanding, it brought him new contacts and Haydn went into local politics; he was a founder-member of Merionethshire Cricket Club. Like his brothers, he blossomed, but for twenty years remained a bachelor, living with his uncles who had bought Pantyneuadd and other farms in 1876. About the turn of the century a scuffling noise in the narrow road behind that house caused him to go out to investigate, to find a young lady had fallen from her bicycle. He assisted her and in conversation learned she was from America but had relations in Bournemouth and Llanegryn: she had come to Wales for a better education than the States could provide. Her father (Lewis D. Jones of Chicago) was a native of Towyn, but her mother was American; she was Barbara Annie Gwendolen Davies Jones and, apart from the long summer holidays, she stayed at Llanegryn. Taking to each other immediately – though he was 39 and she so much younger – they wrote when apart and in due course were married in London in October 1903. He was 40 and she was 19.

Haydn's involvement in Parliamentary and county roles marked him as a man of few spoken words; when he did speak they were well chosen. He preferred people who knew their own minds and did not suffer fools gladly. These traits made him either loved and respected, or disliked and feared, 'everyone was afraid

* Caethlle leased from Ynysymaengwyn Estate.
† From 1894 The County School.

of him'. His father's character shone in him with a close interest in education,* music,† and his Chapel. His employees found him approachable always 'except when we asked for a rise'. He would have no truck with modernity; he abhorred Trade Unions and only suffered the typewriter, but he would not tolerate the telephone. His wife was in some respects a stronger character, more intelligent in other ways, the warmest of persons with immense enthusiasm for creative activities and – as can be said of few – without an enemy in the world. Together they were a formidable team. She died on 4th February 1959.

Shortly before his appearance on the Talyllyn Railway scene, he contested Merioneth as a Liberal in 1910 and (replacing Sir Osmund Williams who had resigned it) won the seat, holding it thereafter for 35 years until he resigned it. By that time he announced that neither Parliament (nor its members) had their former sense of duty towards those who elected it. However, back in 1910, and at 47 and a new MP, he had decided to purchase Quarry, Railway and Abergynolwyn Estate from what he often described as a moral duty towards his constituents in the neighbourhood. He was not confiding, but later admitted he intended only to run these enterprises for ten years,

a decision he did not carry out for he was still the Railway's major shareholder at his death in 1950 as he had become in 1911. Over the years he was often heard to complain that he had provided his locality and tenants with a railway whose facility they did not appreciate or use, preferring the 'bus instead. He usually added that it was costing him £5 per week to continue to indulge them.

Before long the Quarry and Railway found themselves under the influence of his strong local ties and a desire to make his cost of purchase 'work its passage'. McConnel had been a benevolent but often distant owner, and though immediate representation of changed ownership came through the Quarry and Railway Managers, there was no doubting that Haydn intended to sweep with a new broom. In character with most Liberals, he was acutely conscious of his duty to his employees. He deducted an amount from the men's wages (paid fortnightly) towards a Sick Benefit Scheme which he arranged with a local doctor. In consequence a man injured in the Quarry or with sickness in his family had *immediate* medical attention.

He was going to have no truck with organised labour – the Railway employees were a small, scattered force with no organised muscle, but in the Quarry there was a different mood. Some of his early well-meaning gestures reflected the growing awareness of well-disposed Edwardian employers but usually his motives were simply taken as window-dressing measures to prop up his personal supporters. However, his office above the shop made their Member ever available to those seeking help, and beneath a somewhat gruff exterior there was always a streak of compassion (though it was said 'it sometimes needed a Search Warrant to find it'). So in the days when news travelled fastest by telegram or telephone and the telegraph boy on his push-bicycle, Haydn presided in this self-centred, isolated part of the Principality, a near-feudal landowner in surroundings which even the First War failed to alter. It was a setting (for Towyn was similar in this respect to the rest of the county) where Liberal-voting non-conformist males (females were not entitled to vote) had but recently usurped the long-standing landowner situation which traditionally was said to be found – or might be found! – in churches where King James' Prayer Book was in use! Towyn was divided between Whigs in the Chapels and Tories in the Church and even as recently as 1985 the opinion was expressed that Mr. So-and-so must have been an Anglophile and worshipper at St Cadfan's, because he always spoke in English and dressed like a gentleman – the said person was, in fact, a good Welshman, a

A recent view of the east elevation of Pantyneuadd, the Towyn home of Haydn Jones.   AUTHOR

*For some time he was Hon. Director of Education for the County.
† He was Editor of *Can-a-Moliant*, a collection of hymn tunes, published in 1916.

Deacon of one of the largest chapels and a fluent Welsh speaker!

The reason for this background to affairs was historic. The Welsh countryside in general and Merioneth in particular – the most backward of the six North Wales counties – was made up almost entirely of big estates owned by long-established families who, in the district surrounding Towyn included the Corbets of Ynysymaengwyn.

These landlords, though of Welsh nationality, 'scions of ancient county families', and many of whom were joined by marriage, had for hundreds of years enjoyed the support and respect of their tenants. They themselves drew their way of life from English standards which showed in their educational standing, ambition, dress, social life etc. However, the Reform Bill of 4th June 1832 affected town and countryside alike. Apart from giving the small towns representation to Parliament, middle classes of farmers and shopkeepers who owned or rented property of a certain minimum value were given the vote; the Bill 'breached the ancient stronghold of aristocratic privilege'.

The Corn Laws were introduced in 1815 to restrict imports of cheap foreign grain and keep its price up to the scarcity level of the French Wars; landlord and tenant benefited, especially the former. When this artificial tie between them was broken in 1846, the age-old order of things in a part of Wales which was almost a total agricultural society, was gone for ever.

The tenant farmers in these large Welsh estates, be they Towyn or elsewhere, were Welsh-speaking, influenced by the chapel pulpit and politically radical; they drew no inspiration from England. By the time the Bryneglwys Quarry and Talyllyn Railway were operational, Welsh liberalism had found new cells in which to flower – among railwaymen and quarrymen feudalism was fast disappearing. To these the owner of Quarry or Railway (from whatever source he had come) was judged simply by his relations with themselves and principally concerning wages. So it was that it is recalled that the McConnels were concerned employers, as might be expected from a family of Unitarians who had grown from farming background and built their own businesses in a hard school. They had no reason in their time at Bryneglwys to concern themselves with Welsh landowners or their tenants; basically they were an island of commercial enterprise in a foreign setting, economic penetrators on a speculative foray. (Among the 'native' evidence of industry locally were the flour and woollen mills; of the latter, three were in Towyn and two by Talyllyn, all being waterdriven.)

Not so Haydn Jones; his purchase was significant in that the labour force of Quarry and Railway saw in

him one of themselves, namely, a Welsh non-conformist who stated publicly that his purchase was to save them from poverty. Little wonder there was an optimistic mood among the Quarry community at the take-over, and with hindsight, it was no surprise that Haydn would never prove to them the Messiah they expected him to be. There is no doubt that he himself had no illusions from the start, Quarry and Railway were each, in fact, but groups of people in one district, where Haydn represented Welsh Liberalism and another resident, a man of medicine, represented the other political party. Their opposing outlooks, their desire to leave the mark of their convictions, are recalled as a *force majeure* in the community and led to the town being provided with several facilities funded by those same competitors each anxious not to be outdone. Added to this was the megalomania of John Corbett (Ynysymaengwyn) not to be forgotten, and though he failed to provide the anticipated Towyn Pier, his name on promenade and elsewhere will not allow us to forget his influence. The Hospital, Institute, School and Market House are other instances of benevolence attributed to such showering of largesse!

One would not expect the Cambrian Railways, their Towyn station or their local interests to reflect such parochial rivalries, but the Talyllyn Railway, so much dependent on the Quarry, was at times anxious for slate business when Haydn was passing through one of the periods when the quarrymen were trying to promote their case and Haydn was presenting his, with the consequence that the owner closed down the workings and would not re-open until the men had recanted. Luckily, there was usually a stock of slates at the Wharf for customers, but as the quarrymen were responsible for operating the connecting inclines, there were periods when no slate trains ran.

One of Haydn's problems included the adverse publicity Welsh slate was receiving as a result of competition from cheap inferior foreign imports. This reputation spread to *all* slates, good and bad, and architects were turning to other materials – however, the achievement of obtaining an order for slate to re-roof part of Westminster Hall gave Bryneglwys an enormous boost.

About 1912 the Railway's administration was moved from the office at the Wharf where from earliest times the Manager had reigned (except for a time at Brynhyfryd), to 22 High Street, where Haydn could keep an eye on his staff, not one of whom he was prepared to trust implicitly. He himself took charge from the upstairs office which was notable for its three desks overflowing with paper and matters of all description; when one was unusable he simply moved to another less buried in stationery. '... I met him ... in that famous upstairs office of his in his Towyn ironmonger's shop ... here he transacted much of his business ... wearing black striped trousers and frock coat, and with a keen assessive look in his eye'. When the House was sitting (between Monday and Thursday) the Railway business was managed solely by Edward Thomas, who had been moved into the shop from the Wharf; on Mondays he would precede the great man to the Cambrian station for the London train, carrying his bags. On Fridays and Saturdays, Haydn, still in the morning attire of the Commons, would serve his customers with, perhaps, four pennyworth of nails, and weigh them out.

The shop itself was managed by John Parry, a nephew of Edward Thomas and with whom he lived at Trefri, just beside Wharf station. Thomas had bought the land off the Railway in 1908 and built himself a house there. A brother of Edward Thomas, John Evan Thomas, was cashier for all Haydn's businesses, and housed in an office alongside Haydn's. It was his job to bring out daily from a safe under the stairs, the huge Estate Ledgers; Edward embraced his work when John Evan died; the latter 'was as slow as a snail but utterly trustworthy'; his copperplate handwriting was remarkable.

Time and tides in the affairs of men tended to bypass Towyn and it is not surprising that things carried on almost in pre-1914 fashion right up until Sir Haydn's death on 2nd July 1950 (he was knighted for public services in 1937). Almost to the last he continued to give personal and daily supervision to his interests and at his death that veritable mine of local history in his office (which appeared as if it had never been sorted or tidied) was taken out and burned in a corner of the Wharf coal yard by Hugh Jones and Morris Lewis. Edward Thomas supervised the cremation and every time they tried to pick up some nostalgic remnant he would shout 'Go on, go on', as if there was deliberate intent to prevent later generations from finding anything suspect. There is little doubt that this bonfire destroyed personal, Railway and Quarry records for he saw himself as the personal embodiment of a Trinity! Included in this conflagration would be the blueprints of the Fletcher, Jennings locomotives which had long adorned the Wharf office and which over the years had grown more decrepit – this was both shortsighted and stupid, but instructions were instructions, even by dead men in those times, and it must have been seen that with the death of its owner, the Railway would soon follow suit and nothing of this calibre would ever be needed again.

Up at Abergynolwyn, the villagers saw Haydn in a different light, so many being dependent on him for livelihood. For instance, in the mood of a 'Better Britain' after the First War, about half the men were as yet not in a Union and wished to join one. Haydn refused to allow it; if they did so he would close the Quarry. But the men thought they had everything in their favour and joined the Union despite the threat. In 1921 Haydn kept his word and there was much resultant hardship in the village (there had already been a similar stoppage in February 1920). Some men went to Braichgoch Quarry, Corris, to work but were soon disillusioned: in about a month the older men drifted back and later, all the Braich Goch rebels did the same. Those who had not joined the Union were allowed back to work at once, those who did were the last taken on. The Quarry was closed about 3–4 months but Towyn had no such experiences.

His quarrying and farming interests extended beyond the Towyn area – in the mid-1930s he took the leasehold of certain Aberllefenni slate and slab quarries, north of Corris, Edward Thomas being appointed Secretary on 6th April 1935. Haydn insisted on rail transport for this new venture and without it the Corris line might have closed down earlier than it did, certainly pre-World War II.

When at first Haydn became an MP and within a few months had added to his interests, he leaned heavily on Ellis Davis & Co. of Caernarvon (Solicitors) who acted on his behalf in the Freehold & Leasehold of the Quarry, the properties and the shares of the Talyllyn Railway Company. This firm was in fact that of Ellis William Davies (then MP for Caernarvon and a close friend of Haydn – he retired from politics in 1929 and nearly took Haydn with him) and through them Haydn 'purchased 750 £20 shares ... followed by a transfer of 85 shares to friends, relatives or nominees probably to ensure that there was a sufficient number of shareholders to comply with the Provisions of the Company Clauses Act of 1845 as to the meetings of a Statutory Undertaking.'* [When Sir Haydn died, his widow Lady Barbara Annie Gwendolen Davies Jones (sole executrix) generously transferred 650 shares to a Limited Holdings Company formed for that purpose in 1951. However, these were not all the issued shares of the Company; some had largely been 'lost' and Sir Haydn's latter-day solicitors found no trace; the recovery of these takes this narrative into an era outside its coverage.] The legal owners of these shares had, in some cases, never even received their Share Certificates which were retained in the solicitor's office, representing 100 shares in the Company; in all, 20 shares were transferred to five nominees to comply with the Act.

---

*i.e. Haydn was not permitted to own all the shares in the Company: in order to hold a valid meeting of a Public Company there must be a certain number of shareholders in proportion to the capital.

'A rail king in his lair . . . all set for a busy morning keeping the wheels turning' was the fulsome caption to this portrait of Sir Haydn at the age of 86, the year before his death. He sits at one of his famous desks in the overcrowded private office on the first floor above Daniel's shop.   BBC HULTON PICTURE LIBRARY

It would be improper to suggest that Haydn's legal advisers had deliberately failed to carry out their duties to the full, or that on future occasions they did not measure up to the requirements of the 1845 Act, but some nominees were quite adamant that they did not know they held shares in the Company – being mostly successors of deceased original nominees – and received no communication from the Company! As the work in a solicitor's (or) office was quite sufficient to delay the issue of Annual Reports, Notice of Meetings etc. when basically the major shareholder would

continue to control the Company's destiny as he wished, their oversight (if any existed) may be understood.

It could be said that neither Haydn Jones nor his legal advisers recognised that the Railway Company and Haydn Jones himself were, in law, two separate bodies. Whether it was convenient so to do will always remain a mystery. Perhaps it was accepted that because Haydn owned the majority of shares in the Railway and that the balance was held by his relatives and friends, no distinction was made between himself and the Company in the matter – at least this was the opinion given by the Company's legal adviser after Sir Haydn's death. The ultimate confusion did not arise until Talyllyn Holdings Ltd. was formed in 1951 and it was discovered that certain shares – in actuality those owned by the nominees – had not been transferred into that Holding Company.

However, these circumstances may have been to the ultimate benefit of the Railway Company's continuing existence seeing it was but virtually a lifeline of a

Quarry and in this respect would be hard to find another Statutory Company in quite the same position. Certainly if communications to shareholders suffered, so did also the necessary Annual Returns. Would this be the fruits of a little quiet word in the ear of an appropriate Member or Minister in the side corridors of the Commons? Or would the cessation of that yearly reminder that the Railway was still in existence cause the powers-that-be to overlook it both in 1923 and 1948 when, firstly many railways were 'grouped', and

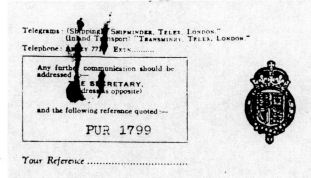

Telegrams: (Shipping) SHIPMINDER. TELEX. LONDON."
(Inland Transport) "TRANSMINRY. TELEX. LONDON."
Telephone: Abbey 7711 Extn..........

Any further communication should be addressed to—
THE SECRETARY,
(address as opposite)

and the following reference quoted :—

PUR 1799

Your Reference ....

MINISTRY OF TRANSPORT,
BERKELEY SQUARE HOUSE,
LONDON, W.1.

18 May, 1949.

Sir,

Talyllyn Light Railway

    I am directed by the Minister of Transport to refer to your letter of 28th April and to state that in the light of the information which you have now supplied, he is satisfied that the Talyllyn Light Railway Company is still in existence, and is entitled to operate the railway.

    The share certificates and transfers enclosed with your letter are returned herewith and I am to say that any inconvenience you may have been caused by this Department's enquiries is regretted.

            I am, Sir,
            Your obedient Servant.

Sir H. Haydn Jones,
    Towyn,
      Merioneth.

secondly, when most survivors were nationalised? If the neighbouring Corris Railway through its bus interests fell into the clutches of the Great Western Railway, why did not the Talyllyn for other reasons? The simple answer would be that they were utterly different in composition however similar in habitat and purpose; the Talyllyn Railway was the personification of Haydn Jones and the Corris Railway was (and had) nobody!

The omission of the Railway from the maw of railway companies which had fallen into the 1948 nationalisation net must have puzzled both the Ministry of Transport and Sir Haydn to the extent that when the former made enquiries as to the survival of the Company, Haydn was convinced it was necessary to send the evidence of share certificates to prove it was! The reply of the Minister is worth reproducing in full, not least the inexcusable error – for the Talyllyn was *never* a 'Light Railway'!

Having covered the exceptional personality of Haydn Jones we now return to the promoters of the Quarry enterprise and its linking Railway; they were carefully chosen. Without exception they came from among the successful commercial class in the greater Manchester area and competitors in the cotton spinning business; friends among the Unitarian movement and John Shaw's Club; neighbours and members of the family were to be found there. It is worth a second look at some of these men. (Business addresses below).

THOMAS SWANWICK of 56 Fountain Street, Manchester (1814–96)

A relative of Frederick Swanwick, who surveyed the Manchester to Stockport railway line under George Stephenson in 1835. He was a well-known American Merchant and a partner in the considerable business of A. & S. Henry & Co. of the city. He was a leading figure in local Unitarian circles and 1865–68 sat on the City Council as representative for the Cheetham Ward. He was the younger brother of John Swanwick, the senior member of the Manchester Royal Exchange.

MURRAY GLADSTONE of 24 Cross Street, Manchester (1813–75)

A founder of the house of Gladstone & Latham .& Co. Prominent businessman who held many public offices and chairmanships. Later lived at Penmaenmawr but his house at Higher Broughton became (1870) the seat of the Bishop of Manchester. A cousin of the statesman.

He was initially a Civil Engineer, [among other interests to the Chester & Birkenhead Railway (inc. 1837)]. He went into commerce in 1844 and to Calcutta (Gillanders, Arbuthnot & Co., Calcutta) in the employ of East India Merchants. Returned to England in 1850 to form Gladstone & Latham. He became a Trustee of the Royal Infirmary, also later the Treasurer – and of the Lunatic Asylum. He was a Governor of Owen's College and Manchester Free Grammar School, Chairman of Manchester & Salford Saturday Bank, Chairman of Royal Exchange,* Deputy Director of Chamber of Commerce and Consolidated Bank, a director of the Indian Branch Co. There is no reference to his Talyllyn Railway interests in his obituary in *The Manchester Guardian* August 1875.

SAMUEL HOLKER NORRIS of Princess Street, Manchester, and Altrincham

Admitted a partner in T. & R. Potter in 1830 (a firm of Attorneys in Princess Street, Manchester) but withdrew in 1836; a Wesleyan family. The Potters were an old family long connected with the cotton industry – originally from Tadcaster; Thomas Potter (later Sir) was first Lord Mayor of Manchester. Edmund Potter President of Manchester Royal Exchange 1860.

By the 1841 census, Samuel had set himself up as a Merchant in King Street, Altrincham and in 1864 was also a member of the Altrincham Local Board.

Of less influential status came three other men:

WILLIAM ORFORD was solicitor to the Talyllyn Railway Company and senior partner in Earle, Son, Orford & Milne of 44 Brown Street, Manchester. He and his son and partner (also William) owned a country house near Bryncrug, called Bronffynnon: his Manchester residence was close to that of William McConnel for whom he acted professionally, and through him it might be that the news that Bryneglwys Quarry was for sale, reached the ears of the McConnel family. Whilst at Bryncrug Mrs. Orford was well-known for her social work, which is still remembered; she started a clinic there which Dr. Jones took over when he bought the estate some time after 1916.†

JAMES STEVENS was a surveyor and architect of 88 Mosley Street, Manchester and his services are likely to have been used before the Quarry acquisition. He was responsible for surveying the Quarry, preparing plans for housing at Abergynolwyn (not all carried out) and when McConnels first acquired the Quarry, he was sent down there and fell foul of Robert Williams. He became Secretary to the Abergynolwyn Slate Co. Ltd. in 1867.

THOMAS ALDRED was the accountant appointed as liquidator of the Abergynolwyn Slate Co. Ltd. in 1883; he worked from 100 King Street, Manchester.

---

* Demolished and rebuilt on same site under Act 29 V.C. I (1866).
† Bronffynnon is now Woodlands Holiday Park.

Bronffynnon was the Welsh home of William Orford, the Manchester solicitor who possibly first made Towyn known to the McConnels.
It is a few miles inland from the coast, and near Bryncrug.   GWYNEDD ARCHIVES

Moving on from the administration: **James Swinton Spooner** was the second son of James Spooner of Portmadoc, and had probably assisted his father along with his brother, Charles Easton, in a survey for the Festiniog Railway in the 1830s. He was born c. 1816 and was educated at 'Mr. Race's School, Altrincham, Cheshire' in 1829 and in the 1850s had left home to work on the railways in the antipodes before returning to Wales by the early 1860s. At the time of his appointment to the Talyllyn Railway he had, along with others, obtained a lease of the Hafod Las slate quarry at Betws-y-Coed, near his later home at Llanrwst. He was involved in this business until 1882 and does not in fact seem to have been associated with railway work after his Talyllyn Railway venture, confining himself to road and bridge work.

The census of 1851 shows him living at Brynllewlyn, Llan Ffestiniog with Julia his first wife from Co. Durham. Two children had been born in the mid-1840s in New Zealand and New South Wales respectively and a further three in Llanbeblig, Caernarvonshire, the ultimate in 1849. His youngest son, Thomas James (1860–1937), served an apprenticeship at Boston Lodge (Festiniog Railway) 1879–83 with Spooner & Co. [this Company then describing itself as 'Civil, Quarry and Mining Engineers, The

Wharf, Portmadoc (also Quarry Proprietors)']. Thomas James became assistant engineer on the Darjeeling Himalayan Railway during the construction of the line and was later on the Indian Midland and Uganda railways in 1902.

In an undertaking as small even as the combined Quarry and Railway, it is hard to see where official titles existed and easy to trace subtle differences in the titles given to administrators from year to year. [The usually-helpful *Bradshaw's Shareholders' Manual* and other Annual Returns which any other company would be bound to submit, cease in the case of the Talyllyn Railway after 1893 and the dates on which persons took or lost office have had to be estimated.]

R. B. Yates was made Chief or General Manager (also Secretary and Engineer) to the Railway in September 1900, continuing in this capacity until the end of the McConnel regime in April 1911, becoming Secretary of Aberdovey Golf Club in 1913. He lived with his wife Charlotte (known locally as Lottie) at Sandilands Hall (demolished in the 1950s).* He seems to have also enjoyed a degree of management over Meyrick Roberts at the Quarry, but the latter remained as local Quarry Manager. He found his Indian re-

---

* Haworth, an architect, had been the last occupier.

creations were absent at Towyn and set about making good this omission, firstly by creating an 18-hole golf course and the formation of the Towyn Golf Club, and secondly by introducing a goodly circle of friends and acquaintances to the delights of the card table. The Golf Club played on the Morfa from 1902 but the course at Aberdovey proved to be a strong competitor. Towyn was requisitioned by the military in 1939 and abandoned, later becoming an airfield.

Yates was a popular figure in the district, a good disciplinarian and a man to see fair play. It was his rôle to report to Haydn Jones every weekend – at the shop or Pantyneuadd – to 'fill in' the Member for Merioneth on his return from London. About 1914 Yates went to live at Moffat: he could claim among the few who came to Towyn in this guise that he is remembered as 'being a proper gentleman'.

One of the most responsible jobs down at King's station was the checking of slates as they were passed out of the Talyllyn Railway wagons into those of the main line. There are no records of such men or others who administered the Railway and Quarry business there, other than the earliest suitable Census Returns of 1871; this reveals **John Roberts** was the Slate Agent and given as 'Managing Owner of the Quarry Co.' – he was born in Penrhyndeudraeth and lived at College Green, Towyn, was 29 and occupied premises down at the wharfside when on duty. In 1876 he is given as General Manager in *Bradshaw's Railway Guide*, and was still in the same post in 1881.

The checking of loads was the duty of **David Humphrey** aged 31, who came from Talyllyn but was now lodging at Brynhyfryd, probably in that part of the house in use for business purposes and not the portion used by T. H. McConnel. His title was Slate Inspector.

The Census also lists **Joshua Sydney Hunt** age 25 from Ringwood, Hants, but now of Neptune Villa, Towyn, described as a Slate Quarry Manager. Of which quarry, or was he an understudy at Bryneglwys? Perhaps McConnel needed an Englishman on those premises?!

Revelation as to who was ultimately responsible for Railway affairs down at King's at a later date sprang from Towyn graveyard where the resting place of 'Hugh Thomas, Slate Wharf, Towyn (November 1842–January 1903)' was noticed. John Parry said that when the Railway first opened, **Hugh Thomas** (then living in Aberdovey) walked daily to the office at Brynhyfryd, used temporarily before the completion of the King's office. Fortunately the Census again comes to our aid, and we find Hugh in 1871 and 1881

PRETORIA at the Wharf pre-1903; the cast is (left to right): Jacob Rowlands, Jonathan Rowlands, Hugh Thomas – with Bob Thomas on the engine.

TALYLLYN RAILWAY CO.

then living in Church Street and described as 'Clerk to the Slate Company' and 'Clerk in the Slate Company's office'. Another lucky discovery reveals him as 'Agent for the Abergynolwyn Slate Co.' in *Sutton's Directory of North Wales (1889–90)*. He was father of Edward Thomas, who joined the Railway Company as Clerk in 1897 as assistant to his father, who 'was Manager at that time'. Hugh would be in his late fifties when McConnel appointed R. B. Yates as Manager, and perhaps this was due to Hugh's failing health – it has been difficult to unearth details of the Thomas family at this time save that they lived in High Street. The same difficulties of title occur; whether as 'Agent', 'Traffic Manager', 'Chief Accountant', 'Manager', 'Clerk' (all these titles having been applied) we may be sure that Hugh Thomas, labouring under any title – appropriate or not – would carry out his duties in whatever sphere the demands of the day required – for such was the nature of the undertaking!

Edward Thomas in his first year with the Company, together with his father Hugh, and Jacob Rowlands — the recorded date is 1897.

J. PARRY

Edward Thomas amid a somewhat pre-arranged chaos of paper (much of it of great archival value today) allegedly checking the ledger in the Wharf office for the benefit of 'Picture Post'. The office was actually kept as neat and tidy as did the Manager keep his own personal appearance!
BBC HULTON PICTURE LIBRARY

In considering these men and their work, and the King's station premises at the turn of the century, on the site of the existing (1988) corner building there (the ex-Gunpowder Store) was formerly a rough wooden shed; it is suggested that this was the Quarry 'office' but that the checker worked at the weighbridge in the main building; there was also a small bothy ('caban') under the lee of Trenewydd railway bridge where the slate loaders took their meals.

Edward Thomas began on the Railway in 1897 and though he retired from full and active participation in 1950 (six months before Sir Haydn's death), he was to remain closely connected with the Company after the period of this book, latterly as a Director. His family lived at 1 Beacon View, High Street (The Dorothy Café) but later he moved to 'Trefri' as previously mentioned and lived there with his widowed sister, wife of 'Captain' Parry whose son John also moved into the shop in 1912 when his cousin Edward went there; John became clerk in the shop and ultimately, the Manager.

Like his father it mattered little what title he carried – his life was to wait upon Haydn's every whim and he moved from shop to Railway office as occasion demanded; there would be many times when he 'wished there were two of him'. Always courteous and attentive, he was largely responsible for ensuring that the Railway did not close down at Haydn's death. He is well remembered as a bachelor, a Church Secretary and Deacon, for his quick light movements when he did duty as guard on the train, nipping from the Wharf office at the last moment before sending off the train with a quick flick of the wrist. At Wharf, he would snatch up the cash box and tickets from the office, despatch the train and slip deftly into the moving van as it slipped past him. He would dispense tickets from that van on the journey and throughout would never waste a physical movement or a word of mouth that was not to some creative end. Only in the coldest weather did he wear an overcoat, and then he never buttoned it.

Jacob Rowlands and his family at Railway View, Pendre found a good friend in him. Haydn Jones would try to find a wife for him, on one occasion telling him to go to Railway View and plight his troth with Miss Jane Rowlands; 'Go on, go on' would insist his employer, until at last he did so, only to be turned down. By now Jane was the last of the family to remain at Railway View. Coincidence or note, either through this disappointment to the menfolk or perhaps to take herself somewhat further away, she made a new home at Piccadilly!

Jane's nephew Edward Chambers would come over from her married sister Mary's home at Criccieth to spend part of the school holidays at Towyn; he was keenly interested in the Railway and she would send him up on the train which he so much enjoyed; despatching him from the house to the station her parting words (intended for Edward Thomas) would be 'Don't let him charge you anything for the fare'.

Edward Thomas had a special way of entertaining his close friends to a conversation in the Wharf office, after the trains had finished for the day. Not for him the cup of tea, or the bottle and glasses in the cupboard, but he would move towards the safe, unlock it and produce a tin of 'Nuttall's Mintoes' . . .

A colourful character, **John Parry** was better known on the Railway in a period following that of this book, when he became Curator of the Narrow Gauge Railway Museum. However, a feature of 'Trefri', appearing in many photographs, was the tall flagstaff in that garden – it was a typical 'John Parry enterprise', being the fruit of one of his proverbial excursions to the shore in search of wreckage; one day he found a 30 ft. spar washed up near Aberdovey and persuading a friend to help him, they carried the spar on two push-bikes from Aberdovey to 'Trefri'. This duly became part of the flagpole.

Meyrick Roberts was appointed Quarry Manager or 'Agent' by the McConnels in 1880 (he also farmed in a significant way), and even after he formally retired in 1922 he continued to be responsible for the wages and delivered them to the Quarry. His predecessor was E. Evans. Of the various features of life at Bryneglwys over this long period, one of his grandsons has clear recollections.

The Roberts were 'on the land' rather than in the quarries: Meyrick moved from Erw Fawr in Llanfrothen Parish, near Portmadoc to come to Bryneglwys where they lived at the Hall, and his wife had ten sons and one daughter, so that the Hall was a very lively place. At lunch time it was nothing to have 14 or more persons sitting down at the table, for McConnel was fond of sending up fellow Scots to see his quarry; he had many friends among Army officers, he himself having served in the Scots Guards. He would also send up relations for a holiday, and all

seemed to enjoy themselves, as much coping with the Welsh language with which they were surrounded. Life at Bryneglwys had not the grim appearance of the ruin it now is. The daughter presented the second Mrs. W. H. McConnel with a set of Crown Derby china from the employees, on the occasion of her wedding.

Also at the lunch table would be representatives and agents who had come up on business; they might be from Ingersoll-Rand, Kynoch or Nobel, for instance. These firms were closely connected with the quarry and mining industries. Kynoch of Witton, Birmingham, were cartridge makers and in later years the Kynoch Works became the base of Imperial Chemical Industries Nobel Division; Kynochs made their own brass cartridge cases. Representatives from Kynoch and Nobel would be anxious to sell explosives (probably through the Kynoch agent, in fact, as Nobels specialised in dynamite, an unsuitable medium, the softer gunpowder being preferred as it did not shatter the rock).

The Ingersoll-Rand Company was of American origin and an amalgamation of earlier firms; they supplied compressors (e.g. one was delivered to Penyrorsedd Quarry before 1900 and survived to the end) and rock drills – and possibly air-powered winches – to the industry as a whole. The matter of equipment in slate quarries has not yet received the ventilation it deserves.

If the doctor was up on a visit, he would arrive by horse from the village. There were frequent small accidents among the men; if a man was killed, his widow received £5 and would be (if suitable) offered a job as a dairymaid, baker, cook or housemaid at Bryneglwys if a place was available.

The working area in the Quarry chambers 'was a mass of compressed air drill piping, and the racket from drills on the rock was intense'.

The small shed in the quarry where the gunpowder was stored was a 'No go' area; children were expressly forbidden to go near it, and it had a red door.

From time to time a photographer came up to the Quarry and the men would assemble on a rubbish heap, a useful 'grand stand' for a photographic group – the Manager could always be picked out from the rest as he sported a gold Albert watch chain. Such pictures were greatly prized and there was scarcely a house in the district which did not display one or more on the wall. That shown on p. 16 was taken on the side of Beudybach, to mark Queen Victoria's Diamond Jubilee.

A curious arrangement in the residential barracks, down in the village or on the farms, was the availability of a wet nurse to suckle children whilst their parents were absent; sometimes children were even kept by the nurse for long periods.

In the long evenings and after the barrack room suppers had been cleared away, the men would entertain each other by candlelight with the singing of hymns.

The McConnels were quite overcome by the Welsh language and tended to come to know best those local residents who were of English descent – somewhat naturally. In this way when Athelstan Corbet was looking for suitable names for two cottages on the Ynysymaengwyn Estate, a McConnel suggested in desperation that they chose English names which at least they could pronounce – in this way Piccadilly and Pall Mall were christened.

The annual Sunday School outing was the one big day of the year for the villagers of Abergynolwyn, and they elected to go to Towyn for it! A special train was provided, and all travelled at the expense of the Quarry owners.

The children of the Meyrick Roberts' family acquitted themselves well in after life; one managed the Deeside Slab Quarries near Corwen, one was a slate agent in London, one was killed in the Boer War, one died as a result of a typhoid epidemic in Towyn, one farmed at Bryncrug, one was a Bank Manager, one became Minister of Health for Wales and also served on the Senate for the University College of North Wales at Aberystwyth, and another farmed on Anglesey. Clearly to be brought up at Bryneglwys was to answer the challenge of life in the world beyond it!

Travel to and from the Hall depended on the Railway and its access, the inclines. Roberts insisted that when travelling on inclines as a family, they should not all occupy the same wagon; the Village Incline seems to have been the scene for most accidents, caused by breakage of the cable. The children were instructed to jump out if the cable broke, before the wagon began to drop, but in every case the men and boys must apply the handbrake, hard. On one occasion these instructions failed to halt the wagon which, whilst they were still in it; careered right into the village, over the road, and hit another vehicle.

On Alltwyllt Incline the family was ascending when Roberts signalled to the brakesman at the top to stop, but this was wrongly interpreted as 'increase speed' which was done, and the jerk broke the cable in consequence. The two wagons started to fly down the slope and the occupants rushed to put on the brakes. 'We flashed by the trolleys coming up from the bottom, and then past the man at the bottom, shot round on the level and hit a stationary railway engine there; this prevented us going over the edge . . . '

Meyrick Roberts' only daughter, who was educated at Dr. Williams' School, Dolgelley, had married P.H.

Evans from her family home at Cantref (now the Midland Bank site). Her husband was articled to the solicitor, William George, Lloyd George's brother in Pwllheli; he did not remain in law but became a journalist with *The Cambrian News* and later with *The Brecon County Times*. The Evans family duly moved to Brecon and came to have connections with Christ College there, Camberley, and later the Royal Navy – a far cry from Bryneglwys. The Meyrick Roberts' children 'all went to the County School, Towyn by train weekly'. There were so many boys they were able to muster a Roberts' XI at football, the last man being made up by a cousin.

Though the Evans family lived away from Towyn, Mrs. Evans returned to her native place every summer, staying with her parents there for six weeks. One of her sons, David, was born on the same day as Haydn Jones' daughter, Eryl, and the respective mothers would proudly push the prams around the town together during those summer weeks. When Meyrick moved his home from Bryneglwys Hall, he went to live at Pall Mall, and later at Cantref in the High Street whilst he built his own house Tegid Villa, next to the Institute. He continued to enjoy a useful life going up to the Quarry on the train most mornings, occasionally with Haydn. The grandchildren would be kept out of the room on the Thursdays when the wages money, by now paid out fortnightly and all in sovereigns and silver, was laid out on a leather-topped table: Mrs. Roberts helped him count out the coins; 'stay out and keep quiet' they were told. The next morning, the money in the Gladstone bags went up with him on the morning train. Haydn had built a bungalow at the Wharf station which may have been intended for Roberts' retirement, but when offered it, he chose Pall Mall instead – probably he thought he would be too convenient if he moved to the Wharf! Meyrick was a Justice of the Peace, a Deacon of Bethel Chapel and a governor of Towyn School. He died on 6th April 1923.

David Evans recalls that the biggest invasion of English people came to Towyn when the Marconi wireless station was set up there before World War I and through it the first news of the success of the Battle of the Falklands was received; he still remembers the incessant rattle of Morse tappers coming from the huts. For some years after the Second War his parents continued to make their annual visits to the countryside which beckoned them. Such was their prestige that a special train or a cleaned-out slate wagon (which they enjoyed) attached to the regular train would be put on so they could re-visit Mrs. Evans' childhood environment. During the Second War there would be children with them in the wagon – not their own but wartime evacuees lodging in Towyn who were about to experience a ride into the Quarry such as few other local children had ever experienced!

Meyrick Roberts and Haydn Jones respected one another. The former spoke openly of the latter's interests; of his chairmanship of the Merionethshire Education Committee he recalled that a thought struck Haydn one day 'We must have an Education Committee in the county ... and I shall run it'. Of Haydn's deaconship at the chapel, he would be found in the big pew at the front of the chapel, reserved for all deacons. Haydn's interest in music had been inherited from his father and he held very strong views as to the appropriate tune for certain hymn numbers – not always that which was published. Often, when the Minister had announced the hymn number, Haydn would jump up and say that it would be sung to tune number so-and-so, and not to that appointed! Of Haydn's visits to the Quarry, Haydn would choose either to ride up on the engine, or sit on the step of the van; guard Jacob Rowlands (of whom more later) took great exception to Haydn doing this in his van, 'It set a bad example'.

Throughout all these years the Quarry was self-supporting; for instance, all bread was baked on the premises in the custom of the times. In the barracks the 'Corris Men' were their own cooks. 'They were a cheerful lot, always singing, even when walking up the Allt Fawr at 6 a.m. on a winter's morning.'

THE ENGINE MEN

Here was a category of employees with the Railway which began in a conventional way only to become less hidebound as the years went by. Starting in 1866 with the usual complement of drivers, fitters, guards and permanent way gangs, supported by a Manager installed in the Wharf (King's) office, and supplemented by a team of slate loaders at the Wharf interchange, (in the manner of most slate railways of the period), the need for economy gradually ate into the numbers on the pay roll until in 1949 the passenger train might be operated entirely by one man (even without a fireman or a guard) and on the days when the train did not run, even he would perforce have to be out on the line, stringing together the wayward track. Surely this was the only Statutory Undertaking running a passenger service with virtually *one* man to do everything? Luckily for the Company, there was no serious accident and nobody reported this state of affairs to the Board of Trade or Ministry of Transport!

First of all, take the Motive Power Department (an impressive term never used at all), the key to bringing slate down from the Quarry and second only in importance to having a railway track maintained to the minimum standard to carry a train at all! In both these Departments the Talyllyn sailed very near the wind for year upon year – if such a metaphor be permitted. By and large, trains were hauled for almost ninety years by the two original steam locomotives, but gravity, manpower, and the use of horses was not despised when things got out of hand.

When the first steam engine was seen at Towyn it would arrive via the new Coast Line, a wondrous sight indeed. But when the first of the two Talyllyn engines came, Towyn would at last have its own personal symbols of the new age, albeit if tradition is reliable, one of them found a home in the engine shed at Ty Dwr above Abergynolwyn, so giving that village an equal share in this wonder.

Imagine too, how much in this Welsh-speaking agriculturally-based community the coming of the railway and all its equipment taxed the local language – never before had it been necessary to describe a locomotive, a point lever or even a narrow gauge railway in the context of the native tongue, and many ingenious terms were contrived, some of them springing from the pseudo-Welsh vernacular derived from the tramways in the slate quarries hereabouts.

But to return to the 'Motive Power Department'. In Talyllyn Railway terms this meant Pendre, where an engine shed suited to one locomotive had been built (this was soon to be extended to accommodate both) where simple repair facilities were provided alongside and most importantly, an adjacent house would be found for the driver. So let us take the men themselves; they included:

William Bousted, sent to Towyn at the age of 28 with his wife Annie, three years the younger, together with their young son Robert then aged 6 and (with Annie pregnant) William about to arrive and be born in this little Welsh town, only similar to their native Maryport ('Merriport' according to the censor) in its proximity to the sea and hills. They would later add James and Annie to their clutch (Sarah was born in 1876 but by 1881 Robert had left home). Bousted had been loaned by Messrs. Fletcher, Jennings & Co., builders of the engines in Whitehaven, to educate the Company in matters of which they had had no experience. Bousted clearly liked the work for he never returned to Cumberland and stayed with the Company until at least 1882 when he emigrated to Australia and one of his sons became a well-known organist. He (Bousted) appears on the 1881 Census as 'Engine Fitter' of Pendref station; perhaps, experiencing the effort of the Quarry Company to sell the undertaking, he felt that security was no longer the factor it had been and preferred to take his chance abroad. Even the use of the Company's house at Pendre was an insufficient tie. Such was his regimented effect on the Railway staff that it is still recalled ... 'No one could move an engine until he came'. The remark, for all its ambiguity, is clear enough.

Working with Bousted were two other drivers – they may have been contemporary and one a man from Abergynolwyn. Possibly this was the man Bousted had been training and the next-in-line being **Hugh W. Griffiths,** he took upon himself the mantle. It must be appreciated that even in a small venture like the Talyllyn, Bousted and Griffiths, and their successors, were something more than pure engine drivers, being nominally Locomotive Superintendents and fitters who drove when circumstance demanded. Griffiths was a native of Towyn, born in 1862 and by the age of 19 already styled himself 'Engine Driver' in the 1881 Census. He learned well from Bousted and 'he was the only one who understood the valve motion of the engines'. Out on a train, *Dolgoch* had failed at Quarry Siding and Hugh was called out. He arrived, and slipped like an eel under the engine, humming a little tune all the while as he was wont to do. He was out from beneath within a couple of minutes and beckoned, 'Try her now' and all was well. In addition, he owned a music shop in Towyn and in due course his son Oswald ran a cycle shop and managed the

cinema there too. To have two places of work was commonplace in Towyn; even quarrymen farmed as well! Clearly the cycle business did not keep Oswald fully occupied either, for his father taught him the tricks of the trade, he became a fireman and later a driver; but he was not a fitter like his father before him. Of Hugh there is some doubt that perhaps – as others who did work on the Railway – he was actually employed by it, latterly. Rolt, who knew his son, was shown Hugh's account book which confirms he was employed on a contract basis to carry out repairs and renewals as they were needed. The detail of his records shows that he – like the general engineering business carried out at Pendre today – was a versatile engineer who included 'chapel organs and cottage pianos' in his repertoire. Hence, no doubt, the music shop. He was able to cast new brasses for the engines from his own wooden patterns, even in the primitive outpost that was Pendre Works.

In the more all-embracing role of fitter/drivers, came **Hugh Jones** who in his turn, had received some instruction from Hugh Griffiths. Hugh Jones was

Possibly taken at Pendre, we have Dick Price (amateur ventriloquist), Hugh 'Gas' Jones and the inevitable Jacob Rowlands. The home-made door used on engines in inclement weather, and the partial closing-off of the cab-opening, betray the weather pattern. Early 1920s.

E. D. CHAMBERS

Hugh 'Gas' peers from the
engine at Abergynolwyn,
August 1935. Is the fire-
man his son, William?
H. F. WHEELLER

never known thus, familiarly he was 'Hugh Gas' as he
had formerly worked in the Towyn Gas Works. He
lived at 9 Station Road (then Plevna Terrace) and ran
a cycle business from a shed in the back garden, power
when required being obtained from a gas engine there.
Indicative of the falling stature of the Railway, there
was insufficient work to keep him entirely at Pendre
and he would often be despatched to the Quarry in
winter where he was inconveniently placed when *his*
successor **Hugh Ellis Jones** had a problem at Pendre
on which he needed urgent advice. 'Hugh Gas' and
Hugh Ellis Jones might share driving in the summer
but after 1936 'Hugh Gas' left to work for the Towyn
& Aberdovey Electric Supply Co. in Happy Valley,
and thereafter it might be said 'the rot gradually crept
in'. 'Hugh Gas' was the last of his line. His son **William
Jones** could be pressed into firing for him even in his
schooldays, but the Talyllyn was too small for him
and, with a sound interest in railway work, he found
employment as an engineman on the Great Western
Railway. He married a niece of Haydn Jones.

Though 'Hugh Gas' is still warmly remembered, it
was his strong physique which impressed his neighbours rather than what he did on the Railway. Though
not a big man, he is best recollected for the tale of how
he underwent an operation on his own kitchen table.
Storytellers insist this was an appendectomy without
anaesthetic; more probably it was to drain an abscess
on the appendix, the patient taking a suitable quantity
of whisky to act as a stupefying agent! Such may have
been the state of medicine in Towyn well into this
century.

An earliest driver proper seems to have been
Jonathan Rowlands, (born 1863) younger brother of

Jacob Rowlands, the long-serving guard; he lived in
Red Lion Street in property now demolished. His
brother **Francis** was a carpenter who helped to keep
the rolling stock in repair. John had begun as a platelayer on leaving school.

Then came **William Lewis** (formerly of
Abergynolwyn) who lived at the sweet shop – which
was run by his wife and daughter – next to the Midland
Bank in the High Street. During the Second War when
sweets were rationed, there were few children who
went away disappointed when his daughter Catherine
was told they had already parted with their ration
coupons! William was an uncle of Hugh Ellis Jones;
he drove from McConnel's into Haydn Jones' time
until the early 1920s. Latterly, with the fall in demand
for slates, he would go up to the Quarry in the winter
months to sharpen saws etc., driving only in the
summer season.

William's son, also **William,** took up the tradition
and after starting as a fireman, sometimes drove as
well but after a time he moved away to work in a garage
in Bala.

It might be expected that as the Haydn Jones' era
developed, the clear-cut duties of employees became
more blurred: if other occupations were more pressing
in the eyes of the owner, Haydn would take the men
off one job and put them on another ... sometimes
away from the Railway altogether. **Dick Price** came
from agricultural origins at Ty Mawr Farm where he
had become a waggoner but when the farm passed into
the lesseeship of the Anwyl family, he left for the
Railway and joined the track gang. Then he moved
into Pendre to learn the fireman's job and soon became
a driver 'and a good one at that'. His wife was nurse

to the young Francis Shuker of Ty Mawr who recollects the joy of being taken up onto the footplate by Dick, and being allowed to blow the whistle!

A second generation of Talyllyn railmen was created when Jacob Rowland's nephew (son of Jonathan) **Robin** became a driver. Unfortunately the work did not suit him as he suffered from asthma; he worked later as a driver on the local 'buses. While on the Railway his proud aunt said of him 'Robin is a very careful driver – he is not fast like the other driver. Robin knows the track is bad'. He may in fact have been over-cautious for his slow movements were well-known and time-keeping was apt to suffer. He lived in Towyn and died in 1957.

There was a hand-to-mouth atmosphere about both fitting and driving in the years of the Second War and after. Hugh Ellis Jones was virtually the 'prop forward' of the undertaking but went to work in the local army camp during that War. When he returned there was a crisis out on the line and he was sent by Edward Thomas to keep the track in shape for trains – a formidable task; but no one else was fitted for the work.

It must not be overlooked that Hugh could not carry on alone the whole burden of running the train – nay the Railway itself when Edward Thomas was unable to leave the shop – even if he had the occasional help

from his younger son Herbert whose schooling was preferably not to be prejudiced. However, his elder son **David Richard Jones** had left Bryncrug School in 1943 and was assisting in the postal round; Hugh's mind was made up, he would approach 'Dai' (as he was always known) and if he was willing to leave the postal duty, see if he would come to the Railway to help him. Dai said he would, but not for less than he was presently earning, namely five pounds per week. (This was a bitter pill for his father to swallow as he himself was then only earning four pounds!) However, the situation was desperate and fortunately Sir Haydn agreed to the appointment: Dai found himself appointed to what was to prove to be the last 'situation' under the old régime. Naturally it was a multi-facet job, as were all Railway tasks at that time, but Dai, like his younger brother, was no stranger to the locomotive for he too had helped out during school holidays. So father and son made their way daily to and from Plas Goch to Towyn. Another small distinction for Dai was that he was one of the few employees in Haydn's time who had never worked in the shop as well! Sir Haydn, always a judge of a suitable man, was well aware of Dai's potential for even as a boy he enjoyed nothing better than his holidays on the engine with Robin Rowlands, then the regular driver;

Ifor Higgon caught Hugh 'Gas' with William Lewis on the footplate at Pendre on 15th August 1931.   I. HIGGON

Sir Haydn's wisdom has been shown to be indisputable! Dai was not on the Railway when Haydn Jones died, having been called up for National Service in 1948.

In 1949, in desperation, Edward Thomas took from the shop, **Idris,** the grandson of Peter Williams who had also done some driving, and put him on the engine, using **Basil Jones,** a young lad from Bryncrug and straight out of school, to fire it. Idris had done some

driving the previous year 'but had little experience'. His career was cut short for 'he liked speed'; he also boasted he had taken *Dolgoch* up The Mineral Extension 'just to see if the rails were still there'. One day in late August 1949, Hugh Ellis Jones was called to the train near Dolgoch viaduct to find the engine nose down with a cracked main frame and the passengers milling around somewhat aimlessly. There was nothing for it but to leave the train there, and later a

The engine crew for the 'Picture Post' event was Idris Williams ('he liked speed') and Basil Jones, captured in the morning light before what was to be one of the busiest days they had known.
BBC HULTON PICTURE LIBRARY

local farmer collected it with his horse team and dragged it back to Rhydyronen where, later still, Haydn Jones sent one of his heavy farm horses to drag *Dolgoch* back to Pendre.

A little detail concerning the use of horses in this manner is opportune. In the latter days of Haydn Jones' time, it is hinted 'they were out on the Railway rather too often.' If failures occurred above Cynfal the horses from Llwynwecws (Brynglas) would be used to drag the offender down to Brynglas; thence, Haydn's horses in the charge of Emlyn Evans, would take over. These horses, quite unused to railway work and unhappy to walk between two rails 'behaved like stubborn mules' and had to be whipped to start them off, the sheer dead weight of a locomotive being a factor to which they were quite unaccustomed. Once in motion, however, all was well.

So from the driver's right hand side of the engine footplate, to the left and the firemen.

The first notice of a 'Railway Engine Stoker' appears in 1881; **Robert Davies,** a native, aged 25 of 8 Athelstan Road, must have been one of the earliest if he made the Railway his first employment. About the turn of the century **Bob Thomas** was at this work, firing to Jonathan Rowlands; he is seen with the oilcan on the McConnel 'special' (deputising for Jonathan who was off ill with rheumatic fever) – he was a frequent driver when there was the need.

Many of the firemen were young boys straight from school and they never graduated to the driver's side of the footplate. Clearly the men who had been described previously as drivers had all begun as firemen but there were two who were firemen for years and were never promoted – possibly because the drivers outlived them! Firstly there was **John Edwards,** seen on the photograph on p.269 alongside *Pretoria* as the boy with the hoop. He left the Railway to work with his father on a coal round, and his cousin **Lewis** ('Keep Fit') **Davies** took over firing duties for a time in the 1940s. Then later came **David Ellis Davies** – known as 'David Ellis' 'one of the best little boys we had on the locomotives; he used to come back to Pendre from Wharf every day at lunchtime and cut firewood' (and on Sundays to clean the engines). He recalled the extra $2\frac{1}{2}$d. given to the fireman for lighting up the Workmen's Train engine at 3.30 a.m. on a Monday. He died in 1981. Another bright lad was William, the son of 'Hugh Gas', who was well trained by his father in the 1930s and who has already received mention. Peter Williams' son **John Williams** ('John Fat'), also fired occasionally, and there was, in the late 1930s, Mrs. Humphreys' son.

At this stage it becomes difficult to trace any more men who worked with the locomotives, and we must return to the best known of all in our generation, Hugh Ellis Jones of Plas Goch, Rhydyronen. His reminis-

cences can at once demolish the neat image of what railways are expected to be and recall working summer passenger trains single-handed, with two engines in steam and Peter Williams as the driver of the other engine! 'Peter Williams'? one may exclaim, (never having considered his usefulness in that category) 'you never told me Peter was a driver'. 'Oh, they had to use

Peter Williams, another faithful servant of the Company; he lived in the cottage behind the Works at Pendre.

anyone in those times who could drive, and there were more passengers than could be carried in one train'. (Actually Peter had had to fire now and again instead of being out on the track). Thus Hugh underlined once more to be wary of the unexpected when considering the Talyllyn Railway.

Hugh Ellis Jones, born at Plas Goch in 1904, seventh son of Dafydd Jones, is the last of the old régime of drivers. He had been in the Quarry's service for 13 years since he left school and was the third generation to work there. His great-grandfather looked after five of the seven horses in the Quarry, and his grandfather Rhys Ellis Jones had been killed in the Quarry aged 37, so that in consequence his daughter, Hugh's mother, who had only been at school for three months, was called home to look after the family. Hugh's mother did not want him to go on the Railway and despite the appeal of the train passing beside the house, together with many footplate trips and the friendship of all the men, when he left Bryncrug School (against the Headmaster's wish) his mother had her way and he started a three-year apprenticeship at the Quarry. He lived in the barracks there for a time, where he was in good company for his two uncles also worked there: in fact, to reduce the pressure of work for his mother, he had lived for a time with one uncle in Abergynolwyn before he left school.

[Hugh also had an elder brother **Rhys Jones** (died 1978 aged 87) who always lived in Abergynolwyn. He, too, started in the Quarry and worked in the South

Wales coalfield also, but later came down onto the Railway to work on the track above Dolgoch.]

Hugh's wife, born Florence Griffiths, hailed from Meifod in Montgomeryshire but came to Pendre, Towyn, when four years old when her father started on a farm there; she died in July 1939. (Their Meifod friends, the Anwyls, had started at Ty Mawr Farm and asked the Griffiths to come to Towyn and help them at Ty Mawr.) These details show how interwoven life was between families in the Quarry and the Railway before the turn of the century.

When 14 Hugh was put into the Old Mill (or 'Blue Mill' where blue slates were dressed – Cantrybedd Mill was 'The Broad Vein Mill'). After ten years there, the dust in the mill made him seriously ill and he was sent to a Dolgelley specialist who said 'keep away from dust'; so for a time he became one of four slate loaders at the Wharf station. However, when the son of 'Hugh Gas' went away to become a footplateman on the Great Western Railway, he was called to Pendre to act as fireman in his place and told to learn all he could. Hugh Jones learned quickly and under 'Hugh Gas' had the advantage of seeing how many repair and maintenance jobs could also be done by a conscientious driver. Consequently in 1935, when 'Hugh Gas' went off to work for the Electric Supply Co., Hugh was now ready to take his place as driver. For a fireman, one of Hugh's sons would be brought from school for the work – a fireman was not always imperative but it was hard work on his own. In winter 1934/5 there was still enough slate in stock to warrant a ten-wagon train running every other day, leaving Wharf about 10 a.m. and returning as ready. When there was no official passenger train, a single coach might be attached if anyone showed up. (The same pattern was used from the mid-1940s when there were no winter passenger trains.)

Hugh's working life was only as primitive as other occupations of that age, but he was expected to produce results almost single-handed. Unless some heavy repairs were needed, he must keep the engines and stock in running order, and during the Second War he had no help for this. The Works were unlit (Edward Thomas would bring candles from the shop, but only two at a time!), tools and lifting facilities were very basic, and the place was wet, cold and inadequate. His own training was that which man had passed to man since the time of Bousted; in 1939 he was paid £2 a week.

The limit of Hugh's ingenuity was reached when *Dolgoch*'s boiler required re-patching to meet the requirements of the insurance boiler inspector, but Hugh was not entirely devolved of responsibility as the engine had to be taken down to the Wharf and, with the aid of the GWR hand crane from Machynlleth, loaded onto a well wagon *en route* for The Atlas Foundry, Shrewsbury.

Things became bleak when *Talyllyn* was no longer fit to be used and had been pensioned off to lie under the haybarn at Pendre. The crunch came when *Dolgoch*'s frame cracked and men from The Atlas Foundry, Shrewsbury were sent for; only they had the required portable welding equipment. To lift the engine and run out the wheels etc. to enable The Atlas men to do this work, Hugh and **James Davies,** the Railway carpenter (also for Estate and Quarry), used screw jacks until wooden packing could be placed underneath and the lift continued sufficiently for the wheel sets to roll clear. There were no trains at all for several weeks. On another occasion a train of empty slate wagons was passing up through Brynglas cutting when some of *Dolgoch*'s tubes burst and the engine had to be stopped and abandoned: not for the first time some heavy horses from Ty Mawr Farm were called out to drag the train back to Pendre. It then fell to Hugh to draw out the old tubes and fit some new – again by candlelight. If springs broke due to the rough track, the engine had to be lifted until the bolts could be released, a bar was removed and the offending spring extracted.

Human memory being what it is, difficulty has been found in dating more accurately the order of events in this phase of Hugh's life, but certainly after the departure of 'Hugh Gas' he was obliged to show every ingenuity and explore every avenue of help to keep the engines running. Among the systems exploited was to cycle down to Hugh Gas's house (Plevna Terrace) or even down to Happy Valley to call for help; 'Hugh Gas' was always ready to assist. Another ploy was to remove various defective fittings from the locomotive not then in service, take them down to the Great Western station and consign them 'by Passenger Train' [sic] to the Britannia Foundry, Portmadoc. There was a good relationship with this firm, for, when things were really serious, an old fitter from that establishment would come down to Towyn on Saturdays and Sundays – presumably in his own time and not representing the firm! – and carry out more major repairs at Pendre over the weekend, including the refitting of any parts which might have been sent north to Portmadoc in the previous period. With things in such a wretched state, it was often necessary to work through the weekend in order to have an engine ready for Monday morning; sometimes repairs went far into the night and Hugh's job was the essential task of holding the candle – sometimes he had little time for sleep before lighting up on Monday morning. His Britannia Foundry accomplice, left to fend for himself, would disappear from Pendre from time to time and find refreshment at The Corbett Arms, only to re-appear again some hours later in a condition less suited to work. It is from such reminiscences that it may be assumed came the illusion that boiler work was done at one (or both) foundries in Portmadoc (Glaslyn or Britannia), the consignment being effected by craning onto a standard gauge wagon at Wharf, taking it thence, to end its journey in Portmadoc by road. The subject is strong on legend and short on fact!

This is a suitable juncture to write more specifically about Sundays and Mondays. Against the Welsh Sabbath background with its strict Calvinistic tradition, Pendre Works was an exceptional place of intensive labour, the more so as equipment required extended maintenance the more venerable it became. For Hugh it was often a day of anxious clock-watching, for once the work was done, it was probably necessary to light up and prepare the engine for Monday immediately. In the usual way, the fireman would come down to Pendre in the early hours of Monday to apply a match to a fire often laid by slipping into the engine shed after Sunday morning chapel.

Long hours were a part of life; for instance, around the early 1900s the summer timetable required four passenger workings, and on Monday morning, the extra Workmen's Train. On a Saturday there would often be a late working. One may imagine, therefore, the extended hours put in by train crew and maintenance staff; there would be many summer weekends when Saturday, Sunday and Monday might see them spend but little time under their own roofs!

Appearing indistinctly in this period is a young man from Abergynolwyn who not only drove from time to time, but also helped 'Hugh Gas'. Perhaps because he died as a young man, information is limited, but his nickname was 'Jack bach'.

During his time as a driver Hugh would cycle along the track from home at Rhydyronen to Pendre. Occasionally his work would be finished before 4.30 p.m. and he would try to leave for home early – this was especially risky on a Friday when Haydn Jones was not in the Commons and might be out in Ty Mawr fields. More than once Hugh was spotted cycling along the line under Ty Mawr bridge, and reported to Edward Thomas. (After the period of this tale, he simply took the engine home with him and used Rhydyronen overbridge as a stable for the engine overnight.)

To help Hugh in the summer, his younger son **Herbert Rhys Jones** was brought from school to fire, but even he could not be relied upon, because when business was at its height in the shop, Edward Thomas had no time to go down to Wharf station to issue tickets or be guard, and Herbert was kept in the shop also. It was left to Hugh to drive, fire, and issue tickets on his own, even though at times pressure was down to 50 lbs. and the fire almost dead. Board of Trade Regulations regarding the working of passenger trains (two men on the engine, a guard etc.) had no meaning when Sir Haydn had other work for the staff to do. If there were slate wagons on the train, these had to be taken to Alltwyllt and the loaded trucks brought back; meanwhile the passenger carriages were left unattended at Abergynolwyn.

The most bitter time for Hugh, who had worked at almost every task on the line, was to find that in the late 1930s and the following wartime circumstances, output from the Quarry was almost at a standstill, the stockyard at Wharf was full, wages were low and there were no orders for the slate there. Soon the passenger train was suspended and there was no call for trains of any kind. Old Peter Williams had been 'retired' but could not be evicted from Pendre. Morris Lewis – like most others – 'had gone to The Camp' (Tonfanau) for better pay, and with no winter railway work, Hugh found himself in Daniel's shop. [When L. T. C. Rolt took over management from Edward Thomas, Hugh obtained work at 'The Camp' too, only to be persuaded to come back for higher wages and continuing responsibility! But this is outside the time of our story.]

MAINTENANCE MEN

A typical relationship between father, son, Quarry and Railway was that of the Evans family. **Griffith Lewis Evans** was Estate Agent for Abergynolwyn to Haydn Jones. They had in addition a small-holding where they lived at Gernos, near Llanfihangel-y-Pennant. One son, young **Griffith,** walked to school over the pass to Abergynolwyn each day but the family moved to Abergynolwyn in 1915 so (World War years excepted) from the age of 9 'young' Griffith remained in Abergynolwyn until 1947. At the age of 14 he was taken on as an apprentice in the Quarry blacksmith's shop, and almost all his work there was done for the Quarry with occasional visits to Pendre by pushbike to carry out repairs before returning to the Quarry again. As the years went on, his time at Pendre increased as maintenance became more necessary! He would take his dinner at Peter Williams' house adjoining – this would be the early 1930s; but he was not the only Quarry employee to help out on the Railway. **'Old Hughes'** the Quarry carpenter would come to Pendre to build 'new' wagon bodies or repair carriages and wagons, for which they would be pushed into the Workshop. When there was insufficient work to keep a carpenter at the Quarry, Hughes (who came from Bryncrug) spent his last years at Pendre where a home-spun sawbench, driven by shafting off the oil engine, was provided. The carpenters' work included making new handles for such items as picks, shovels etc. for both Quarry and Estate. Francis Rowlands repaired carriages and wagons in W. H. McConnel's time.

Young Griffith Evans found much variety in the work at Pendre as an apprentice: one job which was

TAL-Y-LLYN RAILWAY TOWYN.

The Wharf overbridge still had wooden parapets when this picture was taken; the man on the left may be the slate-checker, with a slate-loader beside the first coach. E. D. CHAMBERS

well-remembered was the building of a new rear water tank for *Dolgoch*; he had to squeeze down inside it and hold up the red-hot rivets. 'It was hot and terrible'.

From 1931 **Daniel Evans** (a Caernarvonshire slate merchant with a quarry of his own at Nantlle) was the Slate Agent to Haydn Jones; Evans obtained the services of one **Robert Jones** who would come over monthly from Pen-y-Groes with Evans on his visits, 'and carry out heavy, big work' at Pendre which was outside the experience of Griff Evans and his colleagues; so in this way heavy repairs might be continued – on a limited scale – on the premises. Robert Jones was well suited as he had worked on railways abroad including Australia, and engineering and blacksmith's work was meat and drink to him.

Daniel Evans was said to have 'made a lot of money out of Haydn Jones'. Later on, Evans might send two men from Dinorwic Quarry to Pendre for locomotive repairs there. (These may have been employees of the Port Dinorwic Dry Dock business).

Griff Evans married in 1935 and was put onto war work in a steel business in Birmingham during 1940–1947; he never returned to Haydn's employ but was persuaded to buy a blacksmith's business just outside Pendre Works, so returning to live (after a brief time in Abergynolwyn) in the blacksmith's house there in 1947. His time on the Railway was to come again (outside the perimeter of this account) but meanwhile when the men from the Atlas Foundry came from Shrewsbury to work on *Dolgoch* and *Talyllyn*, they found mutually interesting accommodation with the Evans'!

William John Lewis (whose father was a driver on the Corris Railway as a young man) writes of moving to work in Bryneglwys Quarry – believed to be 1914–1920 – and that 'my father and I spent many a weekend turning the Talyllyn loco's wheels on the lathe . . .', suggesting they came down to Pendre for this work. But in fact the work was done on the Quarry's equipment. He was born in Upper Corris in 1900 and died in October 1982.

GUARDS

One of the earliest guards was **Lewis Owen,** born in Aberdovey in 1852 and probably joining the new Railway on leaving school. In 1881, aged 29, he lived in Wesleyan Terrace and possibly he and his successor, **Jacob Rowlands,** were the only two passenger guards the Company ever had.

Of all the personalities on the Railway, none has received more notice than Jacob Rowlands (1858–18th December 1928) for he *was* 'The Talyllyn Railway'. His appearance (he was the only employee to have a uniform), his manner (his behaviour was of the favoured employee of the management and it was only he who ever took a holiday), and other traits, the subject of constant 'leg-pulling' by his colleagues, gave him the reputation of being a 'management man'.

He was born in Towyn and as a boy he had started work in the Quarry; evidence of some workshop training there or elsewhere was to be found in a number of nicely made teapot stands in brass which were displayed at Railway View. In the 1881 Census he was living in Frankwell Street with occupation of 'Quarry

Miner'. His workmates did not treat him as one of them but he never really appreciated how little respect they gave him! When the train was made up of the four coaches and van he would come up to the engine and with wearying repetition announce, 'Heavy load today.'

The men would often play tricks on Jacob who had the habit of reporting them to the management thus; shooting in Dolgoch woods was but one favourite pastime of driver 'Hugh Gas' who was a crack shot. He would hide the gun in the bunker of No. 1 and, with Dick Price, his qualified fireman, left to drive, he would jump off to make a quick sortie in search of pheasant; if he shot one, his whippet (also to be found on the footplate) would bring the bird to the engine whilst Dick was taking water at Dolgoch station. Jacob would rush up breathlessly to Dick, 'Did you hear that shot . . .?' Whilst thus engaged in conversation, 'Hugh Gas' would slip up onto the footplate again on the far side. His dog was a fine runner and was known to pick up a bird in Dolgoch woods and if the train had left there, rush through the fields alongside, bird in mouth, and beat the train to Abergynolwyn. On *Dolgoch* it was easy to drop and hide a bird through a loose manhole cover in the rear water tank.

Jacob's independent arrangements as regards hiring empty slate wagons for a late-in-day gravity ride back to Towyn, surcharging the Company's rate for the hire, were well known and are recalled on p. 188. The Company charged 2/– for a wagon no matter how many occupants – Jacob would furtively collect a further 1/– per person which every employee in the concern knew would not see its way back to the Wharf office!

His family lived at the house adjoining Pendre Works, known in more recent times as Railway Cottage, and it was his wife's duty to operate the road crossing gates there. The local children found Pendre a great place to play and ride on the wagons: Jacob would chase them off but they knew exactly when he would return from Chapel on a Sunday.

When Haydn Jones bought the Railway in 1911 and knowing of Jacob's close relationship with McConnel (which Jacob boasted *did* exist!) he decided not to take him on, but did so in the event. As already mentioned, when Haydn went up to the Quarry he would often sit on the step of the brake van, to the annoyance and dismay of Jacob to find a passenger beyond his discipline! It is recalled, 'He [HHJ] wore a long black morning coat and carefully spread the coat tails out backwards over the dusty floor of the van. We children would cautiously step on these tails (and leave a footprint) feeling that to have put your foot on a knight's coat was a very daring feat.'

After the time of Jacob Rowlands, no one could follow the guard's duties with quite the same *élan*.

Peter Williams' son 'John Fat' did duty occasionally, and his stentorian 'All aboard' and other instructions were a feature of his work! Perhaps William Lewis was his real successor, he who 'did all the jobs'. Peter Williams himself was no stranger to the guard's van.

PERMANENT WAY MEN (and others)

From times within memory there were four men allotted to the maintenance of the track, whilst there are said to have been twelve in the beginning. As to their work, although renewal of sleepers took place from time to time, it is likely that the rails and fastenings remained largely the originals of the mid-1860s throughout the period under review. There must have been a number of extra rails purchased for emergencies such as a broken one.

The earliest references to a 'platelayer' come in the 1881 Census where **Griffith Rowlands** aged 46 was living in National Street. He was a native of Towyn and maybe uncle to the brothers Jacob and Jonathan in Frankwell Street. Jonathan, aged 18, lived at the same address as his brother Jacob, and was a platelayer with his uncle. In 1881 a **David Jones** aged 47 living at Newtown (Trenewydd) was a 'Labourer/platelayer' but may have been employed on the Coast Line. **Robert Roberts** aged 26 of Pentreucha, Bryncrug and born in Towyn, was also a platelayer.

In the present century **Dafydd Jones** of Plas Goch, Rhydyronen (father of Hugh Ellis Jones currently also of Plas Goch), **Arthur Pugh** of Rhydyronen, **Richard Thomas** and **Edward Davies** were on this work and remained thereon until retirement. Dafydd Jones was in charge and his standards were very high. Sometimes conscientious to the point of sophistry, he would have the men taken up by the early morning Workmen's Train on Mondays; they would alight at Ty Dwr whilst the other occupants of the wagons would rumble on towards the Quarry, lodgers carrying their week's supplies with them. Then, Jones and his men, so it is recalled, would perforce in winter have to linger somewhat aimlessly at Ty Dwr until it was daylight enough for them to start work! Mondays therefore always became the day when maintenance was done on the upper end of the line; on other days it was not possible to arrive before the first passenger train (due at Abergynolwyn 10.10 a.m. – 1909.)

The wooden shed at Ty Dwr took the form of a log cabin and stood on the site of the former engine shed there; it was, however, somewhat smaller in size and might be called a 'rebuild' of the old shed, and there were odd-length rails at the site where shed pointwork in the running line had been ($1\frac{1}{2}$ rail-lengths).

Dafydd Jones was proud of his work and the appearance and safety of the line, and took exception to anyone he found trespassing along 'his' track; he fell out with Jacob Rowlands (who would always turn a blind eye to the practice!) over this. His gang used a small hand-propelled wagon which was often stored on a short 'siding' made of bridge rails at the east end of Dolgoch station, for which a set of lift-out rails were on hand to manhandle it on and off the main line. The trolley could also be found stabled at Rhydyronen (convenient for Dafydd's home), in either of the two short sidings at Brynglas or the short siding at Tancoed or Abergynolwyn, according to need; the stabling point for it at Dolgoch was essential as there were no other sidings between Brynglas and Tancoed. Dafydd was typical of the rural community hereabouts which found itself touched by an industrial revolution elsewhere which reached their locality in the shape, in this instance, of a small railway. In his youth he had worked on a farm at Cynfal and, like many another agricultural worker, moved over to the Railway, starting in May 1900 when he moved to Plas Goch. In 1902 R. B. Yates made him foreman of the permanent way gang and he chose his own men – they would cut grass, and lay hedges besides. He and his like worked long and hard and when 65 years of age had come and gone, they still laboured on. He never retired, but was ill for seven years and left the Railway in 1935.

He was typical, too, of his time; he recognised his employer's position and appreciated the limits of his own responsibility. His ability to speak in English was severely limited but he was often heard to explain 'Jacob, the train .. me, I am the line' so underlining the guard Jacob Rowlands' undisputed sway over all things that moved over 'his' metals.

This story arose as typical of the somewhat uneasy relationship between Jacob and himself. Jacob was a competent English speaker – he had to be in his position as guard – and besides his 'arrangements' about leasing gravity wagons to passengers, he was also owner of the 'mule' tethered to the barn at Pendre station.* Down passenger trains then terminated at Pendre and Jacob would leap from the train before it pulled into the platform, and take the tickets from the alighting passengers, noting which of them had luggage and would be bound for the Cambrian station. He would then offer to take it for them with his mule and cart. Such bona to the family income were denied to Dafydd and his colleagues, but one day he had his revenge when he was working on the track and saw a party of persons walking up the line towards him; he explained in broken English that they were trespassing. The party was not put out, for had they not been given permission to walk down the Railway by the guard? At this the angry Dafydd exploded, 'Jacob, the train . . . me, the track' and forced the visitors to retreat.

---

* A contradictory recollection was that the beast belonged to John Rowlands, and that he operated this private business venture!

Work on the line did not account for the whole family income of the Dafydd Jones' family. His wife Ann (her brother, Edward Ellis was in charge of the Quarry horses) was also involved in the total atmosphere which linked Quarry, Railway, Towyn and the Haydn Joneses; her role was to do the washing which the Haydn Jones' residence at Pantyneuadd created, assisted by her daughter Mrs. Alice Williams, who lived next-door. So a regular weekly part of the Talyllyn van's loading was a large laundry basket delivered to Pendre station and met at Rhydyronen by Ann Jones. She would do the work in the backyard of Plas Goch and the train would duly pick it up again, the basket being collected at Pendre. An obvious omission from this typical instance of Edwardian life-style is that Mrs. Jones probably collected hot water for the operation from the injector overflow of the locomotive – at least, if discipline did not prevent her from doing so, as the sight of trains standing in stations whilst tubs of washing were liberally watered from the injector flow was a worldwide practice in the days of steam!

When the last daily train had come and gone, Ann would slip out of Plas Goch and sweep out the little station; on Haydn Jones' washdays, she would throw the used washing water over the platform shelter's slab floor and mop it down; meanwhile Dafydd would work in his highly productive vegetable garden at the lineside behind the house. So it was for many small railways; the Talyllyn was only typical in these domestic touches.

Dafydd Jones was followed by **Peter Williams** who took on the work as foreman of the track and also did some driving and firing. In the years that followed the track gang was reduced to three and then to two.

Arthur Pugh, 'Blind Pugh', had started on the Railway in August 1900 and worked most of his time with Dafydd Jones (his neighbour in Rhydyronen; he moved there from Pen-y-Bont, Bryncrug) out on the line. He had left school before he was 13 and gone to work for a farmer, John Roberts, near Bird Rock.

One day, when he was 14–15 years of age, he was counting potatoes and his employer had occasion to speak to him; young Pugh replied politely enough but Roberts, thinking the boy was being insolent, struck him on the head with a pole which the local men used for jumping over the irrigation ditches in the Dysynni area. The boy was hit near the optical nerve, blinded and at 19 sent to Manchester where he recovered the sight of one eye. Later, after working on a Llanwrin Water Works scheme, he returned to the Railway where there were four men on the track. One day about 1926, whilst carrying a load of bracken from the lineside (used for packing slates in wagons), they all slipped and the load fell on him; his weakened optical nerve gave way and he was blinded completely. His mother came from Dinas Mawddwy and his wife from Llanegryn; she had died in 1920. They had twelve children (not uncommon in those days); he married his housekeeper in 1924, and died in 1956 age 81.

With Dafydd Jones and Arthur Pugh making such an early start each day, their womenfolk had not made up their dinners before they left home. Accordingly, each had his dinner put into a half-moon-shaped canvas bag which hung from a short rope; depending in which direction the men were working, these 'nose-bags' were collected by passing train (either Up or Down) each morning and dropped off where the men were working. The procedure was that a woman from either household would take stance beside the line, one on each side so that driver and fireman, each extending an arm, could catch up the rope on the bag as the train moved past. Arthur Pugh would never come home for dinner, even if he was working at Rhydyronen itself!

One of Haydn Jones' brothers, the Revd. O. D. ('Lincoln') Jones with his son (both of Bournemouth at that time). Dafydd Jones loads bracken onto a wagon fitted with out-rigging hurdles to carry the greater load. The Revd. Jones was an eminent Congregational Minister and as distinguished in Bournemouth affairs as was Haydn in Towyn.   H. E. JONES

If Haydn Jones thought his other enterprises were more important, then Dafydd Jones and Arthur Pugh would be recruited, as would most other men who worked on the Railway. Thus certain employees might be on the Railway one day and in the ironmonger's shop the next; at appropriate times on his farm all who could be spared from the Railway had to leave it to bring in the hay (etc.) – a pool of labour.

It is impossible to be pedantic where employees of the Railway are concerned. From time to time Dick Price doubled up his duties between working as fireman on the engine and with Dafydd Jones on the track. From the trackside in latter years Idris Williams, also on the line, found himself driver during labour shortages during the Second War; he soon proved himself more reliable in his former capacity! Dick on the other hand, passed from fireman to becoming a regular and reliable driver.

An additional duty of the permanent way men was to cut the grass beside the line and make a haystack at each station; the hay would later be sold. But Haydn Jones himself took most of that stored under the barn at Pendre and it went to his home at Pantyneuadd nearby.

It will be seen that both hay and bracken were used to pack between slates, principally in main line wagons rather than on the Railway itself. Not all the bracken was so used: such was the crop between Brynglas and Dolgoch that it was carefully scythed from the sides of the line, loaded into empty slate wagons to considerable height and taken to Pendre for use as bedding for animals. One customer for it was Richards, the dairyman of College Green, who had a pony to pull his milk cart. Each customer had to negotiate a price with Haydn Jones personally and when the bargain was struck, it was the customer who was obliged to obtain a wagon, cut the bracken and load it. The sight of a moving 'haystack' of bracken, the wagon almost submerged under the load which was limited in size only by the bridge openings on the line, is clearly recalled. Such loads were attached to the rear of the loaded slate wagons and must have been costed on a 'per wagon' basis as the stacking was extreme and only prevented from disaster by considerable roping! This practice may have died before the end of the Second War, but it certainly pertained in the late 1930s.

To increase the capacity of wagons for these bulky loads, the equivalent of the hay frame extensions used on farms was applied, whereby a wooden hurdle which overhung the sides and ends allowed for a considerable 'Cottage Loaf' effect. In certain locations bracken was cut from hill slopes above the line on its south side, and had to be manhandled over the Railway to the other side and then carted down to the farm below. In such cases, of course, no wagons were in use, but it was not infrequently that a train would find the line blocked by a stack of bracken left across the rails, waiting transfer to the field on the north side.

Although not applying in all seasons to every station named, it was usual to find haystacks at Wharf, Pendre, Rhydyronen and Brynglas, that at Pendre being the one in which Haydn Jones had the most interest, having his farm close by.

Peter Williams had **Morris Lewis** of Bryncrug to help him on the line; for many years Morris had worked in the Quarry and came down to Wharf to help to load slates. During the Second War he would accompany Hugh Ellis Jones (driver) with the train on its thrice weekly winter foray up the valley, and help him (who was otherwise single-handed) to work the Alltwyllt and Village Inclines. (The Lewis family were caretakers at The Institute for many years.)

Certain other work such as unloading coal from standard gauge wagons at the Wharf was done by casual labour as required. An illustration (below) shows J. R. Williams the retired Headmaster of the National School, Towyn, and Thomas Jones, a former quarryman, loading a Talyllyn wagon from a stack outside the coalyard compound. (Much of this coal came from The Ocean Coal Co. of South Wales, the colliery owned by David Davies the prominent Welsh railway contractor.)

Arrangements for the professional painting of engines and carriages are not recalled, probably because this work was seldom done and when carried out, was part of the duties of the Quarry painter. However, there was one exception, and it came about in a most unusual way.

J. R. Williams and Thomas Jones — both retired — loading locomotive coal at the Wharf.   J. PARRY

During the First War, sheep were grazed in Hyde Park, London; their owner was George Williams of Glanydon, Towyn who was intent on returning to his native place when the War was over. On one occasion the sheep escaped into the street and a passing pedestrian helped George to herd them back into the Park. He was **George Walter Middleton,** a self-employed coach painter of London and a former boy-chorister at St. Paul's Cathedral. They fell into conversation and George Williams told of his desire to return to Wales at the end of the War, assisted by a scheme to buy ex-Army lorries from the depôt at Slough, convert them into passenger omnibuses and base a bus service on Towyn. Interested, George Middleton agreed to help him and paint them suitably from their drab khaki into a more attractive livery. So in due course both Georges found themselves at Glanydon with a number of lorries to convert and paint, and their bus service began, Towyn's first.

George Middleton's capabilities were emblazoned on every bus as it circulated round the district and in due course Haydn Jones sent for him and suggested he painted the Talyllyn Railway passenger stock, and give it a professional finish which it had probably never received since first it arrived on the line. George asked for a free hand and the same conditions for doing this work as he would have expected in his trade; these included a dust-free atmosphere and a near-level temperature to apply the eighteen coats of paint and varnish which would satisfy his craftsman's upbringing! The work was agreed and it was not long before George and Manager Thomas were at loggerheads about the flying soot and extremes in temperature, inseparable from country railway workshops. However, in one way and another, the job was done and never had the Railway's carriages looked so well! 'All have recently been smartly painted crimson with yellow lining and lettering' (1924). As one bystander put it, they looked really fine and not as the finish on any local farm cart. George's work pleased Haydn immensely and in due course he was given the job of painting Pantyneuadd (built about 1836), Abergynolwyn village, Bryneglwys Hall and the Quarry barracks, but there would be no more lavish painting of road vehicles for Towyn seldom produced the demand for that sort of work. However, Mrs. Wynne of Peniarth had her grey-delivered Wolsley car painted by him, and, as word of his skill moved northward, George found himself at Bangor painting Lord Penrhyn's new Rolls Royce in 1929.

For many years the Middletons were part of the little community at Pandy, Brynglas, and of life there something will be found elsewhere.

The Rowlands family at Railway View had close links with the Railway in every sense. Jacob's eldest daughter Mary was a schoolteacher and taught in

Mary and Jane Rowlands could be the ladies on Pendre platform before the turn of the century. Gas lamps are in position. The loco-motive pit is there but the coal siding has not been added. A leaking water tank inside the shed may account for the ivy growing on the corner.   H. S. BRISTOWE

the Bryncrug Infants School for fifteen years, and at Abergynolwyn for five years. At weekends she came home. When at Abergynolwyn, the train used by the workmen was her weekend transport, but she would be allotted the single first class compartment, in which she travelled in glorious isolation. The atmosphere in the remainder of the coach was unspeakable, due to the thick fug created by men addicted to smoking twist!

In very much earlier times, she and her sister Jane would clean out the carriages when the train returned to Pendre. They especially disliked sweeping out the Lancaster-built coach with the hoods over the wheels which projected above the floor and interfered with the sweeping brush!

Not everyone in Towyn thought the age of enlight-enment had reached the town when the railway and then the motor car arrived. 'I hated travelling on the railway . . . and in cars. And I still do' confessed Miss Pugh (now of Brynhyfryd) looking back over her life. An aspect of the railway personal to her lay in the strict Sabbath code which pervaded most English, Scots and Welsh towns before the Second War. Divine Services took precedence over everything else and each Sunday was marked by a Morning Service, a Sunday School at 2 p.m. and an Evening Service at 6 p.m. Only those like her father, returned to their farms to do what work was necessary for the livestock – and nothing more; he would change from his Sunday clothes for that work, and then don them again. The shortest way from the Pugh farm to the Methodist Chapel was along the Cambrian track, and every Sunday the family would pick its way in their Sunday finery, along the sleepers in each direction – six 'single journeys' in all.

Illustrations showing both engines at once are rare. This one was probably arranged specially. DOLGOCH (newly painted) and TALYLLYN stand in Pendre loop. It was the occasion of Harold Fayle's visit c.1903, and perhaps near the time when DOLGOCH was renamed? The men (left to right) might be Jonathan Rowlands (carrying a heavy spanner in his hand) and Bob Thomas. The light-sheeted cab on DOLGOCH looks somewhat battered.

H. FAYLE

CHAPTER EIGHT
LOCOMOTIVES

AS a centre of widest interest, the two venerable (for some, lovable) railway engines which served the Company throughout this narrative have always held the stage, not least because of their longevity. In some ways this is strange, for neither engine was especially unique and variations of the type which each represented could be found in several rail gauges on industrial sites around the country. But by and large, whilst those few whose familiarity with steam engines at quarries, factories, dockyards and suchlike would find these two old stagers less rare, the many who visited the Talyllyn had no such knowledge and most gazed upon them as something unique. And in many ways they were!

(As to their age: on a wider viewpoint the British Isles was the cradle of the narrow gauge steam locomotive; even in America where development was far more exciting and rapid than here, there was little requirement for steam engines on narrow gauge lines; it was 1874 before one short railroad of 2 ft. $3\frac{1}{2}$ in. gauge acquired a steam locomotive.)

Both engines were ordered by the Aberdovey Slate Co.; the first was named *Talyllyn* before it left the maker's premises, and the second followed about six months later, given the name *Dolgoch* at the time of completion. If names are any guide, we may speculate that *Talyllyn* was so dubbed at the time when the Quarry Company had no thoughts of a passenger service, and *Dolgoch* was thought to be a suitable name after a change of intention to convey passengers. Though neither engine (each very different externally though having many internal interchangeable fittings) was strictly a 'passenger engine', they were destined to spend their lives, turn and about, hauling whatever traffic offered, albeit they were quite suitable to any type of train which was limited to a speed of under 12 m.p.h. as laid down by the Board of Trade Inspector in his wisdom. As to names, down the years the place-name system of bestowing names on engines has brought its problems, and doubtless there have been many in the past who were misled into thinking that a train headed by *Talyllyn* would in fact terminate there: in this regard, the names *Towyn* and *Abergynolwyn* might have been a better choice.

Looking at these engines rationally, it might seem to have been a stupid decision to buy two locomotives of such differing type, especially with Swinton Spooner to call on for guidance. In maintenance terms and to reduce costs, it would have been more sensible if two identical engines had been purchased, and the hypothesis that a second different one was made

necessary by a change in the function of the Railway can be challenged perhaps if *Talyllyn* was not fully satisfactory and the makers were told not to expect the Company to entertain a second engine of the same pattern.

There may be several other explanations; Fletcher, Jennings their builders, may have benefited from the flair of a good local salesman, or perhaps they were prepared to talk of quick delivery or a good discount for cash? Perhaps they were anxious to demonstrate that an engine fitted with their Fletcher Patent (No. 321 of 1864) could be built on a gauge as narrow as 2 ft. 3 in. with a view to wider markets for the type and would give less of a rough ride than the first engine? There must have been good reason why the Company went back to them again.

The Quarry required engines to haul empty slate wagons back to the foot of the Alltwyllt Incline from the Towyn wharfside. A certain tonnage of Up goods would also be carried, including coal, lime, building materials, food etc. for the communities at Quarry and village, and some intermediary traffic. Down traffic would be mainly slate and slab, some 'nightsoil', empty beer barrels etc. The amount of passenger traffic which was at first envisaged would be so small as probably not to be reckoned in the requirements. Apart from short upgrade distances, Down trains would require the engine only as a brake, for hand brakes sufficed on the railway down to 1951. Doubtless the Quarry foresaw that their traffic would virtually monopolise the train service and would not conceive a complete reversion of traffic a century later. Had we the ability to picture the trains of the mid-1860s, they would have been goods and mineral, or 'mixed'. Contrast this requirement with the first engines on the neighbouring Corris Railway which were mixed traffic – destined from the start with larger driving wheel, which gave them a fair turn of speed when suitable.

The Talyllyn engines had several basic features in common, a principal one being to secure the motion brackets to the boiler barrel to act as an effective frame stay and the use of heavy timber buffer beams at the extremities of the frames. (When *Talyllyn* was given extended frames in 1867, this slightly lengthened the unsupported distance.) In these cases, the boiler took up duty as a 'backbone' rather (but not altogether) as in road engine practice, but not so extreme as some industrial locomotives of the period which omitted frames altogether! In the instance of the Talyllyn engines, it might be said that the frame simply located the axleboxes. The boilers, of Low Moor iron, were

THE LOWCA ENGINEERING COMPANY, LIMITED,

Lowca Engine Works, Whitehaven, England.

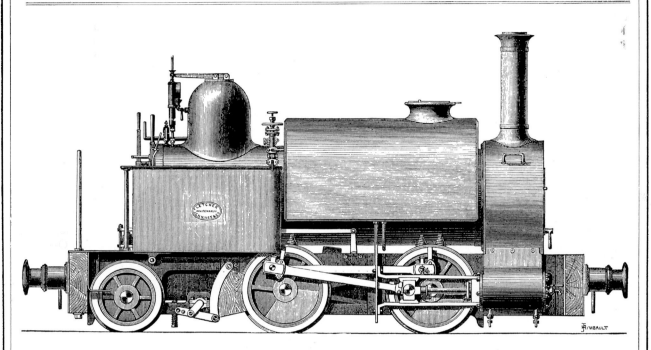

CLASS C.

TANK LOCOMOTIVE ENGINE FOR NARROW GAUGES.

THIS Engine has outside cylinders and six wheels, four being coupled. One with cylinders 8in. diameter is in use on a railway 2ft. 3in. gauge for mixed trains of slate and passengers, consisting of three passenger carriages, each seated for 24 persons, one break or luggage van, and 20 slate wagons. The line is about 8 miles long, and of descending gradients from the quarries to its opposite terminus; these are various, but the greater portion is 1 in 75. Another is employed on a road of 3ft. 0½in. abroad; and several others, rather modified, with all wheels coupled, upon one of 3ft. Swedish.

Dimensions and Prices for Gauges under 3½ft.

Code Word.	Size of Cylinder.	Length of Stroke.	Area of Firegrate.	No. of Tubes.	Diameter of Tubes.	Size of Coupled Wheels.	Size of Trailing Wheels.	Wheel Centres.	Size of Injector.	Diameter of Boiler.	Length of Boiler Barrel.	Gauge of Rails.	Ap'roxim'te Weight when Empty.	Nett Cash Price.
	In.	In.	Ft.		In.	Ft. In	Ft. In.	Ft. In.	No.	Ft. In	Ft. In.	Ft In.	Tons.	
CHARLEMAGNE	8	16	4	66	1½	2 4	2 0	7 6	4	2 6	6 1	⎰ 2 3 ⎱	7½	£700
COBLENZ	9	16	4¾	78	1½	2 9	2 0	8 8	4	2 9	7 3	⎰ to ⎱ 3 6	8¾	£790
CLEMENT	10	20	6	110	1½	3 0	2 4	⎰ 9 0 ⎱ to 10	5	3 0	⎰ 7 6 ⎱ to 8 6	3 6	10½	£900 .

of excellent quality as boilers, but as a substitute (or) for a conventional mainframe, they failed. Smokebox fronts were flat, with horizontally-hinged doors. Smaller fittings common to both locomotives were the tallow cups concerned with the oil feed to the cylinders.

The locomotives were asked to perform about fourteen round trips per week (with extras as the summer passenger service became established over the years)

The engine was Works No. 42 of 1864. (Fletcher, Jennings & Co. of Lowca Works, Whitehaven had taken over the firm of Tulk & Ley in 1857 and, under the ownership of Mr. H. A. Fletcher, continued to trade under that name until 1884 when it became The Lowca Engineering Co. Ltd., Lowca Engine Works. Under a successor they traded until 1912, being wound up finally in 1927. The original Fletcher, Jennings Order Book was loaned to the author in the late 1940s,

One of the earliest photographs of TALYLLYN, carrying its first saddle tank and showing a carriage with 'No. 1'. TALYLLYN's frames, and therefore wheelbase, would be the originals. The personnel are known to be: Jacob Rowlands, Jonathan Rowlands and Hugh Griffiths.
E. D. CHAMBERS

making a total average engine mileage of about 6,000 each per year. Initially, the load would be one or two coaches, the brake van and, say, ten wagons per mixed train, which was well within the engines' capacity. As maintenance declined (and fell sharply with the departure of 'Hugh Gas') it fell at a time when mileages/tonnages were also falling, so that latterly total mileage was only about 3,000 per annum.

Original livery is likely to have been green, the names being painted on. Numbers were not carried in the period of this review and maker's nameplates were missing from one side from the 1920s onwards.

TALYLLYN

This four-wheeled saddle tank engine to the maker's standard design was delivered to Towyn on 24th September 1864. It is legendary that it came by sea to Aberdovey Pier, possibly put on board ship at Whitehaven, a port which had had tramroads before 1730 and had enjoyed railways from earliest times.*

---

* the basis of an 1865 delivery date is obscure; confirmation as yet is lacking and a date in Autumn 1864 would more acceptably fit the timescale.

together with a copy of The Lowca Engineering Co. Ltd. catalogue which still features engravings of their predecessors' engines.) Fletcher, Jennings had failed to excite the interest of the Festiniog Railway Company when they submitted a design for a locomotive in October 1862, being among the twenty-nine manufacturers to tender. It may be assumed it would have been similar to the engine supplied at the time for the Aberdare Iron Co. in South Wales. Among the other tenders received by the Festiniog was one from Thomas Dunn & Co. of Manchester, the firm which supplied the Talyllyn with wagon turntables. Did Thomas Dunn ever build any engines at all? And if the introduction of narrow gauge locomotives onto the Festiniog Railway was to produce such world-wide razzmatazz, why did their delivery at Towyn apparently escape the notice of the newspapers, whilst the arrival of the first carriage there was duly reported? Perhaps the publicity-minded Spooners at Portmadoc had overplayed their rôle and the delivery of a small engine to a more remote Welsh location was no longer news? According to a note in the Order Book, this was the first narrow gauge engine they had 'built with plate frames', a statement which might be doubted by what is to follow herein. The engraving of the engine in their catalogue shows it as fitted with an additional rear wheel set but without detail as to how the frames were extended. The openings in the mainframes for access and lightness are considerable, and have led to the oftsaid comment that this and *Dolgoch* had frames

The engravings of both Talyllyn engines should not be taken too much at face value: *Talyllyn*'s Giffard injector would seem to be fitted in an odd position; three cylinder drain cocks would be unusual but in fact only steam chest cocks were fitted to both engines, and these had to be operated from the front buffer beam!

TALYLLYN must have been fitted with a second saddle tank by the end of 1900; this picture at Pendre is therefore some time in the early 1900s.
NARROW GAUGE RAILWAY
MUSEUM TRUST

which were about as near bar-type as plate-type frames could be! An early edition of the catalogue refers to the type 'As supplied to many Welsh Quarry Railways' (in fact, the Talyllyn was the only one) and to their previous and similar engines supplied to iron companies in South Wales. A later edition of the catalogue omits this reference to 'Welsh Quarry Railways' and substitutes '. . . One with cylinders 8 in. diameter is in use on a railway 2 ft. 3 in. gauge for mixed trains of slate and passengers, consisting of three passenger carriages, each seated for 24 persons, one break [*sic*] or luggage van, and 20 slate wagons. The line is 8 miles long, and of descending gradients from the quarries to its opposite terminus; these are various, but the greater portion is 1 in 75 . . .'. Under the code word *Charlemagne*, the nett cash price for such as was *Talyllyn* was £700. Measurement off this engraving shows a distance of 4 ft. 4 in. from driving wheel to rear wheels, the 1950 figure being 4 ft. This could be explained by failure in some way of the frames of the rebuild of 1867, and their replacement c. 1900 by a set of mild steel frames supplied by Messrs. W. G. Bagnall Ltd.* Mention of this will be made again.

---

* W. G. Bagnall assisted his uncle John at the latter's iron foundry in Wolverhampton from 1865 to 1879. W. G. Bagnall started on his own in Messrs. Massey & Hill, iron founder's premises, Stafford, in 1875.

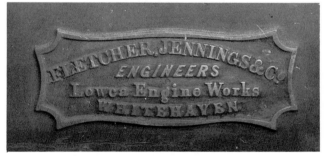

Maker's plate carried by TALYLLYN.   AUTHOR

Features of *Talyllyn* included cylinders and wheels outside the frames, a narrow-waisted firebox dropped between the frames, overhead volute springs to each axlebox, solid disc wheels with spokes cast on the face, brakes to the driving wheels only from a hand screw on the footplate, coal bunkers flanking the firebox, which was topped by a large dome carrying two Salter safety valves, one low and one high pressure injector both of early Giffard pattern, a set of large stubby buffers somewhat uncommon in narrow gauge practice, and finally, a completely exposed footplate at the rear with only a handrail as a safety measure. Stephenson's link motion was fitted between the frames, the valve rods being cranked under the leading axle, and the regulator was of the pull-out type. There

In this unusual viewpoint at Abergynolwyn, the position of the buffer bases on the rear beam of TALYLLYN is yet to be explained.
NATIONAL LIBRARY OF WALES

was no footplate round the engine, which was indeed so small that it was unnecessary. The unusual cylinders had a stroke of twice the bore and may have been of a pattern the makers used on stationary engines.

Comparative dimensions with *Dolgoch* are listed on p. 278.

Captain Tyler had complained about the vertical oscillation of one of the engines and *Talyllyn* was the culprit with its very short wheelbase. From Fletcher's books, there is an entry stating that the engine was back in Whitehaven again by January 1867 and that a pair of trailing wheels was fitted by making a rearward extension to the frames. These wheels were given no sideplay and many problems were to ensue because of this.

Talyllyn returned to Whitehaven a second time about the turn of the century but beyond stating 'Order 1086' Fletcher's surviving records do not enlighten us further. Perhaps a new inner firebox was substituted then? Over the years sundry alterations have been carried out at Towyn where a cab has been fitted, also a partial front footplate, sandbox and a steam stop valve from which steam might be taken to

drive the stationary engine in the workshop. Although not quite so famous as her companion *Dolgoch*, she was always prime favourite with the men, who preferred her additional water capacity and better riding qualities. From a permanent way maintenance viewpoint, the long rigid wheelbase of *Talyllyn* was much harsher on the curves.

L. T. C. Rolt, during his tenure as General Manager of the Railway during the early 1950s, was told that Bagnall of Stafford had supplied a new pair of frames and that they had been fitted at Pendre. Without accepting the full implication of this story, he later discovered that a shaft in the workshop roof had been tried – and found wanting – in the engine-lifting process, thus accounting for its shape! In error, the whole engine, rather than the boiler alone, had been attached to the shaft. Opportunity was taken to move the rear axle forward, making the present-day wheelbase of 8 ft. Back sanding was also fitted at the same time. [There is no reference to this work in *Bagnalls of Stafford*. (Oakwood Press 1973).]

A word about the engine and its predecessors of the same type and from the same maker makes comparison more interesting: that portion of the Order Book surviving began at Works No. 21 of 1858 and if it is accepted that 'narrow gauge' is a measurement less than standard gauge, then the maker's first narrow gauge engine of any type or gauge was to the same design as *Talyllyn*, and supplied to the Aberdare Iron Co. Glamorganshire for their 2 ft. 9 in. gauge tramway, where it was worked over a line about one mile long containing adverse gradients between 1 in 14–29. Over this it successfully hauled 20 'trams' of 5 cwt. each; it was Works No. 28 of 1862 and a repeat order was Works No. 35 of 1864. In May 1875 Aberdare ordered two more but the Company failed (in 1874 the concern was reported as 'almost closed down' due to a shortage of water, but it was the rapid decline in the older iron-

making industry which devastated certain foundries in Glamorganshire) and left the completed engines on the maker's hands; they were ultimately converted to 3 ft. gauge and sold.*

In South Wales, the Iron Works engine was highly successful, to the result that John Brogden & Sons of Bridgend ordered two of the same type, No. 33 of 1863 and No. 69 of 1869, for their 2 ft. 10 in. colliery lines north of that town. (Brogdens were involved in the Lake District, south Manchester and Porthcawl dock/railway construction, also having South Wales mining etc. interests.)

Of the same type again were Works Nos. 38 and 39 of 1864 supplied to the Plymouth Iron Co. of Aberdare, using 2 ft. 8 in. gauge, making *Talyllyn*

Another pre-1900 view of TALYLLYN, carrying its first tank and lined in black. The Abergynolwyn postman stands on the footplate step. The Van attached has horizontal planking, and the lamp bracket (possibly a socket type) has been taken off the rear of the engine.
P. H. WELLS

* *The Industrial Railway Record* (December 1963) has more detail.

TALYLLYN has its second tank and new frames and the quoted date is 1900. The locality is Wharf, so the building behind will be the predecessor of the Gunpowder Shed. Bob Thomas is the fireman. The long handrail has yet to be fitted, but a short one made from a carriage handle is visible at the firebox end.
K. A. C. R. NUNN

At Wharf in 1903, TALYLLYN has been given a rear sandbox (in the footplate floor) and a cover over the reversing lever. Jonathan Rowlands 'up'.
H. FAYLE

TALYLLYN entering Pendre on 4th August 1913. The flared top to the chimney has disappeared; the carriage handle can be seen on the tank but the long handrail is still in the future.

K. A. C. R. NUNN

the sixth Welsh narrow gauge locomotive the makers had provided, albeit reduced and contrived for the narrowest gauge. Thus *Talyllyn* may be seen among its contemporaries. (Fothergill's Plymouth Iron Works, situated at Gadlys, Aberdare, was said in 1874 to 'have little hope' and the business duly succumbed shortly afterwards.) The South Wales engines had 8 in. × 16 in. outside cylinders and 2 ft. 4 in. wheels, the same as *Talyllyn*. The track was combined edge rail and tramplate.

The worst feature of the engine was its rigid 8 ft. wheelbase as the rear wheelset had little side play. This was of limited concern on the main line, but certain pointwork was much sharper than the curves on the main, and the curvature of The Mineral Line was considerable. It became the practice to lay the track to a gauge of between 2 ft. 3½ in. and 2 ft. 4 in. (the platelayer adding the width of his thumb to the track gauge) in order to accommodate the engine. Some stock which enjoyed 3 in. wide wheel treads was quite happy to traverse this increase without falling between the rails; slate wagons were an exception – with 2½ in. treads they were prone to derailment with the gauge at 2 ft. 4 in.

Out on The Mineral Line the sharper curves were given considerable super-elevation to assist the engine round them, though poor maintenance had later tended to exaggerate the height of the outer rail to extreme degree.

A detail of the engine as first supplied was that the rear buffer stocks (no photograph of the front end of that period exists) were fastened to the beam thus ◇ and not in the conventional manner parallel to the beam.

The latter-day chimney — or the old one re-vamped — is restored on TALYLLYN at Pendre on 10th August 1925. (Almost all cameramen seemed to visit in August!)   H. G. W. HOUSEHOLD

A feature of the replacement frames supplied by Bagnall is that they are said to have arrived merely roughed-out and undrilled, so that this had to be done with a hand ratchet drill. In 1881 Hugh Griffiths (aged 19) was already a Fitter and 'Engine Driver'. (see p. 239). There was a last major overhaul at Pendre in the early 1930s, this time by 'Hugh Gas' but, after his departure a few years later, deterioration was slow and sure. By the Second War the engine was already very rough but it was obliged to operate from time to time, failing on a passenger working in 1942 and again in 1945 due to a cracked steam chest.* Boiler inspection showed extensive wasting of the stays (the boiler shell

---

*On the former occasion it is recorded that the passengers returned to Towyn in the wagons by gravity, at a later date *Dolgoch* collected the carriages and engine and drew them back to Pendre, and that *Dolgoch* was not in regular use at that time.

was still the original) and the valve gear had been quite worn out to the extent that it was necessary to jam the reversing lever into any position by hammering in wooden packing to secure it. With a view to complete overhaul, Haydn Jones obtained a report from The Atlas Foundry, Shrewsbury, submitted to him on 15th May 1944.

Dai Jones recalls that he was still at school (the occasion would therefore be prior to summer 1943) when his father, firing to Peter Williams on *Dolgoch*, was involved in a derailment at Fachgoch. It was quite a serious affair by Talyllyn standards, for *Dolgoch* was left straddled across the track with its chimney pointing seawards. Re-railing was beyond the Railway staff

and as many men as then survived at the Quarry were brought down for the purpose. However, such was the damage to the engine that though under steam, it would not move. For some reason the usual method of sending for horses from Ty Mawr was not enacted, and the brave decision to steam *Talyllyn* was taken.

Between them, Dai and his father Hugh, after first pouring a considerable amount of oatmeal into the boiler in order to stem a little of the loss of steam from various escapes, were able to move off up the line and retrieve *Dolgoch*, a salvage operation which took them all day and well into the night. Accepting the fallibility of human memory, this may have been its penultimate steaming, according to how events led up to the fatal

Plenty of water available at Ty Dwr; another viewpoint on the day of the previous photograph. The engine has now received the long handrail to the tank top, and small modifications to the smokebox door will be noted over the years. H. G. W. HOUSEHOLD

On 13th June 1931 TALYLLYN had lost its maker's plate from this side of the engine . . .   G. H. W. CLIFFORD

. . . but it was in place on the other side.   G. H. W. CLIFFORD

TALYLLYN taking water at Dolgoch on 6th July 1936.

S. W. BAKER

'last time' of 1945. (There is a possibility that this event was one and the same as described by Tom Rolt when *Dolgoch* derailed after return from its overhaul at Shrewsbury and *Talyllyn*, which had been holding the fort on slate traffic in the interim, went out to the rescue on what was Rolt's impression of its ultimate mission, and that the events have become confused in memory.)

This is an opportunity to say a little about the 'arrangements' for working trains at this time. It appears that Hugh Jones and Peter Williams, the two leading characters in the plot, would contrive matters to suit themselves. ... in the interest of the Railway, be it added. Sometimes Hugh would be driving, sometimes he would be out on the track. Often they would be on the footplate together and Hugh would fire until he dropped off at some destination to renew a sleeper or other job which was more than overdue for attention. Wharf office paid little heed to all this – if matters

were going with reasonable smoothness, why should Edward Thomas interfere?

The aforementioned accident could have been due to that capricious trait found in Peter Williams, mentioned elsewhere, in his operation (or lack of it) of the drum brake on the Village Incline. Peter tended to drive in a series of fits and starts and, perhaps, spurred on by boredom and anxious to break the monotony of the journey, he put on speed and disregarded Hugh's strictures – so often expressed – that 'the track was bad here' (in Welsh, of course). To effect the complete turnround of the locomotive suggests that he was going quite nicely at the time. Perhaps to spread the work the better between these two men, we find Morris Lewis on the footplate handling the shovel in the late 1940s. He has had mention on p. 250; he never drove, however. The main defects of the design were lack of intermediate frame stretchers, tendency for the front end to 'hang' in consequence so that the cylinder

In the guise of the late 1940s but taken in August 1935, Hugh 'Gas' has TALYLLYN at Abergynolwyn, with the third all-welded saddle tank fitted.

Standing in Pendre loop, TALYLLYN has discarded its wooden 'door'.
AUTHOR'S COLLECTION

The engine had three saddle tanks in the period now considered; the earliest lasted possibly until the mid-1890s and had been modified during its life; it ended its days as a sandstore in Pendre yard. The second also had re-incarnation as part of a 'shelter' near the occupation crossing and 'ballast quarry' at Tancoed. The second tank was replaced in the mid-1920s and the third was extant when the engine was withdrawn from duty. There are certain detail features of these tanks which enable uncaptioned photographs to have at least a rough date put upon them.

assemblies worked loose, long rigid wheelbase and throughout that the steaming rates could never match the size of cylinders provided. These shortcomings would not be so embarrassing in normal industrial service, but the Talyllyn was not such a situation!

No remedial action was taken following The Atlas Foundry report, and at the time of Sir Haydn's demise the engine was laid off within Pendre Works.

Whether *Talyllyn* was a factor or not, there was clearly some impasse in the locomotive situation during 1885 for a note in the Corris Railway minutes (3rd December 1885) reveals that during November Mr. McConnel 'had enquired the price of the spare engine. It was resolved not to sell it at less than the original cost of £700'. Much later (19th March 1918) the foreman of Boston Lodge Works on the Festiniog Railway received a postcard from Haydn Jones asking '. . . to be put in touch with repairing firms . . . especially for boiler work'. Whilst both the foregoing have documentary foundation, over forty years ago (when the writer first knew Towyn) there were other

For one year and eleven months TALYLLYN was off duty after DOLGOCH returned from The Atlas Foundry. Most of that time was spent in this position inside the Pendre Works. Within the period of this book, it was never to run again. 25th August 1948.
H. C. CASSERLEY

THE LOWCA ENGINEERING COMPANY, LIMITED,

Lowca Engine Works, Whitehaven, England.

CLASS Bb.

FLETCHER'S "PATENT" TANK LOCOMOTIVE ENGINE FOR NARROW GAUGES.

THIS Engine is designed for use where the curves are easy, and a long wheel base is in consequence admissible, securing greater steadiness than can be obtained with Engines in which the wheel base is short and the firebox overhangs the driving axle.

The Cylinders are placed outside, and the driving axle is situated behind the firebox instead of before it. The eccentrics which give motion to the slide valves are put upon the leading or front axle instead of the driving one, and a peculiar arrangement of link motion employed.

One of these Engines, with 8-inch cylinders, has been some years at work on a railway, 2ft. 3in. gauge, in North Wales, for the conveyance of minerals and passengers. Up gradients of 1 in 75 and 1 in 66 (the latter half a mile long) its usual load is 33 tons, at a speed of 18 miles an hour.

Dimensions and Prices for Gauges under 3½ft.

Code Word.	Size of Cylinder.	Length of Stroke.	Area of Firegrate.	No. of Tubes.	Diameter of Tubes.	Size of Wheels.	Wheel Centres.	Size of Injector.	Diameter of Boiler.	Length of Boiler Barrel.	Gauge of Rails.	Ap'roxim'te Weight when Empty.	Nett Cash Price.
	In.	In.	Ft.		In.	Ft. In.	Ft. In.	No.	Ft. In.	Ft. In.	Ft. In.	Tons.	
BENBOW	8	16	4	73	1½	2 6	6 6	4	2 6¾	4 9	2 3	8½	£650
BARBEL	9	16	4¾	78	1½	2 9	7 0	4	2 9	5 3	to 3 6	9½	£760
BULBUL	10	20	6	110	1½	3 0	8 0	5	3 0	6 0	3 0 to 3 6	11	£860

Carrying the name PRETORIA, the erstwhile DOLGOCH stands at Abergynolwyn on 26th June 1909.　　K. A. C. R. NUNN

less reliable tales in circulation; he has a notebook entry following a conversation with a loquacious local on the platform at Pendre . . . 'Sir Haydn used to send an engine to Caernarvon each year for repairs – it cost him £400. Wasted money. If he had put half that amount into the track the locos would have been alright. Isn't it?'

Which certainly underlines the pitfalls of factfinding by personal contact!

DOLGOCH

In considering the second locomotive supplied by Fletcher, Jennings to the Aberdovey Slate Co., we find yet another four-coupled tank engine but of a type and conception which was wholly different from *Talyllyn* – in fact, the Quarry Company was to become owner of a pair of machines which approached the design of the steam locomotive in quite differing ways.

One of the problems affecting what had become, in the 1860s, the conventional form of the locomotive, was that to traverse the sharp curves of industrial sites, engines were limited to four-coupled driving wheels on which might be placed a weight restriction: whilst firms found they were often limited to the shortest wheelbase of engine available, they also wanted a

DOLGOCH carried this maker's plate. 1943.　　AUTHOR

powerful unit. Locomotive manufacturers usually met all these problems head-on in the one design! Inevitably that answer was, in most instances, found in an engine carried on four-coupled wheels to achieve maximum adhesion from the weight of the machine and with the axles close together to facilitate passing round a sharp curve. Regrettably one effect was to increase the overhang at each end: a four-wheeled engine with a short wheelbase, when passing round a sharp curve, suffers the disadvantage that the buffers

FIG.1.

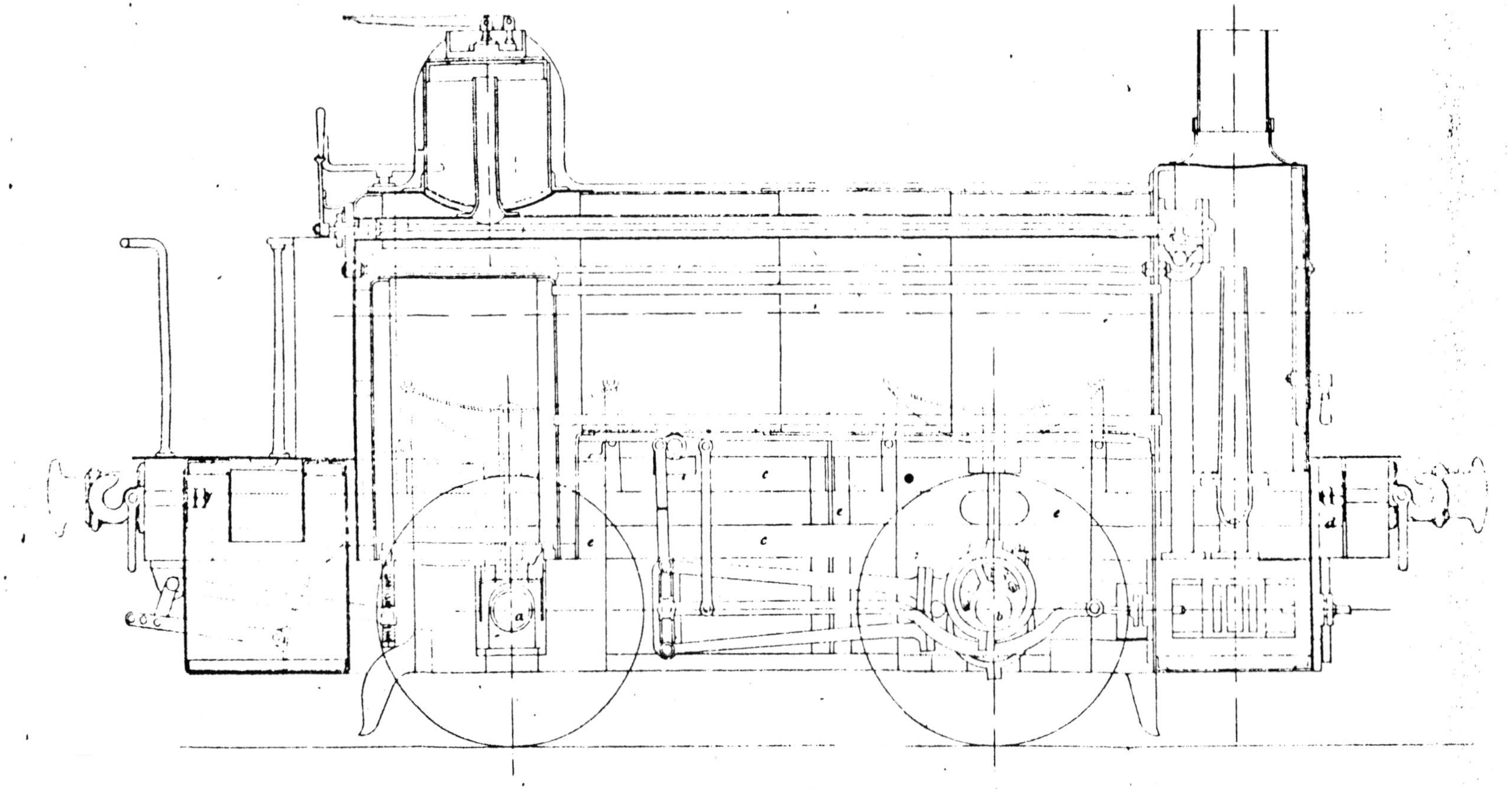

FIG.2.

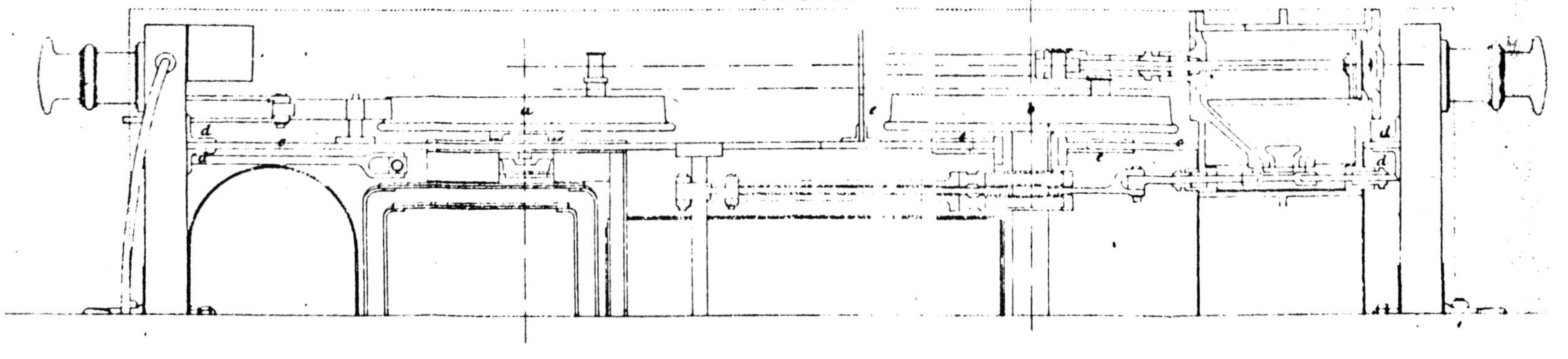

This drawing accompanied the specification for Fletcher's Patent

and drawgear swing wildly from the centreline of the track! This can bring problems for if the engine is pushing wagons round a curve, unless the buffer heads on engine and wagons are of sufficient area, their heads can pass around their opposite number on the curve and when straight track is entered again, they will lock behind each other and cause the wagons (being lighter) to leave the track.

This was but one of various problems that locomotive manufacturers faced so most of them compromised on the difficulties and to reduce costs, evolved one or more 'standard designs' to meet them. Manufacturers then competed with each other by building their own standard designs, often in batches of two or three to achieve economies and then offered 'Ex stock for hire or outright purchase' through such periodicals as *The Engineer*. Over a decade or so Fletcher, Jennings offered three or four standard designs, and *Talyllyn* and *Dolgoch* represented two of them, the former, as delivered, was suited to narrow gauge and similar to

previous products, but *Dolgoch* was adapted and modified from the standard gauge form of a Patent to suit the narrow gauge of the Talyllyn Railway.

Unlike other manufacturers' standard types, this was an engine built to Fletcher's Patent, expressly evolved so as to reduce the overhang by increasing the wheelbase yet not sufficiently so as to prevent the engine traversing sharp curves. Four-wheeled engines built in the conventional manner were usually arranged so that all the working parts which gave movement to the machine (cylinders, valve chests, valve motion, driving rods etc. wheels and axles), were placed forward of the firebox, which could then enjoy all the space now offered between the frames, unencumbered by the aforementioned machinery. So far so good. But consider that there would have to be accommodated behind the rear axle, not only the essential firebox, but also a footplate where the engine crew would stand, and the distance from the rear axle to the rear beam of the engine is now considerably

Again at Abergynolwyn, this pleasant composition was part of an assemblage of various subjects in the former Adams & Whitehouse Collection.
P. B. WHITEHOUSE

DOLGOCH's frames stand in the Works, 'sans everything else'. The boiler, etc., has gone to The Britannia Foundry for repairs. 1935.

L. T. CATCHPOLE

It was either one or other of the engines which might stand for months at a time in the Works; in August 1935 it was DOLGOCH waiting to be stripped down for boiler repairs — see previous picture. H. F. WHEELLER

more than that at the front end, and on a curve all those unhelpful problems just mentioned may arise. Fletcher's Patent, among other things, overcame this difficulty by allowing the firebox to fall between the two axles and permit a nicely geometrical engine with overhangs of equal length at each end. Fletcher's advertised their Patent Engine for many years, but *Dolgoch* apart, the majority was built for the standard gauge (or greater!).

In fact, *Dolgoch* was unlike all its standard gauge sisters in that the foregoing had relatively short wheelbases because the Patent allowed the rear axle to be placed underneath the firebox to greater or lesser extent, whilst *Dolgoch*, with 6 ft. 6 in. wheelbase, has the rear axle completely behind the box. Why couldn't *Dolgoch*'s axle be put under the box as in other cases? It is just that in order to keep the centre of gravity low on a narrow gauge engine, the boiler/firebox assembly will be nearer rail level than in a standard gauge type where the centre of gravity is not so critical; standard gauge Patent engines had their boiler/firebox higher in the frame.

The Patent, was the invention of Henry Allason Fletcher, the senior partner and described as 'Allen's

straight-link motion folded back on itself.' Sufficient to add that by driving the valve gear from the leading axle by means of an arrangement that was acceptable on a standard gauge engine but gave accessibility problems on a narrow one, *Dolgoch* enjoyed a longish wheelbase, gave a steadier ride and imparted its full weight on the driving wheels. If unfortunately, the side coupling rods should break, the engine would be stranded, for the rear driving axle must also operate the front axle which moves the valves to drive the rear driving axle.

A feature of the type, (like *Talyllyn*) is that the boiler acts as a form of frame; again there are no intermediate frame stretchers but there was support from the motion bracket. A water tank is fitted inside the frames below the rear tank, the latter above the footplate at the extreme end of the engine, i.e. a 'back tank'. The 'back tank' holds 100 gallons, and the 'well tank' below (40 gallons) may be a later addition to supplement the meagre original. They are pipe-connected.

On the face of it, it would seem the Talyllyn engine crews had little to choose between their steeds (swings and roundabouts) but humanity being as it is, *Talyllyn* was the preferred engine. *Dolgoch*'s cylinders, wheel-

centres and eccentrics are common to those on *Talyllyn*, and the paint finish was identical; the name was painted on the boiler barrel. Volute springs to each axle were later altered and leaf springs fitted to the leading boxes.* Buffing gear was the same, though a footplate was fitted all round the engine and the boiler top sported a large brass handrail. At some later date a cab was added.

Fletcher's Order Book states that she was similar to *Talyllyn* but had 'shorter tubes'; the Book also gives a few general details of the line in that the engines were designed to haul loads of 33–35 tons up to speeds of 18 m.p.h., the train to be composed of luggage van, three passenger carriages, and twenty empty slate wagons. The grade of the line was given as averaging 1 in 75, the steepest portion being 1 in 66. Until 1938 at least, the Company possessed the blue prints for both engines, and the Delivery Note for *Dolgoch*.

In the Fletcher, Jennings era advertising for the Patent showed a standard gauge version over the caption 'PATENT MINERAL TANK LOCOMOTIVE ENGINES, for mines, collieries, ironworks, branch traffic, contractors etc. In these Engines the Driving Axle is placed under the Fire-box ... Different sizes are always kept in hand or in progress'. By The Lowca Engineering Co. Ltd. era the catalogue page showed *Dolgoch* (or something near it!) as 'Class Bb. FLETCHER'S "PATENT" TANK LOCOMOTIVE FOR NARROW GAUGES' and does stress that it is 'designed for use where curves are easy and the long wheelbase is in consequence admissible ... and a peculiar arrangement of link motion employed'. (The double meaning of the last feature was certainly not intended!) The catalogue engraving ends by adding that 'one of these

Engines with 8 inch cylinders ... at work on a railway, 2 ft. 3 in. gauge, in North Wales ... usual load 33 tons, at a speed of 18 miles an hour'. The nett cash price was £650, and the code name *Benbow*.

The first Patent engine was in fact the engine built immediately before *Talyllyn* (No. 41 of 1864) and was to standard gauge for the Plymouth Iron Works at Gadlys, near Aberdare (and which has already come to notice in connection with *Talyllyn*). An exception came with No. 45 of 1864 which was for the Severn & Wye Railway & Canal Co. (their No. 1) delivered on 1st October 'for a tramway'† of gauge 3 ft. 8 in., and with flangeless wheels only 2 in. larger than *Dolgoch*.

---

* Of these L. T. C. Rolt said, 'The latter are not hung in the normal manner. Instead, their extremities bear against two riveted horizontal cross-members, an arrangement which makes spring replacement almost impossible without dismantling the locomotive ...' (Trans. Newcomen Society XXXIII 1960–1)

† To run on a plateway in fact, but to be convertible to edge rails. Works Nos. 53, 54 and 55 of 1865 to the same design followed.

In all, fourteen Patent engines would be built before *Dolgoch*, which was the fifth narrow gauge engine of any type and the first Patent engine to narrow gauge. (*Talyllyn* and *Dolgoch* were the only 2 ft. 3 in. gauge engines built by Fletcher, Jennings, and also the narrowest in gauge.)

The Patent was of sufficient individuality to warrant specific mention in D. K. Clark's *Locomotive Engineering & The Mechanism of Railways*, a monumental two volume work of 1871 from which the plate reproduced on p.268 is taken. Clark defines the Patent as being suited to locomotives working in industrial situations at low speeds and adds in typically Victorian style '... but the movement is transmitted with some degree of obliquity from the expansion links to the valve spindles, and there is no doubt such obliquity must shake the freely hung pendulous gearing considerably at high speeds.' Not that the Talyllyn would be likely to suffer through such cause ... but the longer journeys of the Railway as opposed to short hauls in industry meant that the gear's inherent weakness, in that it could not be 'notched-up' (and so economise on steam), was more evident.

Whatever the merits or otherwise of the Patent, *Dolgoch* enjoyed the reputation of being 'shy for steam' equal only to that of *Talyllyn*. This might have been due to poor maintenance at Pendre. Experts in these matters have noted that by 1950 the blast pipe diameter had been reduced progressively to one third of its original opening, thus giving a sharper emission from the chimney with a view to improving the brightness of the fire to increase the steaming rate. All this did in practice was to tend to throw half-burned coals from the chimney in an exciting firework display when their heat value had been only partly delivered. The chimney, too, was considered always to have had a diameter larger than it should have been relative to the proportions of the blast pipe. Unburned fuel tended to clog the tubes, vibration due to frame movement loosened fastenings at the front end and air leaked into the smokebox in consequence. Both live steam and blast pipe joints began to leak into the smokebox, cylinders moved on the frames which themselves became warped and cracked in places, and the centres of the cranks and the cylinders seem never to have corresponded – the crank pins were $\frac{3}{4}$ in. too short in

By 1941 DOLGOCH was more in use than TALYLLYN; another occasion of the Messrs. Camwell, Tipper, et al. visit on 26th May 1941, seen here at Brynglas with Peter Williams on the platform.
W. A. CAMWELL

consequence of Capt. Tyler's retrograde recommendation. Other defects by 1950 were that the gauge of each wheelset varied by $\frac{5}{8}$ in., that to prevent a loose wheel two keys had been fitted to it to secure it to the axle, and that (on the same axle) one journal was $\frac{3}{4}$ in. smaller at one end of the axle than the other. A feature of the design was that the same bolts fastened both cylinders and smokebox to the frames; this gave trouble. Among minor issues was the fact that the essential pipework linking the well and back water tanks took all the cut and thrust of the engine in traffic as the well tank was secured to the back buffer beam.

Could any steam locomotive give a century of service with such glaring errors apparently built into the design? Luckily we are not describing modern internal combustion or electrically driven units; the steam engine is not a delicate machine and *Dolgoch*, allowing that many of these faults were simply imperfections with which the crews lived, clearly performed her duties adequately. Efficiency was not a measurable factor on the Talyllyn Railway.

The handrail – perhaps not on the engine when built but showing in the catalogue – was a sensible feature to reduce hazard when going forward to operate the sandbox in the leading splasher on the fireman's side of the engine, and so direct sand onto the rail heads to reduce slipping.

When the boiler lagging was removed – an event which the public rarely sees – these boilers were lagged to reduce heat loss by cladding them in wooden strips $1\frac{1}{2}$ in. × $\frac{3}{4}$ in. thick, the traditional method of those times. Window frames were in gunmetal.

The injector and blower stop valves were placed in a cluster on the boiler top and were closed by climbing on top of the boiler. These fittings dated from the time when the original Giffard injectors were removed.

According to some memories, the name was shown on one side of the boiler and when British troops entered Pretoria during the Boer War (5th June 1900) and the engine was being repainted in the Works, the name *Pretoria* was painted on the blank side, in effect the engine carrying two names. The photograph on p267 proves otherwise. Such patriotism would be much harder to find today. Ultimately the name *Dolgoch* was restored.

As to the engine's history, this relies (as with *Talyllyn*) on the fallibility of human memory, but there is an unconfirmed tale of the engine returning to The Lowca Works about 1913 for heavy overhaul (this might in fact be a First War visit – if official sanction was indeed given for it – and tie in with Haydn Jones' enquiry for help from Boston Lodge). The tradition that the engine went to The Britannia Foundry, Portmadoc for boiler and firebox repairs is partly upheld by pictures of the complete mainframe standing in the workshops sans boiler etc. in a photograph

of 1935; confirmation that it was just the boiler unit which made the journey is lacking.† However, the last major overhaul can be traced with much detail for in March 1945 the engine was taken down to Wharf. Later it was craned onto a standard gauge wagon and consigned by rail to Shrewsbury where a tractor dragged it on a flat wagon through the streets from the GWR yard to The Atlas Foundry in Frankwell.*

The Atlas Foundry was a combination of two businesses about 1902, and on the site of the Frankwell business which henceforward took the leading role. During 1944 the Company acquired its present title 'The Atlas Foundry Ltd.' The undertaking later amalgamated with that of a brother of the owners who ran a blacksmith's shop in Beeches Lane which was concerned mainly with shoeing horses. The Cambrian Foundry at Newtown is also in the hands of the same family, the Davies's. In 1917 the Gazeteer described the firm as 'E. Davies, Engineer, machinist & ironfounder; manufacturer of steam, gas and oil engines etc.' They also turned out threshing boxes and other agricultural machinery.

Edward Davies and Haydn Jones were old and firm friends; they shared a common interest in fishing and the Davies family was a *habitué* of Towyn. It is unlikely that they did much business together before *Dolgoch*'s collapse, but generally the Foundry did not take on railway work, although sons then in the works had heard their fathers speak of work being done on Glyn Valley and Snailbeach engines – probably by sending men out to the job. However, they had much experience with steam road and agricultural engines.

Haydn Jones would have felt entirely at home in that time-evading upstairs office at the Foundry; it was exactly as his own at D. & J. Daniel! Kelly's Directories, 100 years and more of age, catalogues of equal ancestry, Nazi steel helmets of World War II and plug taps for locomotive firebox washout plugs, lay in orderly but thick dust-coated array. It was said that Mr. Davies could lay his hand on anything there and knew in an instant the whereabouts of each.

In 1985 Brian Owen (who came to the Foundry in 1948), said his father had worked on *Dolgoch*. Although the present overhead gantry crane was not there then, there was a shed at the west side of the yard where traction engines were repaired and often converted into steam rollers in order to extend their working life. This was done by placing a top plate, etc. to take the pin which carried the front roller bracket. There had also been an open pit for this work too. *Dolgoch*, however, was brought by the aforementioned

---

† Lewis Cozens states a new boiler was fitted in 1939 – this is not so.

*Edward Thomas wrote on 1st February 1945: ' " *Dolgoch* " will be running on Wednesday February 7th . . .'

Though The Atlas Foundry did not look exactly like this at the time DOLGOCH was sent there for overhaul in 1945 (the overhead crane gantry is more recent) the corrugated iron buildings and the scattering of materials was then as now.
AUTHOR

Lister tractor hauling a low dray and rolled off in the northwest corner; there was no shelter and there the engine was jacked up and work commenced where it rested.

Though completed, no charge was yet made for *Dolgoch*; a cunning ruse was resorted to in order to ascertain what charge should be made. Some devious enquiries were made of The Hunslet Engine Co. Ltd. of Leeds and Andrew Barclay, Sons & Co. Ltd. of Kilmarnock implying that (1) the Foundry wished to contract out some locomotive work and what would the cost be and (2) what would be the cost of a replacement engine (presumably should *Dolgoch* be uneconomic to repair), from which Atlas hoped some guidance as to the figure which could be submitted to Haydn could be given. In the latter case, no doubt Haydn would ask Davies about the cost of replacing the decrepit *Talyllyn* also. 'Both recipients treated this as an enquiry for a new locomotive' and the gist of their replies was that each recommended that it would be better not to do any work on – (Atlas did not name the engine) – but rather to buy a new or re-gauged second-hand locomotive from them.

Ultimately, the Foundry was left to puzzle out a costing for itself, and it is well remembered how the total charges appeared to be so high that a sum considerably less than the total was charged for the work – after all, Davies and Haydn Jones were good friends and the former intended the relationship to remain that way ... and there was the fishing to consider. . . .

This was not the Foundry's only problem, for when the engine was ready for steam test, their customary method of running a road steam engine round the yard

and nearby streets for that purpose was not open to them! However, they had a good friend at Crewe Railway Works and his advice was sought. In consequence, a set of rollers was made and mounted on a wooden frame: the engine was lifted onto these and a stationary test 'run' ensued. The railway cartage service returned, collected the engine, craned it onto a well wagon at Shrewsbury and craned it off again at Towyn Wharf, where the Foundry's manager noted it standing there and saw that all was well.

By September 1945 *Dolgoch* was back in Pendre shed; *Talyllyn* was stored in Pendre workshops and though mechanically run-down, looked externally well cared-for*.

The Foundry did later work (1949) on *Dolgoch*'s cracked frame, but the men were sent over from Shrewsbury and stayed in Griffith Evans' (blacksmith) house next to Pendre Works for that purpose.

Among the work done on *Dolgoch* was the patching of the copper firebox (a job for which they had had plenty of experience with road and portable engines) and fitting of a new set of brass tubes. Some delay was occasioned by the shortage of such materials in those times. Patches were also applied to the boiler and some work done on the motion, for, some years later, a visitor to the Foundry saw a pair of expansion links, clearly intended for the engine, hanging on the wall – they distorted in the hardening process and could not

*Edward Thomas wrote on 11th March 1946: '. . . passenger service was discontinued owing to condition of the track. Labour and materials were impossible to get . . . we run up occasionally for slates . . . output very small . . . Some weeks we do not go up at all . . . "*Dolgoch*" came back from Shrewsbury last September . . .'

be used. The engine was completely repainted. (In more recent times the Foundry has supplied the Railway with brake blocks; these were not consigned per British Rail but by returning hearse to Towyn.)

And what of services during *Dolgoch's* absence, made so much longer by the shortage of materials in wartime? The ailing *Talyllyn* had to take up duty again and was able to provide assistance (with occasional lapses) until the service was withdrawn completely after the trains on 16th March 1945. The next passenger working was at Easter 1946.

Talyllyn continued to stand in the Works and a rejuvenated *Dolgoch* carried on without much complaint until the engine-crew crisis hit the Railway and 21-year-old Idris Williams ('surely one of the youngest

engine drivers in the country ... the engine he controls is exactly four times older than himself') was given the regulator. 'A few days ago the sole remaining engine, the *Dolgoch*, cracked its frames ... the Manager assured me that the damage was being repaired and that the engine would soon be running again. We both wondered, for how long, however ...' said an article on 5th September 1949, headed 'Breakdown on the Talyllyn Railway'. The cause of the accident was, according to those familiar with the circumstance, speed.

Hugh Jones was on trackwork at this time; it was more important than any other feature of the line, for its condition was parlous to say the least. He was called to the shop in High Street and Haydn Jones asked

Pictures of DOLGOCH after 'treatment' at The Atlas Foundry are easily identified by the modifications made to the chimney.

AUTHOR

The same changes and additional pipework at the smokebox sides is evident here, no less the position of the whistle on the first ring of the boiler. This was a historic occasion . . . the last working of the season for 1950 — 6th October.   S. WARD

what he thought could be done about the engine. Hugh said that if Atlas could send men to Towyn – they having the adequate type of welding equipment – he would strip down the engine in the workshop ready for them. Haydn took his advice; Hugh maintained the job was done for £200 but undoubtedly he bore the brunt of the hard work and burned many more candles!

Finally, both *Talyllyn* and *Dolgoch* worked chimney first up the line, the slight upgrade assisting to keep the firebox crown covered by water. It is a moot point as to which was more powerful, but *Dolgoch* certainly had the opportunity of working the heaviest train remembered; *Talyllyn* on such duty would tend to slip. One of the author's earliest trips was on *Dolgoch*, then seventy-nine years old.

'It was impossible to engage either full forward or full reverse gear due to wear in the motion, although the gear had to be used to assist to stop the train, there being only one brake block left. The regulator (push-pull type) offered very little adjustment and the water gauge glass showed some coffee-coloured liquid within. One of the try-cocks was used to fill up the platelayer's billy-can. On the shelf above the firehole door stood two large coloured enamel teapots holding oil: the short handle (9 in.) of the firing shovel was a novelty, no less the bent crowbar for pricking out the coals. The large home-made wooden door (which could be closed in bad weather and transferred to the other engine) was not only amusing but on a later footplate trip (on *Talyllyn*) was welcomed when the engine stopped in a howling winter gale for want of steam in the open fields below Cynfal. The driver, who also had to repair the track, did not like using *Dolgoch* as it played havoc with his frail track. At the time of this trip (1944) *Talyllyn* had been used all the previous season and was laid off for repairs; boiler pressure had been reduced to 70 lbs. and the driver would have preferred to be using her. *Dolgoch* ran at about 10 m.p.h. making an appalling clatter, with the one coach and three wagons loaded respectively with sacks of flour, sacks of coal, and track repairing tools, which pitched alarmingly in all directions behind and appeared as obstinate as a mule which refused to be lugged.

By Rhydyronen pressure had fallen to 20 lbs. and all the company's servants (incuding the author) huddled onto the footplate. There were no passengers so we stopped to "blow up" and the author ate another wartime sausage. Shortly cows and pigs on the line impeded progress, but with every delay – though the young lad who was fireman was sent ahead to drive off the animals – the engine was able to recover breath. *En route* several extra stops were made whilst the driver showed his visitor the beauty spots. Another stop before Abergynolwyn whilst the fireman ran ahead and kicked over the point blades with his foot; he then drove the engine round the coach which was locked and the visitor was invited to drive and propel the wagons to Alltwyllt. Water was taken at Ty Dwr, using the wooden trough . . . water everywhere and some into the tank. Two wagons were attached to the cable, and two loaded ones descended. We brought them down and *en route* stopped to drop three wagons loaded with bricks down the village incline – there were no balancing wagons.

The "new" driver found it difficult to couple gently onto the coach; having no brakes it kept inching away, but the regular and kindly driver leant against the far end of it and the coupling was achieved. So back to Towyn, the regular driver pointing out the worst places and the far end of every rail rising up as the engine rode the joints. Sometimes the new recruit was left alone to drive as the crew made off ahead to scare off livestock . . . Not the stuff out of which steam locomotive nostalgia is born, but an experience repeated many times since but never with the same joy . . .'

Summing up the two engines, here they were in 1950, built with boilers of Low Moor iron and having brass tubes and copper fireboxes; these boiler barrels were now 80 years of age, perhaps enjoying such longevity because the local water supply is very soft. Low Moor iron was highly resistant to corrosion and the water does not cause scale. By modern standards they were crude and simple but built in materials of high quality. Most of the nuts and bolts used the older large hexagon Whitworth sizes, and many did not accept modern spanners. The effect was to require the use of an extended range of tools, to increase repair

Locomotive liveries

	Talyllyn		Dolgoch	Source
1890s	Medium green, black lining (as fitted with first saddle tank)			TRN 120/41
1900	'Red' (?)		as for Talyllyn	T. R. Perkins. TRN 62/40
1901	'Bright Green'		as for Talyllyn	Loco. Mag. 1901
		1904	Engine being painted – name Pretoria given in 1900	
1908	'Green'		as for Talyllyn	Carter p. 253
		Aug. 1912	still carries Pretoria	
1921	Crimson Lake		as for Talyllyn	Rly. Mag. 1927(1) p. 395
1927–31	Nicknamed 'The Black Tankie' (colour not necessarily black)			Hugh Jones
1938	Dark olive green		(in workshop) Black	Rly. Mag. 1938(2) p. 357
1951	'Not recognisable. Perhaps once green, but now almost black'		'smart light green lined in red & yellow following overhaul in 1945 ... akin to LNER green'	TRN 120/41

Sources: *Railway Magazine* articles in 1904 (Fayle), 1925 (Household), 1938 (Woodcock) are quoted where informative.
TRN 120/41 = *Talyllyn Railway News* No. 120 p. 41 (etc.).
Carter, E. F.: *Britain's Railway Liveries* (Burke, London: 1952).

costs, to extend the time required for maintenance, and to widen the vocabulary of anyone involved in repair work. These two machines have a special place in railway history and though they closely resemble what they were, they are today not what they might seem to be!

Gone are those small cocks down on the front buffer beams, which drained the valve chests. The old method of bracketing and riveting an upward exten-

Having no sophisticated sanding gear, someone had to stand on the forward footplating of DOLGOCH in wet weather, and carefully pour sand on the rails in front of the moving engine. Here, young Herbert Jones crouches in the rain whilst engaged on that duty. AUTHOR

sion of the motion brackets to the boiler barrel and so stiffen the frames, is now discarded. The trick of dating pictures of *Dolgoch* after the visit to Atlas, by picking out the lubricator pipes fitted by them on either side of the smokebox, is no longer available – they have been removed. But it is the engines' chimneys into which a little study will reveal the changes and chances of the passing years. *Talyllyn* still retains the original chimney base and the rolled-up and riveted barrel. The cap is a casting and the base a blacksmith's forging. The chimney on *Dolgoch*, though today fitted with a brass collar, was without decoration from 1946 when Atlas removed it and the engine ran until Haydn's death – and after – without one. There must be some reason why a spare one-piece cast-iron chimney was found in the Works in 1950, which was suitable for fitting to either engine, but though chimneys have mouths they have no tongues and cannot recount the story ...

Leading dimensions

	Talyllyn	Dolgoch
Cylinders	8 in. × 16 in.*	8 in. × 16 in.*
Driving Wheel diameter	2 ft. 4 in.*	2 ft. 4 in.
Wheelbase	4 ft. + 4 ft.[1]	6 ft. 6 in.*
Boiler barrel diameter	2 ft. 6½ in.	2 ft. 6½ in.*
Working Pressure	100 lb. sq. in.	100 lb. sq. in.
Grate Area	2.88 sq. ft.*[2]	2.88 sq. ft.[3]
Total Heating Surface	156 sq. ft.	128 sq. ft.
Weight in Working Order	8½ tons[5]	8 tons[5]
Bunker capacity	6 cwt.[6]	6 cwt.[6]
Tank capacity	200 gallons[4]	140 gallons

* figures given in maker's order book
[1] after alteration to 0-4-2 wheel arrangement
[2] Catalogue figure is 4 sq. ft. Decrease of area due to lack of space on Talyllyn Railway locomotive
[3] Catalogue gives 4 sq. ft. (as for *Talyllyn*) but 2.88 is likely to be correct; Catalogue figure probably intended increase due to lack of area on Talyllyn Railway locomotive
[4] Approximate capacity of first of three tanks fitted over the period
[5] These figures are under the precise weight which is not known
[6] Each side

Note: there are many variations quoted to the above, largely due to cylinders increasing in size due to wear, driving wheels diminishing due to wear, etc. By 1950 working pressure was 70 lb. for safety reasons.

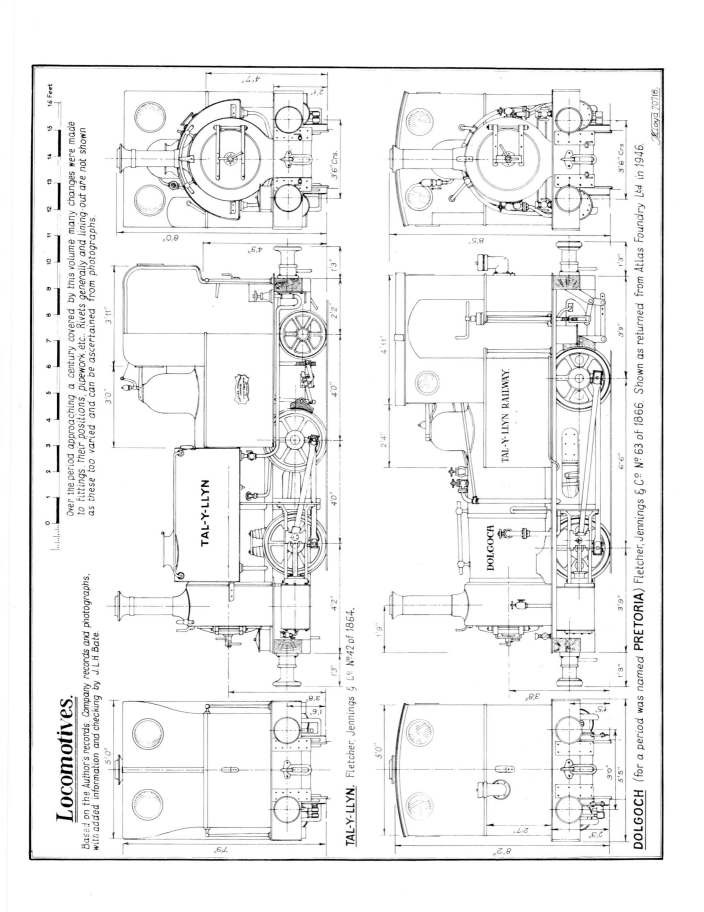

Locomotives.

Based on the Author's records. Company records and photographs,
with added information and checking by J.L.H.Bate.

Over the period approaching a century covered by this volume many changes were made
to fittings, their positions, pipework etc.. Rivets generally and lining out are not shown
as these too varied and can be ascertained from photographs.

TAL-Y-LLYN. Fletcher, Jennings & Cº. Nº 42 of 1864.

DOLGOCH (for a period was named **PRETORIA**) Fletcher, Jennings & Cº. Nº 63 of 1866. Shown as returned from Atlas Foundry Ltd in 1946.

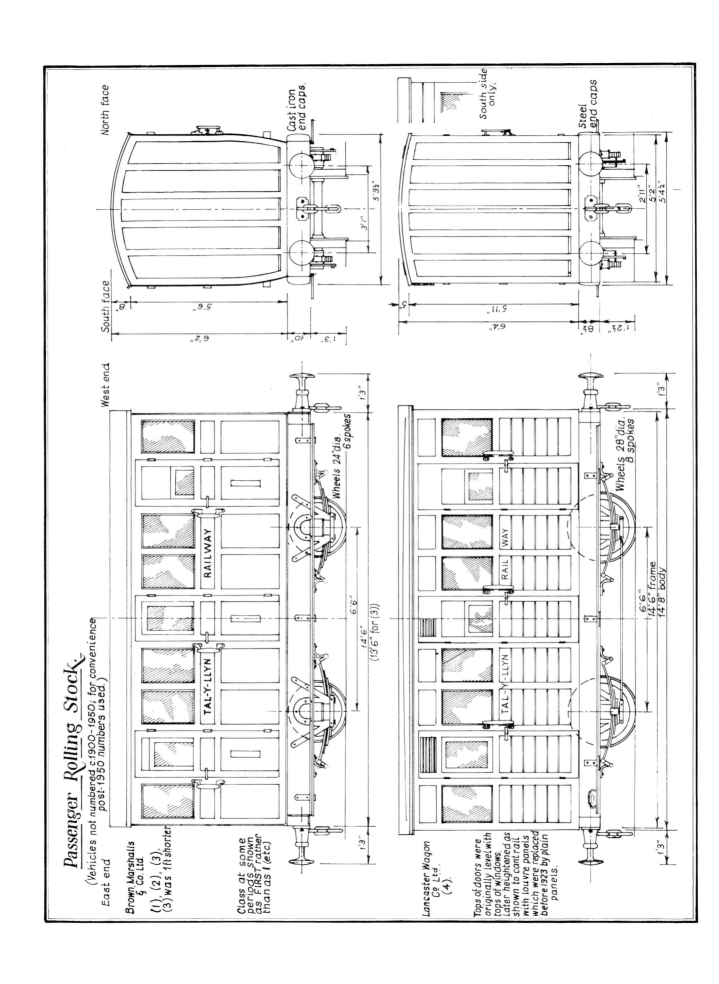

Passenger Rolling Stock.

(Vehicles not numbered c.1900-1950; for convenience post-1950 numbers used.)

East end

West end

North face

South face

Brown Marshalls & Co Ltd.

(1), (2), (3).
(3) was 1ft shorter than as I (etc).

Class at some periods shown as FIRST rather than as I (etc)

RAILWAY

TAL-Y-LLYN

Cast iron end caps.

Wheels 24″dia. 6 spokes

14'6"
(13'6" for (3)).

6'6"

1'3"

1'3"

5'9½"

3'1"

8″

5'6"

6'2"

10″

1'3"

South side only,

Steel end caps

Lancaster Wagon Cº Ltd. (4).

Tops of doors were originally level with tops of windows. Later heightened as shown to cant.rail with louvre panels which were replaced before 1923 by plain panels.

RAIL WAY

TAL-Y-LLYN

Wheels 28″dia. 8 spokes

14'6" frame
14'8" body

6'6"

1'3"

1'3"

2'11"

5'2"

5'4½"

5″

5'11"

6'4"

1'2½"

8½"

CHAPTER NINE

CARRIAGE STOCK

'THE coaching stock is distinctly peculiar, being low pitched and exceedingly uncomfortable to ride in . . . but the brake van is a gem. I fancy it has a sliding door on one side only . . . all platforms being situated on the same side, a door on one side only is necessary . . . this door is not always shut on the journey, so that there is a fair chance of the luggage (especially a bicycle) being jerked out, unless the guard keeps an eye on it.' So wrote A. F. Selby of his impressions in 1909. He was not the first to describe what he saw; Harold Fayle, had written some years before:

> 'The carriages run on four wheels and contain three compartments, each seating six or eight people; the third-class compartments have plain wooden seats, but two of the coaches are composites containing one second-class compartment: the latter is provided with cushions, though probably in comfort it would hardly bear comparison with an ordinary third-class carriage on any standard gauge line.'

No one could quarrel with these impressions, for they were almost wholly accurate, not only of a time from when the Railway was opened up to the time of the occasions, but for all the years after that – on the Talyllyn Railway little changed, save gradually for the worse. By the early years of this century, when these writers came to Towyn, the four-wheeled carriage was already a curiosity, except in railway backwaters. As to the second class comfort, this would be the former first class accommodation, *verb. sap.*! Clearly the proportion and provision of classes made its mark on young Fayle, whose family was then resident in Co. Tipperary.

As to the rolling stock as a *whole*, considering the Company (or Quarry) had purchased almost everything from office stationery to turntables from suppliers in the Manchester district, it is significant that they looked further afield for locomotives, carriages and wagons when there were local firms who manufactured such. Perhaps it was simply a matter of cost? Or was it one of personal contact?

Of the five vehicles which fell into the 'passenger category', four were to come from Brown, Marshalls & Co. Ltd. of Birmingham (founded in 1842 as the Britannia Railway Carriage & Wagon Works) and one

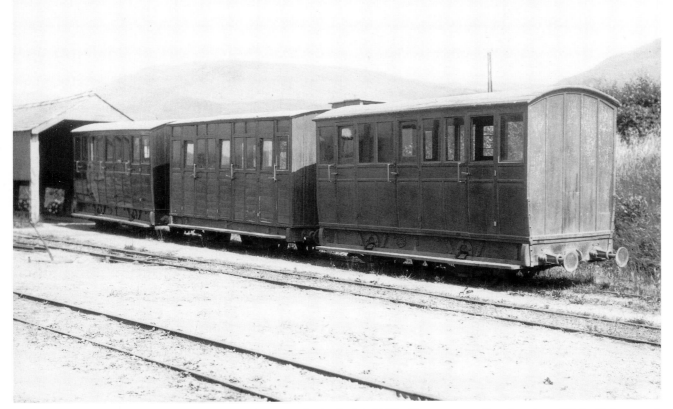

Three of the five 'passenger vehicles' stand outside at Pendre in the late 1920s. The screw couplings have been lifted off the nearest coach.

At some date prior to the previous picture, the rear of the carriages shows them to be shorn of most brassware. Pre-1923.
P. J. GARLAND

from The Lancaster Wagon Co. Ltd. (founded in 1862). In the early years of this century each vehicle had carried a number but not for many years up to the time this narrative ends. For convenience, therefore, the numbering scheme adopted by the Preservation period will be used.

Class	Nominal Body Length
1) $\overline{111}$	14 ft. 6 in.
2) $\overline{333}$	14 ft. 6 in.
3) $\overline{333}$ later $\overline{33}$/2 later $\overline{33}$/1	13 ft. 6 in.
4) $\overline{333}$	14 ft. 6 in.
5) Van	13 ft. 6 in.

The Official Returns to the Board of Trade show all five being in existence from the Return of 1867; there is no question of one being added at a later date. We may hazard that J. S. Spooner's services would have been used not only in the purchase of track components, but in most other technical features; if so, then the notable differences between them and other contemporary systems then purchasing, makes interesting contrast.

Visitors were strictly monitored to ensure they did not travel in a superior class than the ticket they held, the watchful Jacob Rowlands saw to this! However, it was clearly not a case of what category of ticket you held (or even if you held one at all) that mattered if you were a 'local', but what place you held in the Social Order of the district. For instance, 'a certain lady would always be put into the first class compartment at the end of the first class carriage ... officially reserved for the use of Sir Haydn ... the guard always put my mother in it ... but when Mr. H. senior

boarded the train at Rhydyronen ... he was not allowed to join us in the first class ... *we* had to get out and join him in the third. The first class carriage itself I never saw used ...'*

In high season, and especially as these reminiscences pertain to the nineteen-twenties and afterwards, it was usual to put all coaches into one train so that first class (by then restored, ex-second) was available if required. The van, with its booking office conversion, appeared save when the stock was divided into two trains and the driver of one had to issue tickets from the footplate!

Writing of 'The Greatest Trains of all Toy Trains' it was said:

'... there was only one, and it had no second-class carriage. A simple upholstered first-class compartment, usually locked ... and reserved for moths and blue-bottle flies, formed a section of one of its coaches ...'

Official seating capacity was 18 first or 24 third class passengers per one-class coach.

It is a reflection of the times that in this microcosm of a railway separate classes were available at all, instigated in the first instance, no doubt, by a desire of the owners to travel segregated from the *hoi polloi*. As to the exuberances of Guard Rowlands, these were to become a traditional part of the entertainment, being recalled as early in the 1920s by two regular Towyn visitors of that time who delighted in recounting his exploits whilst they travelled with the writer in a steam train mounting the Rothorn in Switzerland in the late 1980s!

---

*Accepting that this verbatim extract contains some mistaken impressions as to the composition of the carriages, the inference is clear enough!

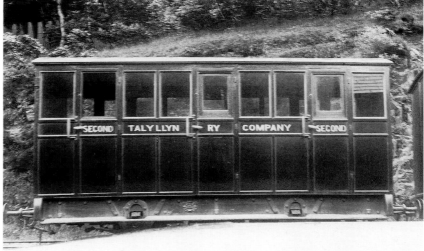

In date order the varying paint styles are apparent. The upper carriage is as on 26th June 1909, and the lower two — the centre one being on 10th August 1925 — are as painted by Middleton.

K. A. C. R. NUNN
H. G. W. HOUSEHOLD
L & GRP

Middleton's brushwork has been superseded by a later hand; stock at Abergynolwyn in September 1940.   J. W. SPARROWE

Very little regard was paid by visitors to the painting of the stock in which they rode — in answer to a general enquiry, the reply was that the carriages were 'red'. 1935.
H. F. WHEELLER

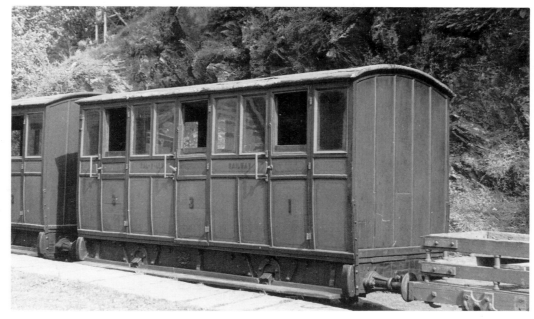

Typical of the assorted appearances of the carriages is the former All Third, long fitted with a partitioned end compartment and upgraded to First. Abergynolwyn; 25th August 1948.
H. C. CASSERLEY

The general outline of Nos. 1, 2, and 3 is similar, save that when examined closely, No. 3 is lower and shorter, with a different roof line. It is probable that No. 3 was the first carriage to be delivered (see p. 46) in January 1866 and a wheelset off it was marked 'P[atent] S[haft] & Axletree 1865'. The bigger Nos. 1 and 2 were possibly delivered in late 1866 also. The style of these panelled and beaded carriages was more akin to standard gauge practices of the day, including the side buffers and (possibly) link couplings. They looked more traditional than the box-like vehicles of those times running on the Festiniog and Festiniog & Blaenau Railways, but comparisons such as these are not creative, for both those lines were of narrower gauge and initially they displayed the overriding desire to keep a low centre of gravity. The Talyllyn coaches showed little regard for this. Each coach had three compartments, plainly fitted out. As built, the divisions between them were only waist high and the later-built single first class compartment in No. 3, which is likely to have been divided off for the privacy of the owners when travelling, was a 'home-spun' affair. No. 3 (the compartment coach) and the van (yet to be described) show evidence of having been used more than the others.

There were footboards and doors on both sides but, perhaps as the result of Captain Tyler's inspection, the doors on the south side were locked, the windows barred, and door (but not certain grab handles) removed. [It seems that at least one grab handle was retained on each south side at first.] Whether this was to prevent passengers de-training on the side where there were no platforms, or to meet Board of Trade requirements where the track was slewed under over-

Screw couplings on narrow gauge stock are not usual. 1943.
AUTHOR

bridges, is not clear. Perhaps both. Axle lubrication was by tallow grease boxes, and evidence again shows they were prone to running hot. The wheels of Nos. 2 and 3 developed hollows in the tread and this unevenness caused the loosely-hinged axlebox lids to chatter incessantly when the carriage was in motion. Wheels were spoked, and the laminated springs were underhung. Certain, if not all, had an outside socket on a window frame onto which a candle lantern could be hung – it probably shone into the interior.

First class was distinguished by either loose cushions or 'chapel runners' on the seats and a padding for the back. Third class was plain and spartan. There were no racks, no heating, and footwarmers were not available either. Strictly, the Rules forbade the running of trains after dark, and it was forbidden to smoke on the train or at stations (locomotives excepted!). The interiors were given a teak-grained

Of all the Railway's passenger carriages, the Lancaster example was the most antique looking.

G. H. W. CLIFFORD

finish known in the north of England as 'scumble'. The ceilings were lined with 'Lincrusta' paper, likely to be a 'Middleton touch', and there was a terse notice on the end panels 'NO SPITTING ALLOWED'. The Company had managed to avoid the Board of Trade's directions to fit continuous brake, so if these coaches were left on a gradient without the van, they had to be 'scotched' – a convenient piece of slate slab under a wheel would be used for this. All the foregoing had oak and pitch pine frames and mahogany panelling on timber framework.

No. 4 was entirely different, and, though probably dating from 1866, it came from The Lancaster Wagon Co. Ltd. (being absorbed in April 1902 along with Brown, Marshalls & Co. Ltd. into the Metropolitan Carriage, Wagon & Finance Co. Ltd.). The tyres are marked '1912' and possibly the oil axleboxes are of the same date. The matchboard sides and vertically-planked ends date from about 1925. When built, it had outside wooden framing, planked sides and ends behind diagonal bracings. The door height was only that of top window level, and, to improve headroom, the top ventilator section was incorporated into the door which was then raised to cantrail level.

The reason for this odd vehicle is not clear; it might have been intended for the use of the Workmen's Train. The wheels are of larger diameter than those of the other coaches and project through the floor, four metal splasher-shaped boxes containing these protrusions which were unpopular with the lady cleaners sweeping out the floors.

No. 5, whose drawing dated 18th July 1866 still survives, is a Guard's Brake & Luggage Van suited to all types of train. As built it had an open balcony at

The wheel hoods on the floor of the Lancaster vehicle (which had larger wheels than the others) were the bane of the Misses Rowlands when they were sweeping out.   H. F. WHEELLER

the east end (as the early view of a train on Dolgoch viaduct shows) and here was placed the handle for the brake. Sliding doors were fitted each side and the running gear was interchangeable with Nos. 1–3. In custom with those times, the brake blocks were of oak. Sometime before 1900 the open platform end was closed in, the small side doors to it fastened off and a sliding shutter through which the brake handle can be reached (as it is outside of it) provided. Ducket-type look-outs were added above where the small balcony doors had been, having narrow glazed slits either side to allow the guard a view along the side of the train; pictorial evidence shows them in place up to 1941 when the ducket on the south side was knocked off by the gate on the Carriage Shed. The sliding doors on that side had been removed by that time, as was the

The Van: in its various guises. Dates are c.1911, 1940 and 1950, and show how the vehicle attracted attention whilst standing at Abergynolwyn . . . to the loss of illustrations of the running gear. G. M. PERKINS J. W. SPARROWE and R. K. COPE

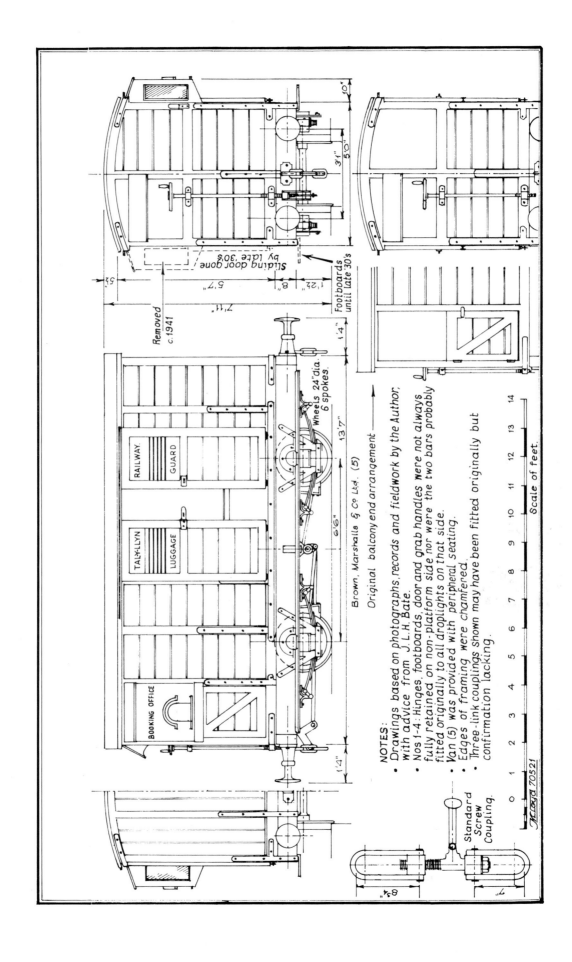

RAILWAY

GUARD

TAL-Y-LLYN

LUGGAGE

BOOKING OFFICE

Removed c.1941

Sliding door done by late 30's

Footboards until late 30's

Wheels 24" dia. 6 spokes.

Brown, Marshalls & Co Ltd. (5)

Original balcony end arrangement

NOTES:
- Drawings based on photographs, records and fieldwork by the Author, with advice from J.L.H. Bate.
- Nos 1-4: Hinges, footboards, door and grab handles were not always fully retained on non-platform side nor were the two bars probably fitted originally to all droplights on that side.
- Van (5) was provided with peripheral seating.
- Edges of framing were chamfered.
- Three-link couplings shown may have been fitted originally but confirmation lacking.

Standard Screw Coupling.

Scale of feet.

JKLloyd 70521

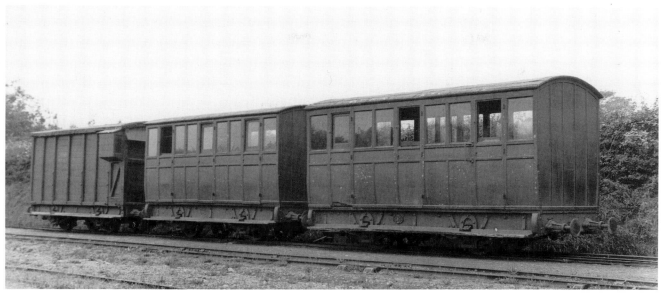

This shows the south sides of the stock in 1936, stabled on Pendre loop.   L. T. CATCHPOLE

footboard by 1939. During the period of Yates' management the north ducket was given a small ticket-
issuing window surmounted by 'Tickets Booked
Here', altered in the early 1930s to 'Booking Office'.
At some periods the ducket did not carry this helpful
guidance of an unusual facility! At the time, only
Wharf station issued tickets, the guard doing so elsewhere; for his convenience a ticket rack and date press
were put in the van which was fitted with seats.

New tyres were fitted in April 1949, the work being
done at The Britannia Foundry, Portmadoc. The van
had not been in service for three seasons prior, being
withdrawn after derailing in Wharf cutting.

**In April 1949 the Van's wheelsets were on the wharf edge
awaiting despatch to Portmadoc — they were back, complete,
by the month end.**   AUTHOR

In the early years of the century a surviving Order
Book of The Glaslyn Foundry, Portmadoc reveals that
a supply of screw couplings was despatched, doubtless
replacements for all the foregoing stock.

Now for a word about painting; firstly, canvas roof
coverings were finished according to the waterproof
medium (usually grey or black) available, but the
growth of overhanging trees did constant damage to
them, and by 1950 they had been re-covered with a
mixture of sheet lead or zinc coated with tar (or) which
itself was not always successful. Below the solebars
the colour seems to have been dark grey or black
throughout life. Bodywork colours can best be tabulated, and it is stressed that source information is
scarce!

Nos. 1–3

June 1912	Crimson lake; black lining out (edged vermilion each side) on panels etc. Lettering TALYLLYN RAILWAY COMPANY in yellow, shaded green [COMPANY later omitted]. Class in full (e.g. waist band on No. 2 reads: SECOND TALYLLYN RAILWAY COMPANY SECOND on both sides of the vehicle.
1943	As for 1912, but darker lake and lining in green without edging colour on both sides. Body ends and beading chocolate brown. TALYLLYN RAILWAY in gold, 3 in. high on waist band. Class numerals (no longer applicable) in gilt on doors.

No. 4

1912	As for Nos. 1–3.
1943	'Post Office Red' shade and not as 1–3 but lettering etc. as for 1–3.

No. 5 (Van)

1943	Dull 'Post Office Red'. Bevelled edges of outside framings gold. TALYLLYN RAILWAY (one word per door) in gold above louvres on sliding doors.

South side: some lettering survived until 1950 on certain
vehicles, (but no panel lining or door numerals).

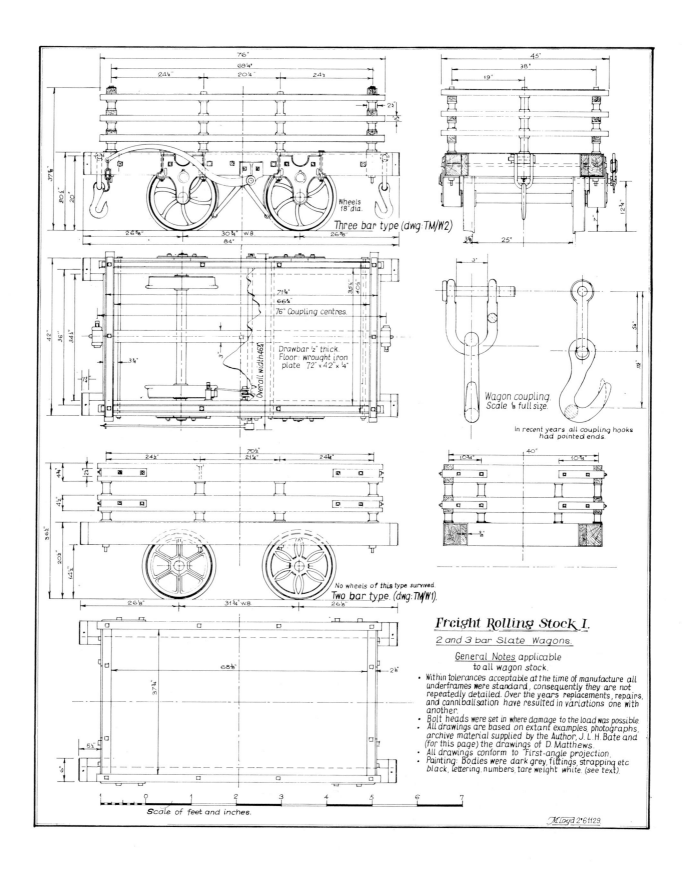

Three bar type (dwg:TM/W2)

Wheels 18" dia.

76" Coupling centres.

Drawbar ½" thick.
Floor: wrought iron
plate 72" x 42" x ¼"

Overall width 46¼"

Wagon coupling.
Scale ⅛ full size.

In recent years all coupling hooks
had pointed ends.

No wheels of this type survived.
Two bar type. (dwg: TM/W1).

Freight Rolling Stock I.

2 and 3 bar Slate Wagons.

General Notes applicable
to all wagon stock.

- Within tolerances acceptable at the time of manufacture all underframes were standard, consequently they are not repeatedly detailed. Over the years replacements, repairs, and cannibalisation have resulted in variations one with another.
- Bolt heads were set in where damage to the load was possible.
- All drawings are based on extant examples, photographs, archive material supplied by the Author, J.L.H.Bate and (for this page) the drawings of D. Matthews.
- All drawings conform to 'First-angle projection.'
- Painting: Bodies were dark grey, fittings, strapping etc black, lettering, numbers, tare weight white (see text).

Scale of feet and inches.

M.Lloyd 2°61129.

CHAPTER TEN
GOODS AND MINERAL WAGONS

UNDER this title, all rolling stock which was not either locomotive or, on any conventional railway, would be classed as 'passenger', is considered. The fact that passengers were carried in mineral wagons is conveniently overlooked!

Wagons which ran on the Railway might, as traffic demanded, be found in the village or the Quarry, having reached such destinations by incline. The nature of their content would include supplies for the village to ensure the survival and well-being of its inhabitants, ranging from bars of soap, bags of flour, barrels of beer, timber for the saw mill or coal coming in, to sawn timbers, sewage and empty barrels coming out. The community up at the Quarry required supplies of similar nature, life in the hinterland being entirely dependent on the Railway as its lifeline, and the way in which all hands turned out to clear the line when blocked by snowfall (mentioned elsewhere) underlines that dependence.

Such traffic was necessary to keep alive the employees of the Quarry and their families but the overall purpose of the Railway was to carry away the products of Bryneglwys and over one hundred suitable wagons were employed on that duty. However, in the 1940s, whilst one might expect to see (when visiting the line) much evidence of these vehicles along the route, they were, in fact, like a disappearing species and became coy and shy, confined mostly to the slate exchange yard at the Wharf, or lurking up at the sorting yard at the foot of Alltwyllt Incline. The casual summer passenger riding between Pendre and Abergynolwyn might be excused for not observing any, and arising from that, having no conception of why the system existed at all. By far the

PRETORIA is about to leave Abergynolwyn for a journey up The Mineral Line; the Incline Wagon behind the engine is possibly destined to be lowered down into the village. At this time the engine carried a lamp socket on the front buffer beam, there being no plain bracket below the chimney. c.1911.

G. M. PERKINS

291

bulk of wagons was retained in the Quarry where, on Cantrybedd or higher levels, they were stored empty ready for loading. Storage facilities on the Railway system itself were so limited that this arrangement was a natural outcome. In a booklet about the line by Lewis Cozens (1948) only the sharpest eye would find a goods or mineral wagon in any illustration: *Railway Adventure* (1953) also fails to feature slate wagons in their correct role. *Verb. Sap.!*

Although not forming a part of the Railway Company's wagon fleet, the wagons used internally within the Quarry must not be overlooked: these would have no business to venture further than the head of Cantrybedd Incline.

To avoid tedium, the stock has been broken down into types and given its English definition; in certain instances the number of vehicles is not known as the Annual Returns required by the Board of Trade did not call for extreme breakdown.

Prior to the turn of the century there were over 115 wagons, by 1937 40 slate and 9 'iron coal' (*sic*), but by 1950 these had dwindled to 16 on the working portion of the line (with but a few 'just usable') and covering all types. The survivors were:* Ten slate, being Nos. 8, 21, 23, 24, 30, 31, 32, 33, 35, 36. Five opens. One bolster. In addition, there was a number of portions of wagons strewn around Pendre yard.

Covered vans had gone, the last taken from service in 1932 and remaining as a body at Rhydyronen bridge. One Gunpowder Van body survived at Pendre for

---

* Post-1950s numbers given. No old numbers were perpetuated.

Wagons and van stand in the village yard; indecipherable stencilled characters defy identification.   TALYLLYN RAILWAY CO.

Slate wagons in use for coal traffic are lined up outside the Wharf coal yard, 1936.
D. COZENS

This Incline Wagon contains one of the removable seats used in the slate wagons for 'overflow' passenger traffic. 30th July 1947.
G. A. HOOKHAM

storing locomotive sand; remains of bolsters might be found, and livestock was by then carried in open wagons covered by netting or sacking, suitably tied down. When the Quarry closed, a number of vehicles was left stranded in the workings and scrapped on site in due course. Eight in the village yard were to suffer similarly.

Wooden underframes (bolsters apart) were common i.e. 7 ft. over dumb buffers and 3 ft. 6 in. wide. Many wagons were fitted with hand brakes, the shoes being curved to conform to the tyre; both wheelsets were braked. All wagons were four-wheeled, none was sprung, and all had link-and-hook couplings. Wheels of 1 ft. 6 in. diameter were of cast iron straight, curved

Another Incline Wagon containing 'small coals' at Wharf in 1943. The loss of the solebar projection, perhaps due to derailment or rot, was a common shortcoming among the surviving wagons at this time. AUTHOR

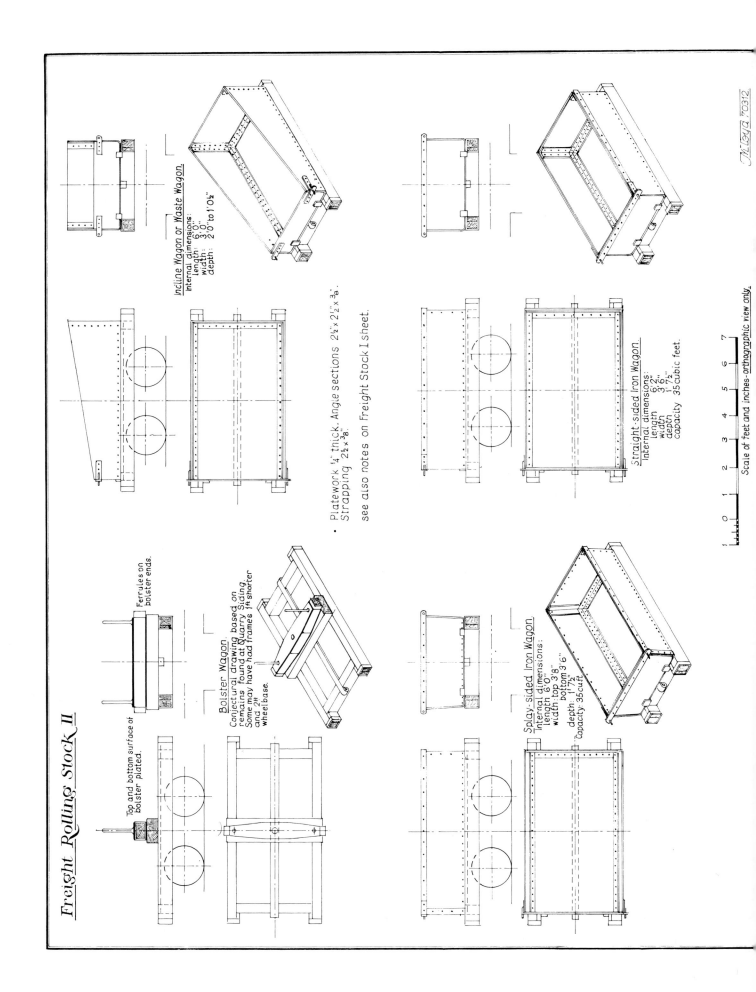

Freight Rolling Stock II

Incline Wagon or Waste Wagon.
Internal dimensions:
length: 6'0"
width: 3'0"
depth: 2'0" to 1'0½"

Straight-sided Iron Wagon.
Internal dimensions:
length: 6'2"
width: 3'6"
depth: 1'7½"
capacity: 35 cubic feet.

- Platework ¼" thick. Angle sections 2½" x 2½" x ³⁄₈". Strapping 2½ x ³⁄₈".

see also notes on Freight Stock I sheet.

Ferrules on bolster ends.

Top and bottom surface of bolster plated.

Bolster Wagon.
Conjectural drawing based on remains found at Quarry Siding. Some may have had frames 1ft shorter and 2ft wheelbase.

Splay-sided Iron Wagon.
Internal dimensions:
length 6'0"
width: top 3'8"
bottom 3'6"
depth: 1'7½"
capacity 35cu.ft.

Scale of feet and inches - orthographic view only.
0 1 2 3 4 5 6 7

Mleya 70312

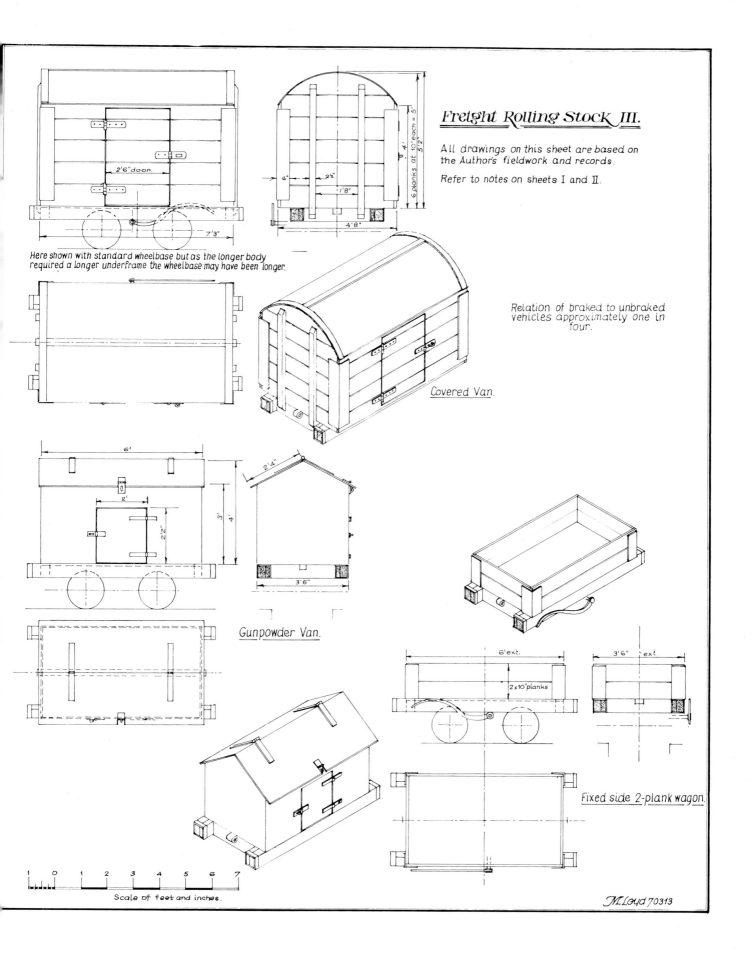

Freight Rolling Stock III.

All drawings on this sheet are based on the Author's fieldwork and records.

Refer to notes on sheets I and II.

2'6" door.

6 planks at 10" each = 5'

5' 2"

4'

6" 2½" 1'8"

4'8"

7'3"

Here shown with standard wheelbase but as the longer body required a longer underframe the wheelbase may have been longer.

Relation of braked to unbraked vehicles approximately one in four.

Covered Van.

6'

2'

2'2"

3' 4'

2'4"

3'6"

Gunpowder Van.

6' ext.

2 x 10" planks

3'6" ext.

Fixed side 2-plank wagon.

1 0 1 2 3 4 5 6 7

Scale of feet and inches.

M. Loyd 70313

These slate wagons on the wharf platform were still carrying out their intended business, little though it was. 1943. AUTHOR

in cast steel, or open-spoked pattern, many vehicles running with mixed sets.†

Painting of wagons was a dark grey (though some slate and wooden open wagons were red oxide), with ironwork in black. Lettering etc. was in white (where it survived), and slate wagon examples included:‡

'No. 27 (Tare: 14 c. 2 q.)' and 'No. 20 (Tare: 13 c. 3 q.)'.

TALYLLYN RAILWAY and wagon numbers had been stencilled on certain wagons; examples of open wagon numbers being 'No. 62 (Tare: 16 c. 1 q.)' [straight sides] and 'No. 77 (Tare: 16 c. 2 q.)' [tapered sides].

Makers of pedestal bearings were principally Isaac's Foundry, Portmadoc, whose cast inscription they bore.

A curious discovery as recently as 1971 was made in the Pendre rubbish tip where three large wagon bearings were found; they had provision for oil lubrication and not the basic grease type as on the Talyllyn wagons, and were possibly of a later date. It is recalled that two iron sheet-sided wagons had come from Caernarvonshire in the latter part of the last century; furthermore, they were the curse of Dafydd Jones's life (he looked after the track), and, though they were said to have been to 2 ft. 3 in. gauge when delivered, they had narrow wheel treads and fell between the rails. He was instructed to ensure that the track gauge was kept exactly, but pointed out that if this was done, *Talyllyn* would not run on it as it was essential to

The last of the covered vans peeps shyly from under the lee of Rhydyronen overbridge.   AUTHOR

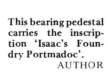

This bearing pedestal carries the inscription 'Isaac's Foundry Portmadoc'. AUTHOR

† No open-spoked survived to 1950: they were noted in 1942.
‡ Pre-1950 numbers given.

keep the gauge to '2 ft. 3 in. and the width of my thumb' to suit this engine. In the end the needs of the engine triumphed, the gauge was kept to 2 ft. 3 in. (plus) and the wagons taken out of service after an almost useless existence at Towyn. This leaves the question – where in Caernarvonshire would use be found for wagons of this gauge?

The wagons were once numbered in separate series with a prefix letter to distinguish them. A development of this was to give the next free prefix (which was the letter K) to any slate wagon which was a free-runner and suited to the gravity passenger wagons. K14 was especially noted for its lively running until some blighter repainted some of the numbers and gave K14 to one of the most sluggish!

For the use of the track gangs there was an old wooden-bodied open wagon which carried a tool box at its east end; in the box was also a chain and padlock to secure it to the running line, if necessary, overnight! A ganger would attach it to the rear of a train and release it when near the place of his work: there was no need for the train to stop. He would then 'pedal'

(sic) the wagon by pushing with one foot on the top of the rail, whilst resting his other leg on the wagon buffer.

There was also a number (quantity not known) of simple trolleys without couplings which were usually left in the sidings at Rhydyronen, Brynglas and Abergynolwyn, and also in the two 'spoon sidings' at Dolgoch and Tancoed.

Finally, two types of wagon were predominant in the Quarry workings: the first, a wooden cradle construction comprising a long narrow frame with four cross-bearers, each surmounted with an iron strap to reduce wear; these were carried on four wheels, the axles running in simple bearings. Frame members were extended to form 'buffers', and hooped with iron to protect the ends. Link-and-hook couplings were fitted and a central tie bar with attendant iron ring projected each side to provide anchorage for fastening chains. Such 'bogies', 'slab wagons', 'sleds', or 'cradles' were used to bring slab blocks out of the workings, and those which have been inspected had once been given a handbrake, workable from either

Seats were arranged in the slate wagons in various forms and these must have been nailed into position to retain them.   L & GRP
Cty. DAVID & CHARLES

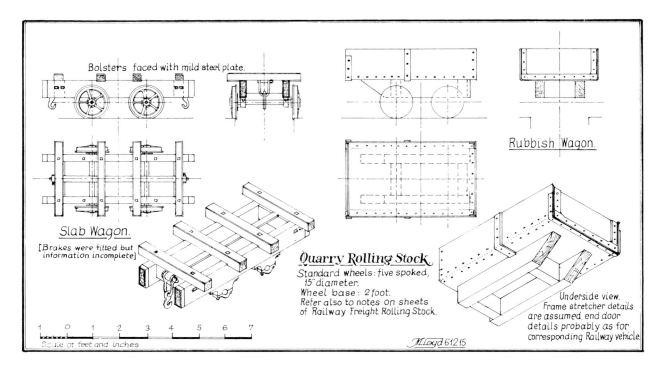

Quarry rubbish wagons did not find their way out onto the Railway; their unsuitability for working between Railway wagons is not contradicted by this one found between slate wagons at the foot of Beudynewydd Incline, 1936.

D. COZENS

side; not enough material survived to describe its working. The overall length of the trolleys was 5 ft. 6 in. to 5 ft. 9 in., width 2 ft. 9 in. to 3 ft., and solebars 2 ft. across faces. They had very short wheelbases of 2 ft.

Secondly, there was a number of open-ended (i.e. two sides and one end) sheet-iron-bodied rubbish wagons on a wooden frame, running on four wheels; some still survive underground. Unlike wagons in most other quarries, these did not have double-flanged wheels, but, either by design or through wear, a groove

had been formed in the wheeltreads. These wagons were without coupling gear and therefore unsuited to travelling over inclines.

Note on iron-bodied wagons. The drawings accompanying the text show sides, ends and bottoms of flat plates riveted to angle-irons. This feature was taken from vehicles which survived until 1950 but in the late 1930s certain sheet-iron bodies were made from one piece of sheet.

Style of wagon	No. in use (where known)	Description	Body	Approx. overall dimensions and capacity
(1) Slate/slab	114 goods and mineral in 1882 and 1890: 70 ditto in 1921	Two side/end wooden members spaced with iron or timber bobbins	Sheet iron floor	Body 6 ft. × 3 ft. 6 in. × 1 ft. 4 in. side height. Nominal 1 Ton 16 Cwt.
(2) Slate/slab		As (1) above, but three wooden side/end members (minority of this type)	ditto	ditto
(3) Incline	5?	General purpose wagon designed to prevent spillage on inclines	Sheet iron inc. floor (tapered sides) Lift-out end door	Body 6 ft. × 3 ft. 7 in. × 2–1 ft. side height*
(4) Open	10 in 1921†	General purpose, straight side/end	Sheet iron (parallel sides) Lift-out end door sheet iron floor	Body 6 ft. 2 in. × 3 ft. 6 in. × 1 ft. 8 in. side height*
(5) Open		2 and 3 plank: fixed sides and ends. 1 ft. 4 in. above floor	Timber with sheet iron floor.	As for (4)
(6) Open		As (4) above, but sides/ends tapered outwards towards the rims	As (4) above	Body 6 ft. 3 in. × 3 ft. 6 in.–3 ft. 8 in. × 1 ft. 8 in. side/end height*
(7) Bolster	4 in 1921	Floorless frame carrying single bolster	Timber bolster	5 ft. × 3 ft. 6 in. (main frame only)
(8) Bolster	?	Evidence suggests a shorter form of (7) existed in earlier years	ditto	4 ft. 3 in. × 3 ft. 6 in. (main frame only)
(9) Covered Van	3 in 1921	Side door on north face only. Roof curvature of varying contour between different vehicles. Last survivor withdrawn 1932.	5 plank side: Timber Zinc sheet roof covering	7 ft. 3 in. × 4 ft. 8 in. × 4 ft. Side height 5 ft. 2 in. floor to top roof. 2 ft. 6 in. wide door
(10) Gunpowder Van	2?	Gable-roofed (hinged one side) with side door opening: vans not quite identical. Last one scrapped c1955	Sheet iron, lined with timber	6 ft. × 3 ft. 6 in. × 4 ft. height from floor to ridge
(11) Pig Wagon	3	Converted from open wagons (6) and given upward extensions of sides in various materials	—	
(12) Sheep or Calf Van	1	Converted from covered van (9); fitted with openings in upper sides, suitably barred. Given replacement barred door	—	
(13) Goods Brake Van	1	Appears only in 1929–31 Returns. No details (may have been clerical error)	?	

* Level load of (say) stone app. 1 Ton 17 Cwt. Load of stacked coal app. 1 Ton.
† In 1921: 3 'Loco Coal' wagons – later 2.

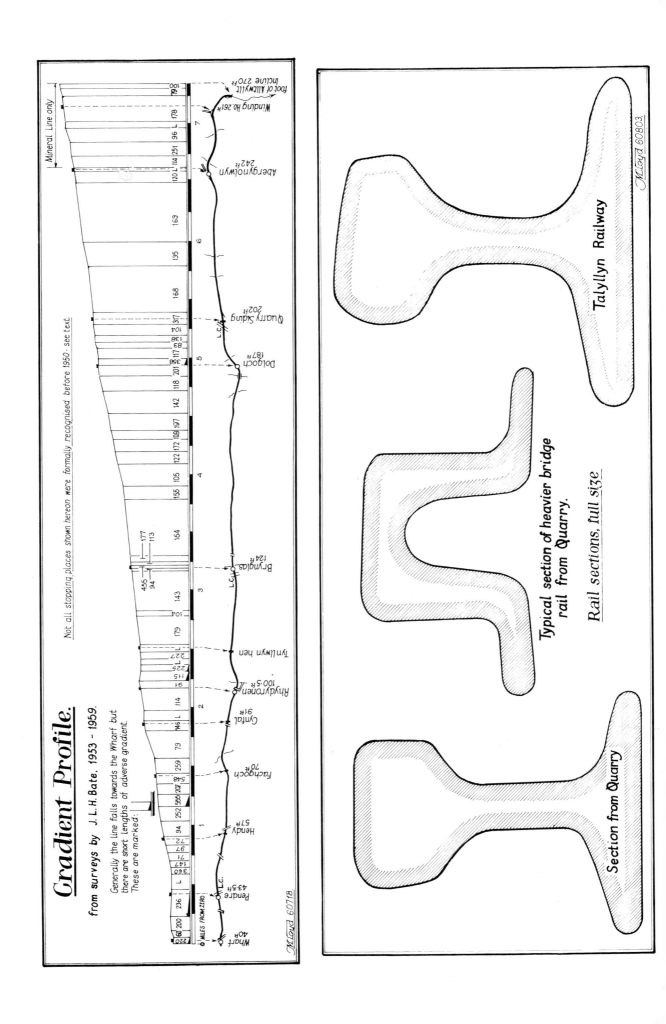

Gradient Profile.

from surveys by J. L. H. Bate, 1953 - 1959.

Generally the line falls towards the Wharf but there are short lengths of adverse gradient. These are marked:

Not all stopping places shown hereon were formally recognised before 1950 - see text.

Mineral Line only

Wharf 40ft
Pendre 43·5ft
Hendy 57ft
Fachgoch 70ft
Cynfal 91ft
Rhydyronen 100·5ft
Tynllwyn hen
Brynglas 124ft
Dolgoch 187ft
Quarry Siding 202ft
Abergynolwyn 242ft
Winding Ho. 261ft
Foot of Alltwyllt Incline 270ft

ℳℒℓoyd 60718

Talyllyn Railway

Typical section of heavier bridge rail from Quarry.

Rail sections, full size

Section from Quarry

ℳℒℓoyd 60803.

CHAPTER ELEVEN
PERMANENT WAY

THIS subject might be easily dismissed by stating that the track was laid throughout from Wharf to the top of the Alltwyllt Incline in wrought iron flat-bottomed rails weighing a nominal 40 lbs./yard, each rail 21 ft. long, and held to wooden sleepers at yard intervals by both keyed chairs and spikes, and that the rails were joined in a larger pattern of keyed chair, the whole shale-ballasted with material obtained from Tancoed Quarry and of limited value in terms of drainage but generally adequate as a supportive medium. Ballasting was at first carried out to the level of the sleeper tops but, as the condition of the track deteriorated, it was brought up almost to the level of the rail heads in order to reduce the amount of lifting when derailments took place! The rails were originally laid to a gauge of 2 ft. 3 in. measured between the railheads but, for longer than memory can recall, the gauge had been slightly widened to accommodate the locomotive *Talyllyn*, a somewhat strange way of going about things as it would have seemed more simple to modify the locomotive.

At turn-outs (of which there were 25 sets on the above-mentioned length), materials were the same but construction was different from the plain track. There were four turntables on the platform edge at Wharf station, which were of 5 ft. diameter.

There was also a larger turntable of 6 ft. diameter behind the winding house at the top of the Village Incline by which stock could be turned off a loop line at the rear of the house and, by means of an acute-angled level track crossing, had access to the head of the Incline. These facilities were unsuited to turning locomotives. All turn-outs were operated by local ground levers, there being no lever frames or locking of a type such as might be required by the Board of Trade for a railway operating a public passeger service.

Of all the technical features (locomotives, carriages, wagons and track), it was the construction of the track which put the Railway into an unusual category. Of the locomotives it could be said there were others like them, and even the Fletcher Patent was, at that time, widely advertised and often found. Of the carriages,

The almost unbelievable state of things towards the end of the Old Order — and along this length trains were passing Up and Down twice a day at least.

R. K. COPE

301

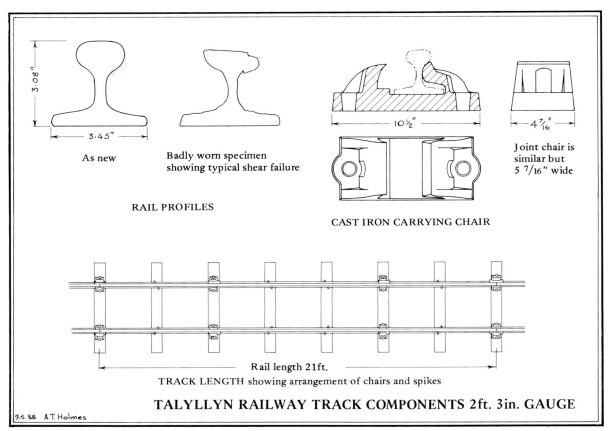

As new

Badly worn specimen
showing typical shear failure

RAIL PROFILES

Joint chair is
similar but
5 7/16" wide

CAST IRON CARRYING CHAIR

Rail length 21ft.

TRACK LENGTH showing arrangement of chairs and spikes

TALYLLYN RAILWAY TRACK COMPONENTS 2ft. 3in. GAUGE

9.5.88 A.T. Holmes

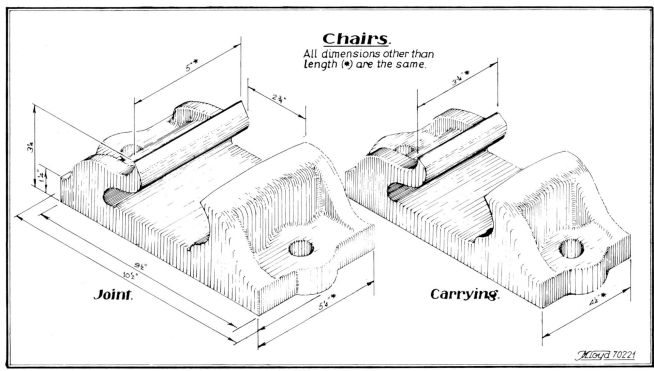

Chairs.

All dimensions other than
length (*) are the same.

Joint.

Carrying.

JLloyd 70221

they were not of the form then coming into vogue, whose outlines declaimed their bodies ran on narrow gauge – often completely obscured below – but rather the opposite, being more scaled down versions of the primitive four-wheelers which were found on the standard gauge up and down the country. Of the wagons, being mostly linked with Quarry work, they were brothers and sisters (but not twins) of the many hundreds already linking Welsh quarries with Welsh ports. But the permanent way was different, for the individuality was, and remained until well after the period of these pages, a feature perhaps almost unique in its longevity.

To understand why this came about is to require some knowledge of world practice in general and slate-carrying railways in particular. By 1864 when the Talyllyn Railway was probably conceived, only one Welsh line of less-than-standard gauge had any lengthy experience of steam working; this was the Padarn Railway with a gauge of 4 ft., but its features were scarcely recognisable as a narrow gauge system. Of those to whom direct comparison may be made, the Festiniog had just embarked on converting from horse-working to steam and its first 1863 engines ran on the old 21 ft. long T-section rails of the horse era (these had been 42 lb./yard since 1852) with such unhappy results that hurried replacements began in 1868. The Corris Railway, also horse-hauled, began with bridge rails and had some T-section rails (in chairs, similar to the Croesor Tramway) by the mid-1860s. The Penrhyn Railway – oldest of them all – had been through a variety of rails but introduced a very light 21 ft. long, 18 lb. version in 1849, which served indifferently until replaced by an entirely new railway to accommodate steam power!

So we may imagine the possible dilemma of James Swinton Spooner, called in to advise, but aware that the foregoing gave him no sense of direction, for the Talyllyn would be a 'Narrow Gauge Railway' from inception, a feature unknown in Wales at the time. However, Spooner's family links with Ffestiniog would familiarise him with the nascent Festiniog & Blaenau Railway (almost an extension of the Festiniog Railway but created by another company) then 'under Starter's Orders'; this undertaking was to use steam and certainly had flat-bottomed rails, probably fish-plated at joints and weighing approximately 39 lb./yard. The F & BR opened in 1868, a vital but later date in the developments of those times, and Board of Trade Returns show it was relaid in 1878, causing a loss on working. It is clear that Swinton Spooner would not find anything helpful in local contemporary practice!

The date on which flat-bottomed rails were first introduced into North Wales is not known. They were

(Upper) A typical carrying chair with wooden key made in the village sawmill, the whole supported (?) on a locally-made sleeper. (Lower) A typical joint chair showing the unsatisfactory accuracy of the running rail surfaces. AUTHOR

hardly to be found in use by railway companies but had been laid in America to a pattern by C. E. Vignoles in 1836. Rolling of them was difficult and there may have been misgivings about them overall. The South Wales Dowlais Foundry was making a flat-bottomed section similar to that found on the F & BR site by the 1870s and may have done so earlier; the F & BR section was smaller in every dimension than the type adopted for the Talyllyn, but it was thicker in the web. It did not have to do duty on its parent site for more than sixteen years, whereas the Talyllyn track was in service for almost a century! (At that time there were no accepted standards for rail sections.)

Swinton Spooner's answer to a problem, the exact like of which had never arisen here before, was a compromise resulting in a hybrid of practices possibly unknown here but often used in America. For instance, by 1840 the Atlantic & St. Lawrence Rail Road used a combination of flat-bottomed rail having some sleepers chaired and others spiked to hold the rail on a frequency of one chaired to two spiked sleepers. Joints were made in chairs, as they were on most American railroads at the time, even if *all* other fastening elsewhere was by spikes. (Undrilled rails were cheaper to buy). Swinton Spooner had been overseas and may have already encountered this arrangement.

In a recent publication concerning the locomotives of the Railway, it is suggested that chaired track may have been adopted so as to counter the rigid wheelbase of *Talyllyn* with its tendency to spread the gauge. A moment's reflection on this will reveal that it could not be so, the tendency could not have been foreseen before the locomotive was delivered, nor would any undertaking add chairs to its railway rather than cure a fault in one vehicle.

Another crossroads (so to speak) had also been reached in the matter of rails. Up to 1860 it had been usual to use wrought iron but in early 1857 steel rails were first rolled at the Victoria Ironworks of the Ebbw Vale Iron Co. and one sample laid in Derby Station for evaluation. The benefits over the wrought iron rails were outstanding, and when lifted in July 1873 the future of this composition was assured.

The materials for the track were ordered by the Aberdovey Slate Co. The rails were likely to have come from a South Wales supplier – about 500 tons of them costing £3,000–£3,500 in those times – and in view of the dates of laying the Railway were probably shipped from South Wales to Aberdovey and thence carried by the new Coast Railway. Their length of 21 ft. was a standard for that time, but some rails are as short as 18 ft. in accordance with the current practice of completing an order according to the output of the rolling mill. Whilst some doubt has been expressed as to the exact composition of the rails – steel included – all were of wrought iron of somewhat indifferent

quality, due to the personal variations in skill of the men in the mill.

Each rail was carried on six sleepers (probably uncreosoted) at approximately yard intervals, and, laid under the ends of each (in addition to the foregoing) a sleeper carrying the joint chair, such sleeper taking its half share of the burden with the adjoining rails. Four of the six intermediate sleepers were spiked but the second and fifth of each length was chaired. In those times, what are now known as 'dog spikes' with their modern outline of a dog's head, were not made; rather they were of $\frac{1}{2}$ in. square bar chiselled at one end and bent over at the other. The laying of this form of track called for new skills, as to pack the sleepers efficiently from below, those which were spiked would be higher in the ballast than those which were chaired. Some original sleepers probably 'remained' for up to forty years.

Captain Tyler's Report gives us little knowledge of the track and says nothing at all about the materials. However, the track as inspected in 1866 was virtually still doing duty in 1950 when this account ends and many of the rails would be in the positions of eight decades previously! However, there had been some alterations in that an attempt had been made to remove the butt-joints by either drilling or screw-punching (this was done by a portable machine known as a 'Bear') two holes in the end of each rail so as to receive fishplates. Legend has it that one or two elderly men set off from the Towyn end but failed to reach Abergynolwyn and so complete the assignment. There were certainly a number of rails which were never given holes – and others which were given holes but never had fishplates – and remained butt-jointed until replaced. Only the line from Wharf to Alltwyllt foot was so treated.

Where fishplates had been substituted, these were four-holed and of curved section so as to fit snugly into the rail web. Such was the squat section of the rail that there was little vertical support in practice (whilst the former chairs gave far more, so long as the joint sleepers were well packed) thus there was considerable drop at joints and resultant 'hogging' of rails developed.

Tyler gave the rail weight as 44 lb./yard, a figure he is likely to have been given rather than weighing for himself! Clearly if the Railway Company had been supplied to an order given by weight (as was usual) then they received more yardage than they expected, for the weight has proved to be approximately 40 lb./yard.

Laying the track would be a comparatively simple operation, with materials handy at the Wharf and rail conveyance from there as the work progressed. The unfinished state of the cutting east of Wharf may have delayed work for a time but this is conjecture. It has

'As the engine moved forward onto the next rail length, the further end of it cocked up into the air, only to sink down again as the weight of the engine was transferred further onwards.'
AUTHOR

been suggested that working the then accepted sixty-hour week, tracklaying could have been completed in 4–5 months and this would include the main line, The Mineral Line to the top of Alltwyllt and the Village Incline.

A feature of all railways laid in physical surroundings akin to the Talyllyn is that the whole railway tends to slide downhill, caused partly by the braking of trains; in certain cases this becomes so excessive that the track has to be anchored to Mother Earth – but things were not so extreme on the Talyllyn. Possibly an early trouble with the chaired joints was that they tended to pull apart due to rail creep and the rail became loose in the joint chair; to overcome this, fishplate holes were given to certain rails at a later date to accommodate a somewhat primitive fishplate made from rolled half-round section iron bar having round holes accepting round bolts – the latter tended to revolve in their holes. This meant removing the joint chairs and re-spacing the sleepers but there was clearly some difficulty in achieving a satisfactory result; the outcome was that although several lengths of rail would be successfully fishplated, there then came a joint where the joint chair was still in use. Presumably because of rail gap, it would have meant making special fishplates for such locations. As to the legendary failure for the work to be completed, there was certainly evidence that The Mineral Line contained both fishplated and chaired rails when lifted in the 1970s. To make matters more difficult to explain, in the latterday of Haydn Jones the replacement of defective rails by others – perhaps by robbing the village trackage (or) – which might or might not be holed, made conclusion more elusive. Certainly an unfortunate feature of the rail was its characteristic to split away in long slivers

along the head, in extreme cases leaving only the top of the web as a running surface! Even the webs were suspect, for, as is well known, the practice of ballasting up to rail head means that the webs are seldom drained and when the ballast is pulled away are wont to show daylight under the rail head. The weight of a vehicle soon crushes the web where such corrosion has occurred, and even if the head is intact, the collapse will signal the replacement of the rail.

Tyler tells us that the sleepers were 4 ft. 9 in. long × 7 in. × 5 in. of rectangular section. (A half-round section sleeper with the flat side uppermost unearthed one foot below the present formation and in the neighbourhood of the gravity siding above the Wharf road bridge is possibly a relic of the construction line. Also found were some timbers laid longitudinally under the permanent rails and carrying the joints; the system of supporting the rails in this manner was carried eastwards for some distance through the cutting beyond where the siding was. The reason for it is likely to be the wet nature of the ground.)

Elsewhere it has been explained that beyond the top of Alltwyllt Incline, bridge rails were laid up into and within the Quarry, save that 'Talyllyn type' rails were also used in the Haulage Way there. It might be assumed that that was an end of it but quite different section of flat-bottomed rail was found by the writer there in the early 1940s and might be explained by the purchase of an odd lot of material at some date.

Deterioration of the line continued faster than remedial work on it. By the mid-1920s the sections just east of Pendre crossing on 'Parry's bank', and generally between Brynglas and Dolgoch, were notoriously dreadful. By the late 1940s, the train might systematically derail in the same place every time it was

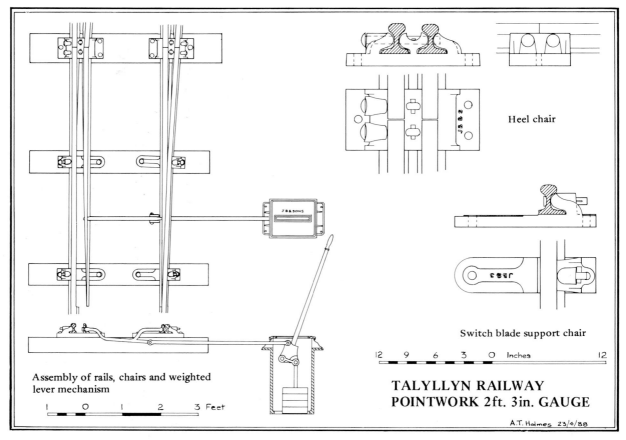

Heel chair

Switch blade support chair

Assembly of rails, chairs and weighted
lever mechanism

```
1     0     1     2     3 Feet
```

```
12   9   6   3   0   Inches        12
```

**TALYLLYN RAILWAY
POINTWORK 2ft. 3in. GAUGE**

A.T. Holmes 23/4/88

traversed. Many years ago an old employee recalled 'that the old driver made soleplates from the floors of redundant slate wagons and these were put into the curve just above Pendre crossing, the chairs being taken out altogether: about 100 yards were so treated. There was some improvement but the sleepers were poor. Later we tried to make sleepers from local oak on Haydn's land, and cut them in the mill at Abergynolwyn.' Certainly there were numerous untreated half-round sleepers of this source in the track at the start of the Second War, and some had rooted and started to grow! A better answer (when Haydn was prepared to spend money) was to use second-hand standard gauge ones.

As to the cast iron chairs, the larger were $10\frac{1}{2}$ in. × $5\frac{1}{2}$ in. wide, weighing c.19 lb.; the carrying chairs were only $4\frac{1}{2}$ in. wide weighing c.17 lb. and they were held on the softwood sleepers by two wrought iron pins per chair, 6 in. long × $\frac{3}{4}$ in. diameter, having round heads; the holes in the chairs were tapered to facilitate drawing from the mould. The sleepers were pre-drilled before the pins were driven in. Hardwood keys (of rounded rather than rectangular section) on the outside were used initially, but later various forms of home-made types emerged from the village sawmill.

With no spare stocks of rail, Haydn purchased some second-hand steel rails from the abandoned Glyn Valley Tramway, Denbighshire, in 1936. Some say he bought sleepers as well. It was some months before he had fishplates and as those breaking up the GVT burned off the fishplate bolts, there was even further delay whilst Haydn made up his mind to proceed and the requisite new nuts/bolts were ordered. By then the materials had been lying near Cynfal, where they were due to be laid, for some time. In due course about 290 yards of line were replaced with this Dowlais 1887 50 lb. flat-bottomed material in 28 ft. lengths, amounting to about 12 tons. Relaying may not have begun before 1938–9, the exact date and certainly the amount paid, not being recalled. The original Talyllyn sleepers and chairs were retained.

In 1949 Haydn bought 8 tons of Corris (then part of the British Railways system, ex-Great Western Railway) rails; these were to be laid as an extension of the GVT length but were never put in, being Rhymney Iron Co. 40 lb. steel flat-bottom section in 24 ft. lengths, dated 1878 (the period when steam locomotives were introduced) and amounting to about 250 yards of line westwards from Cynfal.*

* After 1950 they were laid down as originally intended. A portion of the GVT rails survives in 1987, having been longer in use on the TR than the GVT.

There were certain pieces of
the permanent way which had
lived up to that title; some
were on The Mineral Line.
AUTHOR

It may be added that though it was commonplace to
find maker's marks on rails, none of the Talyllyn rails
had such upon them.

Pointwork required the addition of small quantities
of chairs of two further patterns. One was in the
form of a double chair to take both stock and switch-
blade rails, and provided the position from which
the heel of the switch rails was hinged by means of
one or two horizontal bolts, which passed through the
chair and rail webs horizontally. These chairs were
held to the sleeper by three pins and, at about 43 lb.
weight each, were the largest in use on the railway. A
final form of chair was a more conventional slide
pattern which located the stock rails from the outside
by means of a horizontal bolt passing through that rail
and chair, but on the inner side it had a plain flat surface
to enable the blades to slide over it. Both the foregoing
might be marked (but not inevitably) 'J.B. & S.' There
were usually four slide chairs to a turnout, the blades
of which were 7 ft. long and having a 1 in 6 crossing
and a radius of about 150 ft.

The blades were held by a U-shaped round section
tie rod; its ends were flattened to pass through oval
slots in the blades' webs. At the bottom of the dropped
portion a rod was taken, by means of a further length
of rodding to suit the site, to a ground lever which
actuated the blades. The lever itself was pivoted in the
top of an iron box having a slotted and loose lid through
which the lever protruded. The box was dropped into
the ground almost to lid level to give it stability and
to ensure that the blades fitted the stock rail closely
for the desired 'normal' position of the points, a rod

In general terms, the pointwork was to prove the Achilles' heel
of the whole undertaking, as this crossing shows.
G. A. HOOKHAM

depended from the lever down into the iron box, and on this was threaded a series of cast iron disc weights (each 28 lbs.) sufficient to give the necessary force. To move the point out of the 'normal' position, the lever had to be held over manually. Clearly this did not suit the conventional Talyllyn Railway situation with its minimal workforce, and a number of short lengths of rail (or) were cut which could be arranged to fit under the lever and support it when the lever was in the 'pulled' position – in which it could be left as required! Many of the box lids had 'J.B. & Sons' marked on them.

An issue which the Inspecting Officer raised in 1866 was the risk of derailment should the single tie bar break and it is possible that the dual tie/connecting rod assembly to the levers which could be found here and there, was the answer to his criticism. As to 'Who were J.B. & S?', it has been speculated that the maker may have been John Bagnall & Sons of Stafford but there is no confirmation of this. This type of box and lever was not unique to the Railway, and similar, if not identical, forms have been noted on standard gauge systems, albeit not main lines! Whether these, too, carried the same maker's initials cannot be recalled.

Finally, the frog crossings were cut by trimming and forging the ends of two rails to the degree where the webs could be riveted together. Naturally very considerable wear had taken place at these crossings by 1950, but it is still possible they had seldom been replaced. Checkrails had to be spiked as no special chairs for holding them were provided; cast spacers were used to maintain the flange gap accurately. The pointwork (all original) was the most decrepit feature of the Railway's permanent way in 1950.

Mileposts must have once been provided and maps at the turn of the century show them at 1 and 3 miles from Wharf only; perhaps these were then the only survivors from the complete series?

Very little has changed since this turnout was first laid – probably in c.1865. This example was at the Village Incline loop.   AUTHOR

The turntable at the Village
Incline winding drum.
M. CHRISTENSEN

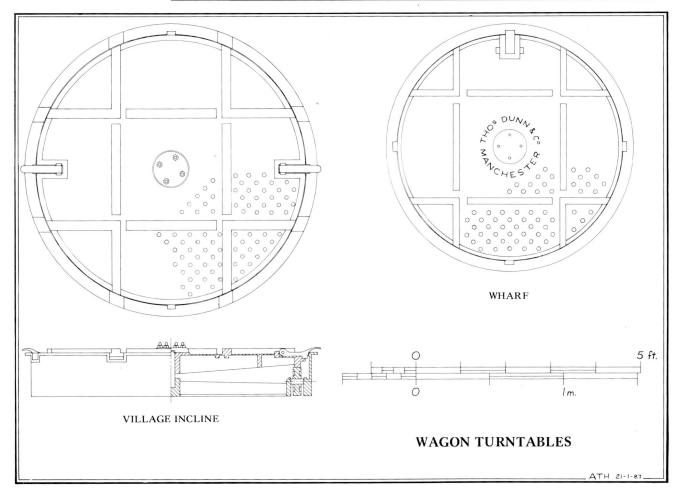

WHARF

VILLAGE INCLINE

5 ft.

1 m.

WAGON TURNTABLES

ATH 21-1-87

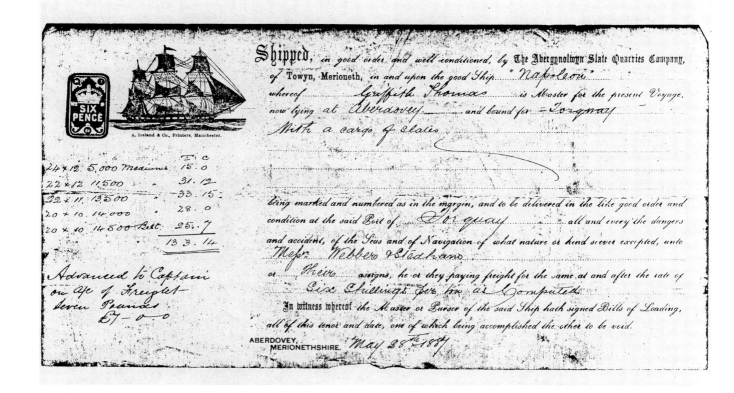

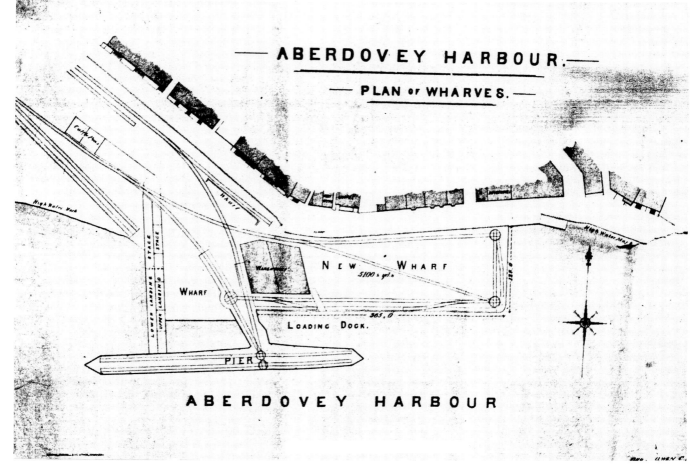

ABERDOVEY HARBOUR

Plan of the Aberdovey wharves by the Cambrian Railways, Oswestry.

APPENDICES

Appendix 1 – PLACES AND SHIPPING

TOWYN

Towyn has its origins in a Maerdref, that is a village which sprang up close to the lord's 'llys' or Court, and where land cultivation was organised. Over the years a subtle change in the function of the cultivators was to provide a service to the rural community surrounding them and offer a market for their convenience. Usually, and certainly at Towyn, the church would be the centre of such a settlement. However, these origins have long been drowned by later developments which have transformed the former 'native' town, and no more so than in the years following the Second World War after which the Welsh character of the town and its inhabitants has been entirely changed by housing developments which have brought in a large influx of English-speaking people to diffuse the old Welsh culture.

The period of this book, however, exists almost wholly before this last-named metamorphosis began but does cover the most formative years when the last vestiges of its Maerdref past transformed it into a small but fully-fledged town. It has been said that the traditional idea of town growth in Wales does not apply in Pwllheli, Beaumaris, Nevin ... and Towyn! Similarly it has been classed as coming into a later phase of Welsh resorts, those lying beside the Chester–Holyhead railway line being the pioneer. It has also been cited as a particularly good example of the way Anglicisation affects a narrow strip along the Welsh coast to the effect that much of the tourist industry is in English hands, and to the detriment of the Welsh language.

The effect of rivers flowing into Cardigan Bay has been to create separate economic units each with its own marketing centre. North–south journeying by land is difficult. Until the coming of the railway each of these areas (Towyn being the centre of that formed by the Dysynni in the north and Dovey in the south), looked in upon itself. Its occupants seldom travelled far afield and even in the Railway Age it was easier to reach Chester, Shrewsbury or Hereford from this Welsh Coast than such large Welsh towns as Bangor, Llandudno, Swansea or Newport. The motor car, hardly a dominant factor in this review, has changed all this and the old jokes about Liverpool, Shrewsbury and Gloucester being the capitals of Wales have lost much of their sting. Fragmentation, returning again after the Beeching Plan cut off so many areas of Wales by rail, has been stayed by widespread car ownership.

Had Edward I's borough for the district come into being, this would have centred on Bere, seven miles inland; but it was never built and Towyn burgeoned instead. When the Coast Railway came, the town began to creep towards the sea in order to demonstrate to those whose patronage it sought, that it was a seaside place, though it never had been. Mention elsewhere has been made of John Corbett's developments on the sea front and hinterland; an effect of the Great Exhibition at the Crystal Palace had been for foundries to produce catalogues offering 'kits' to build seaside piers and was to bring into being on 21st November 1876 The Towyn Pier Co. Ltd., one of a plethora of seaside piers contemplated in consequence. That at Towyn would also 'harbour' steamers 'purchased or hired for the conveyance of passengers'. The pier was to be 400 yards long with a decking 9 ft. 5 in. above High Water Mark, and on 27th December 1876 a line of stakes was driven into the sands and carried through to the Cambrian station, thence into 'the old town'. Bells were rung, the band from Aberdovey blew lustily and a speech by Charles Elliott ['a rascally solicitor acting as agent to the Ynysymaengwyn Estate when Athelstan J. S. Corbet fled abroad to avoid his creditors'] embraced the intention of making Towyn 'the Queen of the Welsh Watering Places', (a title purloined by Llandudno in more recent times). Those promoting the pier were, however, a somewhat dubious bunch of characters even though one or two – innocent enough – had jumped on the band wagon: it was to be three years later before Corbet's executors took action concerning Elliott's activities.

An Act was given Royal Assent* on 12th July 1877 and a foundation stone for the pier was laid the next day and work began; it stopped three months later with perhaps only the stonework and embankment for the pier, and two gate houses being completed. The men then disappeared to do work on the Estate, so suggesting that the pier work was being done at Estate expense. That was all. There were rumours that John Corbett, who had purchased Ynysymaengwyn from the spendthrift Athelstan J. S. Corbet in 1879, had plans to re-start it, but heavy seas soon did their work and it was ruinous by that year, *The Cambrian News* commenting 'Towyn will have to see that Davy Jones does not take the pier into liquidation'. Ultimately the notorious and damaging south-westerly gale along this coast did its work; John Corbett purchased such effects as remained for £450 on 2nd June 1880 and the company was dissolved in 1905. Pier Road and Pier Villas remained as a memorial to intention. A cynical commentator wrote that as the century drew to its end, so did the vitality of the town.

The town stood alongside a piece of higher ground which kept it above the excesses of storms and tides

---

* One of eight watering places so involved.

311

which would, from time to time, invade the coast and flood the hinterland. To its north lay the glacial deposit from the Dysynni, spread out like an apron and making for an almost useless marsh until the Corbets took matters in hand in 1788 and embarked on land reclamation which at last deterred that river from constantly changing its course (but failed to prevent changes in the position of its mouth), and put a stop to shipbuilding by stopping-off and eliminating a useful creek which served the town. Prior to then, when the Dysynni flowed from Rhydgarnedd towards Gwalia and then westward to discharge at Sarn Bach, incoming vessels would moor beside Sylvaen Cottage in Gwalia with limestone which was burnt near the church wall, the church claiming one quarter of its value. Such was the apparent importance of shipping that an Admiralty report insisted that a swing bridge must be provided by the Aberystwyth & Welsh Coast Railway to accommodate vessels of about 100 tons burthen which had been built at Towyn, 'a large town two miles up the river'. The Admiralty must have been misinformed; the timber bridge was made a fixed one and in the early 1860s a Drainage Board was set up which obtained an Act in 1864 and in due course further drainage etc. would make less truthful Lewis's *Topographical Dictionary of Wales* which wrote of Towyn in 1833 '(it) is on the verge of a tract which once formed a very extensive morass ...'. Another local landowner, W. W. E. Wynne, MP, of Peniarth, was more critical of the Drainage Act's achievements, for sixty years later, when all had been long completed, he maintained that for all the expense to date, the achievement was less than one per cent; this was honest for he was one of the ten members of the Drainage Board who qualified to sit from 3rd December 1863 by virtue of owning not less than 20 acres of land within the district. The drainage, carried out by William Bailey of Doncaster for £4,000 deprived the old people of a source of rushes which they collected on the marsh, for candles.

To the south of the town E. Newell built Esguan after buying the Bodtalog Estate (said to be haunted), converting the waste land into a model farm. He inspired the building of the Market Hall to sell local produce; it was a wooden structure, but on the site of the present one.

A comprehensive description of Towyn and district comes in the preamble to the Corbet Estate (Private) Act of 1862 relating to the will of the late Athelstan Corbet (died 26th December 1835) to grant building and mining leases and raise £5,000 for the improvement of the port of Aberdovey and lands adjoining:

'... Tywyn is much frequented as a watering place and its present house accommodation is wholly inadequate to the visitors coming there and the numerous persons engaged in the increasing trade of the town and port of Aberdovey are suffering from the want of proper dwelling houses, and disused stables and dark halls are fitted up as dwellings for numbers of the poorer classes ... and the influx of workmen consequent on the commencement of the Aberystwyth & Welsh Coast Railway close to the said town without the due accommodation for them will produce serious evil.'

The English Presbyterian Church was founded to enable men working on the Coast Railway to have Divine Service.

So much for the town at the onset of the Railway Age. That Age might have been a little more marked if Solomon Andrews (already developing estates at Arthog and Pwllheli) had had his way: his intent to carry out a similar development on what was then the marsh (now the Golf Course) at Aberdovey is revealed in a letter sent by the Cambrian Railways' agent at Barmouth Junction on 16th October 1899 to John Corbett. This disclosed that Andrews was 'about to purchase land adjoining his and construct a passenger Tram Line through to Towyn station ... it could be laid so that its position in future time ... [could be] a Carriage Road'. During May 1900 Andrews took steps towards fencing the land but, through the Commoners Association, the local farmers received 'information from London that grazing belongs to the commoners'. Matters warmed up until 10th November when there was a Day of Action. Shops closed from 2 p.m. and a procession was formed in Aberdovey, to be addressed in the Square. Banners were evident, one reading 'No surrender', and the Chief Constable intervened. Andrews reflected on the message, decided to 'back off' and no more was heard of the concept.

Nor was this the only possible contributor to the Railway Age for Towyn station might have been the junction for a standard gauge 'tramway' branch from its yard for – the article describes the venture in the past tense – the use of a Mr. Jones, Timber Merchant of Aberdovey who, claims the *Carnarvon & Denbigh Herald* of 27th April 1878 'had laid a tramway to carry materials from the railway station ...' Jones was erecting 'a fine terrace of houses ... on the beach near Neptune Hall' so it said. (Possibly this was the same man who applied to lay down a siding at Towyn for the purpose of his business but about which the Cambrian Railways were not over-excited as the junction would have been too far from the station signal box. Just whether either of these lines existed is yet to be proven, for newspaper articles often implied something done when in fact it was only intended; temporary lines do not find their way onto maps either!)

As to the erection of houses, part of Thomas Savin's plan was to build such on the front at Towyn as he had done (for instance) at Borth. But his failure in 1866 led ultimately to John Corbett becoming owner of the necessary land and his building of the promenade and the contemporary terrace houses there.

To avoid tedium, but to emphasise the development around the time of the McConnels' ownership of the

Bryneglwys Quarry, other events may be more conveniently set out in shortened form:

A Local Board was set up in 1858 (the equivalent of a Local Council) being one of the oldest in North Wales. (Towyn was the largest parish in the Diocese of Bangor.)

The original water supply came from two public pumps and public wells; John Corbett reduced the cost of the replacement water and drainage scheme to the inhabitants by contributing much of it himself.

There was an annual Eisteddfod, usually in a marquee on the site of Gray Jones Garage, but in 1893 Mr. R. Bruce built the Assembly Rooms (now the cinema) as a permanent site for the Eisteddfod; it had no gallery when built. The rooms were on the site of the venerable Angel Inn.

There was a final Victorian building boom in 1889–94 when Marine Parade, Brynmair, Idris Villas and Central Buildings appeared.

In 1902 Daniel Edwards embanked the Dysynni on its south side between the Ynys Estate and the Coast Railway bridge.

In 1908 came the Grammar School building; two years later a Wesleyan Chapel at Neuadd Pendre was demolished and a Drill Hall erected. In the nearby former Congregational Chapel a mineral water business was set up but, when moved to larger premises, the chapel became the Roman Catholic Church.

The nearby Marconi Station was built in 1913 and opened the following year. After World War I it moved to Chelmsford.

The Institute, materials all from Bryneglwys, was commenced in 1925 and opened in 1926. It became the Council Offices in 1951.

Roger Corbett donated the site of the Cottage Hospital, opened by David Lloyd George, Prime Minister, in 1928; the hospital was the conception of Dr. J. Alban Davies.

In an age when the medical bath was much favoured, and spas such as Droitwich, Malvern, Cheltenham, Bath (and so on) were advertising their wells or springs so that hydropathic establishments were appearing in such towns, Towyn could not afford to be outdone. Boasting about the curative properties of the ancient St. Cadfan's Well, a trickle of families from the west midland counties came there in search of relief. Many came by coach and were followed by wagons with their furniture and belongings, and certain of them built houses which they occupied during the better weather. All this took place before the Railway Age in Towyn.

St. Cadfan's Well (like the town's drainage, which was installed in the early 1860s to replace an open ditch which ran from Ty Mawr and along the fields into the main street as an open sewer, and then disappeared into the fields not far from the Well (!)) was not all that savoury, so a low, solid slab-walled building with ornate barge boards was erected over it; a plunge bath and surrounds – all duly tiled – was fitted up, and changing rooms provided. Though perhaps somewhat less well-known for cures which the Faithful enjoyed at Lourdes, for instance, nonetheless the Well's healing powers were much sought-after, the evidence being the numbers of crutches hanging on the wall . . . or was this a Confidence Trick?!

Lewis said of it in 1850 that rheumatism, scrofulous and cutaneous disorders were treated; though once open to the weather there were now two baths each 6 ft. square and four dressing rooms attached 'under the care of a person'.

The Well was somewhat tucked away down on the marsh (Morfa) behind the present National Westminster Bank, and much more striking was the number of public houses in the town at this time – 'anyone could open one'. Nonetheless, for over a century Towyn (until a recent mania for residential building for the retired or summer homes for the wealthy) was essentially a seasonal resort so that 'everyone looked forward to spring and the return of the visitors'. The organ in St. Cadfan's is a gift of the Kettles, who built Rhowniar in 1911.

Sir Rupert built (or bought and rebuilt) Glan-y-Don (opposite Neptune Hall) some time before 1884.

Evidence of the popularity of sea-bathing was the considerable line-up of bathing vans along the seashore – many survived through to the 1920s.

ABERGYNOLWYN

Abergynolwyn too is worthy of inspection in a little more detail; it was of course the child of the Quarry and the site of a farm known in earlier times as Cwrt. To meet the growing population of incomers created by the Quarry, the earliest part of its development is said to have had its housing problems solved by a purchase of unwanted wooden prefabricated army huts when the Crimean campaign ended (1856),* these being given outer skins of slab walling brought down from the Quarry. Another legend is that the same huts were not a snap purchase by the Quarry, but rather a prisoner-of-war site. Certainly the earliest buildings, single storeyed, have well-disguised this air of urgency which their present permanent appearance belies. Here were housed not only the Caernarvonshire families, but men from South Wales and Cornwall when employment in their respective mining districts became unattractive. Similarly Abergynolwyn experienced an exodus in its population when business at Bryneglwys was under threat, there being a well-established two-way traffic between the coal pits of

---

* The Crimean War covered period October 1853 to March 1856 notable for its poor administration by both sides, and loss of life by disease.

South Wales and the slate chambers of Bryneglwys. In the preamble to the Corbet Estate Act (1862) concerning housing in both Towyn and Aberdovey people were recorded living in disused stables and dark hovels, whilst the Merionethshire slate mines enquiry of 1894 revealed that the men now lived in 'excellent houses . . . compared with the huts in which men lived in my early days'. Industry brought social improvement to rural Wales at a pace which the old agricultural community could never have attained.

Not surprisingly it was the Mancunian and Unitarian influence which began through the efforts of the Aberdovey Slate Co. in 1864 and 1865: it revolutionised the hamlet and created a close-knit community. In three clusters, over seventy houses (some to the designs of James Stevens) were erected; these stretched across the valley floor to the river bridge near the former tannery. Chapels followed in the late 1860s. Several of the oldest houses had begun to require expense by the turn of the century and in 1909 McConnel offered such tenants outright purchase for £20 each, but no one was tempted to buy. There was a feeling about that he would be pulling out of the Quarry, an eventuality borne out one year later; also at this time families were emigrating to America and elsewhere overseas, to establish a slate trade which survives in some parts today. When Haydn Jones took over and the news spread that he only intended to work the Quarry for a decade, the gloom deepened and the property values slumped even further.

Though referred to elsewhere, the features of the village relating to the Railway may be emphasised: where the Village Branch line came over the river there was, on the left hand, the long low building which had been the Writing Slate Factory, the slate coming from the Quarry but the wooden frames being made on the premises. Later this became the carpenter's shop for the Estate. At the end farthest from the tramway was an undershot wheel which drove the machinery and, when the premises closed, the wheel pit was cleared and became pig sties. The Factory had been served by a branch off the village line leading off a turntable where that line formed a loop. Finished materials were stored in a slab-floored yard, part of which was later used to store coal supplied by Hugh Jones & Co. of Towyn: the yard was walled and the tracks passed through gates into it.

Opposite the Factory had been Pandy Farm; its lands extended up the mountainside behind to Hendrewallog and, when it ceased to exist as a farm, the cowshed was converted into the Estate smithy, and the Estate blacksmith (latterly Griffith Evans) divided his time between working here and at the smithy in the Quarry. At the river end of the farm buildings was an overshot waterwheel, driven by water brought at some height from the river upstream on a wooden

aqueduct carried on slab piers: this drove the saw mill, there being a long belt connection to the saw itself; over half a century ago James David and David Evans put up a slab building to enclose the saw, and their next task (about 1921) was to install a dynamo to be driven by a second belt taken off the waterwheel. This gave enough power to provide lighting (only) for the top of the village; the belt drive was so long that it caused surging but this was overcome about ten years later by disconnecting the belt and putting in a water turbine to replace the wheel. An extension building had to be put up for The Turbine House or, sometimes, The Power Station – this building also contained the Generator Room, switchboards etc. The turbine was fed, not by the old waterwheel launder, but a new pipeline taken from the Gwernol near the Alltwyllt Incline and led along The Mineral Line which had to be re-sited slightly to accommodate it. During its latterday life the pipe leaked badly, but, nonetheless, Abergynolwyn could boast having electricity long before Towyn and indeed some quite sizeable Welsh towns. Unfortunately, the power output was low and was not permitted for heating; its cost to the tenants of one shilling per year was included in the rent and no meters were installed. If tenants were found to be using the supply 'illegally', it was turned off – as it also was in time of drought. Electric fires became as unpopular with Haydn as telephones – the former were the principal illegal consumers in Abergynolwyn. (Mains electricity was installed in 1962).

The sawmill had a long life; its main function was to cut timbers for houses and local farms, Quarry and Railway use. Some railway sleepers of home-grown oak were made, but these gave poor results, lasting only 15 years.

The Aberdovey Slate Co. encouraged the people to work allotments and set aside land at one farthing per square yard per annum; other land was rented where pigs, sheep and cows were kept intensively, one complaint being that pigs were being housed in the outdoor privies whilst their owners had to find alternative accommodation! It was Evan Evans of Brynglas who encouraged this turn of events; he would erect a weighing machine outside the Railway Hotel and buy such animals as met his requirements; they would then be herded up to Abergynolwyn station and loaded into the Railway's 'pig van'. In respect of the available space being earmarked for gardens, some were to be found on the Railway side of the Village Incline river bridge.

The last village amenity during the life of Haydn Jones was the Village Hall (constructed during the late 1940s) for which slab for foundations came down from the Quarry, providing the Incline with one of its last purposes. Haydn Jones prided himself in continuing

Abergynolwyn from the south. The bridge at the foot of the Village Incline crosses the Gwernol on the left; Pandy farm with overshot waterwheel complete the scene.   WYNDHAM SERIES

the social practices laid down by the McConnels. Reminiscences today confirm how plentiful good food was in the village, most people keeping two pigs, every house having bacon joints hanging from hooks in the kitchen to cure, whilst many kept cows to the end of Quarry days. The Railway Hotel (sometimes 'Inn') does not appear in the Census before 1871; Evan Davies, born in Llanbadarn, was licensee. It was possibly licenced under the Beerhouse Act of 1830; a quarryman may at first have held the licence and, whilst continuing his employment in the Quarry, his wife would have managed the premises. The Hotel was the property of the Quarry Company and sometimes acted as a public forum; inquests on Quarry fatalities were usually held there.

There had been a small brewery.

As to just how you saw the village depended on what impression you wished to convey. *Picturesque Wales*, published by the Cambrian Railways in 1891, said

'. . . the sanitary village of Abergynolwyn – foreground to the picturesque Bryneglwys slate quarries – and somewhat formally planned . . . in the shape of an arrow head . . . pointing to a . . . miniature railway which has the backs of the houses turned towards it, serves as a scientific scavenger. It carries away all the offensive matter before harm can be done and as the Moule system of natural deodorisation and disinfection by dry earth is here enforced, epidemics have been virtually banished . . .'.

However, the County Medical Officer's report in April 1897 was unable to 'account for the high death rate' in Abergynolwyn 'unless the Quarry is to blame . . . the sanitation at Abergynolwyn is far from perfect' and later he complained that his recommendations regarding sanitary arrangements had been entirely ignored by the Railway Company.[*] In more recent times the collection of night soil had been put out to tender and was collected by horse cart. It is not clear if the Railway was still responsible for that traffic in the years concluding this narrative, but it seems unlikely.

Local residents still recall how dependent they were on the Railway for all their supplies; an accident with resultant stoppage on the Village Incline was a cause of great excitement, but also of real concern.

A census of the village in 1871 shows how cosmopolitan was its population – using the vernacular of the listing, quarrymen, labourers and miners were mostly Welsh and their young children had been born recently and locally, thus showing that a number of newly-weds had settled there to find work at the Quarry.

Of these people of Welsh extraction, the majority had come here from Caernarvonshire slate quarrying districts; a few came from the Ffestiniog area of Merionethshire, a handful from Denbighshire and

---

[*] Cholera epidemics in Wales, due in part to bad sanitation, were a feature of the mid-19th century, but silicosis among quarrymen might also cause a notable death pattern.

Water Street, Abergynolwyn,
the 'better end' of the village.
GWYNEDD ARCHIVES

Cardiganshire and more from local quarrying areas like Pennal and Corris.

The real 'outsiders', (the lesser half of them being Welsh) included parsons, teachers, mechanics, slate polishers, slate enamellers, excavators and others in the artisan bracket. For instance the mechanic Rogers came from Manchester (and was to be killed in a tragic accident later), excavators from Macclesfield, Cheshire, the Rector from Fishguard, Pembrokeshire and the teacher from Bristol. Many of these were unmarried and lived in lodgings in the village or Quarry, or in the Quarry barracks.

The common denominator was the Quarry ... Abergynolwyn was virtually a New Town exactly in the manner of a present-day Milton Keynes or Skelmersdale (but microscopic in size) and in the manner of Bournville or Saltaire, was a model of industrial paternalism. Although the village might be considered today to have been a rough place akin to an isolated contractors' site on any major project in Victorian times (a suggestion expressed more than once) the effect of Calvinistic Methodism was strong and similar to other young, growing quarrying/mining communities in Mid Wales at the time. Though it might be assumed that links with Towyn would be firmest, the easier road and rail links being obvious, the village also enjoyed strong connections with Corris in both business and pleasure. Not only was there a regular interchange of men working in the slate industry according to demand, but young men took their brides from neighbouring villages too. The main factor which took people 'abroad' was a cultural one; the chapel, music, drama, festivals and sport were the

bonds, with choirs the most dominant. It was music which enlivened the drab side of life and to hear snatches of *The Messiah* ringing through the underground chambers of Bryneglwys was to be expected. Do the factory floors of Japanese-owned South Wales industry reflect anything more than the influence of Radios 1 and 2 today?

ABERDOVEY

To understand the rôle which the Bryneglwys Quarry and Talyllyn Railway played in both the Welsh slate trade and the surrounding community, it is not enough to leave the subject where the slates were trans-shipped into Cambrian wagons at the Wharf; as so many tons of slate were shipped from Aberdovey it is necessary to have a greater appreciation of facilities at that port. It has been a point of shipment for over a thousand years, being recorded as a 'ship haven' in 550 A.D. and again in 1140 as a haven used by those disembarking for the Great Church Conference of All Saints held on 1st November of that year. By 1216 it was regarded as 'the central port of Wales' and by 1565 there were to be seen 'herring fishers from all parts of the realm off Aberdovey'.

However at this last date it was, unlike Towyn, hardly more than a place to take or leave ship on the north shore of the estuary of the River Dovey. Landward, facilities were hardly existent, being but three households.

One might continue with a chronological list of how the place developed into a port, of how agricultural produce came by water coastwise (obviously the most convenient means of communication when land transport was restricted to times when tracks were passable) mainly from out of the Severn or West Wales. By 1600 salt and corn were coming in from northern England and lead ore was being shipped to France, a trade which grew throughout the seventeenth century. At this time Cardiganshire employed about 600 miners in the county's lead workings; the ore was taken down to the shore at Glandovey and loaded into river craft. These unloaded at Aberdovey and the ore was warehoused there; by the middle of the seventeenth century 15,000 tons of lead ore was leaving the port and a small quantity of slate went as well. By the late eighteenth century slate tonnages were increasing, again wholly that produced locally and brought down river to Aberdovey for reloading into seagoing ships. This took its place alongside oak bark, timber, lead ore, silver ore, wheat, barley, oats, butter, eggs, poultry, and copper ore. However, the commodities which excelled in quantity were timber products, such as planks, oak beams, props and oak bark for tanning. Then as the nineteenth century began, the place itself began to grow. In the period 1835 eighty-eight ships of 10–500 tons were built in seven shipyards and yet, even in 1861, the population was but 652 souls. By the late 1870s the boom in slate at least, was over – Aberdovey port only enjoyed that boom for about a decade.

In the 1830s there was coming into Aberdovey – and with only primitive means to distribute – coal, culm, groceries, limestone, bricks and timber not grown locally.

Today the shipping trade is almost forgotten – in 1946 a load of seed potatoes came in from Eire but the last links with overseas disappeared in 1940, accelerated by the Second War. Memories of the sea links which saw three steamers per week coming and going have faded; though the only shelter between Portmadoc and Fishguard, there are virtually no commercial craft surviving in these waters which need to use it. The mouth of the river is tricky and has claimed many lives; the river is not helpful in scouring a deep channel. Even the enticement of a rate for cement at six shillings per ton from either London or Aberdeen, compared with a railway rate of six times that figure, could do nothing to generate business which was no longer there; nevertheless, cement from the Thames was discharged here until 1939. Here was the focus of the local slate trade (and other metal mining ventures) for the whole hinterland of the Dovey estuary; through Aberdovey went thousands of tons overseas – not in such quantities as would make Portmadoc a household name among seafarers, but the vital mecca for those whose business required ships to carry their products over deep waters. Wartime restrictions on coastal shipping, silting of the channel and (1987) the long-distance lorry, have doomed Aberdovey as a port.

The dependence of Bryneglwys Quarry on the port may be judged from tonnages now quoted. The correspondence between the Cambrian Railways and the Aberdovey Slate Co. which would have to rely on Cambrian wagons to carry their output from Towyn to the railway-owned wharf at Aberdovey has already been mentioned (p.43-4). The figures quoted are taken from incomplete port records 1884–1915 and have been presented in a way not used in those records:

Destination	No. of voyages	Total tonnage	Average load (tons)
Gloucester	27	2597	96.1
Sligo	16	2142	133.8
Belfast	17	1911	112.4
Faversham*	14	1682	120.1
Londonderry	14	1611	115.0
Portsmouth	11	1504	136.7
London	9	1199	133.2
Weymouth	12	1192	99.3
Dover	8	1014	126.7

Total 14,852 tons

* Faversham, a north Kent town served by Faversham Creek.

Over the period, 6,591 tons of Bryneglwys slate was despatched from Aberdovey to London and south coast ports, 5,664 tons to Irish ports, and 2,597 tons up to Gloucester via Sharpness and the Canal. In addition, there were 48 other ports of destination; a total of 61 voyages carrying 7,142 tons were made to unnamed ports. Over the years 1883–85 151 shipments were made averaging 50.3 ships per year but this had become 161 shipments in 1885–1915 averaging 5.4 ships per year carrying Bryneglwys slate, among other cargoes, for Aberdovey was unlike Portmadoc and it is unlikely that slate would make up the whole cargo of one ship, although there were over 230 tons in one shipment, average shipment over the period was 114.3 tons of slate.

Up to about 1893 output at Bryneglwys followed the national trend but after this was mostly lower. Many ports of call fell into the once-only class and the whole shipment picture can be summarised:

Destination	Tonnage	Percentage of total
England	18974	53.2
Ireland	8717	24.44
Wales	705	2.00
Antwerp	73	.21
Aberdeen	51	.15
(Unknown)	7140	20.00

All this tonnage would have to pass down the Talyllyn Railway, be loaded onto standard gauge and pass down onto the present (built 1885) Aberdovey Pier, working of which was in the hands of a man with a horse allocated to shunting wagons down there. Of course, the above was not the whole of Bryneglwys output, a larger proportion of which left the district by rail, the proportion growing larger as shipments fell. Detailed examination of ports of call show that there was hardly a place around the coasts of Ireland where Bryneglwys slate did not find a buyer!

Passing mention must be made of the contribution to Aberdovey shipments made by the upstream quays of Tanyffordd, Quay Ellis, Quay Ward and Garreg Creek, all at Derwenlas which took products of mines and quarries eastward thereof and delivered them to Aberdovey for reloading; boats of 70 tons or less might reach these quays. When the standard gauge 'Doveyation' linked Aberdovey with the main railway system, almost 80 ships – mostly sloops – which worked up-river from Aberdovey were no longer employed, some being towed into the Dysynni and sunk under the north bank to form a revetment. Up to 1939, local slates (but not those of Bryneglwys!) were loading for Le Havre, Caen, Rouen, Hamburg, Calais, Stettin, Bremen etc.

When Messrs. William and T. H. McConnel were negotiating for a lease of the nearby foreshore at Trefri in 1868, the port was described as 'good, having an easy entrance but no wharf or proper facility for loading vessels ... only ... a small wooden jetty at which vessels can lie on at a time in calm weather. If the wind rises the vessel must at once move away into the River for fear of being wrecked ...'. Something of McConnel's aims can be ascertained '... if our application should be granted, we hope ... to have a Steam Tug ... the Wharf we contemplate making would enable vessels to moor and load in perfect safety ... and encourage a return trade in Slates, Slabs ... to various places, especially Ireland whence we are now sending considerable quantities of slates ... is the one thing wanted to revive the expiring trade of Aberdovey ... we should have to connect the Wharf with the Cambrian Railway ... maintain a pointsman constantly on the spot and make approaches from the turnpike road ...'.

The jetty in question was that used for the building of the Coast Line north of Aberdovey about four years previously. It had not been improved to the McConnel's satisfaction – perhaps due to the bankruptcy of the Cambrian which lasted from 15th February 1868 to 1st January 1879 – from which naturally sprang the idea of building a new jetty which would give priority to Bryneglwys traffic, and produce income from incoming shipments of all kinds and for all the hinterland. But failing to obtain *both* foreshore and accommodation land for a jetty (the former was acquired), the McConnels did not proceed with their scheme. The Cambrian Railways, however, fell into dispute with the Talyllyn Railway Company over rates for slate from Towyn to Aberdovey Harbour. Until May 1883 this had been 1/- per ton, but was then raised to 1/6d. per ton; previous to October 1870 the

rate had been 8d. per ton and the Cambrian reckoned the traffic was being worked at a loss. The May 1883 increase brought objection from the Quarry Company which the Cambrian failed to meet and under the Railway & Canals Traffic Act of 1873 the Railway Co. gave notice (correctly) 'requiring slates to be forwarded from Abergynolwyn Station on their Line to the Pier at Aberdovey at a through rate of 2/5d. per ton, of which the Cambrian Company should receive 8d.'. The Cambrian approached the Board of Trade with their objection, maintaining that the traffic was expensive 'inasmuch the number of journeys, averaging only about 5 per month, made by the wagons employed is small in relation to the amount of the Toll received and ... the stopping of the trains at the Siding 333 yards nearer Aberdovey than the general sidings at Towyn, at the former of which the slates are transferred from the narrow gauge wagons to the wagons of this Company, involves much additional work on this traffic as compared with the general traffic at Towyn'.

There had also been trouble between the Abergynolwyn Slate Co. over harbour dues at Aberdovey in December 1881, McConnel claiming that these were the responsibility of the Ship Masters and not the Quarry. More than one ship was involved and McConnel lost his claim for repayment by the Cambrian. An opinion formed of McConnel himself after reading the documents revealed that 'he seems to have been determined, ingenious, and hardheaded. He also did not give his solicitor much peace'!!

By April 1884 the Cambrian was campaigning for the Board of Trade to enforce the closing of the existing Towyn trans-shipment wharf and the use of 'general sidings' instead, but was not supported. Following this, the Cambrian suggested (February 1886) that 'a sufficient number of old wagons [be] fitted up to carry the narrow gauge trucks with their loads, to Aberdovey, thereby shortening the time stock is detained at the Abergynolwyn Siding and enabling us to take the better class wagons out of this traffic'.* Further, and as to shunting Talyllyn traffic by horse at Aberdovey Pier, it was pointed out to the Board that before the Cambrian had built its new jetty and wharf (in 1885 by Abraham Williams, a local contractor) the shunting of the Slate Company's traffic was done by 'shippers' who were paid by the Slate Company at 1/- per wagon.

Besides the above, the Cambrian could charge the Slate Company 3/- per day for each of its wagons held at the Wharf trans-shipment siding under load for over

---

*A cunning ruse adopted by the Slate Company was to load directly into Cambrian wagons at Wharf; instead of using the Wharf area for storage, Cambrian wagons would be left standing, loaded, until consigned by Quarry instructions. Thus in effect, the Cambrian was saving the Quarry the cost of double handling.

48 hours (or 6d. per day for private wagons). It had been shown that the Talyllyn Railway Company detained standard gauge wagons for an average of 12 days per wagon, some for as much as 3–4 weeks. Would the Board allow this to continue? Finally, the Cambrian sought steps to extract a sum of £63 4s. 7d. being the sum total of charges against the Slate Company and which the latter had withheld paying since the dispute began on 1st September 1883. (Between 12th July 1884 and 18th February 1885 the Cambrian was bankrupt for a second time.)

Judgement by the Railway Commissioners in February 1886 upheld that the rate named by the Talyllyn Railway Company was reasonable but that the Cambrian was entitled to 2d. per ton for Pier dues, and 5d. per ton to whichever company trans-shipped the slates onto the Cambrian siding at Towyn: furthermore the distance over the Cambrian metals would now be taken at six miles instead of four. The Commissioners felt that even this did not give the Cambrian a fair settlement 'having regard to the special services they perform', and they supported the suggestion that the Cambrian should transport Talyllyn wagons 'on their own trucks and so get the five pence per ton . . . and in the event of this not being agreed to that they should threaten to take up the Siding which they made from their Station at Towyn to the Talyllyn Company's Wharf'.

It was shown that the Cambrian could not insist on handling trans-shipment at the Wharf but that the Talyllyn Company could be pressed into limiting the time and number of wagons held at the Wharf 'and by refusing to shunt them once they were there'. It was added that 'there ought to be no difficulty . . . on transferring the narrow gauge wagons on to the Cambrian wagons . . . and carried to the Pier'. We may sympathise with the Cambrian which wanted to carry TR wagons in pick-a-back fashion, but this would have obliged the TR to build more wagons; nor was the TR willing to lay down more storage sidings in its limited area.

As is usual in these matters, there was a human aspect lying behind these complaints; it seems that a McConnel held a Season Ticket 'at a nominal charge' which in fact seems to have been a Free Pass between Minffordd and Towyn, and which the Cambrian had just refused to renew. Unfortunately neither the address nor initials of the complainant were quoted in the Cambrian minutes which imply McConnel's nearest station was then Minffordd, his original application for the Pass stating that 'I was wishing to take this house so far from my work at Towyn . . .'.

There was clearly no agreement following this fracas and the prospect of transporter wagon traffic between Towyn and Aberdovey Pier faded out of sight. It could

be that McConnel felt he should not allow himself to be more heavily committed to the Cambrian than already. The Cambrian – 'with a new wharf and deep water pier' – sent out a circular from their headquarters at Oswestry dated July 1885 which stated they 'were now in a position to deal expeditiously with Shipping Traffic at Aberdovey'. They had built a new 500 ft. long wharf with rail connections, three turntables, two storage warehouses etc. and a 370 ft. jetty with two railway tracks along it. There were also cattle pens opposite Glandovey Terrace with direct walking access from the ship. They were wooing the traders of the English Midlands to send their goods by sea 'from the best Harbour on the West Coast between Holyhead and Milford Haven'. Aberdovey was stated as 'conveniently situated for trade with the Southern districts of Ireland, being immediately opposite Rosslare Harbour from which it is distant about 96 miles'. The Cambrian was especially looking for cattle traffic; its timber trade was already extensive. 'The Corris and Abergynolwyn Slate Quarries, from which slates are carried at low prices, are in close proximity to the Port . . .'

The Cambrian minutes had hinted at such development for years and there had been discussions with the Manchester & Milford Railway (opened to Aberystwyth 1st January 1866) regarding a joint steamer service between Aberdovey and the Americas of which nothing more was to be heard (the M & MR was hardly any better at keeping out of Receivership than the Cambrian!) An Aberdovey Import & Export Co. Ltd. held its inaugural meeting in Aberdovey on 5th May 1881, thus confirming the Cambrian minute of the previous 20th December that a company 'is being founded for the purpose of working steamers between America and Aberdovey'. There were other signs that the Cambrian was developing the port; on 19th October 1880 they had opened a wagon repair shop and in July 1885 they purchased the steam crane on the wharf from the contractor for £200 . . . no doubt to his delight! However, there were sombre features, one being the discovery that no rent had been paid for the foreshore since 1864 and this would now be due, that the slate business had been poor since 1879 and that the previous winter, 1,200 tons of imported manure had been lying on the wharf awaiting collection – a lack of manure for the adjacent agricultural lands was a current local farming weakness.

Several concerns were formed, encouraged by the improvements in the steamship and the potential of Aberdovey, nearby Aberystwyth being a poor harbour to enter and leave. These included the Aberystwyth Steamship Co. Ltd. of 1882 (working the steamer *Glanwern*), and the Aberystwyth & Cardigan Bay Steam Packet Co. Ltd. of 1884. The impetus for

Aberdovey, however, came from the formation of the Aberdovey & Waterford Steam Shipping Co. Ltd. The Cambrian had obtained fresh powers for new harbour works on 29th June 1883 and in the ensuing three years the pier was widened to accommodate its (and other larger) ships. The A & WSSCL began with two steamers, the *Liverpool* and the *Cambria* (the latter may have been the ex-London & North Western Railway's steamer of that name), both paddlers. The service was inaugurated with *Liverpool* leaving Waterford on 19th April 1887. The Shipping Co. was sponsored by the Cambrian which had shares in it.

The *Liverpool* was a clipper-like vessel which had already had quite an eventful life and was eventually sold and replaced by the former Belfast Steamship Company's vessel, *Magnetic*. Advertising made it clear that the business was mainly in cattle and that the *Magnetic* had 'cattle spaces all illuminated by electric light'. Passengers were also carried, but were probably all too aware that the service was principally operated for four-legged beasts. To encourage the cattle trade, it was added that 'all beasts could be let into a field near Aberdovey' where they could be rested.

The *Cambria* had been built by Nevill & Co. of Llanelly for the Llanelly Steam Navigation Co. in 1866; its tonnage was 134.

What might have been a success turned to disaster when, either intentionally or otherwise to cause trouble, the LNWR Agent at Waterford gave the mate of one of the vessels a bottle of whisky, to the effect that the crew mistook the Cardigan lightship for the Dovey outer buoy and thereby missed the tide. Pandemonium among the cattle was imminent so the ship was turned north along the coast and beached on the shore at Trevena (or Tonfanau, north of Towyn). Such was the condition of the cattle that when they were released, some of them charged up and down the shore, crazed with thirst. Local butchers were rounded up and in due course the whole shipment was slaughtered. The Shipping Company lost the contract and this, together with pressure from both the Great Western Railway and the LNWR who had shipping interests of their own in the Irish Sea, the A & WSSCL went out of business, but not before they tried again. The *Magnetic* was followed by the *Electric* but even these more modern ships were unable to maintain Thomas Savin's dream of using Aberdovey as the main Welsh port for Ireland. Instead the port took on a useful role as a place where the Cambrian itself imported many timber sleepers from the Baltic etc. and steel rails from South Wales. Materials for Liverpool's Vyrnwy Reservoir scheme were also landed here for onward transport to Llanfyllin by rail: later the Birmingham

Corporation Elan Valley reservoirs also brought in materials by sea.

A later development was to be the Aberdovey & Barmouth Steamship Company's *Telephone* and *Dora* which linked with Porthdinllaen and Liverpool for many years: these were destined to be the last steamers to use Aberdovey. They were based on Liverpool and owned by David Jones & Co., the Liverpool wholesale grocers and had been built at Paisley (?) *Telephone* was but 162 ton gross but *Dora* was 300 tons. [*Dora* was sunk by a U-boat on 1st May 1917 *en route* for Liverpool from Belfast.]

Much more might be written about Aberdovey, its development and limitations as a slate port and its oft-uneasy relations with the McConnels. But the subject is too diverse for herein. Ever since the Aberystwyth & Welsh Coast Railway's intentions to make Aberdovey a large and safe harbour had been scotched by Parliament and attacked by shipowners in Scotland, Liverpool and London, its successors the Cambrian Railways had sought the assistance of Irish railway companies to support its Irish sea link proposals, and encouraged companies who looked to America for business. The Cambrian was always especially fearful of the London & North Western Railway which was luring shipping from southern Ireland to Holyhead.

It could be after all, that Aberdovey with its Talyllyn traffic potential which never came to pass, was the victim of inter-director feuds and their support for competitive schemes on the part of the A & WCR and the infant Cambrian, whose Minutes reveal some extraordinary personal line-ups which as yet, have not been published. Perhaps in knowledge of these, the McConnels preferred their Railway to terminate where they had some control!

The Bryneglwys Quarry's own ship *Seven Brothers* has received mention; its links with Aberdovey were basic. In retrospect it was a reflection of the huge demand for slated roofs throughout western Europe that allowed the local Merionethshire quarries to find markets overseas, backed by the wonderful reputation of Welsh slate as a waterproof material. Shipping records confirm that unlike slate ships which left Portmadoc to deliver their cargoes round the world, Aberdovey ships and men, no less hardy vessels and masters of their calling, were more (but not entirely) confined to coastal passages. The fact that Bryneglwys was able to continue in business for over a century is no less coupled with the satisfaction which its products gave to its purchasers and no less ability of local seafarers.

A glance in St. Cadfan's churchyard, Towyn, will reveal how many Aberdovey ships were manned by

Towyn men. However, the lasting impression of a visit to this now-overgrown graveyard is how much of it is shared by those who lived in Aberdovey and the proportion of them who earned their living at sea. Gravestones (naturally in slate slab) of seamen frequently quote the name and type of the ship, and even the widows and children of seamen had this information on the inscriptions. So here, though now deserted by the sea which once lapped the graveyard wall, lie those who, often enough, sea and slate by railway brought together. An epitaph taken from among many, reads:

WILLIAM EVANS   SEAMAN   AGE 23
died 23 March 1870

O'er the turbulent seas I sailed
Until at last from illness failed
My journeys ending here at last
My anchor safely here to cast

A pictorial record of slate-loading at Aberdovey is rare, but this incident of a steamship unloading timber recalls an equally bygone age.
NATIONAL LIBRARY OF WALES

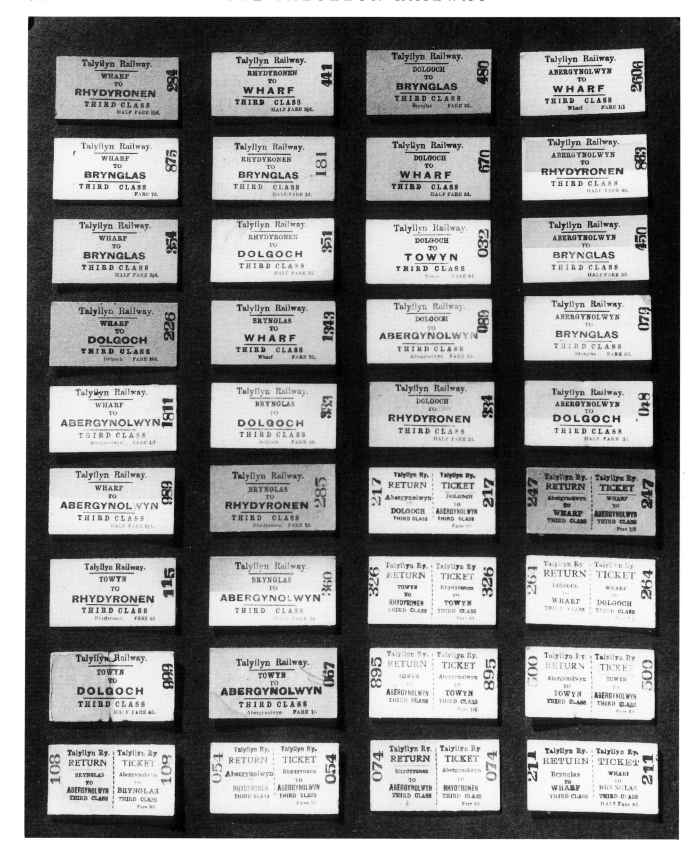

Appendix II – TICKETS

In keeping with its unusual character, the Railway's ticket system had an individual quality. An outcome of this was that when the Preservation Society began to assess the situation before operating a train service, L. T. C. Rolt was to write; 'When we took over the Railway the tickets we collected from the various offices, used or disused, were found to be so baffling in their number and confusion, that it was decided to introduce new issues.' Knowledge on that confusion and a full explanation of the Railway's ticket system has remained limited ever since.

From the start of passenger services, Edmondson-type tickets in card measuring $2\frac{1}{4} \times 1\frac{3}{16}$ ins. were used. There was a system of colours to assist class identification; in 1904 this was First/White, Second/Green, Third/Purple and, as the Company was not a member of The Railway Clearing House, the recommended colours used by its members were not followed by the Talyllyn. With the changes in availability for First or Second Class travel down the years, certain tickets must have become obsolete and it was probably Yates who introduced a system of colours to identify stations between which tickets were valid. Such were the liberties taken after his departure that by 1949 at least five various colours were in use for travel between the *same* stations. By that year, only one series of First Class tickets remained, being the Wharf-Abergynolwyn single at 1/9d. Only in more recent times of Haydn Jones did fares appear on the ticket; the amounts might include a farthing (one quarter of an old penny) and the lowest fare of all was one halfpenny.

On certain singles the destination was printed a second time in small type in the middle of the lower edge to allow that portion to be punched out and convert the ticket into a half-fare for a child – who had to be under 12 years of age. In earliest times tickets were given serial numbers by a stencil process but later the numbers were printed. There were tickets for every combination of stations, but none showed the word 'Pendre'; this stemmed from the time when Wharf was not a passenger station and Pendre was the official start. The word 'Towyn' was used throughout, and meant 'Pendre' until Wharf came into use, and even then Pendre was ignored and tickets were printed 'Wharf' or 'Towyn'. On 26th March 1948 all fares were increased by approximately 50% and existing stocks of tickets were withdrawn. From this time those joining trains at Rhydyronen, Brynglas, Dolgoch (or any intermediate 'halt') paid cash to the person in charge of the train ... who might be the driver!

It has not been established if and when Workmen's Tickets were issued, but certain deserving persons were given a Free Pass, a typical one being that issued to J. J. O'Sullivan, the General Manager of the nearby Corris Railway. This was dated 1914 and signed by H. Haydn Jones. The pass was of folding card type, bound in dark green leather with lettering in gilt – 'TAL-Y-LLYN RAILWAY. Available for All Stations.' The folded size was $2\frac{1}{2} \times 1\frac{1}{2}$ ins.

There were at least two ticket-dating machines, found probably at Pendre and Abergynolwyn booking offices; ultimately they found their way into Wharf and the Booking Office portion of the converted Guard's Van which was Yates' method of dispensing with the issue of tickets at stations beyond the Wharf – necessitating the Guard leaving the train and opening up the little offices at certain stations. Up to Yates' time, there was no check on used tickets and they were not surrendered at the end of the journey. Later in the Haydn Jones' era a form of economy was practised in the high season whereby Jacob the Guard would collect recently purchased tickets before the train moved, and re-sell the same ones as required. Thus the more popular journeys (e.g. Wharf–Dolgoch return) were sanctioned by a limited number of dog-eared specimens which is well-remembered. These economies meant that the train staff were carrying considerable sums in cash, but examination of the careful records kept at Wharf shows that even the casual passenger picked up at a 'halt' had his cash payment duly entered. None of the tickets which so frequently changed hands on the same train/day, was given a date stamp. Some had had the fare, where shown, altered in ink – invariably upwards.

Colours of Third Class tickets included;

	ADULT	CHILD
Single Journey	Light green	Blue (upper) White (lower)
	Brick red	Brick red
	White	Green (left half) White (right half)
	Light blue	Pink (upper) White (lower)
	Dark blue	Dark blue
	Purple	Purple
	OUTWARD	RETURN
Return journey	Blue	White
	White	White
	Green	White
	Purple	Purple
	Brick red	Brick red

Talyllyn Railway.—APPLICATION FOR PRIVILEGE TICKET ORDERS.

No. of Order issued _____

I beg to apply for the following Local or Interchange Privilege Ticket Orders:—

Signed _____ Grade _____

Department _____ Station _____

Description.	No. of Tickets required.	Class.	Single or Return.	Date travelling.	Between what Points.		Railway.	Relationship to Applicant.
					From.	To.		
MALES								
FEMALES ...... (other than Children)								
CHILDREN under 15	Male.	Female.						
CHILDREN 15 and over								

NOTE—All members of a family must be permanently resident with the Applicant, and must not be allowed Local Privilege Tickets if in receipt of more than 15/- per week, or Interchange Tickets if in receipt of more than 10/- per week, and then only at the discretion of the Heads of Departments. Any abuse of the privilege will render the servant liable to dismissal.

Countersigned _____

Acknowledgements

The conception of this book and the support it has received throughout preparation belongs to Paul Karau, without whom the manuscript would have continued to lie unfinished.

Whilst intended to use my own researches and familiarity with the Railway, encouragement throughout the book has been given by the Trustees of the Narrow Gauge Railway Museum (situated adjacent to the Talyllyn Railway) and especially from Jeremy S. Wilkinson and Alan Holmes who have generously provided me with fundamental material, particularly concerning Bryneglwys Quarry.

John L. H. Bate, Engineer to the Talyllyn Railway Company, has placed his special knowledge at my disposal, has led me in the paths of righteousness and considered the manuscript.

Oswald Edwards, Musician of Ruthin, loaned his records of the ancestry of Henry Haydn Jones; Mrs. Eryl Mathias, (Sir Haydn's daughter) recalled her father's life with great patience.

Adding to my information on the Quarry, Commander David I. Evans (R.N.R.) of Wilmslow has given generous detail of life there in the time of his grandfather, who was manager of it.

Hugh Ellis Jones, 'Dai' Richard Jones and Mrs. Mair Spratley-Jones have given me many hours of their time: their forebears were employed for almost all their lives by the Railway Company, as were Hugh and Dai themselves.

Harry Chidlow of Shrewsbury searched the records of The Atlas Foundry for details of locomotive repairs, and Miss Katie Pugh linked these with personalities at Towyn.

Most closely associated throughout has been that small team of 'collaborateurs' which has so enriched all my efforts in this direction: Jeremy S. Wilkinson in so many various capacities, John M. Lloyd for long hours of careful draughtsmanship backed by his own investigations, and my wife Dorothy who has not only created order from chaos at manuscript stage, but has assisted by working through the Census Returns.

Whilst the content, interpretation of documents and fieldwork remain my own responsibility, the final result includes the help not only of the foregoing but of many others, the principal among whom being: John H. L. Adams, Derek Allen, Mrs. D. Banks, Mrs. Olwen Bate, E. D. Chambers, Alan Chorlton, Lewis Cozens, Tristram England, Griffith Evans, C. C. Green, George Hall, Ifor Higgon, Gwynfor P. Jones, R. W. Kidner, Dr. Jean Lindsay, M. E. M. Lloyd, George Middleton, John P. Parry, L. T. C. Rolt, Rev. F. Riley, Councillor T. Rowlands, H. Francis Shuker, John Slater, J. B. Snell, E. K. Stretch, Edward Thomas, J. Graham Vincent, Rodney Weaver, Alan Whatley, Roger Whitehouse, John C. Wilkins, David Woodhouse and last (but not least) to the Principals and staff of the following: University College of North Wales (Bangor) [Tomos Roberts], Gwynedd Archives (Caernarvon) [Gareth Williams], Gwynedd Archives (Dolgelley) [Miss Ann Rhydderch], National Library of Wales (Aberystwyth) [D. Michael Francis].

Acknowledgements – Illustrations

John Adams, John Adams/P. B. Whitehouse, C. P. Baines, B.B.C./Hulton, G. D. Braithwaite, H. S. Bristowe, Burrell Series, W. A. Camwell, H. C. Casserley, L. T. Catchpole, E. D. Chambers, G. H. W. Clifford (per C. C. Green), R. K. Cope, Lewis Cozens, Dennis & Sons Ltd., B. Edgington, Frith & Co., N. Fields, Fine Spinners & Doublers Ltd., George & Sons, Gwynedd Archives, Ifor Higgon, A. T. Holmes, H. G. W. Household, H. E. Jones, Mrs. Mair S. Jones, Locomotive & General Railway Photographs, F. Moore/Locomotive Publishing Co., Narrow Gauge Railway Museum Trust, National Library of Wales, K. A. C. R. Nunn (per Locomotive Club of Great Britain), John Parry, G. M. Perkins (per C. C. Green), Real Railway Photographs, Bernard Roberts, J. B. Snell, J. W. Sparrowe, Talyllyn Railway (per D. Woodhouse), H. B. Tours, Valentine & Sons, P. H. Wells (per L. Somerfield), H. F. Wheeller, I. L. Wright, Wyndham Series.

SOURCES

Documentary
Records of The Talyllyn Railway Company
Records at Gwynedd Archives (Caernarvon and Dolgelley)
Records of Alan Holmes on Bryneglwys Quarry
Records of John L. H. Bate on Talyllyn Railway
The Croft Collection
The Public Record Office
Notebooks of Lewis Cozens – courtesy Narrow Gauge Railway Museum Trust
The National Library of Wales

Bibliographical
History and Survey of the Trinity Port of Aberdovey: T. Wynn Williams
The Cambrian Railways: Christiansen & Miller
The Story of the Cambrian Railways: C. P. Gasquoine
Cambrian Railways Album: C. C. Green
Brief Glory: D. W. Morgan
Slates from Abergynolwyn: Alan Holmes
The Manchester & Milford Railway: J. S. Holden
General View of the Agriculture of Merionethshire: George Kay
Landscapes of North Wales: Millward & Robinson
Packet to Ireland: M. E. Williams
Irish Passenger Steamship Services: D. B. McNeill
History of the North Wales Slate Industry: Jean Lindsay

INDEX